FIFTY YEARS LATER

Cover: Fragment of a water color by A.H.A.H.M. Borret (1848-1888). From a series of water colors made in Suriname. (KITLV, HISDOC collection)

FIFTY YEARS LATER

ANTISLAVERY, CAPITALISM AND MODERNITY IN THE DUTCH ORBIT

Edited by

Gert Oostindie

1996
University of Pittsburgh Press

Published by:
University of Pittsburgh Press
127 North Bellefield
Pittsburgh, Pa. 15260
USA

This book is also published by KITLV Press (Leiden, 1995)

Cover: Marjan Groen

Library of Congress Catalog Card Number 95-62019
ISBN 0-8229-3929-0

© 1995 Koninklijk Instituut voor Taal-, Land- en Volkenkunde

No part of this publication may be reproduced or transmitted in any form or by any means, electronic or mechanical, including photocopy, recording, or any information storage and retrieval system, without permission from the copyright owner.

Printed in the Netherlands

Contents

Preface	vii

Gert Oostindie
    Introduction
        Explaining Dutch Abolition
	1

Seymour Drescher
    The Long Goodbye
        Dutch Capitalism and Antislavery in Comparative Perspective
	25

Maarten Kuitenbrouwer
    The Dutch Case of Antislavery
        Late Abolitions and Élitist Abolitionism
	67

Angelie Sens Dutch Antislavery Attitudes in a Decline-Ridden Society, 1750-1815	89
Edwin Horlings An Economic Explanation of the Late Abolition of Slavery in Suriname	105
Alex van Stipriaan Suriname and the Abolition of Slavery	117

Gert Oostindie
    Same Old Song?
        Perspectives on Slavery and Slaves in Suriname and Curaçao
	143

Robert Ross Abolitionism, the Batavian Republic, the British, and the Cape Colony	179
Gerrit J. Knaap Slavery and the Dutch in Southeast Asia	193
Pieter C. Emmer The Ideology of Free Labor and Dutch Colonial Policy, 1830-1870	207

Stanley L. Engerman
    Emancipations in Comparative Perspective
        A Long and Wide View
	223

Seymour Drescher
    Epilogue
        Reflections
	243

Index	263
The Contributors	271

Preface

The Dutch tend to find a certain reassurance and, even less innocently, pride in quoting negative foreign opinions on the national character. In choosing the title *Fifty Years Later* for this book, I am certainly 'one of us'. There is an apocryphal dictum by Heinrich Heine that he would choose to go to the Netherlands if the world would come to an end: after all, in the country of his Western neighbors, everything happened fifty years later. The late Dutch abolition of slavery has been cited as a case in point, and this book indeed addresses the issue with a wink at Heine. Any perceptive reader will understand the metaphor implied. The Dutch were not the last to abolish slavery, nor did their final Emancipation Act lag exactly half a century behind the first, Britain's. Yet remarkably tardy they were.

This book, published by the KITLV Press in Leiden and the University of Pittsburgh Press, originated from a conference held at the KITLV/Royal Institute of Linguistics and Anthropology on 15 October 1993. Eleven scholars were asked to comment on Seymour Drescher's thought-provoking paper, 'The Long Goodbye: Dutch Capitalism and Antislavery in Comparative Perspective'. After a day of lively debate, I invited the participants to rework their interventions into full-blown articles. Due to time constraints, Ernst van den Boogaart and Peter W. Klein could not cooperate; all others did consent to do so, and – eventually – turned in revised papers. I thank them all for their professional work and their patience with my insistence on including yet another issue, clarification, bibliographic entry, etc.

Fifty Years Later now includes – after my introduction – 'The Long Goodbye' followed by eight chapters each addressing Drescher's essay. These chapters both provide comments on 'The Long Goodbye' and broaden the discussion on slavery and abolition in the Dutch world and beyond. In the following essay, Stanley E. Engerman compares emancipations of unfree labor through time and continents. In the 'Epilogue', Drescher reflects once again on the Dutch case in view of the findings of this book, and concludes by taking up the challenge of Engerman's olympian survey.

One of an editor's lighter and most delightful if at times delicate tasks is that of acknowledging debts collected along the way. There is only one institutional debt, namely to the KITLV, for financing the seminar, co-publishing this book, and generally, for being a superb institution for work on the Caribbean.

I was efficiently and cheerfully assisted in the process of editing by Marco Last. Peter Mason helped to smooth stylistic inelegancies in some of the non-native speakers' contributions. It was a pleasure working with both of them. Ellen de la Rie, of the Department of Caribbean Studies, provided good-humored assistance with the preparation of the index. Harry Poeze and Marjan Groen, of the KITLV Press, were helpful and accurate as ever in the final stages of the preparation of this book. At the University of Pittsburgh Press, Catherine Marshall coordinated publication of the American edition.

I owe thanks also to Pieter C. Emmer and Robert Ross for inadvertently suggesting the *Fifty Years Later* title, and to Professor H.W. von den Dunk for kindly sharing his intricate knowledge of this particular aspect of German-Dutch history, namely, that Heine most likely never made the 'Fifty Years Later' observation, at least not in print.

Finally, I am happy to acknowledge my debt to Seymour Drescher. His article, 'The Long Goodbye', obviously triggered this book, which in turn honors his analysis. On that score, further words of appreciation are superfluous. Even so, I should mention that it was an enormous pleasure working with a scholar whose intellectual range and depth form an exceptional combination with his good sense of humor. I fondly remember his immediate and reassuring fax answering mine in which I accounted for a time delay by half desperately, half pompously mentioning a series of projects – among which another edited volume – in which I was involved: 'Editing two volumes at once must be one of the punishments Dante would have located at the lowest levels of his *Inferno*'. Such messages indeed helped *not* to make the effort infernal.

GERT OOSTINDIE

Introduction
Explaining Dutch Abolition

'I will only remark here that there are many occupations which would seem unjustified if they would not be of particular advantage. An argument here may be the *Slave Trade*, which should be acquitted of all unlawfulness solely because of the benefit it furnishes to the merchants.'[1]

'[...] the colony of Suriname seems to be treated as a Stepchild by its Mother Country, no matter how she treats this Mother with true Children's love [...]. She [The Netherlands] persists in withholding from us the only means by which we can labor in order to boost her riches and prosperity. Perhaps she will deplore this *cruel treatment* no earlier than when it will already be too late.'[2]

Colonial slavery is no admirable chapter in Dutch history; nor is antislavery. Yet crucial they are. Around 1600, while fighting hard to win their freedom from 'Spanish tyranny', the Dutch entered the slave trade. By the mid-seventeenth century, the increasing involvement in the transatlantic slave trade had been accepted as just another business in the newly established republic, and slavery was becoming crucial in much of its overseas territory. In 1814, the slave trade was abolished. The final abolition of slavery itself was only enacted in 1863.

---

[1] 'Alleenlyk zal ik hier aanmerken, dat 'er vele bedryven plaats hebben, welke ongeoorloofd zouden schynen, indien 'er geen byzonder voordeel in te vinden was. Getuige zy hier van de *Slavenhandel*, dien men alleen al door het voordeel, 't welke dezelve aan de kooplieden toebrengt, van onwettigheid kan vryspreken.' (Gallandat 1769:3-4.) D.H. Gallandat was a medical doctor. The quote is taken from his Dutch manual for slavers. I hope to be pardoned for using this chillingly evocative citation twice in one book (see also p. 146). I want to thank Seymour Drescher, David Eltis, Pieter Emmer, Stanley L. Engerman, and an anonymous reviewer for the University of Pittsburgh Press for commenting on an earlier version of this introduction.
[2] '[...] schijnt de colonie van Surinaamen door het Moederland, als een Stieff kind gehandeld te worden, hoe zee zy deese Moeder met waere Kinderlieffde te gemoet treed [...]. Zij blijft ons onthouden de eenige middelen waar meede wij tot vermeerdering van haar rijkdom en welvaart kunnen en wilen arbeiden. Moogelijk beklaagt Zij zig deese *wrede behandeling* niet eerder dan wanneer het reeds te laat zal zijn.' Gemeente Archief Rotterdam, collection Hudig, 215, 20 May 1789; my emphasis. Planter and administrator J. Rocheteau complaining to absentee plantation owner O.Z. van Sandick about the poor supply of slaves to the colony. See also Oostindie 1989:361-3.

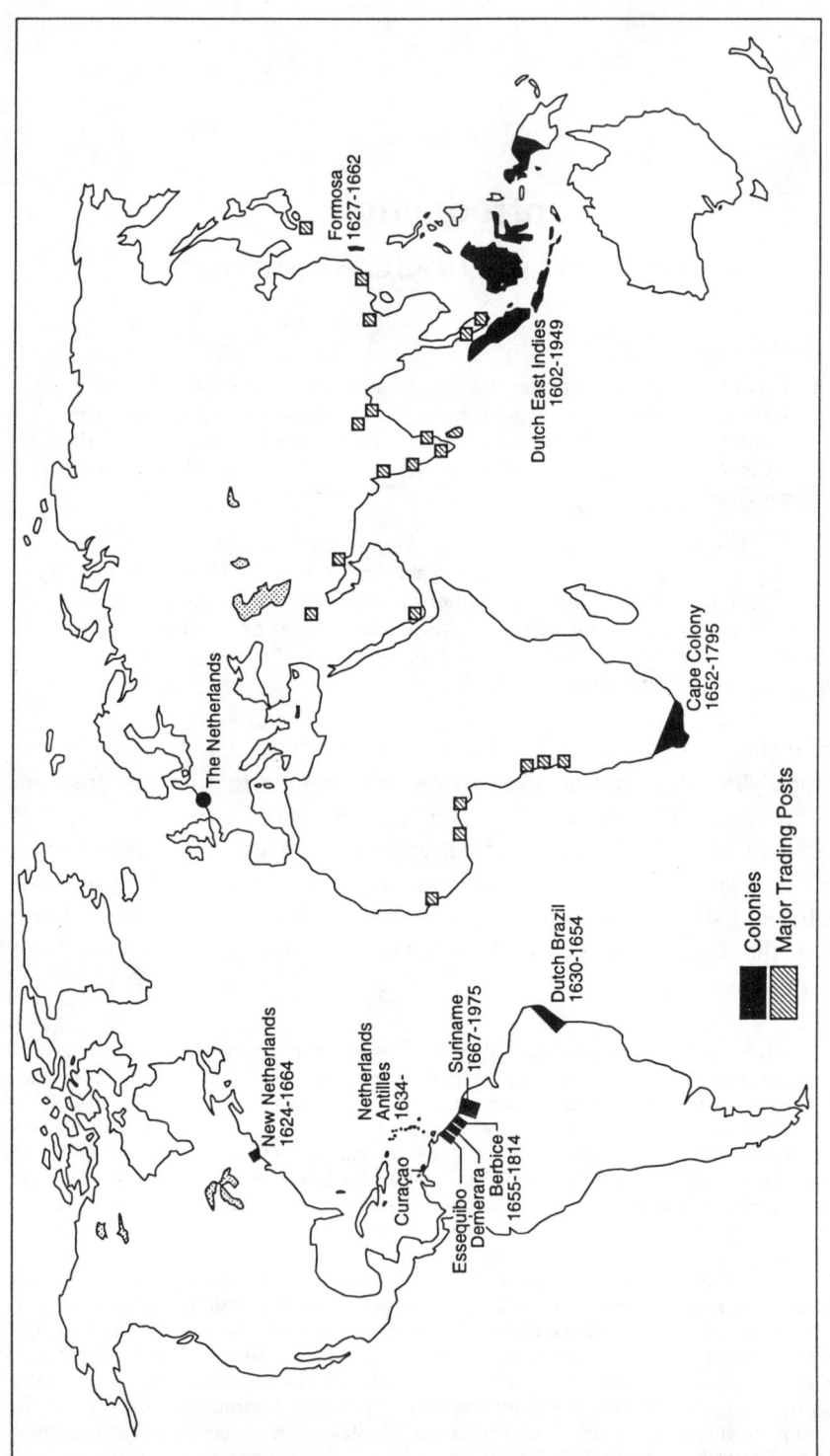

The scope of the Dutch Maritime Empire. (Map by G-O graphics, Wijk bij Duurstede).

If any one country could be called upon to confirm that an intense involvement in the Atlantic slave trade was fully compatible with a record of early capitalism and modernity at home, the Netherlands would be a perfect case. There is no dearth of studies underlining the astonishing economic growth and prosperity of the Dutch Republic. This growth encompassed virtually every sector of the economy, ranging from agriculture through industry to trade and banking. Historians of diverse leanings have concurred in evoking the Low Countries as a pioneer capitalist state. Thus, Wallerstein singled out the Netherlands as the first hegemonic power in the capitalist world-economy (Wallerstein 1980:36-71). Likewise, the recently published, state-of-the-arts economic history of the Netherlands by De Vries and Van der Woude summarizes Dutch economic performance from the sixteenth through the eighteenth century under the heading 'The First Modern Economy'. Measured against the economic performance of Britain – the world's economic leader for a subsequent, and far longer period –, the Dutch record is impressive indeed. De Vries and Van der Woude (1995:814) calculate that per capita income in the Netherlands exceeded the British figure from at least the seventeenth up to the late eighteenth century. In fact, the Dutch per capita income attained around 1670 was not equalled in England until the 1830s.

International trade was an essential element of the Dutch miracle. Though the bulk of this trade was intra-European, colonial expansion too was crucial to the international profile of the Dutch economy. By the mid-seventeenth century, the Dutch colonial empire included the Dutch East Indies; a string of colonies in the Caribbean, of which Suriname and Curaçao were the most important; six trading posts and one colony of settlement in West Africa; as well as short-lived colonies in Brazil, North America, and several factories in Asia (Map 1). With the notable exception of the metropolis, where slave labor was forbidden, slavery was prominent throughout the Dutch colonial empire. In Asia, slave labor was introduced on a modest scale for colonial purposes alongside extant, pre-colonial forms of bonded labor. In Africa and particularly in the New World colonies, African slavery was crucial. As in the other tropical economies of the New World, the sugar and coffee plantations were worked with slave labor; the demand seemed insatiable, and the Dutch Republic was eager to arrange for its potentially rewarding supply. From the late sixteenth through the early nineteenth century, Dutch slavers boarded some 550,000 Africans in the New World, 460,000 of whom survived and were effectively landed. The Dutch share in the total Atlantic slave trade therefore amounted to approximately five per cent (Postma 1990:302). The majority of these African slaves arrived in the Dutch Caribbean, notably in Suriname; the rest were mainly dispersed over Spanish America and, initially, Brazil (Postma 1990:300).

Economic growth and colonial expansion were not the only indicators of the surprisingly prominent Dutch profile in the emerging world order. Again, scholars of different leanings have singled out the early Dutch Republic, depicting it as a place of remarkable political and religious as well as cultural and scholarly achievements. Studies on the 'golden' Dutch era of the seventeenth century such as Schama's *The Embarrassment of Riches* (1988) paint a picture of perhaps ambivalent, but nevertheless strong humanitarian leanings and, at the same time, ongoing experiments with the organization of political and religious freedom. In *The Dutch Republic* (1995), Israel affirms the pre-eminence of the Netherlands in many sectors of intellectual and artistic life.[3] In fact, even as economic and political decline set in during the eighteenth century, the Netherlands would long retain a fame for being prosperous and progressive at the same time. A Dutch reputation and self-image as a liberal nation and a haven for refugees from injustice in other parts of the globe survived well into the present century (Blakely 1993).

There is a sad paradox here. The young Republic acquired a reputation for being democratic and economically precocious, and for displaying a culturally sophisticated and tolerant *esprit*. As Seymour Drescher writes in 'The Long Goodbye', 'The Dutch Revolt of the sixteenth century had already generated an ideology that affirmed the inseparability of freedom of conscience, political liberty, and personal freedom' (p. 34).[4] Yet at the same time, it sustained its businesslike engagement in the slave trade and in slavery itself, a form of labor eradicated from the Low Countries long before. The 1814 abolition of the slave trade was an imposition by Britain rather than the outcome of a national debate. As for the 1863 Emancipation Act, the preceding, flat debates among the Dutch élites were pale reflections of the polemics which had stirred the Anglo-Saxon world starting more than half a century earlier. The Dutch chapters of antislavery indeed confirmed Heinrich Heine's apocryphal dictum that in the Netherlands things happened fifty years later.

---

[3] 'This astounding concentration, in such as small place, not only coincided with, but was linked to, Dutch pre-eminence in commerce, shipping, and finance, as well as in agriculture and technology. Furthermore, none of this could have occurred, or been sustained, had the United Provinces not become one of Europe's military great powers for over a century and one of the world's principal naval powers for longer.' (Israel 1995:5.)

[4] This article was first published in the *American Historical Review* 99 (1994):44-69. The complete text is reprinted – with minor revisions – in the present volume. My references to 'The Long Goodbye' refer to the pages in this volume.

The Antislavery Debate and Drescher's 'Long Goodbye'

Why did the Dutch fail to extend their hard-won liberty and their presumed democratic spirit to their own colonial ventures and subjects? And why, two centuries later, did it take them so long finally to follow the lead of apparently more 'modern' nations by abolishing the slave trade and slavery? Why did this allegedly pioneer modern state fail to do what our conception of modernity would lead us to expect? Why does the Dutch case present the conundrum of 'a society identified as a pioneer of modern capitalism from the early seventeenth century, one unencumbered by serfdom for centuries more before that, yet one that failed to generate a major antislavery movement' (p. 51)?

It took remarkably long for these questions to surface in the historiography of the Dutch Caribbean and of antislavery in general. In hyperbole, 'fifty years later' applies not only to the Dutch abolition of slavery, but equally to the inclusion of the Dutch case in the pertinent historical debate. To be sure, the trajectory of Dutch antislavery and abolition has been addressed by many Dutch and Dutch West Indian scholars. Van Winter (1982) and particularly Siwpersad (1979) carefully reconstructed the long-winded Dutch debates preceding the 1861 passing of the Emancipation Act which came into effect on 1 July 1863. Yet whereas these studies provide a wealth of evidence regarding the Dutch and, to a lesser extent, the West Indian situation, both authors refrained from drawing explicit comparisons to a wider debate on the abolition of New World slavery. Recent monographs on the economics of slavery in the foremost Dutch plantation colony, Suriname, do discuss issues such as the efficiency, profitability, and viability of slavery, yet only cursorily engage with the wider debate on abolition in international context (Oostindie 1989, Van Stipriaan 1989, 1993; see also Oostindie 1993). The authoritative study by Postma (1990) on the Dutch in the Atlantic slave trade is a fairly definitive account of numbers, origins, destinations, mortality, profits, etc. Postma's treatment of Dutch attitudes towards the slave trade and slavery itself, however, is less detailed, and does not attempt to incorporate a comparative perspective. In fact, only Kuitenbrouwer (1978) and Emmer (1980) offered an explicit positioning of Dutch abolitionism within the wider context of international abolitionism. While both articles were published a decade and a half ago, and Emmer's in particular has been widely quoted, the discussion of Dutch abolition in comparative context remained something of a backwater in the burgeoning international debate on capitalism, modernity, and antislavery.

Not until fairly recently did the relevance of the Dutch case to the general debate on the abolition of slavery in the Western world become apparent. It may not inspire excessive chauvinism to state that even in the historiographic debate on Dutch abolition, the Anglo-Saxon world took the lead – but it certainly did so. The historical debate on the abolition of the transatlantic slave trade and slavery in the New World has long centered upon the Anglo-Saxon world, and upon the link between capitalism and antislavery. In the late 1980s, a debate in the *American Historical Review* between Thomas L. Haskell, David Brion Davis, and John Ashworth on the links between capitalism and antislavery in the Western world resulted in an awareness that the hitherto neglected Dutch case could provide valuable comparative insights.[5] In 'The Long Goodbye: Dutch Capitalism and Antislavery in Comparative Perspective', a paper first circulated in 1992, Seymour Drescher took up the challenge to rethink the Dutch involvement with New World slavery, as well as its late abolition, in the broader context of New World slavery and abolition. The present book offers a series of reflections, mainly by specialists in Dutch and Dutch colonial history, on the issues raised by Drescher in this seminal contribution.

In 'The Long Goodbye', Drescher formulates the still unresolved 'bedrock economic question' emerging from this debate as follows: 'Was abolition facilitated by the decline of slave economies and/or the rise of capitalist industrial systems, and how did economic and non-economic considerations figure in this process?' (p. 26). With the initial participants in the *AHR* debate, he advances the Dutch case as a significant opportunity for comparative analysis.

In contrast to most previous scholars, who concentrated on the decades preceding the final Dutch abolition of slavery in 1863, Drescher emphasizes the heuristic value of including earlier periods in the analysis. The first phase is that of feverish capitalist expansion in the seventeenth century, coinciding with the Dutch Republic's emergence and consolidation out of a struggle for national independence. Even more than Britain, the Republic was a precocious and successful capitalist state, dominated by a bourgeois oligarchy. The second pivotal period is the three decades of economic and political distress at home and in the colonies from the 1780s up to the establishment of the Kingdom of the Netherlands in 1814. The third period, finally, runs from the 1814 abolition of the slave trade to the late abolition of slavery itself in 1863. In this period, the Netherlands is characterized by its falling behind the leading European nations in terms of economic growth, political democratization, and imperial expansion. In the first of the two periods cited, the Dutch failed to develop any significant abolitionism,

---

[5] See Davis 1992a:178 and particularly 1992b:294-6, and Haskell 1992:233-4. Excerpts from Davis's work, the *AHR* debate, plus two new essays by Ashworth and Davis are brought together in Bender 1992b. In lieu of the present, all too succinct summary, the reader is referred to this book for the interpretations of Ashworth, Davis, and Haskell; see also Drescher 1993.

whereas in the last term they did enact full emancipation, but remarkably late. As Drescher observes, 'More telling than the virtual absence of abolitionism in the stagnant post-Napoleonic Dutch economy, even with its diminishing dependence upon slavery, is the fact that Dutch abolitionism failed to emerge either in the seventeenth century, when the Netherlands was at or near its peak of economic dynamism, or in the early eighteenth century when the slave trade was an important and growing branch of Dutch trade' (p. 30).

What are the currently dominant interpretations in the general debate on abolition, and how do they apply to the Dutch case? Drescher maintains – in line with the conclusions from his *Econocide* (1977) and subsequent writings – that the presumed obsolescence of slavery is no longer a compelling argument. In contrast to the affirmations of contemporary abolitionists and many subsequent economic historians, slave labor was efficient, productive, and profitable. But then, if there was no inherent weakness in slave labor 'causing' capitalists to opt for abolition, what other economic causal chain may be forged between capitalist ascendancy and abolition?

In general terms, scholars have further scrutinized contemporary notions of the superiority of free over slave labor. Both Davis and Ashworth, among others, argue that a free labor ideology reigned supreme in the centers of metropolitan abolitionism. By stressing the non-viability of slave labor the abolitionist argument underlined the alleged greater efficiency not only of free labor, but of the emergent industrial capitalist order as such. This provided ideological leverage for instilling a new free labor discipline in a people still rooted in an older moral economy. The attack on slavery thus reflected the emergent industrial capitalist class's effort to legitimize this new domestic labor discipline. Drescher argues that the Dutch case does precious little to support this theory. Capitalist from the start, and to a large extent an *industrial* capitalist nation at that, the dynamic Republic failed to produce a significant abolitionist free labor ideology – much less practice – for its colonies. Apparently the early existence of genuine industrial capitalism, implying high rates of urbanization, rising per capita income, and a considerable proletariat, did little to necessitate the formulation of an imperial free labor ideology which would at the same time legitimize capitalist labor relations at home.[6]

The approach advanced by Haskell emphasizes the indirect effect of capitalism on antislavery. The growth of capitalism in Europe caused a sort of quantum leap in terms of mentality. Ever-increasing market activity within the new burgeoning capitalism had a strong impact on values and

---

[6] In fact, free labor had become the norm in the Netherlands ever since the thirteenth century, even before urbanization and 'industrialization' gained further momentum in the 'Golden' seventeenth century.

perceptions, creating a new 'cognitive style'. In this new frame of reference, the slave trade and slavery became unacceptable. Again, Drescher argues, the Dutch do not fit: 'in the Dutch case, the early modern Netherlands fully met the market criteria for a capitalist, non-abolitionist, counter-example' (p. 29), yet failed to conform to the theory. The early start of capitalism in the Netherlands did not produce significant abolitionism, in spite of the eminently international orientation of the Republic and even if a reservoir of ideological and particularly religious antislavery arguments was developed and could have been tapped. There is therefore no evidence that a new cognitive style forced the Dutch to renounce their lucrative slave trade and the benefits of slavery in their colonies.

Yet another theory attempting to link industrial capitalism to abolition is proposed by Blackburn (1988). The emerging new capitalist bourgeois order created new forms of class and political struggles both in the metropolis and the colonies. Where these struggles coincided with a marginalization of the colonial slaveholders, the stage would be set for successful antislavery. The supreme case for this theory is obviously the French one, with its metropolitan revolution and concomitant slave revolution in St. Domingue setting the stage for the first (albeit abortive) phase of French abolitionism. The same 'dynamic density' presumably applied to Britain at several periods. Yet, as Drescher remarks, in the late eighteenth and early nineteenth century precisely the Dutch case should have been Blackburn's obvious candidate for abolition, bourgeois- revolutionary style: 'The Netherlands therefore met all of Blackburn's criteria for abolition: political conflict, economic decline, and slave unrest. It even met one of Eric Williams's major prerequisites for the abolitionist take-off in Britain – relative imperial insignificance.' (p. 41). He therefore suggests that the absence of this case from Blackburn's analysis may be explained by the fact that the Dutch experience challenges the theory.

At various points in his analysis, Drescher notes not only that the Dutch case does not fit the latest theories on Anglo-Saxon antislavery, but that there is nothing so remarkable about this failure to conform. Both the uneventful development of Dutch antislavery and its late success with full slave emancipation place the Dutch case firmly in line with abolitionism elsewhere in Continental Europe. Not only Dutch antislavery, but Danish, Swedish, Spanish, and even much of French abolitionism also sharply diverged from the Anglo-Saxon model: 'Nowhere on the European Continent was abolitionism a durable mass movement and nowhere was the enactment of antislavery legislation used to legitimize the claims of either traditional political élites or new industrial ones.' (p. 37). Thus the analysis of Dutch abolition serves to highlight not the peculiarity of Dutch slavery or antislavery, but rather the exceptional Anglo-Saxon and specifically British case of 'econocide' through abolition. For the other nations involved in slavery, there was little direct gain to be made by following the Anglo-Saxon lead. All subsequent abolitions were enacted in a context of increasing external – including British – pressure to follow the good example.

If Anglo-Saxon antislavery, rather than proslavery and indifference elsewhere, is the exception, why is this so? Drescher argues that a comparison of the Anglo-Saxon and Dutch cases suggests that the crucial difference did not lie in the economic dimension, but rather in the demographic and politico-religious ones. In the emergence of intense transatlantic kinship, religious, and political networks, the case of Britain and its American Continental Colonies sharply contrasts with the case of the Netherlands and, in fact, with most of Continental Europe's colonial experience. The uniqueness of the Anglo-Saxon case derived from the establishment of the Continental Colonies as settler colonies, extensions of 'home' with a majority of inhabitants of the same ethnic background, with replications of metropolitan political institutions and with a similar civil status for the free (white) population. It was not that the British were marked by a particular ethno-religious sensibility from the start; yet the subsequent emergence of intensive transatlantic contact did facilitate the emergence and spread of abolitionist thinking through shared religious dissent, such as the 'Quaker International'. In contrast, the modest antislavery movement in countries such as the Netherlands and even France had little contact with the overseas white population. Moreover, in the British Continental Colonies, abolitionism could also feed on the realistic future prospect of a predominantly white, free labor community. Indeed, no model would have seemed less viable than this one for tropical exploitation colonies such as the Dutch West Indies, which seemed inconceivable without imported forced labor.

In conclusion, then, Drescher argues that capitalism per se seems a poor explanatory factor in accounting for the little and late Dutch response to antislavery, and for the divergent paths of antislavery taken in the Anglo-Saxon and Dutch worlds. 'As with other major cases thus far investigated the economic context offers the weakest possible support for and the strongest counter-abolitionist argument against the [Dutch] antislavery process' (p. 53).[7] What remains would simply be the loose linkage that capitalism may have enabled abolition by bringing alternative forms of labor within reach if slavery became too morally embarrassing or politically inconvenient. Yet Drescher argues that for such embarrassment or inconvenience to become a serious concern, and for this concern to be

---

[7] Elsewhere, Drescher is even more positive: 'The Netherlands turns out to be a killing field for most theoretical linkages between capitalism and antislavery to date' (Drescher 1993:326).

translated into active abolitionism, the crucial conditions were not shaped by the impact of industrial capitalism per se, but rather by the emergence of new forms of social mobilization, new notions of individual and collective rights, and a more expansive conception of liberty. These conditions emerged in capitalist Britain and its Continental Colonies, but failed to do so in the equally capitalist Netherlands.

Probing the Dutch Case

The contributors to this book have used Seymour Drescher's 'Long Goodbye' as an invitation to rethink slavery and antislavery in the Dutch world and, eventually, beyond. In so doing, they have significantly broadened the geographical scope of Drescher's original essay by including the West Indian, African, and Asian parts of the Dutch colonial empire. Moreover, they have accepted the challenge to rethink the general relationship between antislavery, capitalism, and modernization by reflecting on the impact of politics, religion, ideology, and racism, as well as on the meaning of both free and unfree labor.

In establishing the order of the following chapters, I have opted for a thematic organization. The contributions by Maarten Kuitenbrouwer and Angelie Sens focus on the debates and changing political and ideological parameters in the Netherlands itself. Edwin Horlings's paper deals with the economics of both the Netherlands and Suriname. The subsequent articles by Alex van Stipriaan and myself discuss the Dutch West Indian context and its implications for the metropolitan debate. From a similar perspective, Robert Ross and Gerrit J. Knaap discuss slavery in the Cape Colony and Southeast Asia, respectively. Pieter C. Emmer compares post-abolition dilemmas in both the Dutch and British East and West Indies. Stanley E. Engerman provides an even wider comparative perspective on the abolition of all types of bonded labor throughout the world in a period spanning various centuries. In his Epilogue, finally, Seymour Drescher weighs the various arguments expounded by the contributors to this volume against his own conceptualization of the Dutch enigma, and the wider debate on abolition.

Before I review the major issues at stake, a brief presentation of the various contributions seems appropriate. In 'The Dutch Case of Antislavery: Late and Elitist Abolitionism', Maarten Kuitenbrouwer compares the evidence from his own research to the interpretations of, among others, Drescher. Earlier research (Kuitenbrouwer 1978) had already led him to the conclusion that the Anglo-Saxon model did not fit the Dutch case, as 'in the Netherlands industrialization was late and modest, religious nonconformism was at first rather passive and inward-looking, and there was little radicalism to provoke the ruling classes into hegemonic actions'. Whereas he offers various nuances to Drescher's interpretation, particularly regarding the nature of Dutch industrialization and the existence of antislavery undercurrents all through the period under discussion, he does not fundamentally oppose Drescher's analysis. Detailing the long-winded parliamentary debates of the 1850s, Kuitenbrouwer argues that the final abolitionist legislation was not enacted as 'perfunctorily' as Drescher suggests. Yet he fully concurs with Drescher in stating that the abolitionist movement was élitist, as was the political system which belatedly legislated the Emancipation Act.

In her contribution, 'Dutch Antislavery Attitudes in a Decline-Ridden Society, 1750-1815', Angelie Sens reviews the influence of the Enlightenment on Dutch thinking on colonialism, and on slavery in particular. She concurs with Drescher's preference to discuss antislavery in the context of new forms of social mobilization. Particularly from the 1780s onwards, the Dutch Enlightenment did indeed produce a new intellectual élite, advocating a new social morality implicating all social classes as a means to advance the cause of the nation. Yet in contrast to the British and French cases, the Dutch Enlightened debate was grounded in a mainly pessimistic preoccupation with the decline of Dutch society and state since its seventeenth-century Golden Age. Hence, the debate focused on a return to earlier, more prosperous and dynamic times. Antislavery did emerge, but failed to have political consequences. The modest antislavery literature met with relative indifference. The Enlightened Patriot movement reserved the right to freedom to the inhabitants of the Republic itself, as did the Batavian Republic and institutions such as the Nederlandsch Zendeling-Genootschap (Dutch Missionary Society). Whereas in the period 1750-1815 the public debate revealed significant political divergence on other issues, virtually all participants opted for the economic recovery of the Netherlands, including its potentially rewarding slave colonies, rather than the abstract good of abolishing slavery.

In 'An Economic Explanation of the Late Abolition of Slavery in Suriname', Edwin Horlings probes a series of possible links between economics and abolitionism. He argues that from the perspective of the Suriname slave holders, there was no economic need to abolish slavery. A forced transition to free labor could only impair the economic prospects of the relatively promising sugar sector. Rather, the structural modernization transforming the Dutch economy from the mid-nineteenth century on provided a new context in which abolitionism could succeed. In general terms, modernization implied more than strictly economic growth. It also meant a reduction in the relevance of West Indian slavery to the domestic economy, and the emergence of a more efficient institutional context.

Political modernization was an integral part of this process. As sustained economic growth set in, financing Emancipation became less of a problem.

Alex van Stipriaan likewise finds a strictly economic explanation of the abolition of slavery in Suriname, the major Dutch West Indian colony, unlikely. In 'Suriname and the Abolition of Slavery', he demonstrates how none of the major sectors (coffee, cotton, and particularly sugar) benefitted from abolition. In fact, the recovery process of the sugar sector was heavily frustrated by the Emancipation Act. Not surprisingly therefore, after the imposed abolition of the slave trade, the Suriname planters and their modest lobby in the Netherlands strongly opposed the abolition of slavery itself. At the same time, Van Stipriaan argues, slavery was undermined from within. This resulted only partly from the negative demographic growth rate of the slave population and the cost of amelioration. There is also evidence of increasing slave resistance to the pressures of the plantation regime and, particularly after the 1848 Emancipation in the French Caribbean, to the prolongation of slavery itself. The colonial state's repeated support for slaves' protests against maltreatment and harsh labor demands only served to further undermine the system. Van Stipriaan suggests that without the growing manifestation of slave discontent, which did affect metropolitan thinking, the final abolition act would probably have come even later than it did.

In my own contribution, 'Same Old Song? Perspectives on Slavery and Slaves in Suriname and Curaçao', I analyze the West Indian rather than the metropolitan élites' views on slavery and slaves. Not surprisingly, the West Indian élites opposed abolition, and their arguments confirm the flatness of the Dutch abolition debate. Economic arguments dovetailed with 'evolutionist', largely racist stereotypes. Yet not everything was the same old song. In view of the impending abolition of slavery, Suriname planters opted for religious conversion of the slaves almost overnight in the 1830s. They hoped that this new policy would ensure civil order and a regular work force both in the last decades of slavery and in the transition to free labor. In Curaçao, conversion to Christianity had a far longer history, dating back to the Spanish period. Many of its lessons could have served to quell the earlier concern of the Suriname planter that this opening to Western culture would undermine slavery, and that therefore conversion would have diminished the menace posed by abolition. Ironically, antislavery and proslavery authors alike implicitly shared many pessimistic notions of the character of slaves/blacks. Meanwhile, the debates in the two colonies varied both in intensity and in the issues raised. These divergences may be related to the colonies' contrasting socioeconomic profiles; at the same time, they confirm the wide distance separating the metropolis from its colonies, and the colonial élites from one another.

A particularly explicit reformulation of the enigma of late Dutch abolitionism is offered by Robert Ross in his contribution 'Abolitionism, the Batavian Republic, the British, and the Cape Colony'. In line with Drescher's reasoning, Ross argues that the divergent abolitionist histories of Britain and the Netherlands should not be traced to differences in economic profiles, but rather in religious characteristics. Thus the enigma is located in the different workings of Protestantism, rather than capitalism, in the two countries. Part of the article addresses this issue by comparing the metropolitan societies. In accounting for the exceptional British case, Ross agrees with Drescher in emphasizing the significance of new modes of social and religious mobilization. Moreover, he argues that Revolutionary France's occupation of the Netherlands imbued the Dutch Protestant élites with an abhorrence of radicalism. For several decades, abolitionism, perceived as an element of revolutionary liberal ideology, was anathema. In the other part, Ross contrasts one or two lone Batavian abolitionists in the last years of Dutch rule in the Cape Colony with the dominant proslavery currents under Dutch and subsequent British rule. Antislavery was present, but never became an influential movement. In its attitude towards slavery too, the Nederlandsch Hervormde Kerk (Dutch Reformed Church), a pivotal religious institution, actually borrowed from the conservative Protestantism in the former metropolis, and thus helped to isolate Christian liberalism well into the present century.

In 'Slavery and the Dutch in Southeast Asia', Gerrit J. Knaap offers an overview spanning the period from the early seventeenth through the late nineteenth century. At no point did the significance of slavery in the Dutch East match its crucial importance in the Americas. Indigenous slavery had been part of the region's social fabric before colonization, and would actually outlive the colonial variant, which was abolished in 1860, for another half century. The domestic variant, interwoven with debt peonage, was of little economic interest from a colonial point of view. As a means to produce export cash crops, slavery was of significance only in Moluccan nutmeg and mace production. For the Dutch, the real significance of slavery was its 'industrial' use, such as in construction and in the harbors, and for private purposes in their own households. Slavery therefore was a predominantly urban phenomenon. By 1680, half the population in the colony's capital, Batavia, were slaves, mainly imported from the other islands of the archipelago. A faint abolitionism emerged only after 1800, and it took the colonial government many decades more to end slavery. By then, colonial slavery had ceased to be of much importance anyway.[8] In 1860, out of a total population exceeding twenty million, a mere 4,735 slaves were freed. Over

---

[8] Ironically, this Asian case seems to support Eric Williams's economistic explanation of abolition, which has been discarded for the Atlantic case he was addressing.

the previous decades, the colonial state had already learned to make huge profits by exploiting the labor of peasants rather than slaves.

Pieter C. Emmer's paper focuses precisely on such post-abolition colonial policies, and on the question of what the different British and Dutch policies accomplished in the West Indies, West Africa, and Asia. In 'The Ideology of Free Labor and Dutch Colonial Policy, 1830-1870', Emmer supports Drescher's 'econocide' view of British abolition, while broadening the argument to include the initial British hesitation to use indentured labor in India (if not in some of their colonies in the Caribbean and the Indian Ocean). The Dutch provide a pragmatic, calculating contrast to the unique British case. Late in abolishing slavery, they opted for an exceptionally long period of apprenticeship, and then for an immediate transition to Asian indentured labor in their major Caribbean colony, Suriname. Meanwhile, from the 1830s to the 1870s, they deployed semi-bonded labor in Java's spectacularly successful cultivation system. From an economic point of view, the Dutch were absolutely right in only belatedly complying with the British free labor ideology. Both in the West and in the East, bonded labor, whether performed by slaves or under other arrangements, was simply more rewarding than free labor. Therefore, only with the decision to dismantle the Cultivation System in the 1860s did the Dutch succumb to the economically unjustified appeal of the free labor ideology.

Dutch Antislavery in Comparative Perspective

Of the many issues raised in these chapters, I briefly review some which may help to put the Dutch case in comparative perspective, and to encourage a further reflection on the relationship between capitalism, modernity, and antislavery. First, Drescher's observation that in spite of its reputed 'humanitarian sensibility', the Netherlands was late in developing a significant antislavery discourse is not under serious attack. Particularly Kuitenbrouwer and Sens add elements to the 'reservoir of distaste for slavery' discussed by Drescher, yet without fundamentally altering the picture.[9] Even the late eighteenth-century radicals failed to consider abolition seriously – including in the Cape Colony where, as Ross observes, they could have made such ideals prevail during the French period.

The attitudes of those with direct interests in slavery, as analyzed in the contributions by Van Stipriaan, Ross, Knaap, and myself, only underline their denial of a moral problem well into the nineteenth century. I therefore feel that the opening citations to this introduction – the first taken from a doctor's manual for slave traders, the second from the correspondence of a

---

[9] A similar nuance was suggested by Klein in his contribution to the seminar. Compare also Blakely 1993.

Suriname planter linking the idea of 'cruel treatment' not to his use of slaves, but rather to the metropolitan slackness in providing enough of them – capture the dominant spirit among the interested parties painfully well for the period up to, say, the 1820s. Only after that date can one observe an ambivalent change of heart among the élites involved. Slavery finally became a morally and ultimately politically embarrassing issue. Yet the continuing exploitation of unfree labor under the Cultivation System in Java again calls into question both the credibility of humanitarian impulses from the metropolis, and the ideological commitment to the liberal doctrine of the superiority of free over bonded labor. As Emmer argues, the ideology of the economic superiority of free over slave labor never made it to the mainstream as it did in Anglo-Saxon abolitionism. Moreover, as I suggest, both abolitionists and proslavery authors concurred in their scepticism regarding the reliability and respectability which could be expected of the slaves after their full emancipation. The post-Emancipation economic and social developments in the British West Indies only served to strengthen such apprehensions.

Of course, the crucial question is not that of whether individuals objected to slavery, but whether and when such feelings translated into social mobilization and political action and legislation. The lack of such a 'translation', well into the nineteenth century, is at the center of Drescher's questioning of the Dutch experience. In the subsequent essays, there is some nuance to, but little fundamental disagreement with, his position that Dutch abolitionism developed late, lacked a popular base, and to a large extent only reacted to international pressure.[10] The detailed analysis by Kuitenbrouwer recalls both the generally low levels of popular mobilization in the Netherlands and the intensity of some of the mid-century parliamentary debates regarding abolition, yet does not detract from the characterization of Dutch abolitionism as élitist, businesslike, and late.

Why was this so? Sens argues that the élites' prevailing pessimism in the late eighteenth century and their obsession with restoring economic prosperity made a bold move towards full emancipation seem all the more capricious. Ross adds that the legacy of revolutionary France's occupation of the Netherlands imbued the Protestant élite with a strong conservatism, which entailed an unwillingness to engage with the very abolitionism propagated by Protestant leaders and rank and file in the Anglo-Saxon world. Perhaps, in trying to account for the absence of a significant religious antislavery movement, one should also mention the absence of trans-

---

[10] 'International pressure' was obviously primarily a British affair. The role of the pervasive Dutch anti-British sentiment, which was particularly strong ever since the British humiliation of the Dutch in the Fourth Anglo-Dutch War (1780-1784), is a rather neglected theme in this book.

atlantic missionary communities. The effort to convert the subjected slaves to Christianity came late in all colonies except the Antillean islands. The few late attempts were mainly the work of relative outsiders to the Dutch world, such as German Moravians, Catholic Spaniards and Southern Dutch; this precluded the development of a regular flow of information and opinions, and a fortiori of a mobilization for a shared political program.

What about the possible economic motives behind abolitionism? Not one contributor explicitly objects to Drescher's affirmation that, even more than the weakness of abolitionism in the early nineteenth century, its absence in the dynamic seventeenth and early eighteenth centuries falsifies the notion of a direct causality between capitalist development and abolition. The various contributions disclose, in fact, an overwhelming focus on the nineteenth century, and an implicit suggestion that abolition was economically damaging rather than profitable.[11] In this, the authors concur not only with Drescher, but equally with the great majority of contemporary actors and authors.

The argument is not necessarily that slavery in the Dutch world was an eminently successful and profitable enterprise. The detailed analyses of Van Stipriaan and Horlings provide a mixed image of slave profitability in Suriname, whereas no figures are offered for the other colonies, where slavery was much less important anyway. In fact, the Dutch West Indian slave colonies may have been among the least profitable in the region – which, of course, could have provided a motive for early abolition, but in fact did not. Yet the crucial issue is that the alternative of free labor was rightly considered to be more costly and/or less reliable. This explains the consistent resistance to abolition, and subsequent tactics to postpone emancipation, throughout the Dutch world, by both slave owners and their representatives in the metropolis.

The links retained between the economy, and particularly capitalism, and abolitionism are therefore in a sense rather trivial: the growth of the Dutch economy during the nineteenth century, and particularly the success of the (bonded labor!) Cultivation System in Java, allowed for the financing of abolition. Slave emancipation had become less costly anyway because of the negative growth rates of the slave populations after slave trade abolition.

[11] Both Van den Boogaart and Klein, in their contributions to the seminar, questioned the overall economic modernity of the seventeenth-century Netherlands. See also Horlings, in this book. Klein suggests that the seventeenth-century economy was not as clearly 'modern capitalist' as Drescher supposes; likewise, that the Dutch state was anything but a monolithic modern entity, and there was not one dominating 'modern' ideology which would have definitively disqualified slavery as archaic. In fact, forced labor was perceived to be of great utility. Van den Boogaart argues that the embryonic free labor ideology of the founder of the West Indies Company, Willem Usselincx, was quickly dismissed in favor of the calculations of Ottho Keye (1659) demonstrating the greater profitability of slave holding tropical colonies over free labor colonies in moderate zones.

The ever diminishing number of slaves lowered the compensation that had to be paid to slave holders. Yet there is a more general connection between capitalism and abolition, namely, that hesitant modern economic growth was but one facet in a general modernization of Dutch society, which included, among other things, a new and stronger role for the state and a new condition of belonging to the modern Western world with its particular moral standards. Evidently, this is a far cry from economistic causality. In fact, one may well question – with Drescher – whether is is useful to think of economic growth or capitalism as the causal factor here, rather than a more encompassing process of modernization per se.

Did developments within the colonies – other than economic performance – and colonial lobbies matter to the metropolitan debate? Interestingly, even without a strong Suriname lobby in the Netherlands, the slave owners' perspective on abolition reigned supreme up to the 1830s at least. It remained a crucial factor to be reckoned with up to emancipation and beyond, into the periods of apprenticeship and the flawed transition to 'free' labor with Asian indentured laborers. Likewise, slave owners in the Antilles, the Cape Colony, and the East Indies could count on metropolitan support well into the nineteenth century. With one possible exception, there is precious little indication that anything happening in the colonies would have helped to induce metropolitan policy-makers to reflect on abolition. As Drescher has rightly observed, neither the eighteenth-century Maroon nor the 1763 Berbice or the 1795 Curaçao slave revolts had any observable impact on metropolitan policy regarding abolition; nor, one may add, did the particularly negative demographic growth rates of the Suriname slave population, or the bad image of Suriname slavery as a particularly harsh variant of the peculiar institution. At least into the nineteenth century, metropolis and colonies seem to have been worlds apart. Only Van Stipriaan's hypothesis regarding increasing unrest and empowerment of the mid-century slaves links colonial developments, and particularly slave behavior, to a sense of urgency in the metropolitan debate.

Finally, it may be useful to review a series of factors which would seem to have mattered, but apparently failed to have consistent consequences for the emergence of abolitionism – in short, the (non-)issues referred to as the 'Goldilocks model' by Drescher (p. 31). In this category, Drescher places the reasoning that Dutch slavery was 'too big' at one time, 'too small' at another to 'cause' abolitionism. The very performance of the various slave economies may be another such issue. Thus, for instance, one may well question whether Van Stipriaan's sophisticated analysis of the Suriname sugar versus coffee sectors has any bearing in the end on the larger issue of abolition: in both sectors, there was no feasible alternative to slave labor. As Van Stipriaan concludes himself, 'for none of the plantation sectors was there an economically "logical" moment to abolish slavery' (p. 136).

In the same vein, the absence of a strong West Indian lobby in the Netherlands seems, in the end, to have hardly mattered at all. For all the influence wielded by the powerful West India interest in Britain, this lobby failed to stop abolitionism, and eventually lost British protectionism too. In the Netherlands, no such thing as a protected home market for colonial produce existed at all. Since this is often taken as evidence of the absence of a successful Dutch West Indian lobby, there is some irony in the observation that apparently no such lobby was required in the Netherlands to keep the Dutch élites from outlawing for so long an institution which ostensibly was so marginal to their economy.

At the same time, one may detect a rationality of sorts – businesslike indeed – in the enactment of the final emancipations. The process was surprisingly pluriform. First, there was the 1848 half-hearted, semi-legislated emancipation in St. Martin, which produced close to nothing anyway. Next, the 1860 abolition in the East Indies was, in view of the loss of relevance of the peculiar institution, extraordinarily late anyway. Then, we have the 1863 emancipation without apprenticeship in the relatively heavily-populated Leewards Antilles, where, for once, the stagnant economies may indeed have been better off with free labor than with slave labor. Finally came the 1863 emancipation in Suriname with its unusually long, ten-year apprenticeship. Whereas one may be inclined to read these various procedures as further evidence of the lack of commitment of the metropolis, one might also perceive considerable rationality here, to wit, that of a metropolitan policy tailored to local needs.

The presence of a significant black population in Britain has been cited as a factor conducive to raising the awareness of colonial slavery and hence of abolitionism in Britain. The Dutch case, with a negligible black presence in the metropolis, could be taken a further evidence of this linking. But then again, why should such a presence heighten a sense of humanitarism, rather than the other way around (as, indeed, we witness today in Europe)? And why, to stretch the point, did the Iberian peninsula, with its long tradition of black presence, fail to produce significant abolitionism? In the same vein, one may question the general relevance of an awareness of the colonies in the metropolitan mind. In my own contribution, I argue that the limited nature of such awareness was an obstacle to the growth of abolitionism. Even so, it stands to reason to argue the opposite too: if few knew of, and had vested interests in the colonies, it would have been all the easier to boost the battered Dutch sense of success and moral strength to 'do the right thing' at a bargain price. After all, there was little to win in respecting the property rights of slave owners with whom very few felt any affinity at all.

These closing and deliberately inconclusive statements underline the utility of analyzing the specifics of single cases of abolitionism, rather than striving for the encompassing model. A focus on the Dutch cases of late abolition may serve to highlight the unique Anglo-Saxon and particularly British cases, and to place the Netherlands squarely within the continental fold, as Drescher's 'Long Goodbye' and most of the contributors to this collection do. There may be additional heuristic value, though, in comparing these continental abolitions to one another, rather than only to the exceptional Anglo-Saxon variant. Thus, to offer but one suggestion, if indeed transatlantic affinities were so crucial to the emergence of Anglo-Saxon abolitionism, one can see why this type of abolitionism did not originate in the Dutch colonies. But how is one to account for the fact that the Spanish American colonies, which in a way form a category in between the extremes of the Continental Colonies and the Dutch West Indies, failed to develop significant abolitionism before independence, and only hesitantly afterwards? Why, to paraphrase Drescher, were the Anglo-Saxon parameters 'just right' for the emergence of decisive abolitionism, in contrast to those in Spain and the Spanish American colonies? And why did the Dutch and the Spanish end up being almost equally slow in legislating emancipation, in spite of the enormous differences characterizing both the significance of slavery in their colonial empires and their cultural, religious, and political traditions?

Obviously, there are more open questions which should be addressed in future research.[12] Yet at this point, we may move, with Stanley L. Engerman's 'Emancipations in Comparative Perspective: A Long and Wide View', to a radical widening of the perspective. Engerman first explores the roughly coincidental abolition of serfdom in many parts of Europe, which suggests the hypothesis that European economic development and the concomitant demographic, political, moral, religious, and ideological factors translated into a similar abhorrence of systems of labor recruitment previously deemed perfectly normal. Yet the question of why precisely this significant change of attitude occurred – and why not elsewhere, such as in Asia and Africa – remains. An analysis of the widely divergent timings of the abolition of the trade and slavery itself suggests that even within the Western world, one unifying theory is unlikely to encompass the many different factors at play at a local level. The continuing history of other forms of forced labor after the various emancipations again poses intriguing questions, both about the intentions of the abolitionists, about the local and international significance and acceptability of alternative forms of labor, and

---

[12] It is remarkable how little explicit attention the various contributors pay to the (lack of) relevance of class antagonism to the Dutch case; the role of class interest is of course a central issue in the wider debate (Bender 1992a:10-1, Drescher 1993).

about the abolitionist movement's apparently limited capacity to mount new campaigns to eradicate these probably less extreme types of bonded labor. In sum, Engerman's reflections again serve to nuance the tendency to take the British, or Anglo-Saxon, case as a yardstick in explaining abolition.

In his 'Epilogue', Seymour Drescher both reviews the arguments advanced by the various contributors to this book, and reflects on the wider theoretical implications of the preceding chapters. While honoring the contributing authors for providing a wealth of new materials and for further widening the geographic and temporal scope of the debate, Drescher affirms that in the end, the evidence underlines his basic thesis that the abolition of New World slavery cannot be explained by reference to economic interest and capitalism per se. In fact, he asserts, addressing the abolition of both slavery and concurrent Western forms of unfree labor, '[t]he wider the range of societies incorporated into the abolition process, the more tenuous becomes the connection between the abolitions of slavery/serfdom and capitalist industrialization'. Instead, antislavery should be understood as a declaration of faith, not just of religious and moral, but equally of economic inspiration. The abolitionist ideology simply *stipulated* – against many odds, as both contemporaries and later historians have demonstrated – that free labor was always superior to slave labor.

In sum, then, this volume offers not only the most thorough and wide-ranging discussion to date of antislavery in the Netherlands and in the Dutch colonial world, but also adds a new dimension to the ongoing debate on the relationship between abolitionism and economic, political, and cultural modernization in the Western world at large. The book's strength lies precisely in its combination of microhistory and theoretical analysis. As such, *Fifty Years Later* reminds us once more that detailed, empirical research is crucial for enhancing our understanding of an abstract, wider problem such as the relationship between capitalism, modernity, and antislavery. In the introduction to *The Antislavery Debate*, Bender signaled with some disappointment that the shift of focus of the wider Davis-Haskell-Ashworth debate to the Dutch case was a shift 'from concepts, abstractions, and analogues to an actual historical case. For historians such evidence is always the court of final appeal. Yet, as with appeal courts, the case brought before the bar is often resolved in ways that miss some of the animating purpose that sent the case to the high court in the first place.' (Bender 1992a:10). Some of those involved in this debate may indeed have deplored such a shift of focus – though particularly Davis and Ashworth frequently expressed their preference for the analysis of 'hard historical evidence' over abstract conceptualizations. Either way, the present book certainly continues the shift towards a discussion of empirical evidence. Not only do the contributors to *Fifty Years Later* bring more 'real life' into the court of final appeal. They also effectively falsify the idea that this endeavor would either obscure a wider comparative perspective or lack animating purpose.

References

Bender, Thomas
1992a   'Introduction', in: Thomas Bender (ed.), *The Antislavery Debate; Capitalism and Abolitionism as a Problem in Historical Interpretation*, pp. 3-13. Berkeley: University of California Press.

Bender, Thomas (ed.)
1992b   *The Antislavery Debate; Capitalism and Abolitionism as a Problem in Historical Interpretation*. Berkeley: University of California Press.

Blackburn, Robin
1988   *The Overthrow of Colonial Slavery 1776-1848*. London: Verso.

Blakely, Allison
1993   *Blacks in the Dutch World; The Evolution of Racial Imagery in a Modern Society*. Bloomington: Indiana University Press.

Boogaart, Ernst van den
1992   'Comment to Seymour Drescher, The Long Goodbye'. [Unpublished paper, presented at the Conference 'Dutch Capitalism and Antislavery in Comparative Perspective', Leiden, KITLV/Royal Institute of Linguistics and Anthropology, 15 October 1993.]

Davis, David Brion
1992a   'Reflections on Abolitionism and Ideological Hegemony', in: Thomas Bender (ed.), *The Antislavery Debate; Capitalism and Abolitionism as a Problem in Historical Interpretation*, pp. 161-79. Berkeley: University of California Press.
1992b   'The Perils of Doing History by Ahistorical Abstraction; A Reply to Thomas L. Haskell's *AHR Forum* Reply', in: Thomas Bender (ed.), *The Antislavery Debate; Capitalism and Abolitionism as a Problem in Historical Interpretation*, pp. 290-309. Berkeley: University of California Press.

Drescher, Seymour
1977   *Econocide; British Slavery in the Era of Abolition*. Pittsburgh: University of Pittsburgh Press.
1993   'Review essay of *The Antislavery Debate; Capitalism and Abolitionism as a Problem in Historical Interpretation* [Thomas Bender (ed.)]', *History and Theory* 32:311-29.
1994   'The Long Goodbye: Dutch Capitalism and Antislavery in Comparative Perspective', *American Historical Review* 99:44-69. [Reprinted with minor revisions in this volume.]

Emmer, Pieter C.
1980   'Anti-Slavery and the Dutch; Abolition without Reform', in: Christine Bolt and Seymour Drescher (eds), *Anti-Slavery, Religion, and Reform; Essays in Memory of Roger Anstey*, pp. 80-98. Folkestone: Dawson; Hamden: Archon.

Gallandat, D.H.
1769   *Noodige onderrichtingen voor de slavenhandelaaren.* Middelburg: Gillissen.

Haskell, Thomas L.
1992   'Convention and Hegemonic Interest in the Debate over Antislavery', in: Thomas Bender (ed.), *The Antislavery Debate; Capitalism and Abolitionism as a Problem in Historical Interpretation,* pp. 200-59. Berkeley: University of California Press.

Israel, Jonathan I.
1995   *The Dutch Republic; Its Rise, Greatness, and Fall 1477-1806.* Oxford: Clarendon Press.

Keye, Ottho
1659   *Het waere onderscheyt tusschen koude en warme landen, aengewesen in de nootsakelijckheden die daer vereyscht worden [...] om beyde die landen te konnen bewoonen [...] Voor-gestelt en vergeleken met Nieu-Nederlant, als sijnde een koudt landt en Guajana sijnde een warm landt, en beyde gelegen in America [...].* 's-Gravenhage: Hondius.

Klein, P.W.
1992   'The Yelp of the Little Mongrel or the Making of a Mixed Economy'. [Unpublished paper, presented at the Conference 'Dutch Capitalism and Antislavery in Comparative Perspective', Leiden, KITLV/Royal Institute of Linguistics and Anthropology, 15 October 1993.]

Kuitenbrouwer, Maarten
1978   'De Nederlandse afschaffing van de slavernij in vergelijkend perspectief', *Bijdragen en Mededelingen betreffende de Geschiedenis der Nederlanden* 93:69-101.

Oostindie, Gert
1989   *Roosenburg en Mon Bijou; Twee Surinaamse plantages, 1720-1870.* Dordrecht: Foris. [KITLV, Caribbean Series 11.]
1993   'The Economics of Suriname Slavery', *Economic and Social History in the Netherlands* 5:1-24.

Postma, Johannes Menne
1990   *The Dutch in the Atlantic Slave Trade 1600-1815.* Cambridge: Cambridge University Press.

Schama, Simon
1988   *The Embarrassment of Riches; An Interpretation of Dutch Culture in the Golden Age.* New York: Fontana Press. [Original edition 1987.]

Siwpersad, J.P.
1979   *De Nederlandse regering en de afschaffing van de Surinaamse slavernij (1833-1863).* Groningen: Bouma; Castricum: Hagen.

Stipriaan, Alex van
1989   'The Suriname Rat Race; Labour and Technology on Sugar Plantations, 1750-1900', *Nieuwe West-Indische Gids/New West Indian Guide* 63:94-117.
1993   *Surinaams contrast; Roofbouw en overleven in een Caraïbische plantagekolonie, 1750-1863.* Leiden: KITLV Press. [KITLV, Caribbean Series 13.]

Vries, Jan de and Ad van der Woude
1995   *Nederland 1500-1815; De eerste ronde van moderne economische groei.* Amsterdam: Balans.

Wallerstein, Immanuel
1980   *The Modern World-System II; Mercantilism and the Consolidation of the European World-Economy, 1600-1750.* New York: Academic Press.

Williams, Eric
1944   *Capitalism and Slavery.* Chapel Hill: University of North Carolina Press.

Winter, Johanna Maria van
1982   'Public Opinion in the Netherlands on the Abolition of Slavery', in: M.A.P. Meilink-Roelofsz (ed.), *Dutch Authors on West Indian History; A Historiographical Selection*, pp. 100-28. The Hague: Nijhoff. [KITLV, Translation Series 21.]

SEYMOUR DRESCHER

The Long Goodbye
Dutch Capitalism and Antislavery in Comparative Perspective

'Is there any point to which you would wish to draw my attention?'
'To the curious incident of the dog in the night-time.'
'The dog did nothing in the night-time.'
'That was the curious incident', remarked Sherlock Holmes.
Silver Blaze (Conan Doyle 1946)

'If the world were to come to an end, I would go to Holland, where everything happens fifty years later.' Pieter Emmer opens his discussion of Dutch abolition with this apocryphal aphorism, ascribed to Heinrich Heine. Of all the northern European imperial powers the Dutch were the last to legislate colonial slave emancipation, thirty years after their British counterparts across the North Sea (Emmer 1980; Oostindie 1992). They perfunctorily abolished slavery in 1863, after their Swedish, Danish, and French neighbors. Historians of slavery seem to have repeated the procrastination. They have been equally slow to view the Dutch case as a valuable opportunity for comparative analysis.[1]

The relationship between capitalism and antislavery has primarily been debated by historians of Anglo-American slavery. For almost a century and half after abolitionism assaulted the slave systems of the Atlantic economy, the historiography of Anglo-American antislavery was solidly embedded in what has come to be called the Progressive or Whig interpretation of history. Historians assumed that the ending of chattel slavery reflected the modern development of civilized behavior, led by the English-speaking world. Slavery constituted a moral and material fetter which antislavery shattered in one area after another. The process moved from the most

---

[1] For their critical judgement and helpful comments I owe thanks to Robin Blackburn, Natalie Z. Davis, Pieter Emmer, David Eltis, Stanley L. Engerman, William W. Freehling, Peter W. Klein, Gert Oostindie, and Robert L. Paquette; to the Seminar on Caribbean Societies at the University of London's Institute of Commonwealth Studies; to the Workshop on Migration and Missionary Activities at the prior international conference on the interaction between the Low Countries and the Americas, 1492-1992 (Leiden, June 1992); and to the participants at the Conference on the Lesser Antilles in the Age of European Expansion at Hamilton College (Clinton, NY, October 1992).

progressive areas toward the most backward, from the Somerset decision of 1772 in England to Brazil's 'Golden Law' of emancipation in 1888, and then on to the termination of coerced labor in Africa and Asia.

Perhaps the most controversial aspect of the historiography of abolition since the Second World War has been the new prominence accorded to economically based motives, forces and conflicts in accounting for the transition from slavery to freedom. In this linkage of economic development to slavery, Eric Williams's *Capitalism and Slavery* was but a forerunner (Williams 1944:108-77; 1970:280-327).[2] For more than a generation, the historical debate over abolition in Anglo-America has been centered on a bedrock economic question: Was abolition facilitated by the decline of slave economies and/or the rise of capitalist industrial systems, and how did economic and non-economic considerations figure in this process?

It is now clear that in at least one important sense, slavery was no peculiar institution. The slave trade was an 'uncommon market', to use Gemery and Hogendorn's terms, only in that its commodities and capital were human beings, not because buyers, or sellers, or users of slaves and their products behaved differently from those in other markets. Since economically grounded models plausibly account for the establishment and growth of slave systems, many historians were tempted to explain the destruction process by similar economically generated forces. Williams explained abolition in terms of an economically induced decline of British slavery and rise of industrialism in the wake of the American Revolutionary War. Historians of slavery in the USA, the British Empire and elsewhere also explained abolition by recourse to a variety of internal economic contradictions and uncontrollable world market forces.[3]

However, a generation of research on the various slave economies in the Americas has also increasingly shown that slavery was economically viable throughout the age of emancipation, even while it was being hobbled and destroyed in one entity after another. Political processes unraveled economically viable systems of production, often at the peak of their economic

---

[2] For reviews of the historiographical trends, see Drescher 1990; Engerman 1986.
[3] On free labor as the peculiar institution, see Finley 1976; Drescher 1987:x, 17-8. On the economics of the slave trade, see Gemery and Hogendorn 1979. Although Williams's initial work focused specifically upon the destruction of the British slave system by British capitalists, he later extended his thesis to the claim that the hostility of metropolitan capitalism in general was a major factor in the abolition of the other Northern imperial slave systems, including the Dutch (Williams 1970:280-90). Others have suggested an extension of the thesis to the whole Atlantic basin (Manning 1990:171-2). The economic argument for the abolition of slavery took two basic forms. The first was that slavery became increasingly unprofitable. The second was that, whether or not it remained profitable, it became decreasingly important economically in the various political systems to which it was attached. In addition to the references in note 2, see, inter alia, Drescher 1976; 1977; Temperley 1977; Eltis 1987:3-16; Solow and Engerman 1987; Fogel et al. 1992, I:60-80; Davis 1988a:153-5.

significance to the world market. Slave labor productivity was, in short, not economically regressive or inferior, a fact which challenged abolitionist conceptions of progress and abolition.[4]

If no inherent weakness in slave labor led to the rise and triumph of antislavery, however, how else might an economic causal relationship be established? A number of historians emphasized the declining value of the colonies to the imperial metropolis. Some have hypothesized that capitalist élites and intellectuals were so impressed by the economic performance of their own dynamic free labor societies that they simply dismissed equally compelling evidence of dynamism in slave labor economies, and assumed that a transformation to free labor could only accelerate growth and prosperity everywere (Temperley 1977:117-8; Eltis 1987:17-28, 102-6).[5] Others have reformulated the connection in terms of a transformation within metropolitan class relationships during the early industrial revolution. Capitalist industrialization required a new free labor discipline, a discipline widely resisted by working people still rooted in an older moral economy. The pioneers of Anglo-American antislavery legitimized the new discipline by denouncing antithetical labor systems, especially the institution of chattel slavery (Davis 1975:453-68; Holt 1990; 1992:13-53). In this perspective abolition validated both ruling class and capitalist hegemony during a period of severe social and military threats – the period of the French Revolution and Napoleon. Abolitionism acted as a screening device, which simultaneously underwrote the old British aristocratic political order and the new industrial order.[6]

All of these accounts stress what has been called the 'free labor ideology'. Spokesmen of antislavery targeted slavery or coerced labor as inferior in efficiency, motivation, or ease of discipline to wage labor. Metropolitan abolitionism promised the universal superiority of free labor. Thus the antislavery movement, like Adam Smith's transformation of political economy, 'reflected the needs and values of the emerging capitalist order' (Davis 1975:350; Ashworth 1992b).

The free labor ideology, however, is not the only economically based model that has been forged between capitalism and antislavery. In another conceptualization of the connection, capitalism stimulated antislavery not

---

[4] Drescher 1977:162-86; Eltis 1987:3-16; Fogel and Engerman 1989; Fogel 1992:81-113; Davis 1988a:153-5; 1988b.
[5] There is a general assumption that 'it is no historical accident that the rise of the "bourgeois state", with its belief in "possessive individualism" should have led to an attack on various systems of forced labor, such as slavery and serfdom' (Engerman 1992:3). Engerman, however, notes the tension between moral and economic arguments in the attack.
[6] Holt 1990:373. Davis (1992b) also noted that antislavery could appeal to 'various aspiring groups, including skilled workers'. He restricts his emphasis on the hegemonic antislavery of industrial capitalists and political élites to the early industrial period in Britain.

through its relationship to free labor superiority or to class interests but through the impact of market activity on values and perceptions, yielding a new 'cognitive style in Europe' (Haskell 1992a).[7] Humanitarianism in general and British abolitionism in particular arose from the interplay of market-fostered values, not through the dialectic of class conflict.[8]

But while historians' focus on the relationship between capitalism and antislavery inside the English-speaking world intensified, the potential value of other national experiences has become increasingly apparent. Similar or divergent outcomes could clarify the nature of the interaction between 'one of the most palpable realities of Western economic history [slavery] and one of the slipperiest abstractions of the Western intellectual heritage [capitalism]' (Wright 1987).[9] The history of the Netherlands is of particular comparative value for a number of reasons. If the pattern of Dutch economic and political development was not precisely that of Britain and France, the Dutch did anticipate and share with Britain a relative economic precociousness and economic expansion overseas during the first three quarters of the seventeenth century. After a further century of relative prosperity but slackened growth the Dutch standard of living in the 1770s still remained among the highest in Europe. Socially and politically Dutch society was dominated by a bourgeois oligarchy that had broken decisively with the aristocratic landholding ethos of neighboring societies. Throughout the seventeenth and eighteenth centuries the Netherlands was a republic dominated by a narrow political class, and characterized by a high degree of provincial autonomy.

On the other hand, more in the manner of France than Britain, the Netherlands entered three decades of acute economic distress, overseas disasters, and political upheaval between the 1780s and the fall of Napoleon. A discernably new period began with the creation of a kingdom of the Netherlands in 1814, and with the partial restoration of the Dutch overseas empire. The Netherlands now diverged both in its economic, political, and imperial history from those of Britain and France. For more than half a century it lagged behind its near neighbors in economic growth, political democratization, revolutionary challenges, and imperial expansion. It is this 'third' Dutch period, coinciding with the final dismantling of the British, French, and Dutch overseas slave systems, that has been the primary focus

---

[7] See the subsequent discussion by Davis, Ashworth and Haskell in Bender 1992b:161-309. See also Drescher 1993a.
[8] For further explorations of the relationship between British capitalism and slavery, see Solow and Engerman 1987:51-282; Eltis 1987:17-30; Blackburn 1988.
[9] For other international comparisons, see, inter alia, Bolt and Drescher 1984:101-318; Drescher 1987:50-66; 1988; Fogel 1992, I; Holt 1982. On the turn towards Holland, see Bender 1992a:9-10.

of what little comparative use of the Netherlands appears in the literature of antislavery.

Yet, a historiography focused solely on the nineteenth-century Netherlands risks the loss of extraordinarily fruitful comparisons which can be drawn from outside the conventional temporal frame of reference. Presumably, given a market model, a 'strong antislavery movement should have emerged in Holland, which was certainly involved in mercantile capitalism, in long-distance commerce, in world markets, and in complex banking and credit. Surely, the Dutch learned to attend to the remote consequences of their actions, and there must have been as many potential humanitarians per capita in the Dutch population as in Britain or the United States. Yet despite repeated prodding from British abolitionists, the Dutch remained stolidly indifferent to the whole abolitionist campaign.' (Davis 1992a). Even as abolitionism was reaching its peak of intensity in Anglo-America, only the faintest echo could be heard in the Netherlands.[10]

The point is critical because the market was more significant in the fifteenth-century Mediterranean economy ('the birth place of modern plantation slavery') than it was in many areas of nineteenth-century rural and abolitionist America. And in the Dutch case, the *early* modern Netherlands fully met the market criteria for a capitalist, non-abolitionist, counter-example. For the century of its primacy in world trade Holland exemplified a 'market-oriented society, whose members continued to see slavery as nothing worse than a necessary evil' (Haskell 1992b:233-4; Davis 1992b:294).[11] Seventeenth-century Holland, with the largest overseas trade per capita of any nation in the world, was the envy of much larger monarchical states. It had a substantial stake in the Atlantic slave system. It possessed a highly

---

[10] Ironically, the 'decline' of Dutch slavery correlates much more closely with the rise of *British* abolitionism. See Postma 1990:78 and compare Postma 1990:215, 275, 284-303; Drescher 1977:50-66.

[11] One might note that the Dutch *East* Indies would also have counted in Dutch calculations about the fate of slavery. In Batavia there were almost 20,000 slaves in 1812-13, and another 8,000 elsewhere in Java. British emancipation in 1833 coincided with the Dutch introduction of a new coercive labor system, requiring the Javanese population to devote at least one fifth of their land and labor-time to the growing of coffee, sugar, and indigo. In 1834 the Dutch East Indies produced an annual profit of ten million guilders, which shortly rose to twenty millions. In uneven proportions slavery and coerced labor were well-established institutions in the East Indies (Abeyasekere 1983). Haskell's argument, connecting the economic *insignificance* of slavery with the propensity to abolish it, recalls the opposite formulation by Adam Smith, who commented wryly: 'The late resolution of the Quakers in Pennsylvania to set at liberty all their negro slaves, may satisfy us that their number cannot be very great. Had they made any considerable part of their property, such a resolution could never have been agreed' (Smith 1937:366). Smith, and a considerable number of later historians and economic historians, considered the economic insignificance of slavery to be the relevant factor in assuring an early and rapid Quaker abolition. Haskell links slavery's economic insignificance to a *delay* in Dutch abolition. Neither Smith's nor Haskell's arguments work easily for both the Pennsylvania Quakers and the Dutch.

diversified economy, tied to the needs of its commercial hegemony and nourished by the most complex banking and market institutions of its time. Its wage levels and standard of living were the highest in Europe for well over a century (Davids and Noordegraaf 1993).[12]

Moreover, in terms of humanitarian sensibility Holland was internationally noted for its institutions of charity. It certainly experienced no shortage of moral and ideological attacks on the improper accumulation and use of wealth – what Simon Schama has called 'the embarrassment of riches'. The Netherlands' religious spokesmen offered an unbroken criticism of the potential immoralities of commerce. Even more pointedly, the Dutch began their seventeenth-century transatlantic slaving venture with occasional moral doubts about the propriety of trading in human beings, and with legal inhibitions on slaveowning at home. Masters understood that when they brought slaves to the Netherlands they implicitly manumitted them. Yet, for two centuries Holland nurtured few antislavery arguments and no abolitionist movement whatever.[13]

One might usefully distinguish three periods of the Dutch case – generations of expanding capitalism in the seventeenth century, the turbulent decades around the time of the French Revolution, and the period of the nineteenth century. More telling than the virtual absence of abolitionism in the stagnant post-Napoleonic Dutch economy, even with its diminishing dependence upon slavery, is the fact that Dutch abolitionism failed to emerge either in the seventeenth century, when the Netherlands was at or near its peak of economic dynamism, or in the early eighteenth century when the slave system was an important and growing branch of Dutch trade. Between the end of the Eighty Years War (1648) and the end of the War of the Spanish Succession (1713) the Afro-Caribbean trade was one of the Netherlands' three principal 'rich trades'. For six more decades a growing Dutch slave trade and an expanding plantation system no more stimulated the emergence of abolitionism during the eighteenth than it had during the seventeenth century (Israel 1989:296).[14]

If abolitionism was a market-linked phenomenon, one can dismiss the

---

12 See also note 18.
13 Schama 1988:290-371; Davis 1992b:295. On implicit metropolitan manumission, see Ross 1988:209-19, citing Van der Chijs 1885-1900, IV:57; Ross 1983:73-4. According to some historians slaves were legally free on arrival in the Netherlands (Armstrong and Worden 1988:116; Elphick and Shell 1988:210-1). Other historians assert that the Dutch legal system never reached an unambiguous position on the question. All agree that slavery's status within the metropolis was problematical (Oostindie 1990:232-3).
14 The Dutch seaborne empire, the first fully global empire of trade, was also 'the first to combine trade hegemony with great power status on land as well as sea, a pattern again subsequently repeated in the case of eighteenth-century Britain' (Israel 1990:x). On slave trade figures, see Postma 1990:250-1, 280-303, 308-61. Up to the 1770s the Dutch slave system remained a significant component of the imperial economy (Postma 1990:280-3).

Dutch case only by deploying a 'Goldilocks model' of capitalism and antislavery. Before the American Revolution Dutch slavery was 'too big' to be attacked in the Netherlands. After Napoleon it was 'too small' to be noticed. (We will have more to say about the revolutionary and Napoleonic interregnum.) Apparently, however, only in Anglo-America was the salience of slavery 'just right' for capitalist-inspired antislavery in the age of abolition.

If the Dutch case undermines the 'market model' of abolitionism, it also challenges the 'free labor ideology' model, whose supporters should also 'find it puzzling that the Dutch bourgeoisie passed up the opportunity to legitimize wage labor, accumulate moral capital, and bolster its own self-esteem by attacking slavery' (Haskell 1992b:233). This puzzle has led some historians to make a sharp distinction between mercantilist and industrial capitalism as the stimulating economic context for antislavery. The linkage is more precisely located in the new social world created when merchant capitalism was being transformed by industrialization: 'The Netherlands, for all of its precocity in merchant capitalism fell well behind even Belgium in industrialization. It was the difference in the timing of industrialization that most sharply distinguished the British from the Dutch economy.' Is a vital clue to be discovered in the fact that Holland's 'anemic antislavery voices coincided with the country's delayed industrialization'? Significant industrialization came late to the Netherlands, long after the emergence of industrial capitalist surges in Britain, France, Belgium, and the United States (Davis 1992b:296, 308-9).[15]

Industrial capitalism remains the most plausible general context in which to link economic growth with abolition. If antislavery 'reflected the needs and values of an emerging capitalist order' in Britain (Davis 1975:350),[16] the Dutch case might also be used to test the early *industrial* capitalist model of antislavery. However, the distinction between an early industrializing Britain in the eighteenth century and late industrializing Netherlands in the nineteenth century is not the only relevant comparison. The Netherlands' first period of rapid industrial growth anticipated rather than followed Great Britain's. In the mid-seventeenth century, at the time when the Dutch West Indies Company was integrating Afro-Caribbean slavery into Holland's economic empire, the town of Leiden was having its greatest impact on the European textile industry (Israel 1989:260). Around 1650 Dutch industry attained a margin of superiority in the production of fabrics that was to be maintained down to the eighteenth century. At the peak of Dutch economic growth, in the generation after 1650, the cloth industry

---

[15] See also Oostindie 1992. For Goslinga (1990:265) it was self-evident that the ending of Dutch slavery 'was caused by the industrial revolution'. On the limits of Dutch economic development, see Krantz and Hohenberg 1975.
[16] See also Davis 1987:221; Temperley 1977; Eltis 1987; Ashworth 1992a, 1992b.

made a vastly greater contribution to Holland's overseas commerce than during any previous phase of its economy (Israel 1989:260). Dutch machinery was a technological pacesetter in the competitive international textile trade. Leiden and other interior inland towns were actually the source of much of the start-up capital for the Dutch West Indies Company. In general, Dutch industries, geared to export, expanded and grew even more competitive during the last third of the seventeenth century (Israel 1989:348).[17]

This rising tide of Dutch industrialization has important consequences for any hypothesis that links abolitionism to rising industrial capitalism. In seventeenth-century Europe the Dutch Republic was not only the leading center of commercial capitalism. It was also the first European country to have a large urban proletariat, and 'the first in which the urban proletariat formed a large proportion of the total work-force'. Even excluding those who worked at sea, well over 100,000 people were employed in the main urban industries. The 'proletariat' in the broadest sense was larger still (Israel 1989:355).[18]

The Dutch Republic remained the world's economic leader for most of the seventeenth century. In 1700 its per capita income was half again as high as Great Britain's. Only forty percent of the Dutch labor force was agricultural, compared with sixty percent in Great Britain. The Netherlands' international trade was as large as Britain's, with a population only one-fifth as large. Its costs were comparatively low because of its efficient canal system. Its capitalist manufacturing sector was as important a source of Dutch profits then as at present. In 1700 the Dutch economy had a higher proportion of its labor force in industry than the British economy 120 years later. Even with the fastest-growing economy in Europe, eighteenth-century

---

[17] By the 1640s Dutch manufactures geared to overseas trade bolstered 'a burgeoning network of rich trades', and 'attained a margin of superiority in the production of expensive fabrics [...] which was to be retained down to the early eighteenth century [...]'. The value of Leiden's textile production trebled in less than thirty years. The peak of the Dutch silk industry came in the 1680s. Linen production also expanded during the third quarter of the seventeenth century. By the early 1660s Amsterdam refineries accounted for half of Europe's sugar production and the Dutch took the leadership in tobacco blending and diamond processing (Israel 1989:259-69). English travellers were impressed by the productivity, competitiveness, and spirit of enterprise in Holland relative to England or France (Carr 1691:17, 25). See also Brenner 1993; Van Zanden 1993. For some parallels with eighteenth-century Britain, see Drescher 1987:50-66.

[18] For the view of seafarers as a 'proletarian' work force under conditions of early modern capitalism, see Rediker 1987:77-204, and Eltis 1993:1421. In the early eighteenth century the Dutch economy employed 50,000 sailors in the merchant marine, the ocean fisheries, the Atlantic and the East Indies. Some recent studies highlight the long-term tensions in class relations between workers and capitalists in a variety of Dutch industries between 1650 and 1800. See for example Mastboom 1992; Davids 1992.

Britain did not surpass Holland's seventeenth-century performance in income per head.

The Netherlands anticipated Europe's age of industrialization in a number of other ways. By the mid-seventeenth century the Dutch rural economy had acquired characteristics often identified by economic historians as prerequisites for general economic growth. Moreover, one third of the residents of the Netherlands were urbanized, a percentage not approached by Great Britain (or even England and Wales alone) even a century later. England, while far more populous than the Dutch Republic, did not have a greater urban population, even in absolute numbers, before the eighteenth century. The enormous outflow of men into the overseas trades and the high mortality of seamen in the Dutch East and West Indies stimulated a heavy rural and foreign influx. Even in relation to other highly mobile areas of pre-industrial Europe Dutch cities were extraordinary magnets. More than a quarter of all persons marrying in seventeenth and early eighteenth-century Amsterdam had been born outside the Dutch Republic.[19]

Dutch urban industrial growth also exhibited a number of other characteristics that were later repeated in the British case. Women and young girls, who made up about 30 percent of Leiden's labor force, worked harder and for lower wages than the average male labor. In the more crowded industrial towns 'night piecework was necessary to make up a living wage for a household' (Schama 1988:168; Van Deursen 1991:8-9, 17-20). Such centers would seem to have provided an urban context analogous to those areas of late eighteenth and early nineteenth century which became centers of British abolitionism. The Dutch case is relevant to the social stress model of capitalist abolition. Many Dutch social problems including alcoholism, urban crime, prison reform, workhouses for the unemployed, and resistance

---

[19] On comparative Dutch leadership see Maddison 1982:29-35. On urbanization see De Vries 1984:39, 210-2, 361 note 15. In 1675 the Netherlands population was more than 45% urban, its peak before the abolition of Dutch slavery (De Vries 1990:47). See also De Vries 1982:44; 1974:236-43. De Vries finds that the Wrigley-Schofield model of English demographic-economic interaction, suitably modified, 'captures certain features of Dutch society' throughout the period 1500-1820, and the 'Malthusian' package of population constraints, broken in England by the early nineteenth century, had already been 'weak if not altogether absent' in the Netherlands since the sixteenth century. In terms of nutrition, evidence suggests that there was no significant change from the Golden Age to the end of the nineteenth century (McCants 1992). Dutch society, with the large proportion of its labor force dependent upon wages, 'had at its disposal economic policy instruments that could have offered faster, more effective adjustments to change in the economic environment' (De Vries 1986:100-22). As late as 1800, the Netherlands still had the second highest output per hectare in Europe, behind only Great Britain (Bairoch 1989:329). Even in the half-century before Dutch slave emancipation, all of the Continental countries which anticipated the Dutch in abolition (Sweden, Denmark and France), lagged behind the Netherlands in their growth of output (GDP) per head of population (Maddison 1982:43-4).

to falling wages appeared likewise a century later in other nascent capitalist societies. Dutch ideologues also offered similar rationalizations and solace for Dutch social problems.

Other putative preconditions for the emergence of abolitionism in early nineteenth-century Britain prevailed in the late-seventeenth century Netherlands. A plethora of Dutch publications delineated the mutual obligations between rich and poor within an idealized framework of natural harmony. The Dutch Revolt of the sixteenth century had already generated an ideology that affirmed the inseparability of freedom of conscience, political liberty, and personal freedom – freedom of body, goods and mind. Influential writers like Van Beverwijck, Cats, Grotius, and other inventors of the national tradition expounded Dutch culture in terms of a patriotic liberation covenant. These writers abundantly exploited 'the Exodus metaphor (from southern fleshpots to northern freedom)'. In that trope the Dutch people were 'the old/new Batavians, guardians of the *waare vrijheid* [true liberty]. They were the reborn Hebrews, children of the Covenant. Where had they come from? From slavery and idolatry, through ordeal, to freedom and godliness.'[20]

When the Dutch launched the most expansive slave trade of the early seventeenth century in Asia, Africa, and the Americas, they had only recently achieved political independence and developed a tradition of individual freedom and God-fearing righteousness. During their Golden Age some Dutch writers viewed the English servant trade to Virginia with disdain, and involuntary transatlantic migration from the Netherlands remained far below that of England. Although slave trading and slavery had been sanctioned by the Dutch East Indies Company as early as the 1620s, doubts about the morality of the trade existed at the very start of the Dutch West Indies Company and lingered on after the company increased its involvement in African slavery in the 1630s. Thus the working conditions and the ideological arsenal accessible to the seventeenth-century Dutch seem congruent enough with those of late eighteenth-century Britain that the complete absence of *any* abolitionist movement or hegemonic displacement process whatsoever may offer a significant counterfactual condition for testing scenarios linking early capitalist industrialization to antislavery.[21]

---

[20] Schama 1988:68. It should be emphasized that *waare vrijheid* was a political concept with no particular meaning as regards labor relations. (My thanks to Professor Peter W. Klein for this clarification.) See also Van den Boogaart and Emmer 1979; Van den Boogaart 1986; Postma 1990:10-14; Fox 1983. The rise of Anglo-American antislavery is often linked to work-disciplinary prison reform. The Dutch were pioneers in this reform (Spierenburg 1991:2-3). The 'patriotic' dimension of antislavery is of some importance in Davis's account of British slave trade abolition (Davis 1975:449-50; Turley 1991:178-81).

[21] Van Gelderen 1992:119, 142, 161, 257-8; Price 1994:198-9; Schama 1988:45, 68, ii.

Why was the reservoir of distaste for slavery in the Dutch metropolis not tapped by Dutch capitalism? Why was there no utilization of abolition of the slave trade between 1672 and 1713 as an ideological device for a beleaguered and war-weary populace? Why did a critical mass of Dutch libertarian symbolism, industrialization, economic crisis, proletarianization, military threat, etc, not anticipate some major parallel to abolitionism? Abolition could have served the beleaguered Dutch as well against the enslaving 'Pharoah', Louis XIV of France, as it served the British against Napoleon after his victories at Jena and Auerstadt. Indeed, this 'patriotic' dimension (so important to some recent accounts of the hegemonic function of British slave trade abolition) could have been of service during the entire half century of Dutch eminence in the slave trade.[22] The desperate Dutch needed every source of patriotic solidarity they could muster at all-too-many moments between the 1640s and the early 1700s.

Remarkably, even after the British had apparently demonstrated abolition's hegemonic potential, Dutch slave trade abolition in 1814 was not used to create any domestic ideological advantage for the restored House of Orange. The only recorded reaction to Dutch abolition was an internal memo to the King by an unknown author, who was displeased with the royal decree. The government's subsequent moves toward slave emancipation came in hesitant and cautious responses to British, French, Swedish, and Danish emancipations between 1833 and 1848, in the form of cautious

---

[22] Schama 1988:53, 220, 27-77; Davis 1975:446; Drescher 1994:152-5. If the young republic displayed an unusual level of religious tolerance and opened its provinces and colonies to victims of European persecution, that experience did not inhibit its own rapid adaptation to the economic logic of overseas enterprise. By the mid-seventeenth century Dutch policymakers assumed that their wealth and security depended upon maximizing their share of the Atlantic slave system. What Davis writes of the Jews in Dutch America is equally applicable to their Christian neighbors. At the threshold of their own liberation from Iberian imperial and inquisitorial persecution many Dutch Protestants were drawn into the same network of racial slavery as the Catholic empires to the South (Davis 1984:95-101; Wiznitzer 1960; Drescher 1993b). There is, incidentally, no evidence of a Haskellian market-related antislavery tendency among the ranks of Dutch Jewry during the era of Dutch overseas slavery. Given the internal oligarchical structure of the Jewish community in the Netherlands, and the 'ever-present reality of popular hatred', there was little likelihood that Jews would deviate far from the dominant Christian majority opinion on either side of the Atlantic. A vigilant corporate censorship was exercised over everything published in Hebrew, Yiddish, or the Iberian languages, the common languages of Dutch Jewry until the early eighteenth century (Israel 1985:198-9). Moreover, especially in the Netherlands, the New World colonies were regarded as a vital part of the European Jewish escape hatch. At critical moments shiploads of Sephardic refugees fleeing from the Mediterranean to Holland were shipped out to the Dutch Caribbean at communal expense (Israel 1985:203). Because the Dutch Americas were a precarious frontier haven in the mid-seventeenth century, the messianic wave that touched virtually all of European Jewry in the 1660s did not spill over into a discussion of New World slavery any more than did Protestant religious radical discourse during the English Civil War.

administrative and parliamentary proposals (Emmer 1981; Goslinga 1990: 245-313).[23]

Since the relatively more rapid industrialization of Belgium has also been alluded to in relation to the Dutch case, it may be heuristically useful to speculate about the fate of abolition in the Netherlands had Belgium remained part of a united kingdom after 1830. One might begin by noting that the Habsburg Netherlands became one of the last European entrants into the Atlantic slave system. The merchants of Ostend eagerly seized the opportunity afforded to them as neutrals in the American war of independence to gain a foothold in the slave trade. Belgian capital flowed into the French slave system (Drescher 1987:170-1).

In its brief political union with the Dutch provinces after 1814, the representatives of the Southern Netherlands had an opportunity to display their attitudes towards the abolitionist process. Four years after the Royal prohibition of the slave trade, legislation was requested from the States-General to establish penal sanctions against merchants who might be tempted to continue the trade. After a brief debate every one of the small minority of five who voted against the legislation were representatives from the Southern provinces. While it would be hazardous to tie their vote exclusively to their economic orientation, it is significant that they all opposed the motion on capitalist grounds. They were disturbed by the fact that convicted violators would be deprived for life of their *patente*, or license to trade. The opponents of the law regarded this penalty as an attack on the industrious segment ('*l'homme industrieux*') of the nation.[24]

It is clear that the Belgians did not stimulate any antislavery movement down to 1830. It might be argued that Belgium's industrial 'take-off' did not occur until after independence. The incipient dynamism of the South was less evident until then. In 1830 the North was forty per cent urban, the South still only twenty-five per cent, and population was increasing more rapidly in the North. The steady expansion of the Belgian metallurgical and textile industries was most apparent after the post-revolutionary turmoil (Mokyr 1976:26-82; Kossmann 1978:129-35, 210-6).

It seems unlikely that even continued unity would have produced an acceleration of slave emancipation in the generation after 1830. As late as

---

[23] After the passage of British abolition Holland was taunted by English poets for having failed, in an excess of capitalist greed, to extend its own liberties abroad. The result was Dutch degeneration – moral, economic, and political. See Montgomery 1978; Benger 1978. Gert Oostindie (personal correspondence) suggests that slave trade abolition might have been resented as a humiliating condition imposed by Britain. Therefore slave trade abolition could not easily have been used to hegemonic advantage after 1814. In any event, the day of slave emancipation in the Netherlands passed with as little public agitation or celebration in 1863 as had slave trade abolition 49 years before (Van Winter 1982).
[24] *Verslag* 1861:16-24. My thanks to Pieter Emmer for calling this debate to my attention.

the 1880s Belgians showed scant interest in their monarch's acquisition of a vast area of the slave-ridden Congo basin for his imperial new 'Free State' in Africa. When Cardinal Lavigerie visited Brussels in 1888, on behalf of an international Catholic movement against the African slave trade, his sermon berated the Belgian nation 'for not supporting her king's great humanitarian work in Africa'. The idea for an international congress in Brussels to end the slave trade originated in Britain. The Congress met in Brussels because of British fears that an invitation to London would be viewed as still one more hegemonic gambit.[25] As late as 1903, the initial public reaction in Belgium to charges from Britain that the 'Free State' had developed a vast and violent new system of coerced labor, offers little encouragement for any inference that the industrializing Southern Netherlands would have generated more action against slavery in either hemisphere than its Northern neighbors manifested (Louis and Stengers 1968:149).

The profile of Dutch antislavery, whether during the Netherlands' economic primacy around 1650, or at the peak of its African slave trading traffic around 1760, or in its economically retarded phase after 1800 remained closer to its Danish, French, Swedish, and Spanish counterparts than to that of the Anglo-Americans. Nowhere on the European Continent was abolitionism a durable mass movement and nowhere was the enactment of antislavery legislation used to legitimize the claims of either traditional political élites or new industrial ones.

Incorporating the Netherlands into a comparative perspective is fruitful in testing another general theoretical framework that links capitalism to antislavery. In a recent history of the ending of colonial slavery Robin Blackburn attempted to relate the rise and triumph of abolitionism to the dynamics of emerging European bourgeois society. Blackburn rejects the hypothesis that capitalist development directly triggered antislavery, since slavery neither collapsed economically in the Americas, nor was it destroyed by rival metropolitan economic interests. Rather 'slave systems were overthrown in stormy class struggles in both colonies and metropolis'. In this sense the capitalist order created new class struggles and political crises which implicated and destroyed slavery.[26]

---

[25] Miers 1975:205-7. On the role of Anglophobia in the abolition process, see note 49.
[26] Blackburn 1988:520. Holt uses a similar frame of reference. His crucial connection between capitalism and antislavery is located in 'the emerging bourgeois social relations of the seventeenth and eighteenth centuries'. A bourgeois movement and ideology, rooted in the Enlightenment, then assaulted slavery in a dual revolution: 'The political upheavals inspired by the French revolution set the destruction of slavery in motion; the ideology thrown up by Britain's free labor economy provided the model for what should replace slavery' (Holt 1992:xxii, 3-9, 21-6). There is usually little hesitation about characterizing Dutch society

Blackburn's principal nominees for what he termed increased 'dynamic density' in bourgeois society are Britain (at various moments between 1788 and 1838) and France (during the Great Revolution and again in the 1840s). In Blackburn's account the Franco-Caribbean explosion of 1789-1804 was the crucial turning point in the history of antislavery, emerging from an unparalleled metropolitan political crisis and the most successful slave uprising in history.

France in the early 1790s most admirably fulfills Blackburn's optimal conditions for the acceleration and triumph of antislavery. The alleged turning point of Caribbean slave revolution in St. Domingue coincided with the climax of the radical French Revolution in Paris, where all remaining feudal rights, and non-capitalist forms of property were being swept away in an environment hostile to both inequality and great commercial interests. The Jacobins gave slave emancipation their own hegemonic twist, sacrificing a distant and precarious colonial interest to consolidate popular solidarity at home. (The British, with 'proto-revolutionary' situations in the 1790s and 1830s, are classified along with France as a zone of bourgeois capitalist expansion, class conflict and abolitionism; Blackburn 1988:519-20.)

What of the Netherlands' place in this more populist model of capitalist antislavery? Blackburn's *Overthrow* categorizes the Netherlands alongside Spain and Denmark in the category of non-starters – societies that failed to develop antislavery movements and that experienced a retarded development of their industrial bourgeois capitalist order. Blackburn offers no comment upon Holland's precocious seventeenth-century industrialization, nor upon its lead in urban, industrial, commercial, and bourgeois development over France throughout the seventeenth and eighteenth centuries. Many historians have, of course, questioned even France's proximity to an industrial capitalist order in 1789.

Blackburn's most salient criterion, however, is the catalyst of political rupture and class conflict, occurring in circumstances in which the voice of the slaveholders was marginalized. Here the Netherlands probably fit his

---

during the two centuries before the American and French Revolutions as dominated by the bourgeoisie. On the Netherlands as the 'Home of Bourgeoisie Revolution', dominated by capital, see Tilly 1993:52-103. On the Dutch as modernizing bourgeois pioneers see Blakely 1993:5. Regarding even the wealthy 'regents' of Amsterdam, 'for all their airs of *bourgeois satisfaits* or *bourgeois gentilshommes*, bourgeois they were and nothing else'. As for the rest, the phenomenon pervading Dutch society as a whole in the seventeenth century, but still more in the early eighteenth century, was 'the *embourgeoisement* of the entire population' (Kossmann 1978:30). As late as the 1780s, when manufacturing not dependent upon the maritime and the transit trades had fared very badly, activities linked to the re-export of overseas commodities remained viable. Therefore one can hardly speak of an absolute and general economic decline before the French Revolution. The bourgeois structure of the society remained largely intact, and the level of consumption was still the highest in Europe (Mokyr 1976:1-8; Kossmann 1978:26-33; Schama 1977:24-63).

prescription for bourgeois democratic abolition far better than Britain and, in some respects, for far longer than Revolutionary France as well. Blackburn emphasized the impact of the American Revolutionary war in setting the stage for the rise of British abolitionism. Yet how much greater was the impact of that conflict on the Netherlands as a result of the fourth Anglo-Dutch war (1780-1784)? The entire Dutch slaving fleet was captured by the British, a loss from which the Dutch only partially recovered. The war was a disaster for Holland's entire merchant marine and for its free port colonies (Schama 1977:133-4, 158; Postma 1990:165, 284-5).[27] The conflict had scarcely ended when the Netherlands experienced its deepest political crisis in a century.

Recent historians of the eighteenth-century Dutch Republic have discovered a number of other relevant parallels between the contemporary Dutch and British cases. In the Republic, as in Britain, there was an upsurge in popular mobilization. 'In the 1780s [...] there was petitioning in the republic on a scale never seen before' (Van Sas 1992:11), signature gathering by the thousands, and a link of enlightenment participatory politics and agressive nationalism. 'Just as in Britain during the latter decades of the century, the link also existed in the Dutch Republic between political radicalism and what we may describe as an industrial vision' (Jacob 1992: 238). Josiah Wedgwood, the Staffordshire industrialist who furnished the British with the African in chains which symbolized the abolitionist movement, also supplied the Patriots and Orangists with images of their heroes. Wedgwood, who exemplified the industrial abolitionist in Britain, was himself the model for patriotic revolutionaries across the North Sea. There was a conjuncture between the Dutch 'industrial vision' of the late eighteenth century and attraction to the Patriotic cause.[28] The Orangist-Patriot civil conflict and the abortive revolution that ensued were settled in 1787 only by the intervention of foreign troops.

All this conflict was but the harbinger of a generation of national upheavals to come. The next three decades brought one disaster after another: war; invasion; revolution; occupation; naval blockade; levies of tribute; mass conscriptions into foreign armies; and outright annexation into Napoleon's empire. Finally, the revolutions of 1830 entailed yet another crisis and one more national humiliation. The seceding Belgian provinces had been compensation for Dutch acquiescence in British demands for the abolition of the Dutch African slave trade in 1814, and for the surrender of important overseas colonies to the British. Between 1780 and 1830, the Netherlands therefore experienced as much military defeat, economic

[27] The annual average of transported slaves fell to less than one-fifth of the 1770-1779 level in the period 1780-1803 (Postma 1990:295).
[28] On the significance of Wedgwood as an abolitionist industrialist see Davis 1975:460-1.

distress, and political turmoil as any colonial metropolis except (and perhaps including) France (Schama 1977).

As for the marginalization of the colonial planter class, so important to Blackburn's model, before the French Revolution the Dutch slave Caribbean had already afforded more evidence of decline than any other European plantation system. Between 1770 and 1789 the Dutch colonial share of the North Atlantic sugar imports shrank more rapidly than any other sector of the plantation Americas. The relative decline of the Dutch colonies continued into the early nineteenth century (Drescher 1977:48, 77).[29] Even in peacetime, the disastrous collapse of Suriname's speculative boom in the early 1770s meant that its exports could no longer pay the interest on the colony's loans, let alone repay the principal. The West Indies' negative trade balance accounted for much of the reduction in the Dutch slave trade at the end of the eighteenth century (Emmer 1991:93).[30]

---

[29] The Danish, with the only other relatively declining system between 1770 and 1789, had a share-loss less than half as great as the Dutch. The Dutch colonies' share of the Caribbean slave population fell from 9.6% in 1750 to 4.6% in 1830. Only the French, with the loss of Haiti, had a greater relative loss during the same period. On population trends, see Engerman and Higman forthcoming. (My thanks to Stanley Engerman for making this chapter available.)

[30] On the Dutch East Indies Company, see Abeyasekere 1983:286-311. Much of the literature of the period after the early 1770s reflects an increasingly pessimistic mood about Dutch plantation slavery, continuing right down to slave emancipation in 1863. See Oostindie 1993:3-4. The late eighteenth century decline was not the first downturn. For a period following the Peace of Utrecht in 1713, the Dutch Caribbean staple trade seemed to be in a state of irreversible decline, with a correspondingly weak slave trade. Dutch annual slave exports from Africa between 1710 and 1719 reached their lowest point since the mid-seventeenth century. Sugar production stagnated. The stock of the Dutch West Indies Company, which had remained strong until 1712, declined steeply. With a recovery in the 1720s the Caribbean and North America became one of the few bright spots in Dutch trade. The Dutch slave trade, sugar imports, and the Caribbean-based intermediary traffic reached eighteenth-century peaks during the conflicts between Britain and France, and at the beginning of the Anglo-American conflict. However, the Netherlands never again approached its ascendancy of the second half of the seventeenth century. Indeed, 'the transatlantic trade partly concealed the impact of Holland's industrial collapse and the decline of her old world rich trades' (Israel 1989:392-7). On the slave trade figures, see Postma 1990:110. Unlike Great Britain, antislavery agitation did not emerge at any of the high points in the Dutch slave trade. In the British case, the first widespread condemnations of black slavery occurred in the early 1770s, the late 1780s and the early 1790s, all relative peaks in the slave trade. The British slave trade, at 44,500 per year, reached its pre-American war peak at the time of the Somerset Case in 1771-72. In the year before the launching of a national abolitionist movement in Britain 43,000 slaves were carried from Africa, again a peak year for the decade of the 1780s. In 1792, the year in which the first slave trade abolition bill was passed by the House of Commons, the British slave trade hit its all-time peak, with more than 57,000 African slaves transported in British ships. In the Dutch case, high points of the slave trade occurred in the late 1660s and in the early 1670s, when the Dutch were probably Europe's leading carriers (5,600 Africans per year were boarded between 1668 and 1672). An even higher and more sustained peak was reached in the mid-eighteenth century (6,350 Africans per year were boarded in Dutch ships between 1755 and 1774). The peak quinquennium of the Dutch slave trade came in 1770-1774, a period of widespread discussion of slavery in Britain,

After 1795 the parallel occupations of the Netherlands by the French and of the Dutch colonies by the British served to isolate the colonial planters from the metropolis. The long separation probably helps to explain the relative indifference in the Netherlands to the abolition of the slave trade which accompanied the restoration of 1814. 'The country's largest slave-worked colony mattered little to Dutch industry and trade.' There was no collective protest against abolition even by the sugar refiners of Amsterdam. Their imports came from a far wider range of plantations than the Dutch West Indies (Postma 1990:78).

Finally, the threat of collective slave resistance, which plays so large a role in Blackburn's model, was at least as prominent in the Dutch case as anywhere else. In 1763 a slave uprising in Berbice nearly engulfed the whole colony of more than 4,000 slaves. It was probably the largest, the longest and most successful slave revolt in the Caribbean before the St. Domingue uprising of 1791. The Dutch took a year and a half to suppress the Berbice revolt and many plantations were not rebuilt (Goslinga 1985:461-94; Postma 1990:215-7).

The Netherlands therefore met all of Blackburn's criteria for abolition: political conflict, economic decline, and slave unrest. It even met one of Eric Williams's major prerequisites for the abolitionist take-off in Britain – relative imperial insignificance. There was no need to search for an imagined 'swing' of interest to the East in the Netherlands after the 1770s, because for more than a century the Dutch had regarded the East Indies as their prime overseas enterprise. If relative colonial economic decline could be said to have eased the path to abolition anywhere in Europe, Dutch anti-slavery should have been 'overdetermined' during the last generation of the eighteenth century.[31]

The complete absence of the Batavian Republic from Blackburn's account of the 'bourgeois democratic' revolutions is a striking gap in his history of antislavery. The reason is clear. The pre-revolutionary period in the Netherlands produced only the faintest echoes of hostility towards slavery in the form of Latin treatises, anonymous poems, and occasional polemics. These

---

but not in the Netherlands. The record number of British exports in 1792 only stimulated Dutch efforts to *expand* the trade, which reached a post-1775 peak of nearly 3,000 slaves in 1793, just before war again sharply reduced the volume of traffic. The Treaty of Amiens in 1802 made possible a brief and final revival. The resumption of hostilities again removed the Dutch from the Atlantic slave trade. Neither peak moments in British slave trading nor in British abolitionism before 1814 stimulated abolitionist action in the Netherlands. (The British averages are calculate from Richardson s.a. This manuscript was kindly provided by Professor Richardson. The Dutch figures may be found in Postma 1990:35, 110, 285. On Danish abolition and its responsiveness to British events see Green-Pedersen 1975:196-220; s.a. Manuscript kindly furnished by the late author.)

[31] On the supposed British swing to the East after 1780, see Drescher 1977:54, 235 note.

were 'isolated expressions hardly noticed by the general public' (Postma 1990:292-3; Schutte 1974:220-3). In 1789, a year after the first abolition debates in the British Parliament, and just after the French Declaration of the Rights of Man, the Dutch States-General remained committed to efforts to stimulate the Dutch slave trade, for 'as long as no one had thought of a method to provide the colonies with the necessary hands to do the labor the "Negro trade" cannot be separated from the growth and prosperity of these colonies, as well as the commerce which results from them' (Postma 1990:286).

The climactic Dutch political crisis occurred in 1794-95. The Batavian Republic was the first and the most important of the 'sister' republics sponsored by the French Revolutionaries. It was a model for other French satellites and the very first regime (including that of France) to adopt 'Liberty, Equality, Fraternity' as its official motto. The Dutch Revolution was an extension of the Patriot movement of the 1780s, supported by the broad middle stratum of classes, from journeymen to members of the social élite. Dutch 'Jacobins' were eager to abolish privileges and to establish a 'revolutionary government'.[32]

In January 1795 the French seized Amsterdam and the Batavian Republic was declared. The question of colonial slave emancipation, however, was raised only once. In the Republic's constituent National Assembly a motion for slave emancipation and the abolition of the Dutch slave trade received an unenthusiastic reception. The French experience was, if anything, evoked as a warning. Any 'action might very well lead to a violent insurrection as bad as anything in St. Domingue and was bound to bring ruin to many virtuous and patriotic burghers'.[33] The issue was buried.

The French made no effort to pressure their republican allies to adopt a slave emancipation policy for their colonies. On the contrary. Traditionally, the Caribbean island of St. Martin was jointly shared by the two metropolitan powers. St. Martin's French slaves had not been freed by the French emancipation decree of 1794 because of the prior Dutch occupation of the French sector. In 1795, the French took charge of both halves of the island. They promptly planted a tree of liberty on the Dutch side, but the slaves remained slaves. French Revolutionary policy turned out to have been

---

[32] Palmer 1959, II:180. The first Dutch Constitution was composed under the direct influence of the French Ambassador to The Hague. See Verhagen 1949. Note the absence of any reference to discussions of Dutch colonial slavery in Leeb 1973.

[33] Schama 1977:260-1. A proposed plan for gradual abolition by a French colonial official and a Dutch planter in Demerara was included in the Dutch translation of Stedman's *Narrative of a Five Years' Expedition against the Revolted Negroes of Surinam* in 1799-1800 (*Reize naar Surinamen*) (cited in Oostindie 1992:163, note 18). It was not taken up by the government. A recent study on the political mobilization of women in the Netherlands in the 1780s and 1790s does not indicate any antislavery dimension in their activities. See Te Brake, Dekker and Van de Pol 1990.

more strategic and less universalistic than many historians have supposed (Goslinga 1990:146).

When a large-scale slave revolt broke out in the Dutch Caribbean in August 1795, the Batavian National Assembly was not impelled towards any abolitionist initiative whatsoever. At the peak of the Curaçao uprising, the rebels probably numbered 2000, more than a third of the slaves on the island. The French made no move to aid the rebels from their own Caribbean strongholds (Goslinga 1990:1-20). As far as both the Dutch and the French governments of 1795-1800 were concerned, the Batavian Republic's Declaration of Rights stopped at the North Sea. When the French later attempted to seize Curaçao, they proclaimed the *status quo* regarding slavery. When Napoleon Bonaparte restored slavery in the French colonies in 1802, he was merely realigning the French colonial order with that of his Dutch satellite. The last Dutch regime officially to sanction the revival of the African slave trade, following the peace of Amiens in 1802, was the Dutch Republic. In 1814 it was the Netherlands' Monarch who abolished the slave trade, under pressure from the ambassador of His Britannic Majesty.[34]

As far as the Dutch Caribbean is concerned, Batavia's sterile revolution casts a long ironic shadow on the 'meaning' of French revolutionary emancipation. Even when one adds to an already bourgeois society like the Netherlands all of the active ingredients in the bourgeois revolutionary model – successive revolutionary crises; overwhelming military threats; a long-term decline in the economic value of colonial slavery; a past and present threat of massive slave resistance; class struggles; and a patriotic republican ideology – the Dutch still come up short of an abolitionist movement, let alone any memorable page in Blackburn's narrative of abolitionism.

In ironic and precise verification of Heinrich Heine's dictum, the Dutch, after being nudged into slave abolition, waited for literally half a century before implementing slave emancipation. Even then, the dynamic and profitable sector of the Dutch imperial economy, which, in effect, covered the compensation costs of Caribbean emancipation, was the coerced labor system of the Dutch East Indies. Other than in helping to fund slave emancipation, the Dutch East Indies provided little stimulus for moving toward an imperial free labor policy. The dismantling of colonial slavery in the West began during the heyday of the coercive 'Cultivation System' in Java. In the East the decisive shift towards wage labor came only in the 1870s

---

[34] Postma 1990:290. When the Cape Colony was briefly restored to Dutch sovereignty in 1802 the Batavian Republic considered the possibility that slavery was unnecessary there, but colonial administrators generally agreed with Governor Janssens that the abolition of slavery 'would overturn all property' and immiserate the colony. No action was taken. (Elphick and Giliomee 1988:163, 337).

and 1880s. True to their tradition, the Dutch became the last Europeans to sign the Brussels Act of 1890 for the repression of the African Slave Trade. 'The Dutch played out their resistance to the bitter end, signing the treaty only at the last possible moment.' As usual they held out for commercial reasons, in protest against the advantages given by the treaty to Leopold II, king of the Belgians and ruler of the Congo Free State.[35]

From beginning to end the role of Dutch metropolitan capitalism in the abolition of slavery was clearly less than overwhelming. The present consensus is that nineteenth-century Dutch industrialization did not really get underway until Europe's 'second' industrial revolution, well after the ending of Dutch colonial slavery. This casts doubt upon the applicability of an industrial or capitalist-industrial model, in any of its dynamic periods, to Dutch abolition.

Historians, relying on the experience of Britain, France, or the United States, have traced a clear evidentiary path from 'capitalism' in accounting for the origins, the evolution, and the triumph of antislavery. Yet the Netherlands was actually more typical than anomalous in having no major abolitionist movement, and more 'Continental' in moving toward emancipation without great domestic pressure. Capitalism, whether mercantile, industrial, or bourgeois, has thus far offered very little purchase for explaining the timing of Dutch abolition.[36]

The cases of Hispanic American and Brazilian slave emancipation inspire as little confidence in the association of capitalist development and abolition as does the Dutch. A number of historians have noted that although the belated emancipation of Cuban and Brazilian slaves is often attributed to the comparative retardation of capitalist development in Spain and Brazil, the most dynamic economic and technological sectors in Cuba, Spain and Brazil failed to back the abolitionist cause. Rebecca Scott showed that the most successful sugar planters of Cuba clung most tenaciously to the slave system. In Spain the Catalan business lobby, the most market-oriented sector of the Spanish economy, defended both slavery and its own privileged trade with the country's slave colonies. Brazil was, of course, long independent of its Portuguese metropolis, whose economic development was, to say the least,

---

[35] Emmer 1980:83; Mokyr 1976:83. Slave emancipation occurred in July 1863 without fanfare or celebration in the metropolis. See Van Winter 1982:125-6. On the East Indies' labor system, see Dros 1991:133-53; Boomgaard 1989:39. On Dutch resistance to the Brussels treaty, see Miers 1975:287-92. 'The Dutch Foreign Minister, "an honourable man," winced when the British Ambassador smugly informed him that Britain, "unlike others" regarded trading interests as a secondary matter [...].' (Miers 1975:281).
[36] See, inter alia, Drescher 1980; 1987:50-66; Davis 1992b:296. Only Brazilian and, to a lesser extent, French abolitionism on the eve of their respective slave emancipations might qualify as approaching the status of broad social movements (Drescher 1988:450-4; 1991:709-34).

unimpressive. Within Brazil itself, urbanization, improved transportation and foreign immigration were most evident in the expanding slave areas. Regarding manufacturing, Rio de Janeiro was beginning to incorporate slaves into factories when the mid-century abolition of the African slave trade and the coffee boom combined to drain slaves from the cities. Nowhere was abolition particularly associated with economic growth within the Iberian cultural zone on either side of the Atlantic. Capitalists came on board only when the slave systems were in advanced stages of political destruction from international pressures, nationalist uprisings or slave resistance.[37]

One other historiographical trend merits comment. Once one begins to explore the intriguing ground of Dutch retardation in detail, scholarship tends to displace some originally economically grounded arguments by those that explicitly rely on demographics, politics, culture, and religion. Whatever the resemblance and parallels between the Dutch and the English in their metropolitan economic, political, and religious development in the seventeenth and early eighteenth centuries, the Dutch overseas imperial system was far closer to those of the Continent than that of Anglo-America in one crucial respect. Unlike the English, the Dutch never successfully established a colonial zone dominated by its own ethnic group, or replicated the metropolitan political institutions and civil status for the bulk of its laborers. In the century before the age of abolition only the North American British settler empire maintained a preponderance of free over slave labor and developed a 'European' religious, cultural, and political infrastructure beyond the Atlantic.

For the Dutch, as for other Continental Europeans, the majority of the labor force in their zones of settlement remained racially and juridically distinct from the metropolis.[38] By the beginning of the eighteenth century

---

[37] On Spanish and Brazilian abolition, see, inter alia, Blackburn s.a.; Corwin 1967; Conrad 1972; Scott 1985; Scott, Drescher et al. 1988. In the mid-nineteenth century, the industrial interests of Catalonia (the 'Manchester of Spain'), were closely linked to the preservation of the Cuban connection, including their trade privileges and the continuity of plantation staple production. See, inter alia, Carr 1982:199-201, 307-9, 323; Beck 1979:114-20; Hennessy 1962:64-8, and especially, Whitney 1992:20-36. The list of opponents of the first Abolition Bill (for Puerto Rico) 'reads like a "Who's Who" of Spain's most prominent capitalists and political figures' (Whitney 1992:29). Peru, another late emancipating nation (1855), is equally illustrative of the weak link between antislavery and rapid industrialization or the emergence of a 'national entrepreneurial bourgeoisie'. See Blanchard 1992:135-7, 189-207. Venezuela, which remained an agricultural export economy throughout the century before final emancipation in 1854, was equally notable for an absence of abolitionism. It entirely lacked 'the panoply of a crusade', popular abolitionism, or anti-slavery campaigns (Lombardi 1974). Fogel and Engerman (1989:254-7) showed that even by Northern European standards the United States slave South ranked high among the world's industrial and financial economies in 1860. See also Schweikart 1987:254-66.

[38] Before the beginning of the eighteenth century the ratio of black slaves to Europeans in Suriname, the major Dutch colony in the Americas, was already more than 4 to 1. In South

all of their possessions were slave or bound-labor societies. A major reason that the Dutch encouraged foreign settlers and tolerated religious diversity in their overseas colonies was the enormous difficulty they had in luring native Netherlanders into their settlements.[39]

By contrast, the seventeenth-century British colonial venture in North America was decisively aided by the fact that England's net rate of migration reached its peak in the four decades between 1630 and 1670, and was supplemented thereafter by other European immigrant flows. Even in absolute numbers, English migration attained magnitudes not matched again until after the Napoleonic wars. At the beginning of this great English surge, in the early 1630s, the Dutch West Indies Company's directors in Amsterdam were lamenting that anyone in Holland 'with the slightest desire to work will find it easy to make a living here, and thus will think twice before going far from home on an uncertain venture'. For its part, the Dutch East Indies Company (VOC) did not encourage large-scale European immigration to South Africa, the one area that might have replicated the Anglo-American experience of European settlement in a temperate zone.[40]

One must not attribute the emergence of abolitionism to a uniquely

---

Africa slaves outnumbered free white burghers by the second decade of the eighteenth century. By the 1730s the demographic ratio of slaves to freemen in certain areas of the colony was similar to that of contemporary South Carolina. For Guiana estimates, see McCusker 1970, I:601. On the Cape Colony, see Worden 1985:10-2.

[39] Even the New Netherland colony in America remained weak, vulnerable, and ethnically diverse before the British conquest because of the scattered pattern of settlement. It also lacked cultural and political support networks and a cadre of leaders interested in reproducing Dutch culture (Roeber 1991). The Dutch seaborne empire relied heavily on foreigners and recently naturalized citizens, Sephardic Jews, Huguenots, Germans, etc, for its seventeenth-century colonial ventures in Brazil, the Caribbean, the Guianas and the Cape Colony. Until the late eighteenth century Suriname was governed by a quasi-public Sociëteit van Suriname, not directly by the Dutch state. This was an additional buffer against perceptions of metropolitan responsibility. There was no impetus toward abolitionism or emancipation from the colonies themselves. In religious terms Moravian missionaries were active in the Dutch Caribbean colonies from the 1730s onward. For well over a century, however, they ensured their acceptability among the planters by emphasizing (like their evangelical counterparts in the British Caribbean until the 1820s) their 'neutrality' on the issue of slavery. Compare Oostindie 1992:153-9 with Drescher 1987:117-23. The Dutch did not manage to establish a transatlantic communications network like that of the Anglo-Americans by the mid-eighteenth century (O'Brien 1986:811-32).

[40] On English migration flows, see Wrigley and Schofield 1981:219-20. In 1700 blacks represented 36% of the population of British America and 12.5% of the Continental Colonies. On the eve of the Revolution the respective percentages were 32.5% and 25%. On the Dutch West Indies Company's difficulties, see Van Dillen 1982:175. During the Dutch Golden Age the ethno-demographic divergence between Continental North America and the rest of the Americas was still narrow. In 1650, whites composed almost one-eigth of North America's population compared with almost one-tenth of the tropical America's and almost one-sixteenth of the Spanish America's. By the early nineteenth century, however, whites composed four-fifths of North America's population compared with about one-fifth of both tropical and Spanish America's (Slicher van Bath 1986:21).

English ethno-religious sensibility any more than to economic precociousness. It was the Dutch-speaking immigrants of Germantown Pennsylvania who produced the first collective petition in the Americas calling for the prohibition of slavery in the new Quaker settlement. And it was the weighty English Friends who tabled that and other antislavery initiatives for two generations thereafter.[41] The Cape Colony in Africa, which still had almost as many free burghers as slaves in the early eighteenth century, occasionally produced a colonist who wistfully regretted that the introduction of slaves had not been prevented from the outset.

In 1717 the Directors of the VOC asked the Cape colonists whether slaves should continue to be imported into the colony, or whether European labor immigration should be encouraged instead. One respondent offered arguments that were later to be more vigorously and collectively asserted in the British empire: that free labor was more productive than slave, that security would be increased by more free Europeans, and that indentured immigrants would ultimately increase the numbers of small proprietors and expand prosperity. By 1717 however, even that Dutch colony was socially already a slave society. Most settlers responded to the question in cost-benefit economic terms: that it was cheaper to purchase and use slaves; that European immigrants would impoverish the colony because Europeans would regard manual labor in the colony as degrading and would rather remain impoverished than work as slaves.[42] Well before the second quarter of that century most descendants of Europeans in the Dutch imperial world envisioned their societies as irrevocably different from that of Europe.[43]

---

[41] Bruns 1977:3-4; Wolf 1976:129; Soderlund 1985; Nash and Soderlund 1991. In abandoning the notion of a gap between English and Dutch economic development to account for British antislavery, one may still be tempted to posit Anglo-Dutch gaps in communications networks or in national sensitivities to the overseas world. Eltis (1993:1421) concludes that because of their superiority in transatlantic migration, the English 'must have dwarfed' the Dutch both in intensity of transoceanic communications and in popular awareness of the world beyond Europe. However, a historian of Dutch racial attitude asserts that 'the industriousness of the Dutch exposed them to at least as great a variety of new experiences as any other nation in the world' (Blakely 1993:37-8). As for their British neighbors, 'the greatest migration into the English Atlantic between 1675 and 1740 was neither English speaking nor European nor voluntary'. Improving English Atlantic communication expanded slavery (Steele 1986:252).

[42] Worden 1985:16-7; Reports 1918:85-112. The distribution of slaves was as important in the colony as their relative importance as laborers. By 1750 almost half the free male population had at least one slave (Elphick and Giliomee 1988:135, 541).

[43] On the convergence of Anglo-American structures and values, see Greene 1994:129-30, 310. On the role of projected futures in the emergence of autonomous communities in the Americas, see Anderson 1983. Comparing Vermont's Dutch and Yankee communities, Roth (1987:302-4) notes the far greater propensity of the latter to engage in reform movements, including antislavery, during the six decades after 1790. He emphasizes the long-term impact of the distinctive character of pre-revolutionary town life and politics in the Anglo-American world, compared with the more parochial and less voluntaristic Dutch. He notes the historiographic perspective that concludes that the Dutch entered politics primarily to advance or protect economic interests, not to reform society, a pattern typical of ethnic groups of the

Only in the British Continental Colonies, after a century of social experimentation and development, was a completely free labor and predominantly white community imagined as a viable long-term probability. The band of self-governing English colonies with black slave populations which were less than half of the total number of inhabitants produced the first intermittent attempts to reduce slave imports and then to eliminate slavery altogether. Everywhere north of the Carolinas, religious, racial, demographic, and political arguments in favor of restricting or eliminating the further inflow of African slaves, increased after the 1750s. All these arguments rested upon the idea that in one part of the New World it was possible to replicate and even to accelerate the trajectory of civil freedom as it had evolved in Northwestern Europe.

The white inhabitants of the Continental British colonies regarded themselves as participants in, and extenders of, British liberty, and they were so regarded by their counterparts in the metropolis. When, on the eve of the American Revolution, Arthur Young calculated the world's free population, the subjects of His Britannic Majesty were the only people in the overseas world included in his zone of freedom.[44]

Freedom was not merely a passive geographical construction. If envisioning abolition required a century of gestation even in the Anglo-American zone, as late as the 1780s nothing in Dutch (or Danish, or Portuguese, or Spanish) transatlantic discourse matched the decades of transatlantic discussion of slavery in the British imperium. Well before the middle of the eighteenth century one British colonizing society unsuccessfully attempted to establish a non-slave community in Georgia. The American Revolution of 1776 accelerated political actions against the transatlantic slave trade. During the next generation the Northern states of the United States became the first American legislatures to constitutionally undermine slavery or to initiate gradual emancipation. A number of Southern states moved to expand white suffrage, perpetuate slavery, and shut down the avenues to

---

Middle colonies (Roth 1987:385-6, note 6). The case of Vermont serves to undermine the market linkage to antislavery (Davis 1992b:291-2). Furthermore, while Vermonters bemoaned their lagging pace of industrial development compared with Massachusetts or England, the state was becoming the most antislavery state in the Union. On the normative 'slave community' of the Dutch Cape Colony, see Du Toit and Giliomee 1983, I:28. Comparing British North America and Dutch South Africa in the eighteenth century Carter (1991), citing Baldwin 1958:8-18, highlights the analogous implications of religious doctrine within both cultures. Dutch Arminians influenced British and American Protestants, who came to regard Arminianism as a moral protest against slavery. But he is perplexed by the fact that Dutch officials and clerics 'missed the message' of abolition, and by the 'stark contrast' between the emergence of antislavery sentiment in North America's 'open society' and its absence in South Africa's 'closed society.'

[44] Young 1970:20-1. On the Continental Colonies as an imagined community without slaves, see Lee 1764.

emancipation. None of these debates and initiatives had any parallel among the settlements of the Dutch colonial empire.[45]

Evangelicals, lured across the Atlantic by burgeoning European communities in America, had to wrestle with a range of choices about the implications of slavery that was completely absent from the bifurcated world of the Dutch empire, with its free labor metropolis and its bound labor colonies. By the 1780s, The 'Quaker International' and its transatlantic consensus against slavery was reinforced by a thickening network of antislavery religious dissent in Britain and North America.[46] Antislavery was one of the ideological movements that survived and counteracted the political rupture of Anglo-America after the War of American Independence. Not until the St. Domingue revolution of 1791 was there to be comparable transatlantic pressure for abolition. Antislavery in France had little connection with overseas white settlers, and Continental abolitionism remained a fragile social formation even in Revolutionary France (Benot 1988; Tarrade 1989:9-34).

In pre-revolutionary Europe itself, an increasing number of slaves brought from the Americas created an unresolved problem of property in persons. In Britain the courts found it increasingly difficult, and ultimately unfeasible, to reconcile the libertarian thrust of the legal tradition and the requirements of colonial slave law. The influx of freed blacks in the wake of the American war of independence also stimulated the founding of Sierra Leone, the first colonial 'free soil' experiment in Africa. In the case of France the rapid growth of a free colored population in St. Domingue and the presence of an affluent branch of that community in Paris contributed to the

---

[45] On the convergence of Anglo-American structures and values, see Greene 1994:129-30, 310. On the American revolution and antislavery see Zilversmit 1967; Berlin and Hoffman 1983. Blackburn's model of 'political rupture' as a catalyst of political action against slavery would be more compelling for Anglo-America, except that the initial outcome of nation-building by the first independent society in the New World was, to say the least, equivocal on slavery (Blackburn 1988:109-30). The demographic pattern within the US was not static after American independence. As early as the 1790s, Virginia, Maryland, and Delaware were net exporters of slaves, and after 1820, intra-Southern importing was dominated by the trans-appalachian lower South (Tadman 1989:10-1, Table 2.1). The demographic erosion of slavery in the upper South played an important role in political calculations on the eve of the Civil War (Freehling 1994:176-219). For an analogous 'shift' in Brazilian slavery after the abolition of its transatlantic slave trade, see Drescher 1988:437-9. Demography may have affected the discussion of Northern slavery as well. In the most substantial slaveholding states north of the Chesapeake, the terms of the debate over abolition apparently were less egalitarian than in Pennsylvania and New England. The inhabitants of New York and New Jersey wanted to encourage white immigrants, whom 'they hoped would be a more loyal and less contentious labor force' (Hodges 1992:39).
[46] Davis 1975:164-254. On Georgia as an imagined community free of slavery, see Crowley 1974:30-4; Wood 1989:66-79; introduction Trevor R. Reese in Anonymous 1972:183. The flow of slaves from the Dutch colonies to the Netherlands was miniscule compared with the British case. Compare Oostindie 1992:162-3, note 13; Drescher 1987:50-66.

intrusion of racial questions, first into the courts and later into the debates of the French revolutionary assemblies. The flow of black slaves and free blacks into the Netherlands was demographically and socially far less significant and presented far less of a socio-judicial problem than in the cases of England or France. When there was a legal clarification of the status of slaves in the Dutch metropolis four years after the Somerset case in England, it was a 'Continental' response, more akin to the reaction to the eighteenth-century black presence in contemporary France than to the Somerset decision. The States-General decreed that Dutch slaveholders could encapsulate their colonical property in the free metropolis. Black slaves were thereby treated like overseas commodities. They could be legally 'warehoused' for reexportation within a limited period.[47]

The impact of slave resistance on the abolitionist process is also difficult to assess. In the French case the St. Domingue slave uprising of 1791 clearly played a large, indeed the critical, role in the French emancipation decree of 1794. The effects of slave resistance in other colonial sectors and in the process as a whole is more uncertain. For more than a century the Dutch confronted the largest Maroon communities per capita in the Americas. Their Guiana colonies were 'a theater of perpetual war' by the mid-eighteenth century. Yet until well into the following century all the turmoil, uncertainty, and costs of repression generated no abolition movement or state-sponsored programs for terminating slavery. Dutch emancipation was enacted after a very long period of relative quiescence in the slave colonies.[48]

As indicated above, the events of the American and French Revolutions produced no Dutch reorientation on overseas slavery. The Dutch and British cases serve to emphasize the different paths taken by two of the most

---

[47] On the Netherlands, see 'Placaat van de Staaten Generaal [...] 23 Mey 1776' (quoted in Oostindie and Maduro 1986:15-6); see also Oostindie and Maduro 1986:7 and Goslinga 1985:553. On the tensions produced by mobile blacks in Britain and France, see Drescher 1987:25-49; Garrigus s.a.; Peabody s.a. For the French Revolution see Geggus 1989.

[48] Slave resistance models of abolition have also proliferated during the past generation. They emphasize the role and agency of slave resistance in achieving emancipation, or in accelerating metropolitan antislavery action. This model has been most successfully applied to the case of the first French slave emancipation, and there have been attempts to extend it throughout the slave Americas. See, for example, Genovese 1979; Craton 1982; Walvin 1982:123-63; Richardson 1985:27-110; Blackburn 1988:161-264, 331-80. Here too, the Dutch case logically qualifies as the preeminent candidate for a slave resistance model of abolition before 1790. Postma calculated that there may have been up to 300 revolts on Dutch slavers in the course of the transatlantic slave trade (Postma 1990:167). Suriname, according to Price and Price, was 'a theater of perpetual war' (Stedman 1988:xiv). The Maroon population of the Dutch colonies was by far the largest in the Caribbean area throughout the period of slavery. See also Price 1976; Benjamin 1992:97-106. Although Suriname's pre-emancipation period was not preceded by a major slave uprising the metropolitan debates were punctuated by discussions of covert resistance and open unrest at the moments of British and French emancipation (Craton 1992:46).

economically developed, religiously diverse, and politically constitutional societies of Europe in the seventeenth and eighteenth centuries. The Dutch, it turns out, offered an ordinary rather than an exceptional goodbye to slavery. In the insulation of their metropolitan political culture from overseas social arrangements the Dutch remained within the 'bifurcated' world of early modern Europe until far into the nineteenth century (Drescher 1987:1-24). In the imperial preponderance of their tropical and slave colonies, in their persistence as a trading empire in tropical staples, in their dearth of transoceanic religious networks, the Dutch diverged far more in politico-religious than in economic terms from the Anglo-Americans.

The Dutch case may clarify another aspect of the very problematic relationship between economic development and antislavery. Whatever the economic implications of any specific case, it is still maintained that the ideological challenge to slavery 'itself reflects fundamental long-term economic forces.'[49] In other words, over the long term antislavery is still widely conceptualized as a 'superstructure', reflecting an economic 'base'. The Dutch case presents us with the following relevant conundrum: a society identified as a pioneer of modern capitalism from the early seventeenth century, one unencumbered by serfdom for centuries more before that, yet one that failed to generate a major antislavery movement by the standards of the age. Indeed, legally coerced labor continued to exist right down to the twentieth century without being eliminated by the Dutch state.

Half a century's investigations of the relationship between capitalism and antislavery have increasingly uncovered the contradictory consequences of antislavery for British capitalism without a clear determination of whether abolitionism diminished or complicated the birthpains of early industrialization (Ashworth 1992b:286-7). By contrast, the Netherlands case makes clear that Dutch capitalism, whether mercantile or industrial, whether in oligarchical or revolutionary phases, created no significant antislavery moment. Nor did antislavery, at any point, significantly legitimize Dutch

---

[49] In considering the longer term relationship between capitalism and servile labor one can note both the persistence of slavery in the commercialized societies of Mediterranean Europe, and the disappearance of chattel slavery in an economically expanding Northern Europe from the mid-tenth to the mid-fourteenth centuries. The Dutch appropriately present the most paradoxical evidence, illustrated by the early decline of personal bondage in the Low Countries and the late ending of slavery and other forms of bound labor overseas. On the significance of time horizons in the capitalism and antislavery debate, see Engerman 1993. Davis (1992b:291-2) vigorously argues against the long-term causal significance of the capitalist market as a stimulus to antislavery. In considering exogenous pressures, consider that in all cases after 1807 British abolition was both example and threat. British emancipation enhanced the desire among some Continentals to remove the shame of slavery and to associate their own nation with the march of progress. But British post-emancipation colonial difficulties and the heavy-handed British diplomacy often frustrated metropolitan initiatives. For an example of the unstable mix of pressures in France, see Drescher 1991:716-34; Jennings 1988.

capitalist industrialization. Viewed in terms of mutual cause and effect the more closely one investigates the relationship the more trivial the outcome appears.

Nevertheless, the hope of encompassing the century of slave emancipation within the ambit of economic development continues to fascinate historians of slavery. They are inexorably drawn to the institution's termination by collectivities professing the social norms of individual liberty, civil equality, free enterprise, and free labor. Few seem prepared to settle for only the weakest and blandest construction of the linkage – that the wealth generated within the North Atlantic economies allowed for accepting alternative forms of labor if slaveholding, however competitive, became morally embarrassing or politically inconvenient. If inconvenience alone were at issue, Europe could have managed to do without chattel slavery well before the age of abolition.

The Dutch dog that didn't bark now joins a larger pack of non-events that challenge a number of stronger formulations of the relationship between economic development and antislavery. It is not as easy as it once appeared to formulate an empirically satisfactory account of the antislavery consequences of European world-capitalism, whether mercantile, industrial, or bourgeois.

Taken in comparative perspective, the Dutch case enables us to make or to reinforce a number of observations about the antislavery process. First, the seventeenth, eighteenth and early nineteenth centuries do not mark incommensurable 'stages' in Western capitalism and Modern slavery. There were zones of both commercial and industrial capitalism in all three centuries. The various segments of Atlantic slavery were likewise not universally rising or declining during the same period. Less well recognized, antislavery sentiments were not limited to any of these centuries. Indeed, the Dutch were remarkably precocious in having developed a politically effective sentiment against metropolitan slavery centuries before the traditional age of abolition.[50]

It is the context in which that sentiment was nurtured into an overwhelming and irreversible political process which is at issue. Here too, the Dutch case is relevant. Neither a dynamic seventeenth-century metropolitan economy, nor a distressed late eighteenth-century economy on both sides of the Atlantic stimulated Dutch antislavery. Therein lies the chief significance of the Netherlands for the capitalism and antislavery debate. For a period of Dutch involvement extending over almost two and a half centuries, we can audit the economic dimension of the relationship with overseas slavery in the relative absence of strong political, and cultural

---

[50] Postma 1990:11; Drescher 1987:15; Davis 1975:214.

pressures against the system. As with other major cases thus far investigated the economic context offers the weakest positive support for and the strongest counter-abolitionist argument against the antislavery process. In light of the eagerness with which scholars have fruitfully juxtaposed cases of slavery drawn from two hemispheres and three millennia, comparing antislavery among neighbors with close cultural, political, and economic ties over three centuries hardly appears a daunting or fanciful project. Our appetites and our critical sense should be as whetted for comparative antislavery as for comparative slavery.

Comparative regional and national analysis suggests that the breakthroughs to collective abolitionism and the triumphs of antislavery are not to be sought primarily in the impact of the usual economic markers of the capitalist industrial revolution – the shift from agriculture, the rise of the large-scale factory, or the new forms of managerial discipline. Antislavery seems to have been more dependent upon the invention of new forms of collective behavior and by communal expansions of the rights of individuals, of social roles, of public membership, which accompanied the rise of Britain and its settler societies to prominence and world primacy. As the discussion broadens the rise of antislavery has to be imagined less as a correlate of expanding new class domination than as one of the new modes of social mobilization. More expansive conceptions of liberty impacted upon Vermont farmers, Yorkshire women, or Caribbean slaves at least as much as they did upon entrepreneurial and abolitionist élites in the economic capitals of Anglo-America.[51]

In its British and North American variants antislavery did intersect with rapid industrial development in ways that are still much debated. The major retrospective stimulus to clarifying that intersection, however, is that once antislavery was consensually embedded in British, and later American, opinion and law, those nations made it increasingly difficult for other societies to avoid placing abolition on their own political agendas. Only a century after the launching of the British abolitionist movement was the link between capitalism and slavery finally broken in the New World, and well on the way to dissolution in the Old.

---

[51] Compare Drescher 1980, 1987:67-88, 111-61; Magdol 1986:57-8, 137-40; Ashworth 1992a: 189-98, 1992b:274-81; Davis 1992b:291-3. A full discussion of Anglo-American capitalism and antislavery must also articulate differences between antislaveries as well as between capitalisms. There were anti-slave trade, anti-black, humanitarian, egalitarian, religious, and secular variants, sometimes operating separately and sometimes in tandem or tension.

References

Abeyasekere, Susan
1983 'Slaves in Batavia; Insights from a Slave Register', in: Anthony Reid (ed.), *Slavery, Bondage and Dependency in Southeast Asia*, pp. 286-314. New York: St. Martin's Press.

Anderson, Benedict
1983 *Imagined Communities; Reflections on the Origins and Spread of Nationalism*. London: Verso.

Anonymous
1972 *The Most Delightful Country of the Universe; Promotional Literature of the Colony of Georgia 1717-1734*. Savannah: Beehive Press.

Armstrong, James C. and Nigel A. Worden
1988 'The Slave, 1652-1834', in: Richard Elphick and Hermann Giliomee (eds), *The Shaping of South African Society, 1652-1840*, pp. 109-83. Middletown: Wesleyan University Press.

Ashworth, John
1992a 'Capitalism and Humanitarianism', in: Thomas Bender (ed.), *The Antislavery Debate; Capitalism and Abolitionism as a Problem in Historical Interpretation*, pp. 189-98. Berkeley: University of California Press.
1992b 'Capitalism, Class, and Antislavery', in: Thomas Bender (ed.), *The Antislavery Debate; Capitalism and Abolitionism as a Problem in Historical Interpretation*, pp. 263-89. Berkeley: University of California Press.

Bairoch, Paul
1989 'Les trois révolutions agricoles du monde developpé; Rendements et productivité de 1800 à 1985', *Annales; Economies, Sociétés, Civilisations* 44:317-53.

Baldwin, Alice May
1928 *The New England Clergy and the American Revolution*. Durham: Duke University Publications.

Beck, Earl Ray
1979 *A Time of Triumph and Sorrow; Spanish Politics during the Reign of Alfonso XII, 1874-1885*. Carbondale: Southern Illinois University Press; London: Feffer and Simons.

Bender, Thomas
1992a 'Introduction', in: Thomas Bender (ed.), *The Antislavery Debate; Capitalism and Abolitionism as a Problem in Historical Interpretation*, pp. 3-13. Berkeley: University of California Press.
1992b (ed.) *The Antislavery Debate; Capitalism and Abolitionism as a Problem in Historical Interpretation*. Berkeley: University of California Press.

Benger, Elizabeth Ogilvy
1978 'A Poem Occasioned by the Abolition of the Slave Trade in 1806', in: James Montgomery (ed.), *Poems on the Abolition of the Slave Trade*. New York: Garland. [Original edition 1809.]

Benjamin, Ann
1992   'Some Reflections on Hilary Beckles' Article: "Caribbean Anti-Slavery" The Self-Liberation Ethos of Enslaves Blacks" ', *Journal of Caribbean History* 26-1:97-108.

Bénot, Yves
1988   *La Révolution francaise et la fin des colonies*. Paris: La Découverte.

Berg, Maxine
1985   *The Age of Manufacturers; Industry, Innovation, and Work in Britain 1700-1820*. Oxford: Blackwell.

Berlin, Ira and Ronald Hoffman (eds)
1983   *Slavery and Freedom in the Age of the American Revolution*. Charlottesville: University Press of Virginia for the US Capitol Historical Society.

Blackburn, Robin
1988   *The Overthrow of Colonial Slavery 1776-1848*. London: Verso.
s.a.   'Abolitionism and Emancipation in Comparative Perspective'. [Unpublished manuscript.]

Blakely, Allison
1993   *Blacks in the Dutch World; The Evolution of Racial Imagery in a Modern Society*. Bloomington: Indiana University Press.

Blanchard, Peter
1992   *Slavery and Abolition in Early Republican Peru*. Wilmington: SR Books.

Bolt, Christine and Seymour Drescher (eds)
1980   *Anti-Slavery, Religion, and Reform; Essays in Memory of Roger Anstey*. Folkestone: Dawson; Hamden: Archon.

Boogaart, Ernst van den
1986   'The Servant Migration to New Netherland, 1624-1664', in: Pieter C. Emmer (ed.), *Colonialism and Migration; Indentured Labour Before and After Slavery*, pp. 55-81. Dordrecht: Nijhoff.

Boogaart, Ernst van den and Pieter C. Emmer
1979   'The Dutch Participation in the Atlantic Slave Trade, 1596-1650', in: Henry A. Gemery and Jan S. Hogendorn (eds), *The Uncommon Market; Essays in the Economic History of the Atlantic Slave Trade*, pp. 353-75. New York: Academic Press.

Boomgaard, Peter
1989   *Children of the Colonial State; Population Growth and Economic Development in Java, 1795-1880*. Amsterdam: Free University Press. [CASA Monographs 1.]

Brake, Wayne Ph. te, Rudolf M. Dekker and Lotte C. van de Pol
1990   'Women and Political Culture in the Dutch Revolutions', in: Harriet B. Applewhite and Darline Gay Levy (eds), *Women and Politics in the Age of the Democratic Revolution*, pp. 109-46. Ann Arbor: University of Michigan Press.

Brenner, Robert
1993   *Merchants and Revolution; Commercial Change, Political Conflict, and London's Overseas Traders, 1550-1653*. Princeton: Princeton University Press.

Bruns, Roger (ed.)
1977   *Am I Not a Man and a Brother; The Antislavery Crusade of Revolutionary America, 1688-1788.* New York: Chelsea House.

Carr, Raymond
1982   *Spain 1808-1975.* Oxford: Clarendon Press.

Carr, William
1691   *An Accurate Description of the United Netherlands.* London: Childe.

Carter, George E.
1991   'A Review of Slavery, Emancipation and Abolition in South Africa and the United States in the Eighteenth Century', *American Studies International* 29-2:69-76.

Chijs, J.A. van der (ed.)
1885-1900   *Nederlandisch-Indisch Plakaatboek; 1602-1811.* Batavia: Landsdrukkerij; 's-Gravenhage: Nijhoff. 17 vols.

Conan Doyle, Arthur
1946   *The Adventures and Memoirs of Sherlock Holmes.* New York: Modern Library.

Conrad, Robert
1972   *The Destruction of Brazilian Slavery, 1850-1888.* Berkeley: University of California Press.

Corwin, Arthur
1967   *Spain and the Abolition of Slavery in Cuba.* Austin: University of Texas Press for the Institute of Latin American Studies.

Craton, Michael
1982   *Testing the Chains; Slave Rebellions in the British West Indies, 1629-1832.* Ithaca: Cornell University Press.
1992   'The Transition from Slavery to Free Wage Labour in the Caribbean, 1780-1890; A Survey with Particular Reference to Recent Scholarship', *Slavery and Abolition* 13-2:37-67.

Crowley, J.E.
1974   *This Sheba, Self; The Conceptualization of Economic Life in Eighteenth-Century America.* Baltimore: The Johns Hopkins University Press.

Davids, Karel A.
1992   'Artisans, Urban Governments, and Industrial Decline in Holland, 1670-1800.' [Paper presented at the AHA annual meeting on 28 December 1992.]

Davids, Karel A. and Leo Noordegraaf (eds)
1993   *The Dutch Economy in the Golden Age.* Amsterdam: Nederlands Economisch-Historisch Archief.

Davis, David Brion
1975   *The Problem of Slavery in the Age of Revolution, 1770-1823.* Ithaca: Cornell University Press.
1984   *Slavery and Human Progress.* New York: Oxford University Press.

1987	'Capitalism, Abolitionism and Hegemony', in: Barbara L. Solow and Stanley L. Engerman (eds), *British Capitalism and Caribbean Slavery; The Legacy of Eric Williams*, pp. 209-27. Cambridge: Cambridge University Press.
1988a	*The Problem of Slavery in Western Culture*. New York: Oxford University Press. [Revised edition.]
1988b	'The Significance of Excluding Slavery from the Old Northwest in 1787', *Indiana Magazine of History* 84-1:75-89.
1992a	'Reflections on Abolitionism and Ideological Hegemony', in: Thomas Bender (ed.), *The Antislavery Debate; Capitalism and Abolitionism as a Problem in Historical Interpretation*, pp. 161-79. Berkeley: University of California Press.
1992b	'The Perils of Doing History by Ahistorical Abstraction; A Reply to Thomas L. Haskell's *AHR Forum* Reply', in: Thomas Bender (ed.), *The Antislavery Debate; Capitalism and Abolitionism as a Problem in Historical Interpretation*, pp. 290-309. Berkeley: University of California Press.

Deursen, A.T. van
1991	*Plain Lives in a Golden Age; Popular Culture, Religion and Society in Seventeenth-Century Holland*. Cambridge: Cambridge University Press.

Dillen, J.G. van
1982	'The West India Company, Calvinism and Politics', in: M.A.P. Meilink-Roelofsz (ed.), *Dutch Authors on West Indian History; A Historiographical Selection*, pp. 149-86. The Hague: Nijhoff. [KITLV, Translation Series 21.]

Drescher, Seymour
1976	'Le declin du système esclavagiste britannique et l'abolition de la traite', *Annales; Economies, Sociétés, Civilisations* 31:414-35.
1977	*Econocide; British Slavery in the Era of Abolition*. Pittsburgh: University of Pittsburgh Press.
1980	'Two Variants of Anti-Slavery; Religious Organization and Social Mobilization in Britain and France, 1780-1870', in: Christine Bolt and Seymour Drescher (eds), *Anti-Slavery, Religion, and Reform; Essays in Memory of Roger Anstey*, pp. 43-64. Folkestone: Dawson; Hamden: Archon.
1987	*Capitalism and Antislavery; British Mobilization in Comparative Perspective*. New York: Oxford University Press.
1988	'Brazilian Abolition in Comparative Perspective', *Hispanic American Historical Review* 68-3:429-60.
1990	'Trends in der Historiographie des Abolitionismus', *Geschichte und Gesellschaft* 16-2:187-211.
1991	'British Way, French Way; Opinion Building and Revolution in the Second French Slave Emancipation', *American Historical Review* 96-3:709-35.
1993a	'Review essay of *The Antislavery Debate; Capitalism and Abolitionism as a Problem in Historical Interpretation* [Thomas Bender (ed.)]', *History and Theory* 32:311-29.
1993b	'The Role of Jews in the Transatlantic Slave Trade', *Immigrants and Minorities* 12:113-25.

1994 'Whose Abolition? Popular Pressure and the Ending of the British Slave Trade', *Past and Present* 143:136-66.

Dros, Nico
1991 'Javanese Labour Relations in a Changing Rural Economy, 1830-1870', *Economic and Social History in the Netherlands* 3:133-53.

Du Toit, André and Hermann Giliomee
1983 *Afrikaner Political Thought; Analysis and Documents, Volume I, 1780-1850*. Berkeley: University of California Press.

Elphick, Richard and Hermann Giliomee (eds)
1988 *The Shaping of South African Society, 1652-1840*. Middletown: Wesleyan University Press.

Elphick, Richard and Robert Shell
1988 'Intergroup Relations; Khoikoi, Settlers, Slaves and Free Blacks, 1653-1795', in: Richard Elphick and Herman Giliomee (eds), *The Shaping of South African Society, 1652-1840*, pp. 184-239. Middletown: Wesleyan University Press.

Eltis, David
1987 *Economic Growth and the Ending of the Transatlantic Slave Trade*. New York: Oxford University Press.
1993 'Europeans and the Rise and Fall of African Slavery in the Americas; An Interpretation', *American Historical Review* 98:1399-423.

Emmer, Pieter C.
1980 'Anti-Slavery and the Dutch; Abolition without Reform', in: Christine Bolt and Seymour Drescher (eds), *Anti-Slavery, Religion, and Reform; Essays in Memory of Roger Anstey*, pp. 80-98. Folkestone: Dawson; Hamden: Archon.
1981 'Abolition of the Slave Trade and the Mixed Courts', in: David Eltis and James Walvin (eds), *The Abolition of the Atlantic Slave Trade*, pp. 177-90. Madison: University of Wisconsin Press.
1991 'The Dutch and the Making of the Second Atlantic System', in: Barbara L. Solow (ed.), *Slavery and the Rise of the Atlantic System*, pp. 75-96. Cambridge: Cambridge University Press.

Engerman, Stanley L.
1986 'Slavery and Emancipation in Comparative Perspective; A Look at Some Recent Debates', *Journal of Economic History* 46:317-39.
1992 'Coerced and Free Labor; Property Rights and the Development of the Labor Force', *Explorations in Economic History* 29:1-29.
1993 'Chicken Little, Anna Karenina, and the Economics of Slavery; Two Reflections on Historical Analysis, with Examples Drawn Mostly from the Study of Slavery', *Social Science History* 17:161-71.

Engerman, Stanley L. and B.W. Higman
forthcoming 'The Demographic Structure of the Caribbean Slave Societies in the Eighteenth and Nineteenth Centuries', in: Franklin W. Knight (ed.), *UNESCO General History of the Caribbean*.

Finley, M.I.
1976 'A Peculiar Institution?' *Times Literary Supplement* 3877 (2 July):819.

Fogel, Robert William and Stanley L. Engerman
1989   *Time on the Cross; The Economics of American Negro Slavery*. Boston: Little, Brown. 2 vols. [Original edition 1974.]

Fogel, Robert William et al.
1992   *Without Consent or Contract; The Rise and Fall of American Slavery*. New York: Norton. 4 vols.

Fox, J.
1983   ' "For Good and Sufficient Reasons"; An Examination of Early Dutch East India Company Ordinances on Slaves and Slavery', in: Anthony Reid (ed.), *Slavery, Bondage and Dependency in Southeast Asia*, pp. 246-62. New York: St. Martin's Press.

Freehling, William W.
1994   *The Reintegration of American History; Slavery and the Civil War*. New York: Oxford University Press.

Garrigus, John
s.a.   'Blue and Brown; Contraband Indigo and the Rise of a Free Colored Planter Class in French Saint-Domingue'. [Unpublished manuscript.]

Geggus, David
1989   'Racial Equality, Slavery and Colonial Secession during the Constituent Assembly', *American Historical Review* 94:1290-308.

Gelderen, Martin van
1992   *The Political Thought of the Dutch Revolt 1555-1590*. Cambridge: Cambridge University Press.

Gemery, Henry A. and Jan S. Hogendorn (eds)
1979   *The Uncommon Market; Essays in the Economic History of the Atlantic Slave Trade*. New York: Academic Press.

Genovese, Eugene D.
1979   *From Rebellion to Revolution; Afro-American Slave Revolts in the Making of the Modern World*. Baton Rouge: Louisiana State University Press.

Goslinga, Cornelis Ch.
1985   *The Dutch in the Caribbean and in the Guianas, 1680-1791*. Assen: Van Gorcum.
1990   *The Dutch in the Caribbean and in Surinam, 1791/5-1942*. Assen: Van Gorcum.

Grauman Wolf, Stephanie
1976   *Urban Village; Population, Community, and Family Structure in Germantown Pennsylvania, 1683-1800*. Princeton: Princeton University Press.

Green-Pedersen, Sv. E.
1975   'The History of the Danish Negro Slave Trade 1733-1807', *Revue Francaise d'Histoire d'Outre-Mer* 62:196-220.
s.a.   'From Danish Abolition to Danish Emancipation; Some Considerations about the British versus French Influence'. [Unpublished manuscript.]

Greene, Jack P.
1994   *Negotiated Authorities; Essays in Colonial Political and Constitutional History*. Charlottesville: University Press of Virginia.

Haskell, Thomas L.
1992a   'Capitalism and the Origins of Humanitarian Sensibility', in: Thomas Bender (ed.), *The Antislavery Debate; Capitalism and Abolitionism as a Problem in Historical Interpretation*, pp. 107-60. Berkeley: University of California Press.
1992b   'Convention and Hegemonic Interest in the Debate over Antislavery', in: Thomas Bender (ed.), *The Antislavery Debate; Capitalism and Abolitionism as a Problem in Historical Interpretation*, pp. 200-59. Berkeley: University of California Press.

Hennessy, Charles A.M.
1962   *The Federal Republic in Spain; Pi y Margall and the Federal Republican Movement, 1868-74*. Oxford: Clarendon Press.

Hodges, Graham Russell
1992   'Black Revolt in New York City and the Neutral Zone, 1775-83', in: Paul A. Gilje and William Pencak (eds), *New York in the Age of the Constitution 1775-1800*, pp. 20-47. Rutherford: Fairleigh Dickinson University Press; Cranbury: Associated University Press.

Holt, Thomas C.
1982   'An Empire over the Mind; Emancipation, Race and Ideology in the British West Indies and the American South', in: J. Morgan Kousser and James McPherson (eds), *Religion, Race and Reconstruction*, pp. 283-313. New York: Oxford University Press.
1990   'Explaining Abolition', *Journal of Social History* 24:371-8.
1992   *The Problem of Freedom; Race, Labor, and Politics in Jamaica and Britain, 1832-1938*. Baltimore: The Johns Hopkins University Press.

Israel, Jonathan I.
1985   *European Jewry in the Age of Mercantilism, 1550-1750*. Oxford: Clarendon Press.
1989   *Dutch Primacy in World Trade, 1585-1740*. Oxford: Clarendon Press.
1990   *Empires and Entrepots; The Dutch, the Spanish Monarchy and the Jews, 1585-1713*. London: Hambledon Press.

Jacob, Margaret C.
1992   'Radicalism in the Dutch Enlightenment', in: Margaret C. Jacob and Wijnandt W. Mijnhardt (eds), *The Dutch Republic in the Eighteenth Century; Decline, Enlightenment, and Revolution*, pp. 224-40. Ithaca: Cornell University Press.

Jennings, Lawrence
1988   *French Reaction to British Slave Emancipation*. Baton Rouge: Louisiana State University Press.

Kossmann, E.H.
1978   *The Low Countries, 1780-1940*. Oxford: Clarendon Press.

Krantz, Frederick and Paul M. Hohenberg (eds)
1975   *Failed Transitions to Modern Industrial Society; Renaissance Italy and Seventeenth Century Holland*. Montreal: University Centre for European Studies.

Lee, Arthur
1764   *An Essay in Vindication of the Continental Colonies of America from a Censure of Mr. Adam Smith, in his 'Theory of Moral Sentiments'; With some Reflections on Slavery in General.* London: s.n.

Leeb, I. Leonard
1973   *The Ideological Origins of the Batavian Revolution: History and Politics in the Dutch Republic 1747-1800.* The Hague: Nijhoff.

Lombardi, John V.
1974   'The Abolition of Slavery in Venezuela; A Nonevent', in: Robert Brent Toplin (ed.), *Slavery and Race Relations in Latin America*, pp. 228-52. Westport: Greenwood Press.

Louis, William Roger and Jean Stengers (eds)
1968   *E.D. Morel's History of the Congo Reform Movement.* Oxford: Clarendon Press.

McCants, Anne
1992   'Monotonous But Not Meager; The Diet of Burgher Orphans in Early Modern Amsterdam', *Research in Economic History* 14:69-116.

McCusker, John J.
1970   *The Rum Trade and the Balance of Payments of the Thirteenth Continental Colonies, 1660-1775.* [PhD thesis University of Pittsburgh.]

Maddison, Angus
1982   *Phases of Capitalist Development.* Oxford: Oxford University Press.

Magdol, Edward
1986   *The Antislavery Rank and File; A Social Profile of the Abolitionists' Constituency.* New York: Greenwood Press.

Manning, Patrick
1990   *Slavery and African Life; Occidental, Oriental and African Slave Trades.* Cambridge: Cambridge University Press.

Mastboom, Joyce M.
1992   'Guild or Union? A Case Study of Rural Dutch Weavers, 1682-1750'. [Paper presented at the AHA annual meeting, 1992.]

Miers, Suzanne
1975   *Britain and the Ending of the Slave Trade.* New York: Africana Publishing Company.

Mokyr, Joel
1976   *Industrialization in the Low Countries, 1795-1850.* New Haven: Yale University Press.

Montgomery, James
1978   'The West Indies', in: James Montgomery (ed.), *Poems on the Abolition of the Slave Trade.* New York: Garland. [Original edition 1809.]

Nash, Gary and Jean Soderlund,
1991   *Freedom by Degrees; Emancipation in Pennsylvania and Its Aftermath.* New York: Oxford University Press.

O'Brien, Susan
1986   'A Transatlantic Community of Saints; The Great Awakening and the First Evangelical Network, 1735-1755', *American Historical Review* 91:811-32.

Oostindie, Gert
1990   'Prelude to the Exodus; Surinamers in the Netherlands, 1667-1960s', in: Gary Brana-Shute (ed.), *Resistance and Rebellion in Suriname; Old and New*, pp. 231-58. Williamsburg: College of William and Mary. [Studies in Third World Societies 43.]
1992   'The Enlightenment, Christianity, and the Suriname Slave', *Journal of Caribbean History* 26:147-70. [Revised and enlarged version in the present book.]
1993   'The Economics of Suriname Slavery', *Economic and Social History of the Netherlands* 5:1-24.

Oostindie, Gert and Emy Maduro
1986   *In het land van de overheerser, II; Antillianen en Surinamers in Nederland, 1634/1667-1984*. Dordrecht: Foris. [KITLV, Verhandelingen 100.]

Palmer, R.R.
1959   *The Age of the Democratic Revolution*. Princeton: Princeton University Press. 2 vols.

Peabody, Sue
s.a.   'Race, Slavery and French Law; The Legal Context of the "Police des Noirs"'. [Unpublished manuscript.]
s.a.   ' "There Are No Slaves in France"; The Political Culture of Race and Slavery in Eighteenth-Century Paris'. [Unpublished manuscript.]

Postma, Johannes Menne
1990   *The Dutch in the Atlantic Slave Trade 1600-1815*. Cambridge: Cambridge University Press.

Price, J.L.
1994   *Holland and the Dutch Republic in the Seventeenth Century*. Oxford: Clarendon Press.

Price, Richard
1976   *The Guiana Maroons; A Historical and Biographical Introduction*. Baltimore: The Johns Hopkins University Press.

Rediker, Marcus
1987   *Between the Devil and the Deep Blue Sea; Merchant Seaman, Pirates, and the Anglo-American Maritime World, 1700-1750*. Cambridge: Cambridge University Press.

Reports
1918   'The Reports of Chavonnes and his Council; The Historical Context, 1790-1916', in: *The Van Riebeeck Society Publications, vol. 1*. Cape Town: Van Riebeeck Society.

Richardson, David
1985   (ed.) *Abolition and its Aftermath*. London: Cass.
s.a.   'The Eighteenth-Century British Slave Trade; New Estimates of Its Volume and Distribution.' [Unpublished manuscript.]

Roeber, A.G.
1991   'The Origin of Whatever is not English Among Us', in: Bernard Bailyn
                and Philip D. Morgan (eds), *Strangers Within the Realm; Cultural Margins of the First British Empire*, pp. 220-83. Chapel Hill: University of
                North Carolina Press.
Ross, Robert
1983   *Cape of Torments; Slavery and Resistance in South Africa.* London:
                Routledge and Kegan Paul.
1988   'The Last Years of the Slave Trade to the Cape Colony', *Slavery and
                Abolition* 9-3:209-19.
Roth, Randolph
1987   *The Democratic Dilemma; Religion, Reform and the Social Order in the
                Connecticut River Valley of Vermont 1791-1850.* Cambridge: Cambridge
                University Press.
Sas, Nicolaas C.F. van
1992   'The Patriot Revolution; New Perspectives', in: Margaret C. Jacob and
                Wijnandt W. Mijnhardt (eds), *The Dutch Republic in the Eighteenth
                Century; Decline, Enlightenment, and Revolution*, pp. 91-123. Ithaca:
                Cornell University Press.
Schama, Simon
1977   *Patriots and Liberators; Revolution in the Netherlands, 1780-1813.* New
                York: Knopf.
1988   *The Embarrassment of Riches; An Interpretation of Dutch Culture in the
                Golden Age.* New York: Fontana Press. [Original edition 1987.]
Schutte, G.J.
1974   *De Nederlandse patriotten en de koloniën; Een onderzoek naar hun
                denkbeelden en optreden, 1770-1800.* Groningen: Tjeenk Willink.
Schweikart, Larry
1987   *Banking in the American South from the Age of Jackson to Reconstruction.*
                Baton Rouge: Louisiana State University Press.
Scott, Rebecca
1985   *Slave Emancipation in Cuba; The Transition to Free Labor, 1860-1899.*
                Princeton: Princeton University Press.
Scott, Rebecca, Seymour Drescher, et al.
1988   *The Abolition of Slavery and the Aftermath of Emancipation in Brazil.*
                Durham: Duke University Press.
Slicher van Bath, B.H.
1986   'The Absence of White Contract Labour in Spanish America During the
                Colonial Period', in: Pieter C. Emmer (ed.), *Colonialism and Migration;
                Indentured Labour Before and After Slavery*, pp. 19-31. Dordrecht:
                Nijhoff.
Smith, Adam
1937   *An Inquiry into the Nature and Causes of the Wealth of Nations.* New York:
                Dutton. [Original edition 1776.]

Soderlund, Jean R.
1985   *Quakers and Slavery; A Divided Spirit*. Princeton: Princeton University Press.
Solow, Barbara L. and Stanley L. Engerman (eds)
1987   *British Capitalism and Caribbean Slavery; The Legacy of Eric Williams*. Cambridge: Cambridge University Press.
Spierenburg, Pieter
1991   *The Prison Experience; Disciplinary Institutions and their Inmates in Early Modern Europe*. New Brunswick: Rutgers University Press.
Stedman, John Gabriel
1988   *Narrative of a Five Year's Expedition Against the Revolted Negroes of Surinam; Transcribed for the first time from the original 1790 manuscript*. Edited, and with an introduction and notes, by Richard Price and Sally Price. Baltimore: The Johns Hopkins University Press.
Steele, Ian K.
1986   *The English Atlantic 1675-1740; An Exploration of Communication and Community*. New York: Oxford University Press.
Tadman, Michael
1989   *Speculators and Slaves; Masters, Traders and Slaves in the Old South*. Madison: University of Wisconsin Press.
Tarrade, Jean
1989   'Les Colonies et les principes de 1789; Les Assemblées révolutionnaires face au probléme de l'esclavage', *Revue Francaise d'Histoire d'Outre-Mer* 76:9-34.
Temperley, Howard
1977   'Capitalism, Slavery and Ideology', *Past and Present* 75:94-118.
Tilly, Charles
1993   *European Revolutions, 1492-1992*. London: Blackwell.
Turley, David
1991   *The Culture of English Antislavery, 1780-1860*. London: Routledge.
Verhagen, Diederik R.C.
1949   *L'influence de la Revolution Française sur la premiere constitution Hollandaise du 23 avril 1798*. Utrecht: Kemink.
Verslag
1861   *Verslag der Handelingen van de Tweede Kamer der Staten-Generaal, gedurende de Zitting van 1818-1819, gehouden te Brussel*, 9th Sitting, November 12, 1818. 's-Gravenhage: s.n.
Vries, Jan de
1974   *The Dutch Rural Economy in the Golden Age, 1500-1700*. New Haven: Yale University Press.
1982   'An Inquiry into the Behavior of Wages in the Dutch Republic and the Southern Netherlands from 1580 to 1800', in: Maurice Aymard (ed.), *Dutch Capitalism and World Capitalism*, pp. 37-61. Cambridge: Cambridge University Press.
1984   *European Urbanization 1500-1800*. Cambridge: Harvard University Press.

1986	'The Population and Economy of the Preindustrial Netherlands,' in: Robert I. Rotberg, Theodore K. Rabb, Roger S. Schofield and E. Anthony Wrigley (eds), *Population and Economy; Population and History from the Traditional to the Modern World*, pp. 100-22. Cambridge: Cambridge University Press.
1990	'Problems in the Measurement, Description, and Analysis of Historical Urbanization,' in: A.D. van der Woude et al. (eds), *Urbanization in History; A Process of Dynamic Interactions*, pp. 43-60. Oxford: Clarendon Press.

Walvin, James (ed.)
1982   *Slavery and British Society 1776-1846*. London: Macmillan.

Whitney, Robert
1992   'The Political Economy of Abolition; The Hispano-Cuban Élite and Cuban Slavery', *Slavery and Abolition* 13-2:20-36.

Williams, Eric
1944   *Capitalism and Slavery*. Chapel Hill: University of North Carolina Press.
1970   *From Columbus to Castro; The History of the Caribbean 1492-1969*. New York: Harper.

Winter, Johanna Maria van
1982   'Public Opinion in the Netherlands on the Abolition of Slavery', in: M.A.P. Meilink-Roelofsz (ed.), *Dutch Authors on West Indian History; A Historiographical Selection*, pp. 100-28. The Hague: Nijhoff. [KITLV, Translation Series 21.]

Wiznitzer, Arnold
1960   *Jews in Colonial Brazil*. New York: Columbia University Press.

Wood, Betty
1989   'James Edward Oglethorpe, Race, and Slavery', in: Phenzy Spalding and Harvey H. Jackson (eds), *Oglethorpe in Perspective; Georgia's Founder after Two Hundred Years*, pp. 66-79. Tuscaloosa: University of Alabama Press.

Worden, Nigel
1985   *Slavery in Dutch South Africa*. Cambridge: Cambridge University Press.

Wright, Gavin
1987   'Capitalism and Slavery on the Islands; A Lesson from the Mainland', in: Barbara L. Solow and Stanley L. Engerman (eds), *British Capitalism and Caribbean Slavery; The Legacy of Eric Williams*, pp. 283-302. Cambridge: Cambridge University Press.

Wrigley, E.A. and R.S. Schofield
1981   *The Population History of England, 1541-1871*. Cambridge: Harvard University Press.

[Young, Arthur]
1970   *Political Essays Concerning the Present State of the British Empire [...]*. New York: Research Reprints. [Original edition 1772.]

Zanden, J.L. van
1993   *The Rise and Decline of Holland's Economy; Merchant Capitalism and the Labour Market*. Manchester: Manchester University Press.

Zilversmit, Arthur
1967   *The First Emancipation; The Abolition of Slavery in the North.* Chicago: University of Chicago Press.

MAARTEN KUITENBROUWER

The Dutch Case of Antislavery
Late and Élitist Abolitionism

It is easier to explain the existence of a historical phenomenon than its relative absence. I first found this out when, as a student in the 1970s, I was struggling with the Marxist, humanitarian and hegemonic explanations by Eric Williams, Roger Anstey, and David Brion Davis of the early British abolition of the slave trade and slavery, to explain the late Dutch abolition and the lack of mass abolitionism in the Netherlands.[1] My conclusion was that these explanations were only indirectly relevant to the Dutch case in a heuristic way. For in the Netherlands industrialization was late and modest, religious nonconformism was at first rather passive and inward-looking, and there was little radicalism to provoke the ruling élites into hegemonic actions (Kuitenbrouwer 1978:95-8). Now, with some irony, I see such prominent Anglo-American historians as David Brion Davis, Thomas L. Haskell, Robin Blackburn and last but not least Seymour Drescher struggling with the stubborn Dutch case from a comparative perspective.[2] The results of Drescher's present comparative essay confirm my conclusion that neither of the existing explanations of British abolition and abolitionism can fully explain the Dutch case. Drescher rightly points out that the Anglo-American cases form the exception rather than the rule in the capitalist world. Indirectly, however, the various explanations based on the Anglo-American experience remain relevant to the Dutch experience in a heuristic way.

In this essay, I will make only a few remarks on the first period of the seventeenth century discussed by Drescher, and a few more on the second period of the late eighteenth century. I will concentrate on the third period of the mid-nineteenth century. As a general thesis I argue in the first place that the late character of Dutch abolition and the lack of popular abolitionism can best be explained by the gradual character of Dutch capitalist development and political change. Although this perspective has recently been criticized as a Dutch version of the Whig interpretation of history, I

---

[1] Williams 1964; Anstey 1975; Davis 1975.
[2] Drescher 1986:280; Davis 1992a:178; 1992b:294-7; Haskell 1992:233-4; Blackburn 1988:520. Apart from Drescher's present essay these different comparative interpretations are all based on only one contribution, albeit a very rich one, namely, Emmer 1980.

think that it remains a valid perspective for the modern history of the Netherlands.³ Economic and political development was more gradual in the Netherlands than in France and even Britain. Second, I argue that there was some overflow from economic modernization and political change into abolitionism in the Netherlands, but that this process was curtailed from above by financial problems generated by the Dutch state and economy, and from below by the late and gradual character of religious and political mass mobilization in Dutch society.

The Emergence of Abolitionism

To return to the seventeenth century, the first period of comparative analysis distinguished by Drescher, the time when the Dutch slave trade and colonial slavery began: I doubt whether seventeenth-century Holland constitutes a valid comparison with eighteenth-century Britain. The Dutch Republic may have been a pioneer in crafts and manufactures, but it did not experience an industrial 'take-off' as Britain did at the turn of the eighteenth and nineteenth centuries, despite all revisionist writings on the first industrial revolution (Krantz and Hohenberg 1975). In the second place, there seems to have been stronger initial opposition to the introduction of the slave trade and slavery in the Netherlands than in Britain (Kuitenbrouwer 1989:212-3; Davis 1970:145-87). There were both fundamental and practical objections. Calvinist ministers attacked the slave trade and slavery as 'popish' institutions. 'Inhumane custom, Godless rascality!', the popular Dutch poet G.A. Brederoo exclaimed in 1615 (Postma 1990:11). Many merchants found the slave trade and slavery a dangerous, risky business. On the other hand, Dutch humanitarianism during the seventeenth century should not be stretched too far. Immigrants like the Flemish Dutch, the French Huguenots and the Iberian Jews were only welcomed insofar as they brought capital or capitalist skills with them (Gijswijt-Hofstra 1989; Schama 1988:565-609). As Dutch involvement in the slave trade increased, the number of legitimations on religious, economic, and racial grounds multiplied as well (Kuitenbrouwer 1989:214-5; Paasman 1984:98-108).

The relative decline of Dutch trade and finance and the absolute decline of Dutch manufacture should, in my opinion, be stressed more than Drescher does as the context of the emergence of Dutch abolitionism at the end of the eighteenth century. The Coalition Wars against France left the Republic already with a large public debt in the early eighteenth century. In 1713 the Dutch public debt amounted to 240 million guilders, per capita

---

3   Stuurman 1983; 1992. For the gradualist perspective, see Daalder 1990.

three times as high as the English public debt (Zwitzer 1990:40-1). Under conditions of economic distress the population of most industrial centers declined in the course of the eighteenth century. The population of the textile town of Leiden, for example, fell from 50,000 to 30,000 (De Vries 1959:170). After 1806, during the French Period, the national debt soared to 1200 million guilders. For years, half the population of Amsterdam was on poor relief.[4] In terms of 1970 dollars, the estimated Gross Domestic Product per capita declined in the Netherlands from $570 in 1700 to $513 in 1780 and, after further decline, recovered to the 1780 figure of $513 again in 1820. In Britain there was a steady increase of per capita GDP from $380 in 1700 to $457 in 1780 and $519 in 1820 (Maddison 1989:29). Drescher rightly points out that the Netherlands was still a fairly prosperous country by the 1770s. What matters here, however, is not the objective standard of wealth, but the subjective experience of contemporaries. At the end of the eighteenth century the Dutch had experienced a long decline, while the British had experienced a steady increase of income. In the case of Britain the socio-economic context was much more favorable for antislavery than in the case of the Netherlands.

Whether real or imagined, the economic decline of the Dutch Republic during the eighteenth century is the first reason why the Patriot Revolution and the Batavian Republic did not generate more abolitionism than they did. Every kind of economic activity, even the slave trade and colonial slavery, had priority over humanitarian concerns for the Dutch *burger* revolutionaries. In the second place, the Dutch Patriot movement and the Batavian Republic were less revolutionary in character than the Jacobins who abolished slavery during the French Revolution. After the Prussian intervention in 1787 the Patriot movement collapsed 'like a house of cards' in the words of its most recent historian, Van Sas.[5] The Batavian Republic could only be founded in 1795 with the assistance of the French revolutionary liberators and remained dependent on them. As Drescher rightly observes, the revolutionary French did not pressure their Dutch brothers to abolish slavery. In the third place, the Dutch slave trade and colonial slavery became a theoretical issue when Britain occupied all Dutch colonies for a longer or shorter time between 1795 and 1815 (Goslinga 1990:21-54). Moreover, these colonies lacked an immigrant settler population which reflected metropolitan freedom like the English-speaking parts of North America, as Drescher points out. Even in the Cape Colony, where the largest Dutch

---

[4] Schama 1977:503. For the relative and absolute decline of the Dutch economy during the late eighteenth and early nineteenth centuries, see Israel 189:377-405; Krantz and Hohenberg 1975:49-55; De Vries 1959:167-85; Mokyr 1976:1-8.
[5] Van Sas 1992:177. See also Schama 1977:64-138. For a comparision between Dutch and French abolitionism, see Sens 1992.

settler population lived, local Patriots understood the new civil rights primarily as a confirmation of their property rights on slaves (Schutte 1974:60-88).

Against this background it may be considered amazing that Dutch abolitionism received any attention at all at the end of eighteenth century. The traditional legitimations of the slave trade and slavery on religious, economic, and racial grounds became less prominent (Schutte 1979; Postma 1990:284-9). In 1776 the States-General declared slaves under certain strict conditions free on Dutch soil. Not unlike the famous Somerset case in Britain in 1772, however, this ruling had at first a more symbolic than practical effect (Oostindie 1986:14-6; Drescher 1986:36-43). Besides a rising number of Dutch abolitionist tracts many foreign abolitionist publications were translated. According to Paasman, however, most contemporary literature on the slave trade and slavery, both fiction and non-fiction, accepted these institutions as necessary evils, calling for a more enlightened and Christian treatment of the slaves (Paasman 1984:109-21). The political response to abolitionism followed the same pattern. When the radical leader P. Vreede proposed the immediate and complete abolition of both the slave trade and slavery in the National Assembly in 1797, he encountered little fundamental opposition, but the majority formed by the moderate members delegated the matter to a commission which repudiated slave trade and slavery with 'the heart' but accepted it on practical grounds with 'the head' (Paasman 1984:121-9; Schutte 1974:147-9). This configuration of few radical abolitionists, few radical defenders and a majority that accepted the slave trade and slavery only as necessary evils in times of economic distress, seems to have been typical of both Dutch policy and public opinion at the turn of the eighteenth and nineteenth centuries.

Slavery and Antislavery

This period of rather moderate revolution in the Netherlands was followed by a period of mild Orangist restoration under the United Kingdom of King Willem I. The abolition of the Dutch slave trade in 1814 was part of his policy to placate the British government into returning most Dutch colonies. The Dutch slave trade was already declining at the end of the eighteenth century and was completely stopped during the Napoleonic Wars. Its abolition was not opposed in Parliament by any Northern MPs. The Anglo-Dutch treaty of 1818 which introduced joint control of the illegal slave trade was only opposed by some Southern MPs on technical grounds (Emmer 1973:184-96; Van Sas 1985:79-96). After the abolition of the slave trade, West Indian slavery did decline in numbers if not in productivity. As was the case with more reforms initiated during Batavian and French times, the Conservative Colonial Secretaries at first tried to adapt slavery to more modern, economic, and humanitarian standards (Siwpersad 1979:69-127; Kuitenbrouwer 1978:74-5). Until Emancipation, the greater number of Suriname slaves was to receive more attention than the lesser number of Antillean slaves, which had little economic value and which were already assimilated in the Catholic culture and society of the islands (Hoetink 1969).

The Colonial Secretaries successfully encouraged the mission of the Moravian Brethren among the Suriname slaves, because of the quietist, accepting attitude of these missionaries towards secular authority. The attempts to introduce new, more humane and economically rational slave regulations failed, however, because of the strong opposition of the Suriname planters, backed by the absentee owners in Holland. In order to embarrass the Conservative Colonial Secretary J.C. Baud, the Liberal opposition in Parliament under the leadership of J.R. Thorbecke even backed the *cabale* against a reforming Governor of Suriname in the 1840s (Siwpersad 1979:69-127; Kuitenbrouwer 1978:74-5).

In 1844 Baud in a secret report to King Willem II proposed that West Indian slavery should be abolished, particularly in Suriname:

> 'Emancipation is for Suriname [...] a measure of material necessity, without which Suriname will be inevitably ruined, because of the dwindling of its workers. After emancipation Suriname will produce less than before, but in the end it will be saved from complete destruction. In short, emancipation seems to be the only way to save Suriname.' (Cited in Reinsma 1963:92; my translation.)

The British slave emancipation of 1833 in neighboring Guiana played a large role in Baud's reasoning, but the disappointing results of this emancipation for the productivity of the British colonies, together with the financial problems of the Netherlands, made Baud very cautious. In search for models he studied the financially successful Cultivation System of forced labor in the Dutch East Indies and the restrictive 'emancipation by association' plan for French Guadaloupe (Siwpersad 1979:127-55; Drescher 1991: 727-8).

Meanwhile, abolitionism reappeared on the scene in the Netherlands. In the early 1840s two petition movements were started against colonial slavery (Reinsma 1963:5-17; Kuitenbrouwer 1978:75-6). The first emerged from the evangelical Réveil movement within the Nederlandsch Hervormde Kerk (Dutch Reformed Church) assiciated with G. Groen van Prinsterer. At first the Réveil members had accepted slavery in accordance with the letter of the Bible, but after visits by members of the British abolition movement, in particular Quakers, the Réveil members became convinced that slavery was against the spirit of the Scriptures. Their cautious petition to the King, however, asking royal approval for an abolition society, was refused on the advice of Baud. The Réveil petition had

56 subscribers. A more frankly abolitionist petition by 125 Liberal subscribers, mostly academics, demanding a more immediate slave emancipation, was also turned down by the King on the advice of Baud. The Liberal abolitionists continued their activities with the publication of an abolitionist periodical for some years. Compared to Britain these petition movements were of course very small in numbers, but by the Dutch standards of the time they were less insignificant. The largest Liberal club, the Amstel Sociëteit in Amsterdam, had only 200 members during the 1840s (Stuurman 1992:143).

From a comparative perspective one would expect that the Dutch slave emancipation should have been realized in 1848-1849, when a new democratic constitution was carried through and when the first Liberal cabinet was formed under Thorbecke. In fact, impressed by the French and Danish abolition and fearing slave revolts in the Dutch West Indies, the Colonial Secretary ad interim in the transitional administration, Rear Admiral J.C. Rijk, proposed the immediate abolition of slavery. The transitional administration, however, rejected the improvised emancipation scheme and the government loan of ten million guilders as compensation for the slave owners.[6] In Britain the slave emancipation had been intertwined with the agitation for parliamentary reform in 1832-1833. In France the revolution of 1848 placed the radical abolitionist Victor Schoelcher in the position to push through the immediate abolition of slavery in the French colonies (Drescher 1991:730-5). In the Netherlands, however, only 8 out of 1500 petitions for a new constitution demanded the introduction of the principle of slave emancipation (Stuurman 1992:157; Van Winter 1953:71).

There are a number of reasons for this failure of Dutch abolitionism. In the first place, the introduction of the democratic constitution was, like the foundation of the Batavian Republic half a century earlier, to a large extent caused by external events. Impressed by the success of the revolutionary movement in many parts of Europe during 1848, King Willem II decided to give in to the Liberal demands (Stuurman 1992:145-51; Boogman 1978:50-63). Although it frightened the King, Dutch working-class radicalism was weak during the 1840s (Robijns 1967:42-64). In the second place, the large national debt became a problem for the Liberals too when they formed their first government. During the 1840s the Dutch per capita national debt was twice as large as the substantial British one and ten times as large as the French debt (Griffiths 1979:46) Moreover, in the late 1840s about 15 per cent of the

---

[6] Siwpersad 1979:161-7. Only on the Dutch half of the tiny island of St. Martin did the slaves successfully declare themselves free in 1848. In Suriname slave attitudes had changed with the process of 'creolization' from resistance to slavery itself to resistance within the system of slavery; Van Stipriaan 1993:385-7.

Dutch population was on poor relief. Finally, and only indirectly, Dutch political culture lacked the impulses of dynamic industrialization. In the late 1840s Britain could boast thousands of steam engines with in total about 500,000 horse power; 48.1 per cent of the British labor force was working in industry in 1851. The Netherlands possessed only 364 stationary steam engines with a total of 6,537 horse power in 1853. Even the plantation economy of Suriname had more horse power by steam per capita than the Dutch economy (Griffiths 1979:5-6; Van Stipriaan 1993:202). Industry accounted for only 24.1 per cent of the Dutch labor force in 1849 (Griffiths 1979:5). We shall see, however, that industrialization formed only a part of economic modernization in the Netherlands.

The Abolition of Slavery

Although they failed to produce an immediate abolition of slavery, the foreign abolitions and the internal democratization in 1848 made Dutch slave emancipation inevitable in the short run. After the French and Danish abolitions, the Amsterdam absentee owners accepted Dutch slave emancipation in principle. They kept on pressuring the Colonial Secretaries, however, to exact as much money as possible for their slaves as compensation. Suriname planters, on the other hand, clung to slavery until the very end. In the Netherlands, the constitution of 1848 had broadened the role of Parliament in colonial policy. Baud had to resign as Colonial Secretary, but was elected as a Conservative MP. His close aide C.F. Pahud became his Conservative successor in the Liberal Thorbecke Cabinet. Pahud negotiated with the slave owners for new, more humane slave regulations for Suriname. In 1851 he suggested as an emancipation plan the abolition of slavery for newborn children without compensation, but this suggestion was rejected by all parties concerned, both slave owners and abolitionists (Siwpersad 1979:209-17; Kuitenbrouwer 1978:77-9). In 1853 Pahud appointed an official commission of MPs, representatives of the Amsterdam slave owners and former officials under the chairmanship of Baud. This commission was to thoroughly prepare emancipation legislation (Siwpersad 1979:223-7). This new step came after the so-called April movement had brought down the Liberal Thorbecke Cabinet.

This April movement was a popular, antipopish reaction to the restoration of the Catholic hierarchy in the Netherlands by the Thorbecke Government. Dutch historians of all shades and colors see it as an isolated rearguard action by the 'greater Protestants' in the Nederlandsch Hervormde Kerk (Boogman 1978:123-34; Stuurman 1983:120-2). The evangelical Anti-Revolutionaries led by Groen van Prinsterer remained aloof. Even so, a petition with 51,000 signatures enabled the authoritarian King Willem III to replace the Liberal cabinet with a Conservative one, in which Pahud remained Colonial Secretary.

Without any relationship to the reactionary April movement, 1853 also became a crucial year in the history of Dutch abolitionism and slave emancipation. Under the influence of the Dutch translation of *Uncle Tom's Cabin*, the Calvinist Anti-Revolutionaries revived the Dutch abolition movement, known in Dutch under the cumbersome name of Vereeniging ter bevordering van de afschaffing der slavernij (Association to Promote the Abolition of Slavery) (Kuitenbrouwer 1978:81-2; Van Winter 1953:72-3). Groen van Prinsterer became chairman of the movement. This time, Liberals like the leader of the 'colonial opposition' in Parliament, W.R. van Hoëvell, also became members. The movement peaked to 667 members in 1857. Most lived in the larger cities of Amsterdam, The Hague, Rotterdam, and Haarlem. Again, their number may seem few compared to Britain and even France, but the reformist Indisch Genootschap (Dutch East Indian Society), led by Van Hoëvell, had only 200 members during the 1850s (Kuitenbrouwer 1978:81-2).

Even so, only the Dutch bourgeoisie could afford the abolition movement's membership fee of minimal five guilders. The money was used to buy the freedom of Christian slaves in Suriname. The movement published a magazine and sent petitions to King and Parliament to ask for emancipation in the short term. Other Christian and Liberal institutions in the Netherlands did the same (Van Winter 1953:74-5). During the 1850s, nine Liberal and Anti-Revolutionary MPs were affiliated to the abolition movement out of 68 MPs in Parliament (Kuitenbrouwer 1978:82). They represented both urban and mixed urban-rural constituencies from all over the country.

These abolitionist MPs could use some extra-parliamentary pressure indeed. In 1853 Secretary Pahud assured the Liberal and Anti-Revolutionary MPs that the question no longer was 'if' slavery should be abolished but 'how' a 'gradual and cautious' slave emancipation should be carried out (*Handelingen Tweede Kamer* 1853-1854:385). In the meantime one had to wait for the reports of the official commission headed by Baud. A year later Groen van Prinsterer, who had been appointed as representative of the abolition movement, left the commission in disgust, exclaiming that if Baud had his way, the West Indian slaves would not be free until the end of the century. In Parliament, Groen van Prinsterer formed an ad hoc coalition with Van Hoëvell to pressure Pahud for new, more humane slave regulations under strict official control. Pahud had to acknowledge the demands of the majority of Parliament. In 1855 the new regulations were introduced and the Calvinist abolitionist J.W. Gefken was appointed as Attorney General in Suriname to supervise their observance by the slaveholders

(Siwpersad 1979:234-44; Toes 1992:69-78). According to Gefken, the new regulations and the strict controls had already broken Suriname slavery before emancipation.

Meanwhile, Pahud refused to introduce further emancipation legislation before the official commission published its reports. Van Hoëvell wrote a fiercely abolitionist book to pressure the commission into action (Van Hoëvell 1854). It must have had some influence on Dutch public opinion because it was reprinted twice. It was not only applauded by bourgeois abolitionists but also by the radical working-class journal *Asmodée* (Waaldijk 1959:82-95). The book consisted of a series of highly dramatized descriptions of Suriname slavery. Van Hoëvell opposed the preference of Pahud, Baud and other members of the official commission for a gradual emancipation, because it would leave too much power over the slaves in the hands of the planters.

Van Hoëvell tried to refute the racial pessimism underlying the gradualist approach by presenting his own brand of racial optimism. 'Don't believe this presumed lack of mental powers of the negro race', he declared: 'On the contrary, although the negro is on a lower scale of mental development than the European, his natural ability exceeds that of the Malay, native American and other races' (Van Hoëvell 1854, II:221). Van Hoëvell singled out the Jewish slaveholders in Suriname as the harshest masters. This unsubstantiated claim was often made by abolitionist writers (Van Hoëvell 1854, I:80-7; Oostindie 1993:7). Van Hoëvell's attacks on Jewish slaveholders provoked the Suriname lawyer B.E.C. Belmonte into an angry reaction, the only publication in which slavery was defended outright during the 1850s (Belmonte 1855; Waaldijk 1959:95-103).

The two reports of the official commission on Suriname and the Antilles were finally published in the course of 1855 and 1856 (Staatscommissie 1855, 1856). Baud's proposals to abolish West Indian slavery turned out to be conservative indeed. In the Antilles the slaves, and in Suriname both the slaves and the plantations were to be expropriated by the state. The former slaves had to pay back the required fifteen million guilders in compensation for the former owners to the state. Until then, they had to work under strict state control on the plantations. Afterwards, these plantations would become their collective property. The main reason for these very restricted proposals was the disturbing results of the British slave emancipation in neighboring Guiana. According to Baud and the majority of the commission, these results showed that the former negro slaves were inferior in civilization and mental faculties. They would only work under compulsion (Staatscommissie 1855:16-7, 149-50). Pahud's successor as Colonial Secretary, P. Mijer, another close aide of Baud, introduced the major proposals of the commission as Emancipation Bills in Parliament in 1857.

This Conservative legislation was soundly rejected by the Liberal and Anti-Revolutionary majority of Parliament during the first readings. The legislation was branded as 'a socialist utopia', 'a copy of the Cultivation System' and 'an emancipation in name only' (Kuitenbrouwer 1978:84; Siwpersad 1979:228-32). Two of the three subsequent Emancipation Bills introduced by Mijer's Conservative successor as Colonial Secretary, J.J. Rochussen, were also rejected by the Liberal and Anti-Revolutionary majority of Parliament. Rochussen's second proposal had been acceptable for the majority at the first readings. It was fiercely opposed, however, by the Suriname planters because of the relative leniency of the apprenticeship for the former slaves and the lowering of the compensation sum for the owners. Governor C.P. Schimpf of Suriname backed the planters and resigned in protest. Rochussen then withdrew this rather liberal piece of legislation and introduced a third set of Emancipation Bills, which were again unacceptable for the majority of Parliament, this time because of their restrictive, conservative character (Siwpersad 1979:244-55; Kuitenbrouwer 1978:84-5).

Like Baud, Rochussen turned out to be a racial pessimist in his defense of a long and severe apprenticeship for the former slaves. 'If the emancipated mass of negroes in Dutch Guiana is left to its own strength, or rather its own weakness, what else can one expect for the future than a decimation of its numbers by misery, leprosy and venereal diseases?', Rochussen rethorically asked the members of Parliament (*Handelingen Tweede Kamer* 1861-1862, Bijlagen:221). By 1860 emancipation policy had reached a deadlock. Dutch public opinion began to lose interest in the endless debates between Conservative Ministers and Liberal and Anti-Revolutionary MPs on the issue. The abolition movement declined in numbers. An attempt by Liberal members to revive the Calvinist abolition movement by broadening its base was rejected by thirteen to three votes during a meeting in 1861 (*Tijdschrift Nederlandsche Maatschappij* 1860-1861:28-34; 1861-1862:29). According to Groen van Prinsterer, whose Anti-Revolutionary *adagium* was 'in isolation lies our strength', the Christian character of the movement was more important than a large membership. The deadlock in the emancipation legislation could only be broken from within. This became possible in 1861 when J.P. Cornets de Groot van Kraayenburg was appointed as the first Liberal Colonial Secretary.

Cornets de Groot appointed a new, small official commission without any representatives of the slave owners. The situation in Suriname added some urgency to its proceedings, because the colonial government reported 'increasing unrest' among the slaves. Compared to the Baud commission this new commission made more liberal proposals (Kuitenbrouwer 1978:86-7; Siwpersad 1979:255-7). First, it lowered the compensation to the owners to

12.8 million guilders, to be paid by the Dutch government and not by the slaves. Second, a less restrictive apprenticeship of ten years for the slaves was proposed. Finally, the commission called for the immigration of new contract labor supervised by the state, following the example of British Guiana. Cornets de Groot's Liberal successors J. Loudon and G.H. Uhlenbeck accepted these proposals and introduced the new emancipation legislation in 1862 in Parliament. At the first readings it turned out that the proposed legislation was still not liberal enough for the majority of Parliament. The ten years' apprenticeship was strongly criticized, in particular for the Dutch Antilles. Some MPs believed that the former slaves in Suriname should also be free to leave the plantations, even if they wanted to go abroad to Haiti or Liberia. Colonial Secretary Uhlenbeck accepted the suggestion to deny the slave owners the legal, positive right to 'compensation', but he did not lower the actual 'accommodation' sum for the owners. He also refused to abandon the immigration plan supervised by the state and the ten years' apprenticeship for the former slaves (Kuitenbrouwer 1978:87; Siwpersad 1979:258-9).

When the two Emancipation Bills for Suriname and the Antilles were publicly debated in Parliament in 1862, Groen van Prinsterer and Van Hoëvell had already left their seats, but the abolitionist coalition of Liberals and Anti-Revolutionaries was still functioning. By amendment they lowered the compensation sum for the owners to twelve million guilders and repealed the ten years' apprenticeship for the Antilles. Their amendment to shorten the apprenticeship for Suriname to four years was narrowly defeated, however. On the other hand, they succeeded in repealing the immigration plan supervised by the state. The amended bills were passed with a large parliamentary majority. Because of the ten years' apprentice period for Suriname, some abolitionist MPs had voted against that Bill. In the more Conservative First Chamber, on the other hand, the liberal amendments were deplored, but Colonial Secretary Uhlenbeck managed to obtain a majority for the Emancipation Bills by invoking government reports about the increasing unrest among the Suriname slaves. In 1863 the 33,000 slaves in Suriname and the 12,000 slaves in the Dutch Antilles were finally freed (Kuitenbrouwer 1978:87-9; Siwpersad 1979:259-66). That was not the end of bonded labor. When the ten years' apprenticeship for the former Suriname slaves ended, the Dutch Parliament accepted a new immigration scheme by the state. This way, 34,000 British Indians and 33,000 Javanese were contracted for the Suriname plantations in what has been called 'a new system of slavery' (Tinker 1974; Kuitenbrouwer 1989:227-8).

The late and incomplete Dutch abolition of slavery and its élitist form of abolitionism has been placed firmly in the fold of 'Continental' European antislavery by Drescher, as opposed to the early and mass variant in Britain and Northern America (Drescher 1980:43-4). Although it failed to attract a mass following, Dutch abolitionism was well represented in Parliament. During the 1850s slave emancipation was a real issue in Dutch politics, dividing Conservatives on the one hand, and Liberals and Anti-Revolutionaries on the other. Between 1853 and 1863, slavery attracted more parliamentary attention than issues like the Cultivation System in the East Indies or poor relief in the Netherlands (Kuitenbrouwer 1978:89-95). Of these three issues, in the early 1850s poor relief had received most attention. After 1854, however, when the compromise Poor Law of the Conservative Liberal Minister G.C.J. van Reenen was enacted, this issue quickly receded. The other colonial question, the abolition of the East Indian Cultivation System, only became a dominant issue after 1862, when the 'young Liberal' I.D. Fransen van der Putte replaced Uhlenbeck as Colonial Secretary. During the 1850s and early 1860s, the Liberals were still caught in a dilemma (Fasseur 1975:127-8). On the one hand, the Cultivation System was at odds with humanitarian and economic principles, but on the other hand it produced handsome state revenues which the Liberals could use for poor relief, railway building, and the abolition of West Indian slavery. In the case of West Indian slavery, the Liberals were not caught in such a dilemma, because the Dutch West Indies did not produce a surplus, but a chronic deficit on the colonial budget.

During the 1850s, slave emancipation was, in Baud's words, a controversy between 'passionate supporters, cautious supporters and secret opponents who pretend to be supporters' (*Handelingen Tweede Kamer* 1853-1854:1397). Because of this controversy, one cannot argue that Dutch slave emancipation should have happened ten years earlier in 1853, when all parties involved accepted abolition in principle. Even then, it would have been a late abolition by 'Continental' standards. Now the deadlock between Conservative Colonial Secretaries and a majority of Liberal and Anti-Revolutionary MPs over the implementation of emancipation delayed the Dutch abolition of slavery for another ten years.

As we have seen, Dutch abolitionism had parliamentary influence, but as a movement it lacked numbers. Even within the 'Continental' variant, the French artisans and workers had been more active against slavery than the Dutch ones (Drescher 1992:729-35). Under the census suffrage of the 1848 constitution, about 10 per cent of Dutch males had the right to vote in parliamentary elections. This was no less a percentage than in Britain before 1833 and in France before 1848, but during the 1850s and 1860s the mass of the so-called 'people behind the voter' was not yet mobilized. The anti-popish April movement of 1853 formed an isolated outburst in this respect. It only temporarily helped the Conservatives to a return to power. The artisan class which is identified by Drescher as the socio-economic base of

British and French abolitionism was only organized in the Netherlands under Calvinist, Catholic and Socialist banners from the late 1870s onwards (Stuurman 1983:125; Drescher 1986:129-35). In 1866 per capita newspaper circulation, which can be considered as an important precondition of mass mobilization, was about the same in the Netherlands as in France, but still much less than in Britain (Schneider and Hemels 1979:178).

With regard to the socio-economic factors determining the lack of mass mobilization in the Netherlands, both in general and in particular with regard to antislavery, it is tempting to point again to the modest level of industrialization. Yet, for the 1850s and 1860s, the situation is far more complicated. The Dutch may have been industrializing on a modest scale only, but they were busily modernizing the other sectors of their capitalist economy: the infrastructure, agriculture, and the service sector.[7] Thanks to the surplus generated by Java under the Cultivation System, the national debt declined. During the 1850s the Dutch government cashed in 267 million guilders from Java, about 30 per cent of all government income (Fasseur 1982:183). All the same, the modernizing of the infrastructure, like the building of railways and the digging of canals, required much government money. The young Calvinist abolitionist J. Wolbers had a point when he blamed 'railway fever' for the lack of enthusiasm for abolitionism among the Dutch bourgeoisie (Wolbers 1970:746). Some Liberal MPs were abolitionists on the cheap. The danger of higher taxes for the bourgeois voters was alluded to during the emancipation debates by some Liberal MPs. By lowering the compensation sum and repealing the immigration of contract labor by the state, this danger was averted. Now, as usual, 'the Javanese and the *jenever* drinkers payed for everything', as the progressive Liberal S. van Houten bitterly remarked (Stuurman 1993:171; Kuitenbrouwer 1978:87-8).

Griffiths has pointed out that, compared to Britain or Belgium, the Dutch economy was 'different', 'behind' in some respects like industrialization, but not 'backward' during the nineteenth century (Griffiths 1980). This may be a fitting epigraph for the Dutch abolition and Dutch abolitionism: different from and behind Britain in the timing of the abolition and in the élitist character of its abolitionism, but not backward in emancipation legislation compared to Britain. It would have been if the Conservatives had had their way, but thanks to the Liberal and Anti-Revolutionary MPs who shaped the final emancipation legislation, the Netherlands was not really backward in antislavery. Britain was the first country to abolish negro slavery permanently, but it was in Britain and its West Indian

---

7   Kuitenbrouwer 1991:59-60. See also Knippenberg and De Pater 1988:17-49; Griffiths 1982. Even in Britain industrial interests had less influence on nineteenth-century overseas policy than is often supposed; Cain and Hopkins 1993.

colonies too that a reaction of racial pessimism and the immigration of Asian contract labor originated (Bolt 1971:75-101; Green 1976:261-95).

In the Netherlands even young N.G. Pierson, the future Liberal opponent of the Javanese Cultivation System, Dutch member of the Cobden Club and a reforming Minister of Finance and Prime Minister, was susceptible to the new climate of opinion. On a business trip to the American South to learn the cotton trade, he wrote his deeply abolitionist Réveil parents in 1859 that *Uncle Tom's Cabin* was 'much exaggerated' and that an immediate abolition of slavery would be an 'unmitigated disaster' for the United States. On British abolitionism he remarked: 'If Britain wants to clear itself of the blame of playing a comedy and committing the greatest hypocrisy with its antislavery system, it should stop its coolie trade'.[8]

Conclusion

The Dutch case of antislavery, characterized by late abolition and élitist abolitionism, is rather different from the Anglo-American and the French cases of antislavery. At first sight the various historiographical interpretations of these cases seem only to highlight the absence in the case of the Netherlands of factors which were in various degrees present in other countries. A closer look, however, reveals some indirect, heuristic relevance of these interpretations even in the Dutch case of antislavery. This applies in the first place to the interpretations by Williams, Davis, Blackburn, and to some extent Haskell, which all focus on the political economy, mutual differences notwithstanding. They all identify slavery mainly with the old, commercial form of capitalism, and antislavery with the new, industrial form of capitalism.

Seen from this perspective it is telling that during the emancipation controversy in the Netherlands the declining Suriname slavery was represented by only one absentee owner MP from Amsterdam, A.F. Insinger, who remained completely silent throughout all parliamentary debates on the issue. Even more fitting, the old merchant capitalists of Amsterdam were represented by the former Colonial Secretary and Conservative MP Baud, the spiritual father of the very restricted Conservative emancipation proposals. Equally, Baud's main opponent, the Liberal MP Van Hoëvell, whose views eventually prevailed in Dutch slave emancipation, represented the new, industrial center of Twente. However, as we have seen, these connections may be fitting, but they are not fundamental and conclusive. Neither Baud's Conservative voters from Amsterdam nor Van Hoëvell's

---

[8] Van Maarseveen 1990:125; see also 98-100. Pierson's rosy picture of slavery in the American South was not completely without substance; Fogel 1989:114-54.

Liberal voters from Twente showed an active interest in the emancipation issue.

For the same reason the emancipation issue had little potential in terms of class hegemony in the Netherlands. Indeed, it was not the emancipation issue, but the reactionary, antipopish April movement of 1853 which enabled the traditional Conservative élites to oust the new Liberal government of Thorbecke and to return temporarily to power. Even so, the emancipation issue had some connections with class hegemony in the Netherlands. This can be gauged from some Radical and Conservative responses to bourgeois abolitionism. The small Radical movement supported on the whole the bourgeois abolitionism of Van Hoëvell, the main parliamentary representative of the new industrial interests in the Netherlands. In the radical working-class newspaper *Asmodée*, Van Hoëvell's abolitionist book was welcomed in the issue of 24 January 1855 as 'a jewel for all people with feelings and minds'. Van Hoëvell presumed that Dutch workers were much better off under free labor than Suriname slaves and Javanese peasants were under forced labor. Indeed, according to Van Hoëvell, a former Protestant minister in Batavia, it was because of this fortuitous condition that the Dutch had a 'calling' towards their colonial subjects: 'Teach those deeply sunken peoples which you rule material happiness, teach them to make life more pleasant, to soften unhappiness, to develop their minds, cleanse their religious feelings, hallow their lives; educate them and lead them to the blessings which art and science and religion render to you; become the herdsman of those strayed sheeps, the guardian of those wandering children' (Van Hoëvell 1849:15).

It was such a 'platoon fire of words', heard at an abolitionist meeting in the Netherlands, which made the famous writer Multatuli, the radical champion of Javanese peasants and Dutch workers, propose with Cobbett-like sarcasm to introduce legal, regulated slavery for Dutch wage earners (Multatuli 1970:116-8). The Conservative MP F.B.H. Michels van Kessenich also presumed that West Indian slaves were better off than Dutch workers. 'The slaves in the West Indies are, I believe, not that unhappy', he said during the parliamentary debate on the final emancipation legislation: 'They do not need clothing and they get their food. We have here in our country people who do slave labor, but do not even get the food they need. Now the fate of those slaves in the West Indies is deplored while the fate of our own is forgotten' (*Handelingen Eerste Kamer* 1861-1862:265).

The modest scale of industrialization in the Netherlands helps to explain both the existence of such responses to the emancipation issue and the fact that they remained marginal. The level of industrialization should not be applied mechanically to the analysis of the Dutch case of antislavery, however. When Blackburn explains the early French slave emancipation of

1848 by the impact of industrial class struggle and the late Dutch slave emancipation of 1862 by the lack of industrial class conflict, he overlooks the fact that both in France and in the Netherlands the same portion of the labor force, about a quarter, was employed in industry (Blackburn 1988:520). Moreover, when socialism finally emerged as a mass movement in the Netherlands during the 1880s, it attracted mainly pre-industrial artisans and rural workers.

The Dutch case of antislavery is even more damaging to Haskell's explanation in terms of a new cognitive, moral style caused by the rise of market capitalism. As Davis rightly observed, Dutch capitalism was geared to a variety of markets when the slave trade and colonial slavery were introduced during the seventeenth century. Nor was political liberalism lacking in the Netherlands during the nineteenth century when the slave trade and slavery were abolished, as Haskell seems to think (Haskell 1992:233-4; Davis 1992b:293-6). This brings us to the relevance of political and ideological factors in accounting for the Dutch case of antislavery.

During the 1840s, when Baud as a Conservative Colonial Secretary first proposed to the King to abolish Dutch West Indian slavery, the Liberals and the Calvinist Anti-Revolutionaries still formed a parliamentary minority. After the constitutional reform of 1848 they formed a parliamentary majority which effectively blocked the restrictive emancipation legislation of Baud and his Conservative successors as Colonial Secretaries. In the end, the abolitionist views of the Liberals and Anti-Revolutionaries prevailed in the Emancipation Acts. Therefore the Liberal and Anti-Revolutionary movements in the Netherlands may be compared to the liberal political and evangelical Protestant movements which, according to Anstey, determined the abolition of the slave trade and slavery in the British case (Anstey 1975:403-14).

Indeed, some contemporaries made this very comparison. The Anti-Revolutionary abolitionist leader Groen van Prinsterer was called the 'Dutch Wilberforce' by a Calvinist admirer, while the Liberal abolitionist leader Van Hoëvell was compared by a Liberal to C.J. Fox (Kuitenbrouwer 1978:96). However, when the young Calvinist abolitionist Wolbers proposed to follow the British example directly by organizing a 'people's petition' for the abolition of slavery, this proposal was rejected by the elderly, cautious leadership of the Dutch abolition movement as 'premature'.[9]

The same political and ideological forces were operating in Dutch abolitionism as in British abolitionism. This made Dutch abolitionism quite influential on the parliamentary level, even if it lacked the mass appeal of

---

[9] *Tijdschrift Nederlandsche Maatschappij* 1858-1859:23; 1860-1861:101. Characteristically, Wolbers became one of the founders of the Calvinist labor union Patrimonium, but that was more than ten years after the abolition of slavery.

British abolitionism. As we have seen on numerous occasions, this was in accordance with the élitist character of Dutch politics in general. Only from the late 1870s onwards were the Dutch 'people behind the voter' organized in mass movements like Wolbers's Patrimonium. The existence of an abolitionist mass movement in Britain and its absence in the Netherlands does explain to a large extent the early slave emancipation in the British case and the late one in the Dutch case. Nevertheless, in the end the abolition of slavery in Britain was not decided by the abolitionist movement as such either, but by Parliament and Government. Although Parliament and Government agreed on the principle of slave emancipation from 1853 onwards, the ten following years of controversy on the ways and means between Conservative Colonial Secretaries, on the one hand, and Liberal and Anti-Revolutionary MPs, on the other, was real enough. Dutch slave emancipation was not 'perfunctory' enacted, as Drescher maintains. Perhaps the dog did not bark in the Dutch case, according to Drescher's telling quote from Arthur Conan Doyle's Sherlock Holmes, but it certainly made some noise.

References

Anstey, Roger
1975   *The Atlantic Slave Trade and British Abolition 1760-1810*. London: Macmillan.
Belmonte, B.E.C.
1855   *Neêrlands West-Indië in zijne belangen en Dr. W.R. van Hoëvell in zijne 'Slaven en vrijen'; Slavernij - emancipatie - kolonisatie*. Leiden: Van den Heuvell.
Bender, Thomas (ed.)
1992   *The Antislavery Debate; Capitalism and Abolitionism as a Problem in Historical Interpretation*. Berkeley: University of California Press.
Blackburn, Robin
1988   *The Overthrow of Colonial Slavery 1776-1848*. London: Verso.
Bolt, Christine
1971   *Victorian Attitudes to Race*. London: Routledge and Kegan Paul; Toronto: University of Toronto Press.
Boogman, J.C.
1978   *Rondom 1848; De politieke ontwikkeling van Nederland 1840-1858*. Bussum: Unieboek.
Cain, P.J. and A.G. Hopkins
1993   *British Imperialism; Vol. 1: Innovation and Expansion 1688-1914*. London: Longman.
Daalder, H.
1990   *Politiek en historie; Opstellen over Nederlandse politiek en vergelijkende politieke wetenschap*. Amsterdam: Bakker.

Davis, David Brion
1970 *The Problem of Slavery in Western Culture.* Harmondsworth: Pelican Books. [Original edition 1966.]
1975 *The Problem of Slavery in the Age of Revolution, 1770-1823.* Ithaca: Cornell University Press.
1992a 'Reflections on Abolitionism and Ideological Hegemony', in: Thomas Bender (ed.), *The Antislavery Debate; Capitalism and Abolitionism as a Problem in Historical Interpretation*, pp. 161-79. Berkeley: University of California Press.
1992b 'The Perils of Doing History by Ahistorical Abstraction; A Reply to Thomas L. Haskell's *AHR Forum* Reply', in: Thomas Bender (ed.), *The Antislavery Debate; Capitalism and Abolitionism as a Problem in Historical Interpretation*, pp. 290-309. Berkeley: University of California Press.

Drescher, Seymour
1980 'Two Variants of Anti-Slavery; Religious Organization and Social Mobilization in Britain and France, 1780-1870', in: Christine Bolt and Seymour Drescher (eds), *Anti-Slavery, Religion, and Reform; Essays in Memory of Roger Anstey*, pp. 43-64. Folkestone: Dawson; Hamden: Archon.
1987 *Capitalism and Antislavery; British Mobilization in Comparative Perspective.* New York: Oxford University Press.
1991 'British Way, French Way; Opinion Building and Revolution in the Second French Slave Emancipation', *American Historical Review* 96:709-35.

Emmer, Pieter C.
1973 'Engeland, Nederland, Afrika en de slavenhandel in de negentiende eeuw I'. *Economisch- en Sociaal-Historisch Jaarboek* 36:146-215.
1974 'Engeland, Nederland, Afrika en de slavenhandel in de negentiende eeuw II'. *Economisch- en Sociaal-Historisch Jaarboek* 37:44-144.
1980 'Anti-Slavery and the Dutch; Abolition Without Reform', in: Christine Bolt and Seymour Drescher (eds), *Anti-Slavery, Religion, and Reform; Essays in Memory of Roger Anstey*, pp. 80-98. Folkestone: Dawson; Hamden: Archon.

Fasseur, C.
1975 *Kultuurstelsel en koloniale baten; De Nederlandse exploitatie van Java, 1840-1860.* Leiden: Leidse Universitaire Pers.
1982 'Nederland en Nederlands-Indië 1795-1914', in: *Overzee; Nederlandse koloniale geschiedenis 1590-1975*, pp. 166-94. Haarlem: Fibula-Van Dishoeck.

Fogel, Robert William
1989 *Without Consent or Contract; The Rise and Fall of American Slavery.* New York: Norton.

Gijswijt-Hofstra, M.
1989 'Een schijn van verdraagzaamheid; Proeven uit vijf eeuwen Nederlands verleden', in: M. Gijswijt-Hofstra (ed.), *Afwijking en tolerantie in Nederland van de zestiende eeuw tot heden*, pp. 9-41. Hilversum: Verloren.

Goslinga, Cornelis Ch.
1990   *The Dutch in the Caribbean and in Surinam, 1791/5-1942.* Assen: Van Gorcum.

Green, William A.
1976   *British Slave Emancipation; The Sugar Colonies and the Great Experiment 1830-1865.* Oxford: Clarendon Press.

Griffiths, R.T.
1979   *Industrial Retardation in the Netherlands 1830-1850.* The Hague: Nijhoff.
1980   *Achterlijk, achter of anders? Aspecten van de economische ontwikkeling van Nederland in de 19e eeuw.* S.l.: s.n. [Inaugural lecture, Free University, Amsterdam.]
1982   'The Creation of a National Dutch Economy; 1795-1909', *Tijdschrift voor Geschiedenis* 95:513-37.

Handelingen Eerste Kamer
1848-1862   *Handelingen van de Staten-Generaal.* 's-Gravenhage: Staatsdrukkerij.

Handelingen Tweede Kamer
1848-1862   *Handelingen van de Staten-Generaal.* 's-Gravenhage: Staatsdrukkerij.

Haskell, Thomas L.
1992   'Convention and Hegemonic Interest in the Debate over Antislavery', in: Thomas Bender (ed.), *The Antislavery Debate; Capitalism and Abolitionism as a Problem in Historical Interpretation,* pp. 200-59. Berkeley: University of California Press.

Hoetink, H.
1969   'Race Relations in Curaçao and Suriname', in: L. Foner and Eugene D. Genovese (eds), *Slavery in the New World; A Reader in Comparative History,* pp. 178-89. Englewood Cliffs: Prentice-Hall.

Hoëvell, Wolter R. van
1849   *Eene epidemie op Java en de cholera in Nederland.* Amsterdam: Van Kampen.
1854   *Slaven en vrijen onder de Nederlandsche wet.* Zaltbommel: Noman. 2 vols.

Israel, Jonathan I.
1989   *Dutch Primacy in World Trade, 1585-1740.* Oxford: Clarendon Press.

Knippenberg, Hans and B. de Pater
1988   *De eenwording van Nederland; Schaalvergroting en integratie sinds 1800.* Nijmegen: SUN.

Krantz, Frederick and Paul M. Hohenberg (eds)
1975   *Failed Transitions to Modern Industrial Society; Renaissance Italy and Seventeenth Century Holland.* Montreal: University Centre for European Studies.

Kuitenbrouwer, Maarten
1978   'De Nederlandse afschaffing van de slavernij in vergelijkend perspectief', *Bijdragen en Mededelingen betreffende de Geschiedenis der Nederlanden* 93:69-101.
1989   'Afwijking en tolerantie bij slavenhandel en negerslavernij, 1600-1863', in: M. Gijswijt-Hofstra (ed.), *Afwijking en tolerantie in Nederland van de zestiende eeuw tot heden,* pp. 211-37. Hilversum: Verloren.

1991 *The Netherlands and the Rise of Modern Imperialism; Colonies and Foreign Policy 1870-1902.* Oxford: Berg.

Maarseveen, J.G.S.J. van (ed.)
1990 *Briefwisseling van Nicolaas Gerard Pierson 1839-1909; Vol. 1: 1851-1884.* Amsterdam: Nederlandsche Bank.

Maddison, Angus
1989 'Dutch Income In and From Indonesia, 1700-1938', in: A. Maddison and G. Prince (eds), *Economic Growth in Indonesia, 1820-1940*, pp. 15-42. Dordrecht: Foris. [KITLV, Verhandelingen 137.]

Mokyr, Joel
1976 *Industrialization in the Low Countries, 1795-1850.* New Haven: Yale University Press.

Multatuli
1973 'Ideeën, tweede bundel', in: G. Stuiveling (ed.), *Multatuli; Verzamelde werken*, vol. 3, pp. 44-382. Amsterdam: Van Oorschot. [Original edition 1864-1865]

Oostindie, Gert
1986 'Kondreman in Bakrakondre; Surinamers in Nederland 1667-1954', in: Gert Oostindie and Emy Maduro, *In het land van de overheerser II; Antillianen en Surinamers in Nederland, 1634/1667-1954*, pp. 1-133. Dordrecht: Foris. [KITLV, Verhandelingen 100.]
1993 'Voltaire, Stedman, and Suriname Slavery', *Slavery and Abolition* 14-2:1-34.

Paasman, A.N.
1984 *Reinhart; Nederlandse literatuur en slavernij ten tijde van de Verlichting.* Leiden: Nijhoff.

Postma, Johannes Menne
1990 *The Dutch in the Atlantic Slave Trade 1600-1815.* Cambridge: Cambridge University Press.

Reinsma, Riemer
1963 *Een merkwaardige episode uit de geschiedenis van de slavenemancipatie.* 's-Gravenhage: Van Goor.

Robijns, M.J.F.
1967 *Radicalen in Nederland (1840-1851).* Leiden: Kok.

Sas, Nicolaas C.F. van
1985 *Onze natuurlijke bondgenoot; Nederland, Engeland en Europa, 1813-1831.* Groningen: Wolters-Noordhoff.
1992 'The Patriot Revolution; New Perspectives', in: Margaret C. Jacob and Wijnandt W. Mijnhardt (eds), *The Dutch Republic in the Eighteenth Century; Decline, Enlightenment, and Revolution*, pp. 91-123. Ithaca: Cornell University Press.

Schama, Simon
1977 *Patriots and Liberators; Revolution in the Netherlands, 1780-1813.* New York: Knopf.
1988 *The Embarrassment of Riches; An Interpretation of Dutch Culture in the Golden Age.* New York: Fontana Press. [Original edition 1987.]

Schneider, M. and J. Hemels
1979   *De Nederlandse krant 1618-1978; Van 'nieuwstydinghe' tot dagblad.* Baarn: Wereldvenster.

Schutte, G.J.
1974   *De Nederlandse patriotten en de koloniën; Een onderzoek naar hun denkbeelden en optreden, 1770-1800.* Groningen: Tjeenk Willink.
1979   'Zedelijke verplichting en gezonde staatkunde; Denken en doen rondom de slavernij in Nederland en koloniën, eind 18e eeuw', *Documentatieblad 18e eeuw* 41/42:101-15.

Sens, Angelie
1992   'De neger, slavernij, abolitionisme en het Nederlandse "enigma"; Een vergelijkend onderzoek naar de opvattingen in Frankrijk en de Republiek, circa 1750-1800'. [MA thesis Utrecht University.]

Siwpersad, J.P.
1979   *De Nederlandse regering en de afschaffing van de Surinaamse slavernij (1833-1863).* Groningen: Bouma; Castricum: Hagen.

Staatscommissie
1855   *Eerste Rapport der staatscommissie, benoemd bij Koninklijk Besluit van 29 november 1853, no. 66, tot het voorstellen van maatregelen ten aanzien van de slaven in de Nederlandsche koloniën: Suriname.* 's-Gravenhage: Van Cleef.
1856   *Tweede Rapport der staatscommissie, benoemd bij Koninklijk Besluit van 29 november 1853, no. 66, tot het voorstellen van maatregelen ten aanzien van de slaven in de Nederlandsche koloniën: de Nederlandsche West-Indische eilanden en bezittingen ten kuste van Guinea.* 's-Gravenhage: Van Cleef.

Stipriaan, Alex van
1993   *Surinaams contrast; Roofbouw en overleven in een Caraïbische plantagekolonie, 1750-1863.* Leiden: KITLV Press. [KITLV, Caribbean Series 13.]

Stuurman, S.
1983   *Verzuiling, kapitalisme en patriarchaat.* Nijmegen: SUN.
1992   *Wacht op onze daden; Het liberalisme en de vernieuwing van de Nederlandse staat.* Amsterdam: Bakker.

Tijdschrift Nederlandsche Maatschappij
1854-1862   *Tijdschrift uitgegeven vanwege de Nederlandsche Maatschappij ter bevordering van de Afschaffing der Slavernij.*

Tinker, Hugh
1974   *A New System of Slavery; The Export of Indian Labour Overseas, 1830-1920.* London: Oxford University Press.

Toes, Jaap
1992   *Wanklanken rond een wingewest; In de nadagen van de Surinaamse slavernij.* Hoorn: Drukkerij Noordholland.

Vries, Joh. de
1959   *De economische achteruitgang der Republiek in de achttiende eeuw.* Amsterdam: Ellerman Harms.

Waaldijk, E. Theodoor
1959 *Die Rolle der niederländischen Publizistik bei der Meinungsbildung hinsichtlich der Aufhebung der Sklaverei in den westindischen Kolonien*. München: Steinbauer/Hagemann.

Williams, Eric
1944 *Capitalism and Slavery*. Chapel Hill: University of North Carolina Press.

Winter, Johanna Maria van
1953 'De openbare mening in Nederland over de afschaffing der slavernij', *West-Indische Gids* 34:61-90.

Wolbers, J.
1861 *Geschiedenis van Suriname*. Amsterdam: De Hoogh.

Zwitzer, H.L.
1990 'The British and Netherlands Armies in Relation to the Anglo-Dutch Alliance, 1688-1795', in: G.J.A. Raven and N.A.M. Rodger (eds), *Navies and Armies; The Anglo-Dutch Relationship in War and Peace 1688-1988*, pp. 33-49. Edinburgh: Donald.

ANGELIE SENS

Dutch Antislavery Attitudes in a Decline-Ridden Society, 1750-1815

Within European historiography certain aspects of Dutch history have frequently been regarded as anomalous, different, and out of line with other Western and Northern countries. Sometimes the Dutch are considered to be ahead of the rest of Western Europe, as in the seventeenth century. However, when it comes to the eighteenth and nineteenth centuries, they are seen as being late or lagging behind, especially when compared to Great Britain and France. The Dutch Enlightenment, for example, used to be considered too parochial and not radical enough to deserve the name Enlightenment, although more recently it has received the attention it rightfully deserves.[1] In relation to one of the central issues raised by the enlightened search for individual freedom and human rights, the issue of slavery, the Dutch version of Enlightenment continues to baffle historians. The comparison of the Dutch Republic with Great Britain and France suggests a range of questions. Why did the Dutch not show any signs of an abolitionist fervor? Why did they not follow the example of the Quakers in England and America, or the French Société des Amis des Noirs?

The ongoing debate on the relation between 'capitalism and antislavery' has primarily been an Anglo-American affair. British abolitionism has become the model for research on antislavery in other countries. One of the central themes in the debate is the hypothesis that British abolitionism was closely linked to the development of industrial capitalism, at least from the end of the eighteenth century. The now famous debate between D.B. Davis, Th. Haskell, and J. Ashworth (Bender 1992) is a case in point. The result of the debate was that the relation between 'capitalism' and antislavery was reaffirmed, despite, or perhaps as a result of, the different viewpoints of the debaters. 'Capitalism' turned out to be a very elastic, overarching concept, including economic, cultural, ideological, and even 'psychological' aspects. However, none of the explanations provided by Davis, Haskell, and Ashworth applies to the Dutch case. Even after Davis introduced the 'enigmatic' Dutch case and proposed further research on political, cultural, and econ-

---

[1] A good, recent overview is provided in Jacob and Mijnhardt 1992.

omic developments in the Netherlands, the British model of a link between capitalism and antislavery did not come under attack. Davis (1992:296) suggested that it was 'the difference in timing of industrialization that most sharply distinguished the British from the Dutch economy'.

Since the Dutch abolished slavery as late as 1863, and since the Dutch industrial 'take-off' supposedly took place in the last quarter of the nineteenth century, another consequence of applying the British model to the Netherlands is that until recently most attention has focused on the nineteenth century. The eighteenth century has been more or less neglected because of the alleged lack of a Dutch antislavery debate and the actual absence of an abolitionist movement.[2] The point I want to make here is that the applicability of the British case to other European countries can be profoundly problematic. In studying Dutch opinions on slavery during the eighteenth century, it becomes clear that the Dutch case cannot be explained by hypotheses derived from Anglo-American research.

The Concept of 'Social Mobilization' as an Alternative

In *Capitalism and Antislavery*, Seymour Drescher examined the impact of British mobilization on antislavery and compared this to developments on the European continent (Drescher 1986). He only briefly touched upon Dutch abolition. As Drescher rightly pointed out, the British antislavery movement was probably an anomaly rather than a model for the elaboration of the discussion in other European countries. In his present article, 'The Long Goodbye', Drescher extends his comparative analysis to include Dutch antislavery. In his view, the Dutch case supplies even stronger evidence for the fact that 'the economic context offers the weakest positive support for and the strongest counter-abolitionist argument against the antislavery process'. Drescher prefers to discuss antislavery against the background of what he calls 'new modes of social mobilization'.

Despite the vagueness of this – in my opinion complex – concept of 'social mobilization', it seems worthwhile to explore it further and to examine it for the eighteenth-century Dutch Republic. We may well opt for a broader definition of this concept of mobilization than a merely political one. 'New modes of social mobilization' refer, then, to the larger spectrum of eighteenth-century Dutch enlightened culture, which includes such fields as politics, religion, science, and literature. Between circa 1750 and 1780 the emergence and further development of the learned, philosophical, and literary societies (Mijnhardt 1987; 1988; 1992) and the rise and growth of the

---

[2] Slavery only became a topic in Dutch historiography after World War II. See particularly Emmer 1980; Goslinga 1956, 1985; Oostindie 1992; Paasman 1984; Postma 1990; Priester 1987; Schutte 1974, 1979; Sens 1992.

periodical – spectatorial – press contributed to an enlightened infrastructure in which a new Dutch political and cultural agenda was proposed. Until 1780, these 'mobilizing instruments' were in general non-political in character. The 1780s, the years of patriotic fervor, marked a decisive shift to a politicization of Dutch society and culture (Van Sas 1987, 1992). Non-political cultural expressions did not disappear, though. On the contrary, during the 1780s and 1790s and well into the nineteenth century, there were numerous cultural periodicals available and people kept on organizing along the lines of philosophical and literary societies for non-political reasons.

Defining the participants in this new Dutch enlightened culture is another, more complicated matter. Frijhoff has recently argued that a new 'intellectual élite' emerged, advocating its 'design of a new social morality involving all social classes'. The core of this group of reformers consisted, according to Frijhoff, of clergymen (Protestant and Catholic), educational professionals, and members of the free professions. One of their targets was the 'uncivilized' poor, who had to be enlightened by means of 'moral' education (Frijhoff 1992:292-4, 301). These cultural newcomers also directed their criticism towards members of the existing economical and political élite, considering them as obstacles to social reform. To make things more complicated, members of the 'old' élite also participated in the new cultural life, and even figured on the side of the Patriots. Te Brake has argued, referring to the political dimension of the Patriotic revolution of the 1780s, that the coalitions in what he calls the 'popular movement' could vary considerably on a local level. In some places members of the ruling élite indeed participated in a patriotic coalition (Te Brake 1990:353-4).

We may suppose that the structures of and the participants in the new Dutch networks of communication and organization were not that dissimilar to those in the British case. However, the central issues on the Dutch political and cultural agenda differed from the principal British, and for that matter French concerns. Dutch issues were all linked to the problem of Dutch decline, in the field of economy as well as of foreign policy, and the possible solutions to it. The peculiarity of the country's political and cultural debate is one of the crucial explanatory factors for Dutch eighteenth-century attitudes towards slavery. This article seeks to address the question of why the Dutch debate differed and where issues such as slavery and antislavery fitted in, if at all. To illustrate the mobilizing forces of the 1780s and 1790s, two examples will be given of organized groups that tried to gain public support on important contemporary issues: the Dutch Patriots, active in the 1780s and 1790s, and the Nederlandsch Zendeling-Genootschap, NZG (Dutch Missionary Society), founded in 1797. Both groups of reformers responded within a new framework, incorporating enlightened culture and the concern about economic decline. Moreover, we might expect both groups to have come up with opinions on slavery, if not outright antislavery attitudes.

Colonies, Slavery and Enlightenment in the Dutch Public Debate

Dutch culture and the self-image of the Dutch in the eighteenth century were characterized by a strong sense of retrospection, not so much in the sense of longing to get back to times gone by, but rather in the sense of trying to understand the conditions and foundations that had made the Dutch Republic the prosperous, free, and Protestant state it had been from the seventeenth century up to the second half of the eighteenth century. One dominating theme characterizes the eighteenth-century 'public' debate: a strong perception of and preoccupation with the decline – alleged or real – of the Dutch state and society. Spectatorial periodicals modelled on London's *The Spectator* stressed civil virtues and offered education and civilization as solutions to moral decline. Authors inspired by Christianity pointed to the religious decline and promoted a deepening of the faith as the solution. The Patriots emphasized the political and economic decline that, in their opinion, threatened the very foundations of the Dutch Republic. Their solutions consisted of demanding broader political participation and control as well as, in the field of economics, a liberalization of trade and commerce.

The Republic faced enormous problems. Solutions to the Dutch decline were moderate in character, and were often couched in religious terms. This does not imply that the proposed solutions were set in a pessimistic tone. On the contrary, 'decline could be answered with Enlightenment and moral rearmament became the slogan' (Van Sas 1989:474). Dutch cultural life in the 1780s and 1790s was vivid indeed. A decline-ridden agenda led to a strong reflection on and preoccupation with purely national problems. The attachment to the fatherland became a crucial feature of Dutch culture. In the words of Jacob and Mijnhardt: 'The coincidence of decline amid Enlightenment produced a new national consciousness that drew its inspiration from the past. Its aim was to restore the morals that were thought to have been the very basis of the seventeenth-century Golden Age' (Jacob and Mijnhardt 1992:13). Despite the decentralized structure of the Dutch Republic, an awareness of belonging to the same 'nation' increased. In fact, the decentralized structure of the Republic had stimulated the emergence of a consensus society.

The Dutch Republic, headed by the States-General as sovereign power, was not formally a colonial power in the sense in which the British and French states or their sovereigns were. The Dutch overseas possessions were private property. Of course, the States-General exercised authority over colonial affairs by means of laws, rules, and regulations, and by giving financial aid to the settlements and the trading companies, mostly in the form of loans, but the trading companies and colonies had a large degree of autonomy in handling their own affairs. When the financial problems of the colonies and the East and West Indies Companies increased from the 1770s onwards, the States-General neither could nor would continue to support them any longer in the traditional way. Monopolies were discontinued, credits to the trading companies were withdrawn. This marked the transition to state ownership of the colonies.

Before the 1780s there was no serious debate on the possession of colonies or their productive importance to the Republic. The trading role of the Dutch Republic was given priority, and the relevance of the Dutch overseas possessions was mainly related to their significance for Dutch trade. Compared to Britain and France, the Dutch had relatively few settler colonies, and the problem of chattel slavery played only a relatively small role in the broad field of writings on the problems of the day. In fact, Schutte (1974) concluded that lack of knowledge of the colonies was one of the reasons for the Dutch indifference to slavery.

More recently, however, Paasman has demonstrated that this argument of ignorance does not hold. He collected an abundance of seventeenth- and especially eighteenth-century Dutch writings and translations on slavery and the colonial world in general. Even if there was not as much material as in Britain or France, there had certainly been enough – fictional and nonfictional – material around to inform the Dutch public about the overseas world (Paasman 1984:211). From the seventeenth century onwards, a body of travel accounts emerged, factual as well as fictional. Furthermore, there were the manuals for slave traders with information on the situation on the West African coast, on the treatment of the slaves on board the ships, and on the ways of selling slaves. West Indian slave holders sent requests to the West Indies Company and/or the States-General to discuss their problems connected with the insufficient delivery of slaves. Theological tracts also mentioned the problem, defending as well as attacking slavery. The Herrnhutters or Moravians likewise supplied information to the Dutch public. Scientists like Petrus Camper (1722-1789) reported on their research on primates and Negroes, and established the fact that blacks were humans with the same faculties as whites. Literary and philosophical societies organized essay contests on topics such as how to convert Indians and blacks (both slaves and free) to Christianity, or whether the slave trade was necessary and in accordance with Christianity. Periodicals published articles on the problem of the slave trade and slavery. A trickle of novels, plays, and poems addressed the subjects of slavery and the situation in the colonies.[3] In addition, a number of foreign writings on the subject were translated into Dutch.

What were the main themes of these writings? First of all, nearly every author discussing slavery stressed the importance of possessing colonies. Colonies, world trade (of which the slave trade was a part), finances and banking were seen as the pillars of Dutch wealth and public welfare. The eighteenth-century self-image of the Dutch leaned heavily on the country's glorious seventeenth century, especially so in the troubled period after 1750. The seventeenth-century merchant was extolled as the ideal republican and virtuous citizen. The foundations of the Dutch Republic – freedom, citizenship, religion – were stressed over and over again. Even critics of the colonial system did not attack the slave trade and slavery as unacceptable institutions. Instead, they pointed out the abuses and wrongdoings within the system and colonial society at large. Defenders of the slave trade and the plantation system, on the other hand, were willing enough to acknowledge the natural rights of every human being, whether black, brown, or white, but these (Christian) natural rights were overruled by historical developments, whether or not guided by Providence. Implicitly, abolishing the slave trade and slavery seemed to be an attack on the economic foundations of the Dutch Republic, if not on God himself.

Religious arguments played a major role in Dutch slavery and antislavery literature. Biblical arguments were used by both defenders and critics of slavery. The curse of Cham even found a defender in the person of a black, Leiden-educated minister, J.E.J. Capitein. He distinguished between spiritual freedom and freedom of the body. Slavery was acceptable because first and foremost there was freedom of the mind, namely, in being a Christian (Capitein 1742; Paasman 1984:104-5). Another minister, J.G. Kals, stressed the importance of setting up mission posts in the West Indian colonies. Kals is known as one of the few critics of slavery in the first half of the eighteenth century, yet he did not oppose slavery as such; he proposed a better treatment of the slaves and above all the permission by the government to convert the West Indian slaves to Christianity (Kals 1756).[4] This is what humanitarianism towards slaves meant: better treatment and an opportunity to learn about and accept the Christian religion.

As in the British case, 'religious' arguments were used by all kinds of authors, whether orthodox Calvinists, liberal Protestants, or writers who did not primarily publish out of religious conviction but rather for political or economic reasons. Even certain publishers felt that they had to use

---

[3] Women writers such as Elisabeth Post, Betje Wolff and Petronella Moens had a relatively large share in literature of this kind.
[4] See also Paasman (1984:105) and Van de Linde (1956:82).

'religious' arguments to defend their publication policies, as was the case with the translation of *The Life of Olaudah Equiano*, which appeared in 1790. Its publisher, P. Holsteyn, emphasized the fact that this ex-slave was properly converted to Christianity.[5]

However, the humanitarian argument, largely of Christian origin, could cut both ways. A humane approach (better treatment) was also prescribed by defenders of slavery, mostly in combination with economic arguments. The high mortality rate and the low fertility rate of the slave population made it necessary to improve the treatment of the slaves. This was especially the case at times when the acquisition of new slaves was obstructed, as in wartime when contacts with the colonies were difficult or impossible, and after the financial crash of 1773 when Suriname planters lost their possessions or lacked the financial resources to buy new slaves.[6] In 1790, a defender of the slave trade and of slavery mixed economic, religious, and humanitarian statements. Motivated by 'healthy self-interest' intended to make a profit, slave owners treated their property well, even very well. Other slave owners, prompted by 'detestable self-interest', did not convert their slaves or stop treating them cruelly. Moreover, it would be impossible to find enough whites who would be willing to do the work of slaves (Barrau 1790:370-85).

What was seen as the moral decline of Dutch society had to be solved by education and civilization. This sense of 'moral teaching' can also be found in Dutch writings on the overseas world. The non-Western world was like a mirror held up to the Dutch public in its search for explanations of the Republic's bad fortune. Life in the colonies, far from the mother country, undermined the habits of a virtuous life. The hot climate, the daily contacts with uncivilized people, and the hunger for luxury and wealth induced the white inhabitants of the colonies to 'non-Christian' behavior. Atrocities towards slaves and sexual misconduct were the results of such immorality. In contrast, Indians and blacks could also be held up as examples of innocence and purity, portrayed as children in need of paternal guidance. Whites could only fulfil the latter task by regaining a purity they seemed to have lost. If they failed to do so, white colonists would be punished: a slave uprising could be one of such castigations.[7] There was always this tension between leading a life of godliness and the necessity of contributing to the national wealth through trading and producing colonial products.

---

5   Holsteyn also wrote that 'the despised and ill-treated Negroes were not insusceptible of education, and that they, by good examples, a mild treatment, and wise education, could be molded as useful members of human Society [...]'. 'Voorberigt van den uitgeever', in Equiano 1790.
6   On the eve of the Patriotic movement of the 1780s, the Dutch West Indian possesions faced major economic difficulties (Van de Voort 1973:72, 201-3). Moreover, the Dutch share in the slave trade decreased after 1773 (Postma 1990:284-303).
7   Brief 1764:234-6, 242-5. See also Keyser 1985 and Paasman 1984.

Writings for the purpose of reflecting on one's own society invariably pictured the non-European world as rather homogeneous, as primarily different from one's own world. Within this homogeneity, however, there was a certain hierarchy in the image of other continents and peoples. The keyword in this hierarchy was 'civilization', as expressed in Christendom, world trade, the written word, the arts, civil virtues, and connected with this in one way or another, color of skin. It was acknowledged that there were other civilized, even older, cultures besides European civilization, but compared to the Western world these cultures, especially the Chinese and Islamic, had reached a sort of standstill. They were static, ruled by despots, barbarous and cruel. Religion became the predominant criterion for the advance of civilization, and religions other than Christianity were seen to be both morally wrong and a cause of backwardness.

Religious dissenters, who were so important in the British antislavery movement, hardly played a role in stimulating Dutch antislavery. There were small Protestant groups such as the Mennonites, whose emphasis on the inner light of the spirit made their religious sensibility similar to that of the Quakers. All the same, in view of their modest numbers,[8] and the widespread availability of British and French writings on a wide range of humanitarian subjects, they did little to contribute to an indigenous, vibrant Dutch antislavery movement. To sum up, even if slavery and antislavery were dealt with in various genres of Dutch writing and literature, even if the 'reading public' expanded gradually and a 'public opinion' came into being, the problem of relative indifference still remains. An analysis of the Patriots and the Nederlandsch Zendeling-Genootschap may help to explain this lack of commitment.

The Patriotic Movement of the 1780s and 1790s: Politics and Colonies

From the 1780s onwards, the Dutch Patriots[9] redefined terms such as freedom, the public good, and welfare, and demanded a broader participation in public and political affairs. Their criticism was directed against the usurpation of power by, and the corruption of, the oligarchical *regenten*. The Patriotic movement incorporated elements of the enlightened agenda set before the 1780s and elevated them to a 'national' level. The Patriots employed already existing networks. Moral education as a reforming instrument was retained on the agenda, but it now became part of a specific political discourse.

---

[8] It seems that the Mennonites themselves faced internal problems: they lost about 80% of their total membership between 1700 and 1800 (Groenveld, Jacobszoon and Verheus 1993:148).
[9] I am aware of the relative diversity of 'the' Dutch Patriots, but for present purposes it seems acceptable to consider them as a single group.

What was the Patriot attitude towards the colonial world? A prime concern was that abuses within the colonial and trading system which were held responsible for the economic decline had to be addressed. The royalist ruling élite had to be replaced by Patriots and there had to be a degree of liberalization in trading and commerce. Propositions like this were set against the background of a new 'national interest' in which the colonies were included (Schutte 1974:105, 214). New definitions and interpretations of freedom and property had to be applied to the white colonial inhabitants. Patriots in the motherland, as well as those residing in the colonies, agreed on the importance of continuing the slave trade and slavery. Abolition would cause total ruin to the overseas possessions and, as a consequence, ruin to the Dutch Republic itself. This tendency to 'nationalize' individual and collective ideas and interests proved to be a very important feature of the mobilizing force of the Patriot movement. Patriot authors of the 1780s and 1790s often used the notions of 'freedom' and 'slavery' in their writings. With a few exceptions, they always referred to the white inhabitants of the Dutch Republic. 'Slavery' was used as a political concept to pinpoint the enslavement of the citizens by the ruling élite.

The 1780s and 1790s witnessed a debate on the status of the colonies, their relation to the mother country, and the position of the trading companies. Discussions in the 1780s focused on the question of monopoly versus free trade, on breaking the power of the ruling élite, and on the support of the colonies in financial and military matters; all this with a view to the welfare of the national state. After silencing the Patriot movement in 1787, the restored Dutch government took up several ideas on colonial affairs as developed by the Patriots, including proposals to nationalize the East and West Indies Companies. In 1791, the West Indies Company was indeed nationalized, as was the East Indies Company during the Batavian Republic (1795-1806). The government took over an existing system of overseas trade and colonial administration. Commercial capitalism, operating within a national framework of decline and stagnation, worked to inhibit the formation of a national consensus on the evils of slavery.

Yet the Batavian Revolution did create new opportunities to put issues such as the status of the colonies, the slave trade and slavery on the political agenda. In the debates on the new constitution(s) which dragged on from 1796 to 1798, the question of abolishing the trade and slavery was raised, notably by Pieter Vreede, but it did not have enough priority to mobilize more than a handful of representatives in the National Assembly. Vreede stated that blacks were as human as whites and that keeping them enslaved was against natural rights, freedom, and brotherhood. He therefore proposed to abolish the trade and slavery.

However, successive National Assemblies gave priority to the many practical and more urgent problems the Republic faced. The colonies became state property, and the regulation of the political and civil rights of the colonial inhabitants was postponed until the national and international problems had been dealt with effectively. These problems were indeed enormous. For several decades the colonial economy had been declining. As a result of the wars in the 1790s, the Republic lost several of its colonies to either Britain or France. Communication and trade with the overseas possessions became very difficult, if not impossible. State debts increased and the Republic had to impose serious budget cuts in an effort to make ends meet. The government sold, for instance, nearly everything the former East Indies Company had owned in the motherland, such as ships, wharves, and buildings.

Between 1796 and 1803, successive governmental committees on colonial affairs worked on drawing up a colonial charter. The result was the Charter of 1804,[10] which would not be put into effect properly until 1814. During the French domination and occupation of the Netherlands (1806-1813) it was out of the question to revise colonial policy, much less to put the issue of abolition on the agenda. The only real priority the government pursued was trying to secure the transport of colonial products to the Netherlands, an effort which met with little success (Van Eyck van Heslinga 1988:37-62).

The Nederlandsch Zendeling-Genootschap (NZG)[11]

During the optimistic, at times chaotic, revolutionary years several ministers of the Nederlandsch Hervormde Kerk (Dutch Reformed Church)[12] founded the Nederlandsch Zendeling Genootschap (NZG, 1797), modelled on the London Missionary Society. The Church itself did not want to participate in the NZG, partly because the NZG strove to be ecumenical, or rather 'interconfessional', like its London counterpart – an aim the Nederlandsch Hervormde Kerk found too progressive.[13]

Up to the end of the eighteenth century, ministers of the Hervormde

---

10   The original draft of the Charter of 1804 by Dirk van Hogendorp was more progressive than the final result. Van Hogendorp intended to abolish the old privileges of the former trading companies that still existed in the colonies. He also proposed to give some rights to the indigenous people inhabiting, in this case, Java and surrounding islands. These proposals were left out of the final Charter.
11   The history of the NZG between 1797 and 1820 is analyzed in Boneschansker 1987.
12   The Nederlandsch Hervormde Kerk was the privileged church until the Batavian Revolution, even if not an officially established Church of the State.
13   This ecumenical idea was primarily aimed at Protestant denominations and sects. In these times of hardship, as the NZG saw it, Protestants should unite on missionary affairs. The NZG did not strive to unite the Protestant world as such (Boneschansker 1987:46-7, 152-62).

Kerk were the 'official' religious personnel in the colonies. They depended on the church and the trading companies for their salary and facilities. Their main task was to serve the white Protestant inhabitants of the colonies. At the same time, various other Protestant and Catholic missionaries were active in the colonies. Missionaries focusing on the indigenous population and imported slaves were severely hindered by the trading companies, colonial administrators, and colonists. Criticism of these obstacles had already been raised during the eighteenth century. In a more systematic way, the NZG now tried to mobilize as many 'true' Christians as possible to spread God's word, not only among non-European heathen peoples, who were the primary target, but also among the increasing number of European 'renegades', contaminated by the secularizing turmoil of the revolutionary wave. Despite its moderate and even conservative ideas, the NZG did stress its modern enlightened character, and molded this into a religious framework. Its organization too was 'enlightened', modelled on the various eighteenth-century 'societies'. Much time and energy was spent on mobilizing the public for the good cause, mainly through the NZG media. In this context mention may be made of its publication *Berichten en Brieven* ('Reports and Letters'), reporting on the activities of the missionaries and the ways in which they handled the mission in the colonies.

Since other missionaries, especially the German Moravian brethren and the Catholics, had directed their attention to the Indians and blacks of the Dutch West Indian colonies, the NZG considered it more appropriate to focus on colonies where their missionaries could start their work without too many difficulties, notably in the Cape Colony and the possessions in the 'East'.[14] The NZG faced major problems in sending missionaries to the colonies until the end of the war in 1813-1814. Partly as a result of this, the 'inner mission' was emphasized more than the effort to convert overseas heathen. The influence of the NZG on the colonial world was therefore rather small during the first fifteen years of its existence. Nevertheless, the NZG kept on developing ideas about its future missionary activities. Its perspective on Asiatic, Amerindian, and African peoples was clearly stated. The main goal was obviously to enlighten the whole world with God's word. However, it seemed necessary to develop different strategies for the Asiatic peoples and religions, on the one hand, and the 'primitive' peoples of Africa and parts of America, on the other. University-educated missionaries should be used to convert the more 'civilized' Muslims, Buddhists, Hindus, and Confucians. For the American Indians and blacks, it sufficed to send missionaries who could read and write and teach some craft.

[14] In 1800 the NZG intended to send missionaries to Curaçao (where Catholic missionaries were active) to convert the 'heathen slaves'. The ongoing war, however, obstructed the execution of this plan. *Handelingen* 1800:21-5, 1801:19-21; Boneschansker 1987:75-8.

Preaching and teaching were also the means of creating obedient, hard-working and therefore useful members of colonial society. If the NZG mentioned the issue of slavery, it was only to point out that plantation owners and local colonial governments would not permit missionaries to preach to the slaves. By 1814 the NZG stated it had felt itself oppressed by the successive governments of the Batavian and French period. Predictably, the society rejoiced when Willem I became king. The NZG did not change its moderate tone though, referring to the abolition of the slave trade in the following words: 'Whether the slave trade will be abolished or not [...], whether this will happen gradually or immediately, we all long for the moment that we will be given permission to work among the slaves over there [...].' (*Handelingen* 1814:64).

After 1815, the Dutch Catholics too took up their missionary activities in a more systematic way.[15] Freedom of religion, established during the Batavian Revolution and restated in the constitution of the new monarchy, created unprecedented opportunities for the Catholic Church. Similar to the NZG, the Catholic 'revival' included both an 'inner mission' and the mission aimed at non-Christian peoples. The overseas mission soon became one of the spheres of competition in which Protestants and Catholics tried to outdo one another. Despite their various incompatibilities, they agreed on one point: converting heathen would mean strengthening their own church. During the first decades of the nineteenth century, priority was given to conversion and the attempt to obtain permission to work among slaves. From the 1830s onwards, particularly in Suriname, plantation owners began to allow missionaries of both denominations on their premises. The colonists now acknowledged the disciplinary advantages of the Christianization of their slave work force.

Conclusion

Slavery and antislavery were relatively minor issues in the eighteenth-century Dutch Republic. There was sufficient information at hand on the subject, but this did not result in fervent public debate. I have tried to explain this relative indifference by looking at the broader context of Dutch eighteenth-century 'reality'. This reality was a mixture of an actual and an imagined decline of state and society, perceived within an enlightened context. Moreover, the peculiar history and structure of the Dutch Republic determined attitudes toward man and society. Moral, political, and economic arguments were intertwined. Solutions offered to remedy the decline were expressed in an optimistic, self-assured way, whether they came from

---

[15] A recent overview of the Catholic mission in the early nineteenth century is Rietbergen 1990.

politically orientated Patriots or zealous Protestant ministers. But these reformers were all preoccupied with their own, at times conflicting, notions of how the future Dutch nation should be, and most importantly, they had to try to reach a consensus on this issue. Both an imagined decline and a real decline, especially the rather depressing political and socio-economic situation between 1800 and 1814, helped to inhibit the development of other issues than national ones.

I have tried to analyze Dutch attitudes towards slavery by using the concept of 'social mobilization' in a broad cultural sense. My tentative suggestion is that the groups involved in the mobilization process and the instruments they used to obtain their goal were not that dissimilar to the ones involved in the British case. However, unlike the latter, the Dutch case indicates the relative irrelevance of slavery in the debates. As Drescher has suggested, British abolitionism was indeed an anomaly.

Nevertheless, the problem remains of how the Dutch case fits into a comparative analysis. In order to avoid notions such as 'to be ahead of' or 'to be late or behind', it may be worth conducting further research on various national and regional cases, not on the basis of strictly formulated models, but with a flexibility in addressing the relevant questions. We may then better appreciate the peculiarity of the eighteenth-century Dutch Republic, where antislavery expressions could indeed be a part of enlightened ideas and attitudes, but failed to become an issue capable of mobilizing a broader public.

References

Barrau, A.
1790 'De waare staat van den slaven-handel in onze Nederlandse colonien', *Bijdragen tot het menschelijk geluk* 3:341-88.
Bender, Thomas (ed.)
1992 *The Antislavery Debate; Capitalism and Abolitionism as a Problem in Historical Interpretation*. Berkeley: University of California Press.
Boneschansker, Jan
1987 *Het Nederlandsch Zendeling Genootschap in zijn eerste periode; Een studie over de opwekking in de Bataafse en Franse Tijd*. Leeuwarden: Dijkstra.
Brake, Wayne Ph. te
1990 'How Much in How Little? Dutch Revolution in Comparative Perspective', *Tijdschrift voor Sociale Geschiedenis* 16:349-63.
Brief van Kakera Akotie
1764 'Brief van Kakera Akotie, een Fantynsche Neger aan zynen Broeder Atta op de kust van Guinea; Over de elende der Slaaven, die van daar naar Amerika gevoerd worden', *De Denker*, 82-2:234-6, 83-2:242-5.

Capitein, J.E.J.
1742   Staatkundig-godgeleerd onderzoekschrift over de slaverny, als niet strydig tegen de christelyke vryheid; Uyt het Latyn vertaalt door H. de Wilhelm. Leiden: Bonk.

Davis, David Brion
1992   'The Perils of Doing History by Ahistorical Abstraction; A Reply to Thomas L. Haskell's *AHR Forum* Reply', in: Thomas Bender (ed.), *The Antislavery Debate; Capitalism and Abolitionism as a Problem in Historical Interpretation*, pp. 290-309. Berkeley: University of California Press.

Drescher, Seymour
1987   *Capitalism and Antislavery; British Mobilization in Comparative Perspective*. New York: Oxford University Press.

[Equiano, O.]
1790   *Merkwaardige levensgevallen van Olaudah Equiano of Gustavus Vassa, den Afrikaan, door hem zelven beschreeven [...] Uit het Engelsch vertaald*. Rotterdam: Holsteyn.

Eyck van Heslinga, E.S. van
1988   *Van compagnie naar koopvaardij; De scheepvaartverbinding van de Bataafse Republiek met de koloniën in Azië 1795-1806*. Amsterdam: De Bataafsche Leeuw.

Frijhoff, Willem Th.M.
1992   'The Dutch Enlightenment and the Creation of Popular Culture', in: Margaret C. Jacob and Wijnandt W. Mijnhardt (eds), *The Dutch Republic in the Eighteenth Century; Decline, Enlightenment, and Revolution*, pp. 292-307. Ithaca: Cornell University Press.

Goslinga, Cornelis Ch.
1956   *Emancipatie en emancipator; De geschiedenis van de slavernij op de Benedenwindse eilanden en van het werk der bevrijding*. Assen: Van Gorcum.
1985   *The Dutch in the Caribbean and in the Guianas, 1680-1791*. Assen: Van Gorcum.

Groenveld, G., J.P. Jacobszoon and S.L. Verheus (eds)
1993   *Wederdopers, menisten, doopsgezinden in Nederland, 1530-1980*. Zutphen: Walburg Pers.

Handelingen
1799-1854   *Handelingen in de buitengewone Vergadering der Directeuren van het Nederlandsch Zendeling Genootschap*. Rotterdam: Cornel.

Jacob, Margaret C. and Wijnandt W. Mijnhardt (eds)
1992   *The Dutch Republic in the Eighteenth Century; Decline, Enlightenment, and Revolution*. Ithaca: Cornell University Press.

Kals, Joannes Guiljelmus
1756   *Neerlands hooft- en wortel-sonde, het verzuym van de bekeringe der heydenen, aangewesen en ten toon gespreit door drie leerredens gedaan en gemeen gemaakt door drie der voornaamste kerk-voogden in Engeland [...]; Uit 't Engelsch vertaalt, en met aanmerkingen verrykt [...]*. Leeuwarden: Koumans.

Keyser, Paula
1985   Suikerriet, suikerverdriet. Culemborg: Educaboek.
Linde, J.M. van der
1956   Het visioen van Herrnhut en het apostolaat der Moravische broeders in Suriname, 1735-1863. Paramaribo: Kersten.
Mijnhardt, Wijnandt W.
1987   'De Nederlandse Verlichting', in: F. Grijzenhout, W.W. Mijnhardt and N.C.F. van Sas (eds), Voor Vaderland en vrijheid; De revolutie van de patriotten, pp. 53-79. Amsterdam: De Bataafsche Leeuw.
1988   Tot heil van 't menschdom; Culturele genootschappen in Nederland, 1750-1815. Amsterdam: Rodopi.
1992   'The Dutch Enlightenment; Humanism, Nationalism, and Decline', in: Margaret C. Jacob and Wijnandt W. Mijnhardt (eds), The Dutch Republic in the Eighteenth Century; Decline, Enlightenment, and Revolution, pp. 197-223. Ithaca: Cornell University Press.
Oostindie, Gert
1992   'The Enlightenment, Christianity, and the Suriname Slave', Journal of Caribbean History 26:147-70. [Revised and enlarged version in the present book.]
Paasman, A.N.
1979   'Reinhart, of literatuur en werkelijkheid', Documentatieblad 18e eeuw 41/42:40-61.
1984   Reinhart; Nederlandse literatuur en slavernij ten tijde van de Verlichting. Leiden: Nijhoff.
Postma, Johannes Menne
1990   The Dutch in the Atlantic Slave Trade 1600-1815. Cambridge: Cambridge University Press.
Priester, Laurens R.
1987   De Nederlandse houding ten aanzien van de slavenhandel en slavernij, 1596-1863. Middelburg: Commissie Regionale Geschiedbeoefening Zeeland.
Rietbergen, Peter J.A.N.
1990   'Aan de vooravond van "het groote missie-uur"; Een onderzoek naar de Nederlandse missiebeweging gedurende de eerste helft van de negentiende eeuw en de rol van "missietijdschriften" daarin', Nederlands Archief voor Kerkgeschiedenis 70:75-108.
Sas, Nicolaas C.F. van
1987   'Opiniepers en politieke cultuur', in: F. Grijzenhout, W.W. Mijnhardt and N.C.F. van Sas (eds), Voor Vaderland en vrijheid; De revolutie van de patriotten, pp. 97-130. Amsterdam: De Bataafsche Leeuw.
1989   'Vaderlandsliefde, nationalisme en vaderlands gevoel in Nederland, 1770-1813', Tijdschrift voor Geschiedenis 102:471-95.
1992   'The Patriot Revolution; New Perspectives', in: Margaret C. Jacob and Wijnandt W. Mijnhardt (eds), The Dutch Republic in the Eighteenth Century; Decline, Enlightenment, and Revolution, pp. 91-120. Ithaca: Cornell University Press.

Schutte, G.J.
1974 *De Nederlandse patriotten en de koloniën; Een onderzoek naar hun denkbeelden en optreden, 1770-1800.* Groningen: Tjeenk Willink.
1979 'Zedelijke verplichting en gezonde staatkunde; Denken en doen rondom de slavernij in Nederland en koloniën, eind 18e eeuw', *Documentatieblad 18e eeuw* 41/42:101-15.

Sens, Angelie
1992 'De neger, slavernij, abolitionisme en het Nederlandse "enigma"; Een vergelijkend onderzoek naar de opvattingen over slavernij in Frankrijk en de Republiek, circa 1750-1800'. [MA thesis Utrecht University.]

Voort, J.P. van de
1973 *De Westindische plantages van 1720 tot 1795; Financiën en handel.* Eindhoven: De Witte.

EDWIN HORLINGS

An Economic Explanation of the Late Abolition of Slavery in Suriname

Unlike most other colonial powers, the Dutch did not abolish slavery until after 1860.[1] At first sight this appears to fit in with the traditional interpretation of Dutch economic development in the nineteenth century. This view focuses attention on the alleged long-term stagnation and late industrialization of the Netherlands, which was caused by unfavorable economic circumstances or by the so-called *Jan Salie* spirit, the absence of a modern, dynamic mentality. In this line of reasoning, it came as no surprise that the Dutch were late with Emancipation as well.

In his essay 'The Long Goodbye: Dutch Capitalism and Antislavery in Comparative Perspective', Seymour Drescher sets out to confront the late emancipation of the Suriname slaves with the pattern of Dutch economic development. He wonders if there was a connection between the abolition of slavery and the rise of 'modern industrial capitalism'. This relationship would find expression mainly in the belief in the superiority of free labor or – in general – in the development of moral standards incompatible with the existence of slavery. On the one hand, he looks upon the Dutch Golden Age (c. 1580-1670) as a period of industrialization and modernization. Nonetheless, no attempts were made to abolish slavery until the nineteenth century. On the other hand, the timing of Emancipation seems to correspond with the (alleged) late industrialization of the Netherlands. Drescher followed a similar line of reasoning in his examination of British abolition. At the time of Emancipation, colonial slavery was more important to the British economy than ever before; if the strength of proslavery economic interests was crucial to the explanation of the timing of Emancipation, then slavery should have been abolished much earlier (Drescher 1977:183-4). These are some of the main foundations of his statement that 'the economic context offers the weakest positive support for and the strongest counter-abolitionist argument against the anti-slavery

---

[1] I would like to thank the participants of the conference on 'Dutch Capitalism and Antislavery in Comparative Perspective' (Leiden, KITLV/Royal Institute of Linguistics and Anthropology, 15 October 1993) for their comments on the original paper. I owe special thanks to Gert Oostindie and Jan-Pieter Smits for their many comments and suggestions.

process'. Instead, Drescher attributes the emancipation to changes in ideology which made slavery both morally and politically unacceptable. In this respect his remarks on the nature of abolitionist movements deserve special mention. In Great Britain, even if this movement did not gain momentum until the end of the eighteenth century, Emancipation was pursued by a mass movement with considerable political influence. In the Netherlands and elsewhere on the Continent, pro-abolitionism was never 'a durable mass movement'.[2]

Views of long-term economic development have changed considerably in recent years. For one thing, the process of economic growth is no longer identified solely with industrialization (Cameron 1985). Agriculture and services have gained in theoretical significance, as have non-economic factors such as demographic changes or political and institutional structures. A second and more fundamental theoretical innovation concerns the formulation of theories of economic development in the very long run. The prevailing approach to this problem is still Simon Kuznets's theory of modern economic growth. He defined this type of growth as a rapid increase in per capita income accompanied by a strong growth in population. The modern nature of this process is determined by the structural transformation of the economy which precedes and explains the growth of income; growth is seen as a result of an increase in productivity rather than a more intensive use of the factors of production.[3] Naturally, the next question must be that of what characterized development before the onset of modern economic growth. One of the main features of premodern economies that is currently at the center of attention is the political and institutional context of development. From this perspective, slavery may be considered as part and parcel of the operation of premodern economies (Kuznets 1969:26-7, 63, 72-86; Persson 1988; Van Zanden 1991).

From this theoretical point of view the Golden Age was not a period of 'modern' development. Growth was concentrated in a few sectors only, namely international trade and transport as well as export-oriented processing industries. There was no evidence of a general increase in productivity or of far-reaching demographic shifts. Although the economy of the Netherlands – Holland in particular – had some modern characteristics, its structure was not radically transformed.[4] Conversely, the modernization of the Dutch economy in the nineteenth century seems to correspond to the abolition of Suriname slavery: the process of modern

---

[2] Compare, apart from 'The Long Goodbye', also Drescher 1977:184-5; Oostindie 1992:159.
[3] In addition, growth must be *sustained*, which means that the long-term increase in income is not fundamentally interrupted by business cycles.
[4] See the special issue of *Economic and Social History in the Netherlands* 4 (1992) for an overview of the state of the art in the historiography of Dutch economic development in the Golden Age.

economic growth appears to have begun in the 1860s. Thus, the possibility of a relationship between the abolition of slavery and the rise of 'modern industrial capitalism' remains.

This essay will explore the economic background of the late emancipation of slaves in Suriname. It is not my intention to suggest that economic changes underlie all societal developments. This approach merely allows for a short and transparent analysis. The examination centers on two questions: why slavery was abolished; and why this emancipation did not take place much earlier. The first section examines the hypothesis that the abolition of slavery was the outcome of developments in the Suriname economy itself. The next sections attempt to link the emancipation to external influences: changing relations in the world market and Dutch economic development. The final section discusses to what extent the various economic factors explain the late timing of emancipation.

The Profitability of the Suriname Plantations

Several authors have pointed out that the Suriname economy was fundamentally undermined by the scissor-movement of falling output prices and rising costs of production (Van Zanden 1991:24-5; Van Stipriaan 1993:100-13; Oostindie 1989:121-2). The plantations depended on a steady supply of cheap slaves. During the second half of the eighteenth century the price of slaves began to rise. This trend was reinforced by the ban on the slave trade, and especially by the introduction of slave registers in 1826. The supply of slaves dwindled and dried up. This forced entrepreneurs to utilize their labor force more carefully. Work load was lowered and the maintenance of slaves improved. However, while the number of inactive slaves (mostly women and children) increased, the death surplus remained. As a result, the size of the labor reserve declined continuously. The combination of a decreasing labor force at higher costs and falling output prices put unremitting pressure on the profit margins of the plantations. Van Zanden implicitly attributes the abolition of slavery to this development. In his view, the increasing pressure on the cost effectiveness of plantations was not counterbalanced by technological or organizational improvements (Van Zanden 1991:103-8). Ultimately, this had to result in the end of slavery.

However, a separate analysis of the sugar and coffee sectors of the Suriname economy shows that the profitability of the enterprises could not have been a reason for abolition (Van Stipriaan 1993:266-75). Both in current and constant prices, profits per slave in the sugar sector displayed an upward trend after 1800, while only the profits of coffee plantations continued to decline. Other indicators of the development of productivity, such as the output volume relative to the number of field slaves or to acreage, show a similar diverging trend. If the development of production is compared with the total weighted input of land and labor – both factors of production weighted according to their share in the stock of capital goods[5] – it becomes clear that the sugar plantations became increasingly productive between 1770 and 1863, whereas coffee producers employed their factors of production ever less efficiently.

It is therefore not surprising that the share of sugar in Suriname exports steadily increased until coffee had become irrelevant around 1860. Moreover, the sugar plantations increased in scale throughout the period. This was to a large extent a function of the technological and organizational innovations that characterized this sector. As a consequence, in 1863 the Suriname sugar sector was among the most productive and most advanced in the Caribbean (Van Stipriaan 1993:140).

From a macro-economic point of view, the Suriname entrepreneurs behaved rationally. In the course of the nineteenth century, an increasing part of the available resources was employed in the sector with the highest expected returns. Constant improvements in the process of production were needed to compensate for the deteriorating relation between output and expenditure. However, the stagnation of the volume of production after 1836 and the downward trend in exports per slave show that these innovations could not have saved the plantation economy in the long run (Van Zanden 1991:100-1). Still, in 1863 there was no reason for entrepreneurs to abolish slavery, especially because there was no alternative source of labor.[6] Individual plantation owners may have been forced to shut down their enterprises in the face of the need for continuous expansion and innovation, but the transition to a system of free labor was not an absolute necessity. An economic explanation for the late date of Emancipation will have to be sought outside Suriname.

---

[5] The weight of labor was assumed to be 63 per cent for sugar plantations and 49 per cent for coffee plantations. Between c. 1800 and 1862 the joint factor productivity of sugar plantations increased by +0.5 per cent per annum, whereas productivity in the coffee sector decreased at an annual rate of -1.8 per cent. These calculations are based on data taken from Van Stipriaan 1989 and Van Stipriaan 1993.

[6] In order to ease the transition to free labor, it was deemed necessary to oblige the former slaves to work on the plantations for another ten years after Emancipation under the apprentice system ('Staatstoezicht') (Brugmans 1961:248-9).

Graph 1. The Contribution of Suriname to Dutch Imports of Sugar and Coffee, 1815-1870

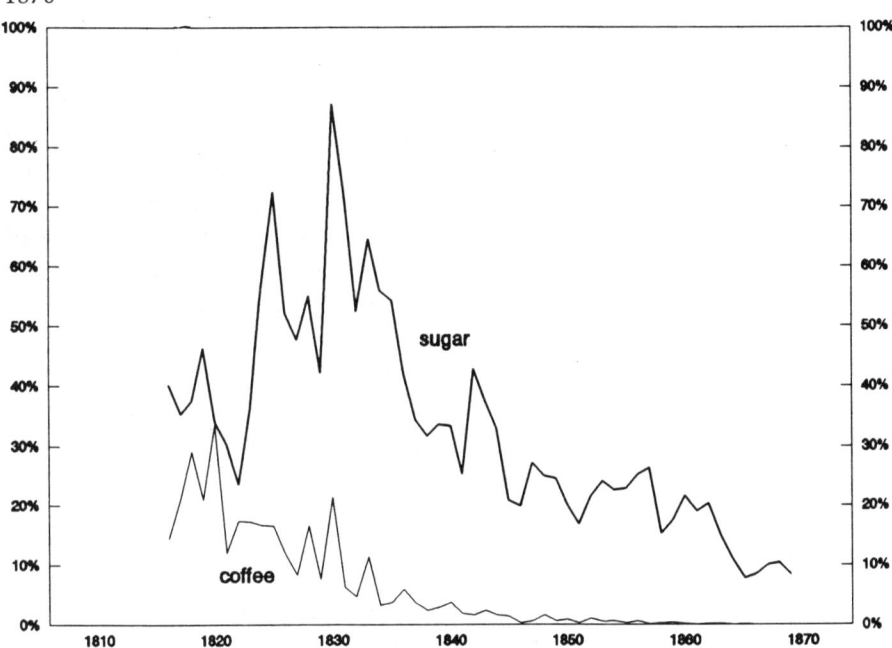

Note: A comparison of general exports from Suriname and imports for domestic consumption in the Netherlands can only approximate this contribution. The development of the share of Suriname is more important.
Sources: Van Stipriaan 1993:429-33; Smits 1994. Dutch international trade figures for the first half of the nineteenth century are derived from my own current research.

Changing Relations in the World Market

The first external cause of the abolition of slavery could have been the development of the world market for tropical arable products. In the nineteenth century, a number of new important areas of production emerged, particularly Cuba, the United States, and the Dutch East Indies. This led to a remarkable increase in the supply of sugar, coffee, cotton, and other products. As a consequence, the price level of these products continuously declined. Moreover, unlike Suriname, output per slave increased considerably in several other Caribbean plantation economies after 1800 (Van Stipriaan 1993:128-44).

The rapid growth of exports from competing areas of production reduced Suriname's share in the world sugar market. Until 1848, efforts to improve its position were thwarted by the obligation to export all products to the Netherlands. Here of all places, the importance of Suriname declined heavily as a consequence of the enormous imports of sugar, coffee, and other tropical goods from the East Indies after the introduction of the Cultivation System – a system of forced cultivation of export crops – on Java in 1832. Graph 1 shows the decline in the importance of Suriname to the Dutch trade in sugar and coffee. After 1850, the produce of the plantations could be exported to those markets where prices were most favorable (Van Stipriaan 1993:266). However, at the same time the productivity of the Suriname plantations remained more or less stagnant, whereas their competitors became increasingly efficient. Meanwhile, the importance of tropical arable products to Dutch international trade decreased (Lindblad and Van Zanden 1989:263-4; Horlings and Van der Bie 1993:143-5). On balance, Suriname continued to lose ground in the world market after 1850.

Of course, the aim of the Suriname entrepreneurs was not to maintain their share in the world market per se, which had never been large anyway; in the mid-nineteenth century, when sugar was the main export product of Suriname, the colony's total production placed it in the lower-middle category of Caribbean sugar producers (Van Stipriaan 1993:29). They were mainly concerned with the preservation of their profit margin at a time of declining prices. Entrepreneurs responded to the long-term fall in prices by raising the level of productivity and substantially increasing the volume of exports compared to the relatively stable level of the eighteenth century (Van Stipriaan 1993:128-44; Oostindie 1989:120-5).

Moreover, it can be demonstrated that the development of output prices cannot in itself explain the precise timing of Emancipation. The price of sugar – the main product – was very high during and after the Napoleonic Wars. If 1863 is set at 100, the sugar price was 372 in 1815. After 1815 the sugar price declined, but from the 1850s to the 1870s – the period in which the emancipation was enacted – there was a slow rise in prices. Although the steady fall in prices placed a persistent burden on the profitability of the Suriname economy, this development explains neither the abolition of slavery nor its timing. The analysis will therefore turn to the economic development of the motherland itself.

Modern Economic Growth and the Abolition of Slavery

There is general agreement that the economic structure of the Netherlands underwent fundamental changes during the nineteenth century. Until recently, economic historians associated these changes with a process of industrialization. The late growth of industry – according to De Jonge (1968), the growth of industry did not accelerate until the 1890s – tempted historians to typify the Dutch economy as 'backward' or at least 'lagging behind' neighboring countries. In an attempt to provide a more precise analysis of this transition, the project 'Reconstruction of the National Accounts of the Netherlands, 1800-1940' was set up. The aim of this project is to examine the development of the Dutch economy on the basis of a comprehensive quantitative base. The following picture emerges from an analysis of the initial results.[7]

Until about 1860 per capita income increased slowly, but this growth was concentrated mainly in international services and export-oriented industries related to the colonial trade (such as shipbuilding, textiles, and sugar refineries). There was little room for sustained growth in the domestic market. Aggregate demand was inadequate, and the lack of integration of the various regions prevented the achievement of economies of scale (Griffiths 1982). Nevertheless, the basis for the changes that took place in the second half of the nineteenth century was laid in the period before 1850. The Netherlands became a politically unified nation state, institutional changes (such as the abolition of the guilds) began during the Napoleonic Wars, and in any case the trade policy regarding the Dutch East Indies provided an enormous inflow of capital.

The 1860s and 1870s were characterized by a number of radical changes that mark the beginning of a process of modern economic growth. After a long period of stagnation the rate of urbanization increased during the second half of the century, while the demographic transition began in the 1870s. Moreover, as a consequence of an increase in productivity growth occurred in all economic sectors. The growth of purchasing power was an important factor in this process: excises on bread, meat, and other primary foodstuffs were abolished, and nominal as well as real wages increased. In addition, infrastructural improvements were of decisive importance in increasing the scale of the domestic market. Government played a crucial role in these changes. As a result of the reorganization of the public debt, the burden of interest payments was lowered and the central goverment's financial room to manoeuvre increased. Moreover, the expansion of the power of the central state meant the lessening of the political and economic influence of local interest groups. From now on, Dutch economic development was more and more strongly determined by the domestic market, while international trade and transport were increasingly connected to the domestic production of goods (Smits 1994). The climate for investment in the Netherlands improved considerably; at the same time, large amounts of capital became available due to the reduction of the national debt, large remittances from the Dutch East Indies, and the growing income from foreign investments.

---

7 These results were presented for the first time in Horlings, Smits and Van Zanden 1994. For an extensive analysis of the growth process in the second half of the nineteenth century see Smits 1994.

How was the transformation of the Dutch economy in this period related to the abolition of slavery in Suriname? At first sight there are three possible explanations. These relate to the supply of capital, the role of government, and the impact of Dutch economic development in general.

First, the emergence of alternative investment opportunities in the Netherlands may have attracted capital away from the colonial economy. In the eighteenth century the opposite can be observed. The economic growth of Suriname was accompanied by a large flow of capital from Holland. This correlates with Van Zanden's description of the economic development of eighteenth-century Holland as 'accumulation without growth': a sizeable increase in income from wealth in a period of aggregate economic stagnation (Van Zanden 1992:17). Excess capital was directed towards the few sectors that experienced growth: investments abroad and the East Indian and West Indian colonies. During the nineteenth century, the West Indies became both economically and politically less important to the Netherlands. Still, continuous improvements in the production process necessitated a steady flow of capital to the colony. Did the process of modern economic growth in the Netherlands make the Suriname plantations unattractive for investors and entrepreneurs now that they could expect higher returns on their capital elsewhere? This would have starved the colony of capital.

Three objections can be raised to this hypothesis. First, the plantations made a modest profit, which could be used to finance innovations to some extent. Second, capital was insufficiently mobile to be moved quickly between different alternatives. Capital invested in plantations was mostly tied up in land, slaves, and infrastructure. Likewise, Dutch merchant houses could not easily abandon the Suriname plantations in view of their large investments in loans and mortgages for the plantation economy (Oostindie 1993:7). Third, if investors and entrepreneurs made their decisions mainly on the basis of expected returns, why had there not been a large flow of capital from the colony previously, in the 1830s, when enormous profits could have been made from trade and transport to the East Indies? The sugar sector continued to expand, while the large drop in the number of coffee plantations after 1836 was the result not of a lack of capital but of a decline in profitability combined with entrepreneurial failure (Van Stipriaan 1993:133, 143).

The second possible explanation of a relationship between the development of the Dutch economy and the abolition of slavery in Suriname concerns the role of government. After 1850, the Dutch central government was finally able to pay the indemnities entailed by Emancipation. In the period 1863-1874, a total sum of 12.8 million guilders was paid to the slave owners (of which 10 million alone in 1867). This was less than 1.5 per cent of the gross domestic product. If the abolition of slavery had occurred in the 1830s, this share would have amounted to more than 2.5 per cent. The difference becomes more pronounced when these costs are compared to total government expenditure. In the 1830s the indemnities would have amounted to about 20 per cent of expenditure, while the national debt and the war effort consumed the greater part of government revenue. In that period, financing Emancipation would have meant a sizeable sacrifice on behalf of a colony that was relatively unimportant to the Dutch economy. In the 1860s the Emancipation still accounted for about 15 per cent of government expenditure, but by now the government could afford such an expense more easily.[8]

Finally, it could be argued that the modernization of the Dutch economy was itself the main explanatory factor. It is striking that sweeping changes occurred in other areas of the economy as well (Smits 1994). In the 1850s and 1860s, the excises on primary necessities were abolished; in 1868 the regular service (*beurtlijst*) of the Nederlandsche Handel Maatschappij (Dutch Trading Company) was discontinued and shortly afterwards the Dutch monopoly of the East Indian market came to an end; international trade and transport were increasingly liberalized; and government became actively involved in the improvement of the Dutch infrastructure, such as in the canals in Overijssel and the building of railways. From this perspective, the abolition of slavery could be interpreted as the outcome of a general process of change in institutional structures and labor relations. However, it is unlikely that modern economic growth brought about a change in mentality in such a short term.

The Timing of Emancipation

The preceding sections suggest that the causes for abolition cannot be found in the development of the profitability of the Suriname plantations or of their share in the world market. There does appear to be a significant relation, though, between economic changes in the Netherlands and the abolition of Suriname slavery. This leaves the question of why the abolition of slavery was not enacted at an earlier moment. What would have happened if the transition to a system of free labor had been made earlier, say in the 1830s, when the supply of new slaves had been cut off?

Presumably, the average wage of a free laborer would have been higher than the cost of maintaining a slave, and the pressure of work could not have been as extreme as it was under conditions of forced labor. All the same, the mortality surplus would have turned into a natural increase. Entrepreneurs would no longer have been responsible for the support of the

---

[8] I am grateful to René van der Voort for providing me with data from his doctoral thesis on the development of Dutch government finance in the period 1850-1913.

inactive part of the population. Along the lines of a merchant capitalist system of labor mobilization (Van Zanden 1991:18-20), entrepreneurs could even have decided to keep wages below the level of the costs of reproduction and rely on the subsistence sector of the Suriname economy to complement the needs of the population, provided the slaves were willing to work on the plantations. Also, alternative sources of labor, such as contract labor, might have become a realistic option.

It is, however, understandable that Emancipation did not occur before 1860. During the Golden Age, when Holland became the most advanced economy in Europe, slavery had been merely a 'natural' means of labor mobilization consistent with premodern modes of production (Van Zanden 1991). Abolition was even less likely to occur in the eighteenth century. While domestic production stagnated, overseas investments and colonial trade (with Suriname as well as the Dutch East Indies) flourished, particularly during the second half of the century. The lack of alternative investment opportunities in the Netherlands ensured an abundant supply of capital, also for the plantations in Suriname. The French Revolution could have been a turning point, but even during the Napoleonic Wars, when the ideal of freedom was considered of paramount importance, motions to abolish slavery were rejected. Moreover, the Dutch colonies had been captured by the British, and the newly centralized government of the Netherlands was utterly powerless outside its borders. The major issue is therefore why Emancipation did not occur shortly after 1815 or during the 1830s.

First, it is quite clear that the late date of Abolition cannot be explained by entrepreneurial failure. Plantation owners did not base their decisions on expected returns in the very long run. They could not dispose of a macroeconomic overview that can so easily be constructed with hindsight. What is more, the switch to a system of free labor was not necessary nor attractive from the point of view of the Suriname plantation owners. Expected returns were high in the 1820s when sufficient slaves were imported. In the 1830s and 1840s, the enormous growth of the Dutch trade in sugar and coffee may have kept the hope of a future recovery alive. Even if this did not result in spectacular growth rates, it was clear that the plantations could survive within the system, albeit with great difficulty. The development of the cost effectiveness of the plantations cannot explain either Emancipation itself or its timing.

In the end, the economic development of the Netherlands does not provide a full explanation for the late date of Emancipation. If however the changes in the role of government in economic life and in the distribution of political and economic power are considered as an integral part of the process of modern economic growth, then one more connection has been made. Before 1850, when the merchant elite was still prominent, attempts to abolish slavery would have encountered strong resistance. Special interest groups, notably of urban merchants, may have had enough influence on political decisions to block any attempt at Emancipation.[9] Moreover, government policy during the first half of the nineteenth century was aimed at a restoration of eighteenth-century structures, notably the staple trade of Amsterdam. Colonial exploitation served to provide trade and shipping with a sizeable supply of goods, while generating a significant flow of capital to the treasury. Nonetheless, government finances were insufficient to afford more than a token compensation.

The enigma is that Abolition occurred after the moment that would have been the most rational choice for entrepreneurs (around 1830) and before the time when 'modern' economic developments could have induced the necessary change in mentality (after 1870). Bearing in mind the potential influence of non-economic factors – such as a change in mentality or in moral values – the late emancipation of slavery in Suriname may have been no more than a political decision based on the fear of a loss of international prestige and on increased financial possibilities. All the same, it can hardly be accidental that it coincided with a major structural transformation of the Dutch economy. Sweeping institutional changes, the creation of an integrated national market, and a general process of economic growth altered the relationship between the Netherlands and its colonies. Changes in the political system were a part of this transformation. This may provide a sufficient explanation for the timing of the Suriname emancipation.

---

[9] For example, the Holland bourgeoisie was sufficiently powerful to stop the Ministry of Colonial Affairs and the Nederlandsche Handels Maatschappij from ending the protection of trade and shipping with the Dutch East Indies (see Chapter 5, Smits 1995).

References

Brugmans, I.J.
1961   *Paardenkracht en mensenmacht; Sociaal-economische geschiedenis van Nederland, 1795-1940*. 's-Gravenhage: Nijhoff.
Cameron, R.
1985   'A New View of European Industrialization', *Economic History Review* 38:1-23.
Drescher, Seymour
1977   *Econocide; British Slavery in the Era of Abolition*. Pittsburgh: University of Pittsburgh Press.
Griffiths, R.T.
1982   'The Creation of a National Dutch Economy, 1795-1909', *Tijdschrift voor Geschiedenis* 95:513-37.

Horlings, Edwin and R. van der Bie
1993 'Dutch Economic Development and International Trade; A Small and Open Economy in an Ever Changing World, 1850-1913', in: M. North (ed.), *Nordwesteuropa in der Weltwirtschaft 1750-1950*, pp. 129-62. Stuttgart: Steiner.

Horlings, Edwin, J.P.H. Smits and J.L. van Zanden
1994 'Structural Change in the Dutch Economy 1800-1913'. [Paper for the Eleventh International Economic Congress, Milan, 1994.]

Jonge, Jan A. de
1968 *De industrialisatie in Nederland tussen 1850 en 1914*. Amsterdam: Scheltema and Holkema.

Kuznets, Simon
1969 *Modern Economic Growth; Rate, Structure and Spread*. Third edition. New Haven: Yale University Press.

Lindblad, J.Th. and J.L. van Zanden
1989 'De buitenlandse handel van Nederland, 1872-1913', *Economisch- en Sociaal-Historisch Jaarboek* 52:231-69.

Oostindie, Gert
1989 *Roosenburg en Mon Bijou; Twee Surinaamse plantages, 1720-1870*. Dordrecht: Foris. [KITLV, Caribbean Series 11.]
1992 'The Enlightenment, Christianity, and the Suriname Slave', *Journal of Caribbean History* 26:147-70. [Revised and enlarged version in the present book.]
1993 'The Economics of Suriname Slavery', *Economic and Social History in the Netherlands* 5:1-24.

Panday, R.M.N.
1959 *Agriculture in Surinam 1650-1950; An Enquiry into the Causes of Its Decline*. Amsterdam: Paris.

Persson, Karl G.
1988 *Pre-industrial Economic Growth; Social Organization and Technological Progress in Europe*. Oxford: Blackwell.

Smits, J.P.H.
1995 *Economische groei en structuurveranderingen in de Nederlandse dienstensector 1850-1913*. [Forthcoming PhD thesis, Free University, Amsterdam.]

Stipriaan, Alex van
1989 'The Suriname Rat Race; Labour and Technology on Sugar Plantations, 1750-1900', *Nieuwe West-Indische Gids/New West Indian Guide* 63:94-117.
1993 *Surinaams contrast; Roofbouw en overleven in een Caraïbische plantagekolonie, 1750-1863*. Leiden: KITLV Press. [KITLV, Caribbean Series 13.]

Zanden, J.L. van
1991 *Arbeid tijdens het handelskapitalisme; Opkomst en neergang van de Hollandse economie 1350-1850*. Bergen: Octavo.
1992 'Economic Growth in the Golden Age; The Development of the Economy of Holland, 1500-1650', *Economic and Social History in the Netherlands* 4:5-26.

ALEX VAN STIPRIAAN

Suriname and the Abolition of Slavery

African slaves, American plantations, and their owners were the major actors involved in nineteenth-century abolition of New World slavery. However, the debate on the explanation and analysis of abolition focuses mainly on Europe. Of course, Europe had introduced plantation slavery in the Americas and as the still dominant power was also the one to abolish it. Still, it strikes one as odd that the subjects of abolition only play their part in the debate as peripheral economic factors in overwhelmingly metropolitan developments, and have hardly been given a voice of their own. The debate on the late Dutch abolition is another case in point. However, a focus on the immediate actors may shed new light on the dynamics of abolition. Therefore, in this article I attempt to look at the question of Dutch abolition from a 'West Indian' point of view.

The Dutch Antilles

During the eighteenth century, the Dutch Antillean islands, particularly Curaçao and St. Eustatius, were flourishing commercial centers.[1] Within the entire Dutch West Indies, however, they never played a dominant role, mainly because they produced no items for the world economy in significant quantities. At the end of the 1840s, salt was the most important export commodity, representing an average total value of only 365,000 Dutch guilders a year.[2] Dutch St. Martin was the only sugar producer of the six islands, but the total output of its eighteen plantations did not even equal that of one average Suriname sugar plantation during the same period.[3] From a colonial point of view, then, Suriname was far more

---

[1] In particular, the slave trade (101,000 slaves were traded between 1675 and 1775) and semi-legal intra-Caribbean trade (so-called *kleine vaart*) were moneymakers (Goslinga 1985: 156-231).
[2] During the years 1847-1850, Curaçao produced an average of 34,820 barrels of salt per annum, Bonaire 57,982, and St. Martin 311,114, while the average price was some ƒ 0,90 per barrel (calculations based on Renkema 1981:61, 356, and Paula 1993:34).
[3] The average annual sugar production of these eighteen plantations during the period 1838-1847 was 155,981 kg (calculations based on Paula 1993:37-8 and 133). A sugar plantation in Suriname produced an annual average of 158,058 kg around 1836 and 187,566 kg around 1854 (Van Stipriaan 1993:135).

interesting. The export value of its plantation products varied between an annual average of 6.6 million Dutch guilders during the 1830s, to 4.1 during the 1840s, and 4.8 million during the 1850s (Van Stipriaan 1993:437). Compared to other Caribbean colonies, the Suriname plantation economy was of medium size and never played in the same league as Jamaica, St. Domingue or Cuba (Table 1).

Table 1. Selected Caribbean Plantation Economies, 1775 and 1850

colony	slaves at Emancipation	production (in metrical tons)			
		sugar		coffee	
		c 1775	c 1850	c 1775	c 1850
Cuba	199,885	10,000	246,251	?	16,646
Haiti	480,000	62,595	–	20,000	19,000
Jamaica	311,070	43,355	30,605	900	3,350
Barbados	31,150	5,446	26,627	–	–
Suriname	36,484	6,610	14,786	7,927	298
Antigua	29,121	7,385	8,551	–	–
Grenada	23,638	8,784	4,945	–	–
St. Vincent	22,266	2,670	7,868	–	–
St. Kitts	8,815	7,934	4,773	–	–

Source: Van Stipriaan 1993:28-9.

In 1863, about 48,000 slaves were emancipated in the Dutch Caribbean, of whom no more than one-quarter lived in the Antilles.[4] This figure included the almost 1,900 slaves of St. Martin. With the cooperation of their 'owners', but without the formal consent of the Dutch government, they had lived as freedmen since 1848, when slavery on the French part of this island was abolished (Paula 1993:96-135). In Curaçao and the other Dutch islands, the slaves – and their owners – depended on developments connected with emancipation in Suriname, because all public and political attention was focused on that colony. Neither colonial authorities nor slave owners in the Dutch Antilles expected substantial problems to arise out of abolition. They waited patiently for events to take their course in Suriname (Renkema 1981: 149-50). Many Dutch Antillean slave owners were even in favor of a prompt abolition with a view to the anticipated financial compensation which many desperately needed to pay off their mortgages (Paula 1993:143-8; Renkema 1981:212-8). Some slave owners had too many mouths to feed with expensive imported foodstuffs, particularly during the frequent droughts and bad harvests. Part of the demanding slave force had become superfluous as its owners increasingly made their money in non-agricultural and less labor-intensive activities like shipping and trade

---

[4] See for the Antillean figures Goslinga 1990:282.

(Renkema 1981:239-43). Emancipation with compensation therefore served their interests well.

Initially, the colonial authorities in the Antilles had worried about the slaves' future because, unlike the situation in Suriname, there was not enough work on the plantations or fertile ground to provide them with after emancipation. This problem was solved by the introduction of a system of share cropping, called *paga-tera* (Renkema 1981:150-1). From now on, no serious objections to emancipation were raised in the Dutch Antilles.

The Suriname Plantation Economy by Sector

In Suriname, as in several other Caribbean plantation economies during slavery, sugar was not the only, and sometimes not even the dominant export crop. The oldest plantations invariably produced sugar, but during the second quarter of the eighteenth century coffee proved to be more profitable, and this crop soon came to dominate the economy of Suriname. Most of the coffee planters did not belong to the old plantocracy. Taking advantage of the abundance of metropolitan capital available during the third quarter of the eighteenth century, aspiring new planters 'without a penny in the world' seized the opportunity to obtain generous loans to start and expand plantations of their own (Van Stipriaan 1993:207-15). As coffee was the most promising cash crop and needed less complicated technology than sugar, this sector expanded rapidly and soon outgrew sugar. The importance of sugar production declined even more at the turn of the eighteenth century, when cotton emerged as another booming plantation sector. Suriname became a multi-sector plantation economy, in which each sector was to have its own social and economic dynamics.

Table 2. Differences in the Suriname Plantation Economy by Sector

	sugar	coffee	cotton
demographic performance of slaves	extremely negative; improving considerably	negative; improving slowly	relatively good
debt situation and new capital after 1800	medium, new opportunities coming up promising	hopeless	
attitude towards innovation and reproduction	generally positive	negative	medium positive

Source: Van Stipriaan 1993:146-92, 205-56, 316-4.

Differences between the plantation sectors were partly due to different kinds of 'production mentality' (Table 2). For example, the management of coffee plantations by this new group of planters was definitely exhaustive, aiming at quick benefits without taking the reproduction of production factors into proper account. Consequently, before the turn of the eighteenth century these planters had exhausted the soil and trees as they used no rotation cycles or fertilizers; they had exhausted their slaves (surplus of deaths over births and no sufficient imports); and they had exhausted their credits without even being able to pay the interest. No innovation whatsoever, whether labor-saving or aiming at increased productivity, had been introduced. The only way in which these coffee planters tried to counter the deteriorating productivity of their plantations was by planting and harvesting from a maximum number of trees. Obviously, this policy worsened the problem of soil exhaustion.

Before the turn of the eighteenth century the rapid expansion of the coffee estates had reached its limits (Table 3). At the same time, the first substantial pieces of land on those estates had to be abandoned because they had been exploited too long. The slaves working the fields had to work even harder as a result of an increase of coffee-growing land and of the number of trees per worker.[5] Particularly after the 1770s, when planters no longer had the means to buy new slaves and the average death deficit in the coffee sector was 18.7 per 1,000 slaves a year, the number of field slaves – approximately half of the total slave population on a coffee plantation – dropped substantially (Van Stipriaan 1993:128, 318).

Table 3. The Average Coffee Plantation, 1750-1830

	acreage			field slaves	one fieldslave works	
	total (ha)	coffee (%)	abandoned (%)		coffee (acres)	coffee (trees)
ca 1750	235	18	1	41	0.9	825
ca 1770	295	28	2	68	1.1	1,262
ca 1790	301	30	7	50	1.7	2,116
ca 1810	300	27	14	45	1.8	2,405
ca 1830	335	19	27	46	1.4	1,997

Source: Van Stipriaan 1993:60-1, 129.

One reason why planters urged slaves to increase production was the financial slump in the sector. Since the end of the 1770s, the majority of the coffee sector was heavily burdened with debts; at the same time, the price of

---

[5] Between c 1750 and c 1825, the average number of coffee trees per hectare increased from 966 to 1458 (Van Stipriaan 1993:128).

coffee on the open Dutch staple market had fallen dramatically.[6] In this context, the Dutch investment structure revealed its fundamental shortcomings. Between 1765 and 1775 some thirty million guilders were pumped into the Suriname plantation economy by Dutch investment funds – so-called *negotiaties* – directed by merchant bankers, who offered easy obtainable plantation mortgages to aspiring planters. Many grabbed the opportunity, dreaming of the easy fortunes they would make. Obviously there were risks. The mortgage maximum was therefore generally limited to five-eighths of the appraised value of the plantation, and the interest rate was five to six per cent, twice as high as in the Netherlands. Furthermore, the planters were obliged to conduct their entire trade via the merchant bankers in Amsterdam or Rotterdam. These merchants were in a very favorable position. Without having to risk their own capital – they only directed a fund paid by others – the merchants charged commission on every commercial transaction performed for the mortgaged plantation. More production meant more commission, irrespective of the eventual financial benefit to the investors. Another shortcoming in the investment structure was that planters could obtain a higher mortgage as soon as the estimated value of their plantation rose, on the (not always correct) assumption that the productive capacity had expanded as well.

As coffee proved to be the most promising cash crop since the 1740s, most of the easily obtainable Dutch credit had been used to lay out and expand coffee plantations. A new plantation sector arose, built by planters without any capital of their own, and often lacking the specific knowledge required to run a coffee plantation. As long as the estimated value of their plantations increased, they were able to obtain more credit to buy slaves and plant more trees, helping them to a substantial income sufficient for the required debt servicing.

As mentioned above, one weakness was that credit was linked to the estimated value of the plantation without taking into account its real productive capacity. Planters regularly had their enterprises revalued, always securing a higher figure which permitted them to obtain more credit. Such increases in value were to some extent the result of the expansion of the coffee acreage and the slave force, but particularly in the investment flurry around 1770 speculation and even fraud were evident too. Either way, part of the credits were spent on conspicuous consumption.

The system started to falter when a growing number of planters were unable to pay their interest. It collapsed completely the moment this new generation of planters had to start paying off their mortgages, which happened to coincide with falling coffee prices. Many went bankrupt; the coffee

---

[6] The average price during the years 1765-69 as well as 1770-74 was 92 cents per kg, whereas in the next five years it fell to 62 cents per kg (Van Stipriaan 1993:434-5).

sector now entered a period of decay. Ownership often passed into the hands of the unfortunate suppliers of credit. They could not immediately sell off these plantations as there were no serious buyers. Instead, they opted for trying to get as much as possible out of their properties for as long as possible. New investments were not a serious option any longer.

This arrangement continued to be profitable for the merchant bankers, because their risks were minimal and commission still came in, though less than before. Even for those investors who did not panic and kept their shares in the *negotiatie* funds, the final outcome was less disastrous than might have been expected; eventually they saw some return on their capital. An earlier emancipation would not have helped them. Free labor would not have stopped the exhaustion process. Perhaps an awareness that emancipation would entail compensation for the owners would have won some investors for this solution, for they could have used this money to convert the plantations for the production of cash crops which were still sustainable on the exhausted coffee estates, such as sugar. All this is hypothetical: emancipation had not yet become a political or public issue in the Netherlands.

The situation in the sugar sector was quite different. When Dutch capital was abundant in the colony, no more than half of the sugar planters mortgaged their plantations to secure their share of the abundant credit pie. Those who did borrow substantial sums generally spent it productively rather than on conspicuous consumption. The sugar sector had a long-standing tradition of innovation, ranging from the *polder* system and the use of hydraulic energy to the introduction of new cane varieties and steam power (Van Stipriaan 1989:96-103). Again in contrast to the coffee sector, even the first sugar plantations in Suriname had been laid out by experienced planters – particularly Jewish refugees from Brazil in the mid-seventeenth century. Most sugar plantations were established (long) before the credit bubble and had at least partly been financed by the planters themselves. The sugar sector was generally managed with a more efficient and prudent productive mentality than the coffee sector. Sugar planters who did not innovate and expand, mortgaging their plantations in the same way as their colleagues in the coffee sector, only formed a minority which indeed failed to survive.

Table 4. Type of Mill and Viability of Sugar Plantations, 1755-1857*

	animal traction	water traction	steam traction	sugar production abandoned
ca 1755	34	9	–	–
ca 1780	15	26	–	2
1857	–	11	18	14

* Sample of 43 plantations.
Source: Van Stipriaan 1989:97.

A representative sample of forty-three sugar plantations (Table 4) shows that fourteen did not survive until the mid-nineteenth century. Ten of these were operated by an animal traction mill until the very end. On the other hand, of the twenty-nine surviving plantations at least eight had installed a more advanced – and thereby more productive – type of mill during these years. The largest shift from animal to water traction – a very costly affair – was made precisely during the credit bubble of the 1760s and early 1770s. Therefore, after the turn of the eighteenth century the sugar sector faced a brighter future and was not as burdened with debts as the coffee sector (Table 5). Sugar was even able to attract new capital and new private and governmental initiative.[7]

Table 5. Profitability by Sector, 1775 - 1855

period	coffee sector		sugar sector	
	average profit per slave*	number of plantations	average profit per slave*	number of plantations
ca 1775	ƒ -51	295	ƒ -15	111
ca 1795	-50	248	23	102
ca 1815	40	235	21	100
ca 1835	4	137	8	105
ca 1855	3	62	17	91

* Based on samples of 4-23 (coffee) and 6-11 (sugar) plantations. As slaves were the most important and most constant 'capital goods', the average yearly profit is related to the number of slaves per plantation. Profits are inclusive of interest payments and redemptions of mortgages and other debts.[8]
Source: Van Stipriaan 1993:268-71, 438.

The drop in profitability in the sugar sector during the 1830s (Table 5) was not so much due to the continually falling sugar price,[9] as to the conversion of water mills to steam engines and other modern machinery, which entailed heavy investments. However, these innovations apparently did

---

[7] For example, in 1827 Inspector General Johannes van den Bosch was sent to Suriname to see how the plantation economy could be made more profitable. He strongly advised the authorities to promote the sugar sector combined with steam technology, and to found a private bank to finance those plantations (Van Stipriaan 1993:246-52).
[8] These figures should be employed with the utmost care, particularly those of the coffee sector. The reason is that we only have archival material at our disposal for plantations that did not go bankrupt (immediately). These (atypical) plantations are therefore overrepresented in the nineteenth-century samples. For example, the all-time high profits (because of all-time high prices) in the coffee sector around 1815 are in striking contrast to the process of exhaustion or the fact that since the 1770s more than one-fifth of the plantations had stopped producing coffee and many more were to follow.
[9] The average price of sugar during the 1820s was 39 cents per kg, during the 1830s 31 cents per kg, and during the 1840s 25 cents per kg (Van Stipriaan 1993:268).

pay off, as despite a further decline in sugar prices, profitability increased once again during the last decade before Emancipation. Clearly, then, under these circumstances 1863 was not the most appropriate moment to abolish slavery.

The cotton sector occupied an intermediate position between the coffee and sugar sectors. Part of the cotton estates were former coffee plantations where a (timely) switch to cotton had been made. The rest of this sector was completely new, including new capital and a new group of planters, both for the major part from Britain. The section of the cotton sector originating in the languishing coffee sector was characterized by exhaustion, while the other, newer section was marked by innovation and reproduction.[10] Either way, this sector could not survive in the long run because of ecological problems (ocean flooding, insect plagues), and the fall in prices since the 1830s. There was no indication that free labor would have been advantageous to the survival of this sector. The cotton from the major producer, the United States, was all slave-grown, and Suriname's neighbor Guiana saw its cotton production decline even faster after slavery was abolished in that colony (Mandle 1973:18).

No more new plantations[11] were laid out in Suriname after the early 1820s, and the total number of plantations dropped from 383 in 1810 to 161[12] just before Emancipation. Particularly the coffee and cotton sectors of the plantation economy seemed to account for this decline, as the number of sugar plantations remained roughly the same. However, the situation was a bit more complex. From the early 1820s until Emancipation, some thirty-five coffee and cotton plantations switched to sugar production, while during the same period some fifty plantations stopped sugar production. On most plantations the switch to sugar production had been made during the 1820s and 1830s. Even so, eight plantations only switched around 1850, while the first, and for a long time the only central sugar factory was also installed around that time.

---

[10] Van Stipriaan 1993:140-4, 186-91. On the other hand, eleven of the remaining twenty-six cotton plantations in 1856 were operated with a steam engine, and the introduction of new cotton varieties seems to have been almost common practice (*Koloniaal Verslag* 1856; Van Stipriaan 1993:187).
[11] The word plantation is used only for large-scale agricultural enterprises where cash crops were grown for an international market. I do not include large-scale timber plantations, nor cattle or food crop plantations.
[12] This figure includes twenty-three cacao plantations.

Table 6. The Suriname Plantation Economy, 1810-1862

year	plantations	slaves	sugar under cultivation (ha)	production (1,000 tonnes)
1810	100	10,108	6,425	8,8
1825	95	12,352	6,459	11,4
1836	105	17,659	8,674	16,6
1849	92	?	7,989	16,1
1854	91	17,884	8,750	17,1
1862	86	19,789	8,903	16,9

year	plantations	slaves	coffee + cotton under cultivation (ha)	coffee production (1,000 tonnes)	cotton production (1,000 tonnes)
1810	283	27,660	?	3,0	0,7
1825	251	25,653	21,087	2,4	1,0
1836	189	19,487	12,187	1,3	0,7
1849	115	?	8,766	0,5	0,4
1854	92	10,681	7,026	0,3	0,4
1862	52	6,443	3,464	0,1	0,2

Source: Van Stipriaan 1993:311, 438-9 and *Koloniaal Verslag* 1849.

After its long eclipse by coffee, sugar entered its second youth during the first decades of the nineteenth century. Between c 1810 and 1862, the slave population of this sector almost doubled, as did production. Profitability rose 1820s and 1830s. The Suriname sugar sector had always ranked among the most productive and technologically most advanced of the Caribbean.[13] Suriname sugar planters therefore saw no advantage in duplicating the abolition of slavery announced in the British West Indies. The second phase of expansion, which started around 1850, was aborted by the now impending Emancipation in Suriname. For the Suriname sugar sector, Emancipation came at the worst moment imaginable. The second phase of expansion and innovation started in Suriname at roughly the same time as it did in the

[13] Average Annual Sugar Output of Caribbean Slaves, 1820, 1830

	kg/slave (c 1820)	kg/slave (c 1830)
Barbados	186	242
Jamaica	474	413
Grenada	521	539
Antigua	431	362
St. Vincent	727	781
Trinidad	531	851
Guiana	437	926
Suriname	926	941

Source: Van Stipriaan 1993:139.

free-labor sugar sector of neighboring British Guiana and the slave sugar sector of Cuba, by then the two most advanced sugar producers of the Caribbean.[14] During the 1840s the Guianese planters had abundant capital at their disposal – partly state-financed compensation payments for the loss of their slaves – which were used for the modernization of sugar production (Adamson 1972:173; Green 1976:203). In Cuba, where the abolition of slavery seemed a distant probability, substantial innovation in the sugar sector only got underway in the 1850s, when a new wave of credits was made available to the planters (Watts 1987:489). In Suriname, the overall modernization of the sugar sector failed to gain momentum, because in anticipation of Emancipation, few potential creditors remained seriously interested in the colony.

Suriname Planters and Abolition, 1800-1848

Not surprisingly, the Suriname planter class opposed abolition, and made this point repeatedly. For example, a group of planters stated in a note referring to the first official Emancipation proposal that

> 'all this artificial emancipation of people with a civilization which has not yet climbed up to the [required] level for freedom is untimely, dangerous, and unfavorable to the state'.[15]

However, this generalization does not help us much in understanding the late timing of emancipation in Suriname. First, the Suriname planters can hardly be considered as a single, homogeneous class. A substantial part had lived in Suriname for generations and did not have many ties with the Netherlands, such as Sephardic and Azhkenazi Jews, or the descendants of French Huguenots. Others had only recently become planters in Suriname and had no ties with the Netherlands either, such as the British group. Next, there was the powerful group of administrators, some of whom merely acted as representatives of absentee owners, while others owned plantations themselves. Finally, there was a small but growing group of planters and administrators of mixed black and white descent, anxious to play their part in colonial society, but held in low esteem by their white colleagues.

There were other lines of division too. The interests of coffee planters differed from those in the sugar sector, which did not parallel cotton interests either. Thus, in the course of the nineteenth century, it became clear that the coffee sector was doomed. Nevertheless, many coffee planters

---

[14] Around 1860, the output per hectare of total cane acreage was 1,899 kg in Suriname, as against 1,861 kg in Cuba, and 2,931 kg in Guiana (Van Stipriaan 1993:138-40, 181-2).
[15] Cited in Siwpersad 1979:184. All quotations in this text are translated from the Dutch original by the author.

had a direct interest in the continuation of slavery, because the slackening pace of work on their own plantations enabled them to hire out their slaves at a good margin to sugar plantations. On the other hand, not all sugar planters were as fervently opposed to the abolition of slavery as it might seem. Some of their spokesmen used free contract laborers from Madeira and China alongside their slaves almost a decade before Emancipation.[16] The main issue for these planters became that of financial compensation for the loss of their human capital. This money could be employed to expand and modernize their enterprises.

Not surprisingly, the sugar lobby was most outspoken. Between 1848 and 1857, seven influential missives were sent to the Dutch king or the Minister of Colonial Affairs, signed by various groups of owners and/or administrators of Suriname plantations residing in the Netherlands or Suriname. The most influential opinion leaders numbered no more than twelve, even though they spoke on behalf of many more.[17] In 1853 this group of twelve had interests in thirty sugar plantations, ten coffee estates, and five cotton plantations. They represented one-third of the sugar sector, but no more than one-sixth of the other sectors.[18] Their sugar plantations were among the most advanced in Suriname.[19] Quite understandably in view of the decline of these sectors, neither the coffee nor the cotton sector had such influential spokesmen.

In the end, it seems that in colonial Suriname substantial changes in this plantation economy were only implemented when there was no alternative and/or in response to serious external pressure. This phenomenon persisted throughout the nineteenth-century history of slavery. It may first be observed in the formal acceptance of the abolition of the slave trade as one of the conditions under which England returned Suriname to the Dutch

---

[16] Around the mid-1850s, H. Wright and E. van Emden, two leading sugar planters, both employed some thirty laborers from Madeira along with 112 and 257 slaves, respectively, on their plantations 'Boxel' and 'De Drie Gebroeders'. In 1858, they were among the twelve planters who contracted twenty-five laborers each from the first shipload of Chinese indentured laborers (Van Sypesteyn 1854:98-9; *Almanak* 1859:76-7, 130-1).

[17] See, for example, the petition by Van Emden in 1852 on behalf of 105 'colonists'; the others were G.C. Bosch Reitz, R. Le Chevalier, P.C. Gulcher, J.J. Poncelet and Co., H. Wright, C.L. Röperhoff, H. Bijlaart, U.H. Wilkens, D. Taunay and Insinger and Co. (Siwpersad 1979:158, 181, 186, 211-4).

[18] That is, 30 out of a total of 91 plantations, employing 37 per cent of the slaves in that sector. The totals for the coffee and cotton sectors were 62 and 30 respectively (Van Sypesteyn 1854:96-147).

[19] Particularly 'De Drie Gebroeders' (Van Emden), 'Hooyland' and 'Alkmaar' (Wright), and 'De Resolutie' (Bijlaart and Röperhoff) were well equipped and year after year ranked among the ten best producing sugar plantations of the colony. In 1858-1860, these four plantations produced more than ten per cent of Suriname's total sugar output (*Koloniale Verslagen* 1855-1862).

king in 1814. As a consequence of the Napoleonic wars, Suriname had been occupied by the British during the years 1799-1802 and again in 1804-1814. When Britain abolished the slave trade in 1808, this measure therefore included Suriname. Some protests were uttered at the time (Van Stipriaan 1993:318; Wolbers 1861:546), but no more planters' protests were voiced after 1808, and upon the return of Suriname to the Kingdom of the Netherlands in 1814 the Dutch Crown accepted the fait accompli without significant opposition. The absence of subsequent planters' protests may have been due partly to the continuing illegal slave imports, despite British control; some 1,000 slaves were estimated to be smuggled into Suriname each year.[20]

Upon the return of Suriname to the Netherlands the Dutch king not only confirmed the abolition of the slave trade with Africa at the special request of the British ambassador in The Hague, but he was also made to accept the installation of a mixed Anglo-Dutch court in Paramaribo to supervise its compliance (Emmer 1974:184). The one exception to this rule may have satisfied the demand of Suriname planters for 'fresh' slaves. A provision was made that intra-Caribbean slave trade between countries that had also abolished the slave trade with Africa was not forbidden. Unintentionally, this provision implied that wherever traders managed to import African slaves illegally, they could proceed by legally selling them to other colonies. In this way, particularly via the French West Indies, Suriname planters were able to import another 12,000 new slaves until 1827, when registration of all the slaves and further British pressure finally put an end to the slave trade (Van Stipriaan 1993:107).

The consequence of the full abolition of the slave trade was that the demise of slavery itself became inevitable. On the one hand, there was the factor of a structural demographic decrease of the slave population. On the other hand, measures to counter this decrease, such as an amelioration policy towards the slaves, would in the long run also make the system disappear, or at least undermine it. Any improvement in the conditions of slavery had a price, financially as well as psychologically. A better-fed slave could work harder, but would also be able to demand more food – which was exactly what happened, as will be demonstrated below.

Even so, when Britain abolished slavery in 1834 there was no need for the Suriname planters – nor the Dutch government – to follow this exceptional example. Irrespective of the outcome of the debate on slavery, the coffee sector was doomed. The cotton sector did not 'know' yet that it had just entered a downward spiral, whereas the sugar sector was innovating and on its way up again. All other interested parties simply aimed at getting as much out of the plantations as they could for as long as they could. In sum,

---

[20] Wolbers 1861:547. The total slave population of Suriname in 1813 was 44,000 (Van Stipriaan 1993:311).

no calculating entrepreneur needed or wanted the change to free labor or the obvious instability that went along with it. There was no point in following the British example, particularly as no other nation joined the United Kingdom.

The dominant attitude towards Emancipation among Suriname planters seems to have been evasive. The plantocracy did not react until it thought itself unjustly attacked by outsiders who pleaded for abolition by depicting or concocting the 'horrors' of slavery.[21] In fact, occasionally a planter even spoke out precisely in favor of Emancipation.[22] The high colonial officer W.H. Lans drew up several emancipation models during the 1830s and 1840s, but his long-term plans were too far-reaching and/or too costly to convince the Dutch government or the colonial authorities.[23] During the early 1840s there was an ongoing (parliamentary) discussion about the introduction of substantially improved slave regulations, which were seen by many as a first step towards Emancipation. Plantation owners who joined the debates sent one memo after another to the metropolitan parliament, advising Dutch policy-makers not to interfere in these colonial matters, redressing their negative image, and arguing that the slaves were not yet civilized enough to benefit from full freedom (Oostindie 1992). The case in favor of amelioration as a prelude to Emancipation was defended by such prominent spokesmen as the Governor of Suriname, B.J. Elias, and the Minister of Colonial Affairs, J.C. Baud. Their support for amelioration, however, was fiercely contested. In 1845, Elias resigned as governor of Suriname

---

[21] For example, the accusations made in a circular by the Moravian missionary Otto Tank about the maltreatment of slaves in Suriname were countered in a publication by the three influential planters and administrators E. van Emden, H.G. Roux and J. Frouin. Likewise, when the Dutch member of parliament Van Hoëvell published his Suriname version of *Uncle Tom's Cabin* (Van Hoëvell 1854), he was rebuked by the lawyer and administrator of the colony's first private central sugar factory, B.E.C. Belmonte. The latter provocatively defended the slave owners of Suriname against Van Hoëvell's accusations of their barbarious behavior, but in the end he came up with an emancipation model of his own which was not even that conservative (Van Winter 1953:76-7; Siwpersad 1979:213).

[22] For example, in 1839 J.J. Bueno de Mesquita, the owner of two vast timber estates and one coffee plantation, sent a request to the Dutch king for the creation of a reserve fund to pay for the emancipation of the slaves in Suriname. According to him, abolition was unavoidable now that the British had shown the way (Siwpersad 1979:181). Nothing was ever heard of this request.

[23] Lans's first Emancipation proposal dates from 1833 and was stimulated by the ad interim Minister of Colonial Affairs, G.G. Clifford. In this proposal he stated that in order to keep the emancipated slaves working, the sugar plantations would have to be converted to the production of less demanding crops such as coconuts and vanilla. His 1844 Emancipation model – which was supported by the Minister of Colonial Affairs, J.C. Baud – suggested that all slaves and plantations should be expropriated by the state and that the former owners should be compensated with bonds worth ƒ24.6 million. All plantations were to be planted with sugar cane and worked by slaves, while the processing of sugar would take place in thirty-seven central factories (costing another ƒ3.5 million). In this scheme, the slaves became free once all bonds had been paid off (Siwpersad 1979:6-8, 134-54).

without having obtained acceptance of amelioration policies (Siwpersad 1979:115-23). Perhaps by then amelioration was indeed accepted as wise management, but Emancipation continued to be seen as something for the distant future. Meanwhile, the plantocracy simply begged to be left alone by those European 'philantropists' who did not know anything about the colony, where the planters themselves were trying to bring civilization and prosperity to all.[24]

Despite such petitions and discussions, the public debate on questions of slavery and emancipation was meager up to 1848. The only serious publications in favor of emancipation were those by M.D. Teenstra (1842), J. van Ouwerkerk de Vries (1841), and J. de Neufville (1841); the latter received an anonymous reply by 'a Colonist' (Kolonist 1842). All this changed after 1848, during the fifteen years leading up to Emancipation in 1863, when at least twenty-five book(let)s[25] were published in favor of the abolition of slavery, against some fifteen defending the status quo.[26]

Planters, Slaves, and Emancipation, 1848-1863

Until 1848, British Emancipation had been the exception. In 1848, however, as a consequence of revolutionary changes at home, the French suddenly followed the British example. The Suriname planters were shocked, not in the least because they were now surrounded by plantation colonies where slavery was abolished.[27] As one planter wrote:

> 'Now a new and very eminent danger threatens us. I mean the emancipation of the slaves in the French colonies. This information will soon blow over to Suriname from the neigboring colony of Cayenne.'[28]

After 1848, Suriname planters were not so much concerned with the question of whether Emancipation would come, but how soon and how. The latter in particular became their main concern: how would they be compensated by the Dutch government? All planters agreed that there could

---

[24] Indeed, medical care, food, housing, and labor conditions on the plantations were gradually improving during the nineteenth century. As a consequence, birth rates rose from 18.6 per 1,000 plantation slaves around 1800 to 28.9 per 1,000 during the 1850s, and mortality declined during the same period from 40.7 to 34.6 per 1,000 plantation slaves (Van Stipriaan 1993:323, 332).
[25] Of twenty pages or more.
[26] Counted in Waaldijk 1959:78-128. One-third of the fifteen pro-slavery tracts were anonymous.
[27] Except, of course, for Brazil, but the enormous Amazon jungle separating Brazil and Suriname made this country seem farther away than Europe.
[28] Letter from the planter Vereul to the Minister of Colonial Affairs (in Algemeen Rijksarchief (ARA): Ministerie van Koloniën (1814-1849) 1853, 6 May 1848; my translation.

be no Emancipation without a 'fair compensation'.[29] This indeed was one of the few causes in Suriname history on which all planters agreed.

Discussions of fair compensation seemed to continue endlessly. Meanwhile, with the new slave regulations of 1851 and 1856, 'amelioration' had become the official policy. The 1851 regulations were the immediate result of the events of 1848. The revolutionary government in France proclaimed the abolition of slavery on 27 April 1848. Less than three weeks later, on 15 May the Dutch Minister of Colonial Affairs ad interim, J.C. Rijk, sent a circular to the 'Suriname interest' in Amsterdam[30] in which he warned that 'to stick stubbornly to the principle of slavery in the way it still exists in Suriname [is] highly dangerous' (cited in Siwpersad 1979:157-8). He continued by summoning the planters 'to soften the fate of the slaves in order to diminish motives for rebellion and desertion', for which he gave a long list of practical ameliorations. The answer of G.C. Bosch Reitz and twenty-five other interested persons shows how shocked they were by the 1848 events. Quite timidly they replied that 'after mature deliberation and after having taken into consideration the signs of the times', they were now willing to submit to the Minister's recommendations with only a few alterations (Siwpersad 1979:158).

In 1851 these regulations were formalized as a slave law, which prescribed an amelioration in the formal conditions of slavery. However, according to a growing number of politicians and some Christian social movements, the influence of the planters' interests was still too visible; the law did not provide for Emancipation in the near future. After further parliamentary discussion this criticism was met by the installation of a Staatscommissie in November 1853. The term Emancipation was not mentioned in its instructions. However, the Commission report published in August 1855 not only helped to further improve the slave regulations (1856), but also precipitated the final abolition of slavery (Siwpersad 1979:223-8). That the final decision was postponed until the early 1860s was entirely a financial matter.

For many planters and their representatives in Amsterdam – as well as for some conservative politicians – the enactment of improved slave regulations was reason enough to postpone Emancipation. In the meantime slave owners could try to obtain maximal compensation for the future loss of

---

[29] See, for example, the petitions of G.C. Bosch Reitz et al. (1848) and Van Emden et al. (1852) in Siwpersad 1979:180-7, 212-3.
[30] A group of thirty to forty absentee plantation owners or their representatives, mainly resident in Amsterdam. Its spokesmen were G.C. Bosch Reitz (owner and administrator), J.J. Poncelet and Co (merchant, owner and administrator), and A. Brugmans (a barrister specialized in Suriname cases). In 1853, 57 per cent of the 189 Suriname plantations producing for export were absentee owned, mainly by Dutch. This Amsterdam-based interest group was crucial to the Suriname plantation economy.

their slaves, whereas the politicians would have time to think about the cheapest possible way to emancipate the slaves. One factor, however, increasingly put pressure on the timing of Emancipation, a pressure neither planters nor the authorities could ignore: the slaves themselves. Characteristic of these developments was a 1849 letter from Suriname, published in a Dutch newspaper:

> 'The [plantation] director, who used to have moral power over the slaves, is now being treated by the slaves with disdain. The subordination is completely undermined. Now the servants are beginning to scare the masters. Let us hope that the government will soon take measures to proclaim the abolition of slavery here. The negroes live in hopes of soon shaking off their yoke, yet if this would not be realized I am fearful of the consequences.'[31]

These words were true. The slaves were certainly aware of the fact that the planters had become increasingly dependent on them, particularly since the import of new slaves had come to an end. They used this situation to create more room and rights for themselves in everyday plantation life, and gradually began to behave as a relatively independent proto-peasantry.[32] To mention just one example, the food supply of the free population came to depend increasingly on what the slaves produced in their own time, on their 'own' subsistence land, for their own profit. An overseer or director who did not respect the slaves' 'rights' to this business was confronted with obstinacy – to say the least – and often had to be fired or transferred to another plantation.

Moreover, the slaves' rights were now actively supported by the colonial authorities. With a view to maintaining law and order and to keeping the slaves from rebelling, they did not want the improved slave regulations of 1851 and 1856 to remain a dead letter. Consequently, from 1853 on an annual average of forty-five plantation managers or owners – ten to twenty per cent of the total – received an official warning about not having (fully) observed the slave regulations. An average of eight were brought to trial every year, mainly for imposing more severe punishments than the law allowed (Van den Boogaart and Emmer 1977:209). Even if the authorities would have preferred to close their eyes to the violations of the slaves' rights, the victims forced them to look. During the years 1848-1863, at least thirty-nine plantations witnessed a combination of rioting and running away. In twenty-four cases the slaves did not run away to hide in the woods but went to Paramaribo to complain to the Attorney General about the violation of their rights, maltreatment, or related grievances (Kool 1993:75). A striking example of this new attitude on the part of slaves and at least some officials alike happened in 1857. A female slave, Sanna, complained to the Attorney

---

[31] Cited in Toes 1992:27.
[32] See for example Van Stipriaan 1992, and 1993:385-407.

General that her mistress had unjustly beaten her in the face. The only thing that had happened, she claimed, was that when her mistress had reprimanded her for spoiling a basket full of flour, Sanna had told her that freedom was near and that slaves and masters would soon be equals. In former times Sanna would have received a severe punishment for such 'impertinence'; now Sanna's mistress had to pay a fine of twenty guilders (Toes 1992:155-7).

Slave rebelliousness had indeed become a national and chronic phenomenon in Suriname by that time (Table 7).

Table 7. Rebelliousness on Suriname Plantations, 1820-1862*

period	number of plantations involved
1820-1833	24
1834-1847	27 (1841: general unrest and rebelliousness because of Emancipation rumors)
1848-1862	61 (1857: general unrest and rebelliousness because of Emancipation rumors)

* (strikes, Marronage and/or riots of at least 10 slaves).
Source: Van Stipriaan 1993:448-9 and Kool 1993:137-43.

The rebellions and Maroon wars of the eighteenth century have overshadowed nineteenth-century slave resistance in Suriname. Not only was the latter less spectacular or dramatic, but, more importantly, the objectives of the slaves had changed. In the mid-eighteenth century, almost three-quarters of the slave population were still born in Africa, whereas a century later the majority were born in Suriname and some were even third- or fourth-generation Surinamers. This evolution had direct repercussions. When eighteenth-century slaves ran off to the woods to join the Maroon communities, they mostly did so because they had reached the limits of what they could take and because they had little to lose. In the woods, far from colonial society, they had an opportunity to start a new life; though hard, it was free and resembled life back in Africa. Since the end of the eighteenth century, after the major Maroon communities were either formally recognized by the colonial authorities or chased away from the colony, chances for new runaway slaves to join the Maroons were no longer good.[33] Nevertheless, nineteenth-century slaves ran away from the plantations on a larger scale than ever before. Paradoxically, it might be claimed that they did so precisely to help them stay on the plantation. The slaves now had more to lose because they had strong roots on the plantations. The

---

[33] For the colonial authorities, the most important part of the peace treaties with the Ndjuka (1760), the Saramaka (1762), and the Matawai (1767) Maroons was the condition that every newly-arrived runaway had to be handed over immediately.

plantation was the place where they were born, where they had relatives, and where they had built up a common culture, undeniably African-based, but combined with a variety of European elements and adapted to Suriname plantation life. This creolization process, in which a heterogeneous West-African 'crowd' turned into a rather homogeneous Afro-Suriname 'community' (Mintz and Price 1992:18), made the slaves stronger and more independent. This in itself implied a structural threat to the slave system. Moreover, the plantation increasingly became a place where slaves made some money for themselves by way of a variety of small-scale agricultural and craft activities.

To defend this proto-peasant type of life within the slave plantation system, slaves used all kinds of resistance, including running away. However, they no longer marooned desperately to leave colonial society behind. On the contrary, they ran away temporarily as a way to obtain more space within the system, or to show that their rights had been violated; after a while, most runaways returned to their plantation. Sometimes a complete slave population withdrew from its plantation in protest and stayed in the woods until its demands were satisfied, or at least heard. Such actions resemble labor strikes in industrialized Europe later that century. In Suriname, these strikes had become a mighty weapon in the slaves' hands long before 1848. Just like the creolization process, this struggle was not directly aimed at the abolition of slavery, but it severely underminded the system and boosted the emancipation of the slaves.

An example may underline this point. In 1828, one of the absentee owners of the Potribo plantation came to Suriname to visit his estate. Five field slaves used the opportunity to run away after first having spoiled some of the recently produced sugar. No causes were given in the reports on these events, but it is plausible that the plantation director wanted to impress his superior because of the expected visit and pressed the slaves to work harder than usual. The runaway slaves returned to the plantation after some time and were severely punished, together with the black overseer whose 'misbehavior' was held responsible for 'the existing confusion and irregularity'.

After his visit, the owner concluded that the sugar production of Potribo could be expanded considerably. This was immediately put into practice. Between 1828 and 1835, the sugar acreage doubled from 47 to 94 hectares; already in 1830, the administrator reported that he could hardly recognize the plantation.[34] The same year, however, the owners in Amsterdam received 'bitter complaints about the recalcitrant and rebellious behavior of the negroes'. Some time afterwards, they received a message that the plantation's complete slave population, with the exception of old women and

---

[34] Gemeente Archief Amsterdam (GAA): PA-600/544.

children, had retreated to the forest hinterland of the plantation. The administrators then investigated the plantation's management, and concluded 'that this man had given the slaves no other cause for discontent and misbehavior than his persistence and pressing for orderly and industrious work'.[35] Nevertheless, they saw no solution except to replace this director. At this decision, the entire slave force returned to the plantation. The slaves were apparently not unwilling to lay out more sugar fields; afterwards, with the assistance of newly bought slaves from another plantation, the expansion was realized without any recorded protest. The extra help must have been crucial. In the earlier phase, they may have felt that the obligation to work harder without rewards was a violation of the established routine, because it meant less time and energy for their own activities – an infringement they were not willing to accept. The impact of such strikes – Potribo was no exception (Van Stipriaan 1992) – must have been considerable. News travelled fast among the plantations, and such actions encouraged other slave forces to stand firm in their own struggles.

After 1848, when slavery was abolished in most Caribbean countries, and more particularly in neigboring British and French Guiana, the Suriname slaves became even more restless and were anxious for their own Emancipation. In 1841 and 1857 this led to almost nationwide unrest and rebelliousness on the plantations, when the proclamation of formal ameliorations in slave labor conditions invoked the rumor that Emancipation was imminent.[36] The slaves' hopes were strengthened by the fact that their voice was indeed acknowledged now and by the amelioration process itself, which had assumed a rhythm of its own. What they most probably did not know was that, in the country where the decision on the abolition of slavery had to be taken, their rebelliousness as well as comments on ill-treatment were used as arguments in a sort of press campaign.[37] Although this campaign was not a decisive factor in the abolition of slavery, it certainly played a role in The Hague (Van Winter 1953:86-7; Toes 1992:168-76). Without these pressing circumstances, the abolition of slavery in the Dutch West Indies would probably have taken even longer than it did.

---

[35] Gemeente Archief Amsterdam (GAA): PA-600/544.
[36] The new slave regulations of 1856 stated that working during the night – which was sometimes necessary during harvest – was only permitted if those nights were compensated with a day off. At first the slaves interpreted this as a prohibition on work after six p.m. In the resulting labor unrest, rumors about an imminent Emancipation spread quickly.
[37] Toes 1992:168-76. Governor C.P. Schimpf in fact admitted that the fear of further rebelliousness was an argument used in favor of abolition when he spoke about those 'wrong notions, that when a general emancipation is delayed a rebellion of the slaves would have to be feared' (cited in Toes 1992:153).

Conclusion

Why, then, were the Dutch so late in abolishing slavery in Suriname? First of all, at no point in the history of this plantation colony would abolition have been logical from an economic point of view. The Suriname plantation economy was not ruled by king sugar, but consisted of three major sectors, each with its own dynamics. The least unlikely moment might have been around 1780, when the coffee boom was over its zenith, the plantations were burdened with heavy debts, and the dwindling slave imports combined with the structural death deficit resulted in a continually diminishing slave population. Perhaps coffee could have survived as a peasant crop, while sugar could have been produced by free labor on the plantations – even if there is no indication that this would have meant the cheaper production of sugar.

Anyway, around 1780 abolition was not yet on the agenda. When Suriname was returned to the Netherlands after the British interregnum (1799-1816), coffee had already entered a cul-de-sac, and emancipation did not offer a way out. For the cotton sector, a change to free labor was of no importance either. After the flourishing 1820s, this sector slowly deteriorated as a consequence of ecological disasters and the dominance of the market by the cheaper, slave-grown cotton from the USA. Finally, during the 1820s and 1830s, the productivity of slaves in the Suriname sugar sector was higher than in any British Caribbean plantation economy, profitability was reasonably good, and a new phase of innovation had started. A switch to free labor might have given these favorable developments an extra stimulus, but it was not exactly required. Moreover, the cloud of the coffee sector disaster was still hanging over the plantation economy and scared away potential creditors; Emancipation would probably have worsened the colony's credibility. When Emancipation was finally enacted, it came at an untimely moment during the second phase of innovation and expansion in the sugar sector.

In sum, for none of the plantation sectors in Suriname was there an economically 'logical' moment to abolish slavery. From this point of view, any date for Emancipation was as good or bad as any another. There was no need to do the same as the UK, particularly not as the British had already forced the Dutch to abolish the slave trade. Why follow the exception of Britain, rather than sticking with France, Spain, Denmark, Brazil, or the USA? Keeping a low profile and avoiding revolutionary changes was probably felt as the best remedy for the recovery of the Suriname plantation economy.

Another factor to explain the late timing of abolition, mentioned by Seymour Drescher too, is the fact that neither Suriname nor the Antilles were specifically Dutch colonies. In 1737, for example, at least half of the plantations were owned by people of non-Dutch origin, mostly Portuguese Jews from Brazil and former Huguenots from France (Van Stipriaan 1993:32). They were later joined by German Jews, while at the beginning of the nineteenth century a group of British planters entered the scene prominently, specifically in the cotton sector. The Suriname planter class and other interested parties had no strong ties with the politico-economic élite in the Netherlands. Moreover, the different 'production mentality' and interests per sector made the planters even less united than they could have been culturally, which again kept them from forming a front in their relations with the mother country. The market side of the relations between Suriname and the Netherlands provoked a lack of mutual commitment as well. Suriname products were never protected on the Dutch market like British West Indian produce. On the contrary, the Dutch market was open to any rival of Suriname, and Suriname sugar or coffee was never in a position to dominate this market.[38]

Drescher is therefore right in stating that economically, Suriname was never important enough, nor were its ties with the metropolis strong enough, to give birth to a strong abolitionist movement – nor to strong anti-abolitionist feelings, for that matter – in the Netherlands. More importantly, as a consequence of the same circumstances, a powerful Suriname or Dutch West Indian Interest never developed in Amsterdam or The Hague. This may be the crucial issue: perhaps a strong abolitionist movement could only develop if there was an influential planter lobby, such as the British West India interest. As such links between the Suriname plantation economy and Dutch politics never really matured, the Suriname lobby remained weak. Only after the 1840s, when particularly plantation owner G.C. Bosch Reitz and A. Brugmans, a barrister of 'Suriname' cases, became the self-appointed spokesmen of the Amsterdam-based absentee plantation owners or their representatives, could one speak of a more or less organized 'Suriname interest'.[39] By then, some successful Suriname administrators had made

[38] During the second half of the eighteenth century the Suriname share of sugar on the Dutch market fluctuated between 20 and 34 per cent, and that of coffee between 44 and 50. The rest came mainly from the French West Indies. This competition ended after the Haitian revolution, but then came the rise of Java. At the beginning of the nineteenth century, the two colonies' exports were almost of the same volume. At mid-century, Suriname produced some 15,000 tons of sugar but hardly any coffee, whereas Java exported 104,000 tons of sugar and 71,500 tons of coffee (Van Stipriaan 1993:263-4).

[39] For example, the 1849 official 'Commission of interested parties in Suriname agriculture', headed by Bosch Reitz. He was actually in favor of emancipation – he even designed an emancipation model – but, as a parliamentary commission put it, his protests at least suggested that his only goal was to get maximal compensation (Kuitenbrouwer 1978:77). Nevertheless, he was respected and, with Brugmans, he was appointed in the Staatscommissie of 1853 to represent the plantation owners. An abolitionist member of this commission resigned in 1854 because of Brugmans's inflexibility in aiming 'at an emancipation which could be

enough capital to retire to the Netherlands and become part of the Dutch élite. They helped to close the gap between the interested parties on both sides of the ocean.[40]

In the early 1840s the abolition movement finally gained momentum with the start of two petition actions against colonial slavery.[41] However, its impact was very limited (Van Winter 1953:61; Siwpersad 1979:191-2). It is telling that even this flurry of Dutch abolitionism, a paradoxical coalition of progressive Liberals and Evangelical Christians, was triggered by British abolitionists and Quakers (Van Winter 1953:65-6; Kuitenbrouwer 1978:75-6).

It was only in 1848 that the tide started to change, again as a consequence of outside events. Now Suriname became one of the remaining anomalies in the Caribbean and found itself surrounded by 'emancipated' plantation colonies. The abolition of slavery became inevitable, though the Suriname interest on both sides of the Atlantic, united for once, managed to postpone the final verdict for another fifteen years. It might have taken even longer, had it not been for the slaves who had already undermined the system for a long time. This process was no 'liberation struggle' like the eighteenth-century Maroon wars on the periphery of the plantation economy. It took place in the heart of the system, in the plantations, where creolization and (proto-)peasantization made the slaves claim and win increasingly more room for maneuver and rights. They knew Emancipation was coming, although twice they rejoiced too early. It is not surprising that at first they could not believe the news that on 1 July 1863 their Emancipation had indeed become a reality. 'Only [...] when the Attorney General would come

---

realized perhaps in a thousand years' (cited in Van Winter 1953:77).

[40] For example, the earlier mentioned reply to the 1848 circular of Minister Rijk to the 'Suriname Interest' in Amsterdam was signed by six people, three of whom had been administrator in Suriname; one was represented in Suriname by a relative. R. Le Chevalier and P.C. Gulcher had inherited some plantations, carried out the Dutch administration of a few others, and had probably never set foot in Suriname. U.H. Wilkens was born in Suriname; not long before coming to the Netherlands he owned two plantations and administered twenty-four others. D. Taunay was also born in Suriname, where his father had owned two plantations and administered thirty-eight others in the 1820s. E.G. Veldwijk, who left the colony in the early 1820s when he was about thirty-seven years old, owned one plantation and had administered at least ten plantations there. Finally, G.C. Bosch Reitz had probably never seen Suriname with his own eyes, but his interests in that colony – eight plantations, which he owned, had a share in, or administered – were represented there by a G.J.A. Bosch Reitz (Van Stipriaan 1993:295-9; Koninklijk Instituut voor de Tropen Amsterdam: Collection Van Breugel; Public Record Office London: CO 278/15).

The greater flexibility of the planters in Suriname is striking. When the abolitionist Attorney General in Suriname wrote to one of the abolitionist politicians in the Netherlands one month before Emancipation, he noted that the planters were rather dejected, but resigned themselves far better to the decision of parliament than the 'Suriname Interest' in Amsterdam, headed by Brugmans, who had never expected that the change to Emancipation could be decided upon without their consent (Van Winter 1953:88).

[41] See Kuitenbrouwer's article in this volume.

to the plantations to announce it, only then would they believe it.'[42] One cannot blame them: who would not have been cynical after such a long road to abolition?

[42] Letter by Attorney General J.W. Gefken, cited in Van Winter 1953:88.

References

Adamson, Alan H.
1972   *Sugar Without Slaves; The Political Economy of British Guiana, 1838-1904.* New Haven: Yale University Press.
Almanak
1788-1912   *West Indische Almanak/Surinaams(ch)e Almanak.* Amsterdam/'s-Gravenhage/Paramaribo: [various publishers].
Belmonte, B.E.C.
1855   *Neêrlands West-Indië in zijne belangen en Dr. W.R. van Hoëvell in zijne 'Slaven en vrijen'; Slavernij - emancipatie - kolonisatie.* Leiden: Van den Heuvell.
Boogaart, Ernst van den and Pieter C. Emmer
1977   'Plantation Slavery in Surinam in the Last Decade before Emancipation; The Case of Catharina Sophia', in: Vera Rubin and Arthur Tuden (eds), *Comparative Perspectives on Slavery in New World Plantation Societies,* pp. 205-25. New York: Annals of the New York Academy of Sciences.
Emden, Egbert van, H.G. Roux and J. Frouin
1848   *Onderzoek ten gevolge der circulaire van den heer Otto Tank [...].* Paramaribo: Muller Az.
Emmer, Pieter C.
1974   *Engeland, Nederland, Afrika en de slavenhandel in de negentiende eeuw.* Leiden: Brill.
Goslinga, Cornelis Ch.
1985   *The Dutch in the Caribbean and in the Guianas, 1680-1791.* Assen: Van Gorcum.
1990   *The Dutch in the Caribbean and in Surinam, 1791/5-1942.* Assen: Van Gorcum.
Green, William A.
1976   *British Slave Emancipation; The Sugar Colonies and the Great Experiment 1830-1865.* Oxford: Clarendon Press.
Hoëvell, Wolter R. van
1854   *Slaven en vrijen onder de Nederlandsche wet.* Zaltbommel: Noman. 2 vols.
Koloniaal Verslag
1856   *Koloniaal Verslag; Bijlage van het Verslag der Handelingen van de Tweede Kamer der Staten-Generaal.* 's-Gravenhage: Algemeene Landsdrukkerij.

Kolonist
1842 *Een woord ter wederlegging van het schrijven des heeren de Neufville over de vrijlating der slaven, in het bijzonder voor zoo veel zulks de kolonie Suriname betreft; Door een Kolonist.* Amsterdam: Diedericks.

Kool, Linda
1993 'Rechtvaardigheid en onafhankelijkheid; De ontwikkeling van het Surinaamse slavenverzet in de 19e eeuw'. [MA thesis Erasmus University Rotterdam.]

Kuitenbrouwer, Maarten
1978 'De Nederlandse afschaffing van de slavernij in vergelijkend perspectief', *Bijdragen en Mededelingen betreffende de Geschiedenis der Nederlanden* 93:69-101.

Mandle, Jay R.
1973 *The Plantation Economy; Population and Economic Change in Guyana, 1838-1960.* Philadelphia: Temple University Press.

Mintz, Sidney W. and Richard Price
1992 *The Birth of African-American Culture; An Anthropological Perspective.* Boston: Beacon Press. [Original edition 1976.]

Neufville, Jacobus de
1841 *De vrijlating der slaven in hare gevolgen beschouwd en op de Nederlandsche volkplantingen toegepast.* Amsterdam: Groebe.

Oostindie, Gert
1992 'The Enlightenment, Christianity, and the Suriname Slave', *Journal of Caribbean History* 26:147-70. [Revised and enlarged version in the present book.]

Ouwerkerk de Vries, J. van
1841 *Het godsdienstig onderwijs der negers en de bloei der kolonie Suriname in groot gevaar; Een bedenkelijk voorval in de mogelijke gevolgen beschouwd.* Amsterdam: Ten Brink and De Vries.

Paula, A.F.
1993 *'Vrije' slaven; Een sociaal-historische studie over de dualistische slavenemancipatie op Nederlands Sint Maarten 1816-1863.* Zutphen: Walburg Pers.

Renkema, W.E.
1981 *Het Curaçaose plantagebedrijf in de negentiende eeuw.* Zutphen: Walburg Pers.

Siwpersad, J.P.
1979 *De Nederlandse regering en de afschaffing van de Surinaamse slavernij (1833-1863).* Groningen: Bouma; Castricum: Hagen.

Stipriaan, Alex van
1989 'The Suriname Rat Race; Labour and Technology on Sugar Plantations, 1750-1900', *Nieuwe West Indische Gids/New West Indian Guide* 63:94-117.
1992 'Het dilemma van plantageslaven; weglopen of blijven?', *Oso* 11:122-41.
1993 *Surinaams contrast; Roofbouw en overleven in een Caraïbische plantagekolonie, 1750-1863.* Leiden: KITLV Press. [KITLV, Caribbean Series 13.]

Sypesteyn, C.A. van
1854   *Beschrijving van Suriname; Historisch-, geografisch- en statistisch overzigt uit officiëele bronnen bijeengebragt.* 's-Gravenhage: Van Cleef.

Tank, Otto
1848   'Circulaire: Aan de Heeren Eigenaars en Administrateurs van plantaadjes in de kolonie Suriname', *Berigten uit de Heiden-Wereld* 6:93-6.

Teenstra, M.D.
1842   *De negerslaven in de kolonie Suriname en de uitbreiding van het christendom onder de heidensche bevolking.* Dordrecht: Lagerweij.

Toes, Jaap
1992   *Wanklanken rond een wingewest; In de nadagen van de Surinaamse slavernij.* Hoorn: Drukkerij Noordholland.

Waaldijk, E. Theodoor
1959   *Die Rolle der niederländischen Publizistik bei der Meinungsbildung hinsichtlich der Aufhebung der Sklaverei in den westindischen Kolonien.* München: Steinbauer/Hagemann.

Watts, David
1987   *The West Indies; Patterns of Development, Culture and Environmental Change Since 1492.* Cambridge: Cambridge University Press.

Winter, Johanna Maria van
1953   'De openbare mening in Nederland over de afschaffing der slavernij', *West-Indische Gids* 34:61-90.

Wolbers, J.
1861   *Geschiedenis van Suriname.* Amsterdam: De Hoogh.

GERT OOSTINDIE

Same Old Song?
Perspectives on Slavery and Slaves in Suriname and Curaçao

Explaining abolition has long been a central concern in the historiography of the Americas.[1] Not so for the Dutch Caribbean, where the ending of the slave trade was imposed by the British and where slave Emancipation came late but apparently undisputed. In fact, the belatedness of Emancipation was the most remarkable fact about it all. The Dutch government accepted the inevitability of the ending of slavery only in the 1840s; and even then little progress was made. By 1861, two years before Emancipation, the Dutch historian J. Wolbers scorned the lukewarm abolitionists for having forsaken the noble cause. Slavery was still a reality. Yet the abolitionists now slumbered, self-congratulatory for once having contributed to the good cause and deaf to 'the shrill cries of the tortured slaves [as] it became so tedious to hear time and again of those negroes living so far away' (Wolbers 1861:746). Subsequent historians have consistently remarked on the absence of a passionate public debate on abolition in the Dutch world. David Brion Davis summed it up with the cursory remark that Dutch Emancipation was 'businesslike' (Davis 1984:285).[2]

The question then seems to be not so much why the Dutch abolished the slave trade and slavery but rather, as Seymour Drescher rightly reformulates the issue in this book, why so late and in so laggard a manner as they did?[3] Why was Dutch society, with its presumed conscience-stricken tradition of questioning the gathering and deployment of wealth, so little responsive to

---

[1] An earlier version of this paper was published in 1992 in *The Journal of Caribbean History* 26:147-70, under the title 'The Enlightenment, Christianity and the Suriname Slave'. I thank the editors of *The Journal of Caribbean History* for permission to use these materials in the present article. Seymour Drescher, Pieter C. Emmer, Sidney W. Mintz, Richard Price, and Tracey Thompson kindly criticized the earlier version. In the present version, I have lightly revised the sections on Suriname, while adding a new section on Curaçao and rewriting the conclusion. The writing of the earlier version was facilitated by a Fulbright Research Fellowship, awarded by the Netherlands America Commission for Educational Exchange.

[2] See also Van Winter 1953:61; Kuitenbrouwer 1978:98; Siwpersad 1979:xiv; Emmer 1974, 1980:80; Postma 1990:291-4; Buisman 1992:307-42.

[3] See Drescher's contribution in this book.

the abolitionist cause? Short of an immediate answer, suffice it to question here the notion of a chronic Dutch *Embarrassment of Riches* (Schama 1988), and to recall that the Dutch were not unique in their apathy. In the context of the times, the British rather than the other participants in the Atlantic slave system were the exception to the rule. Britain provided the momentum in Dutch abolition by simply imposing the ending of the slave trade at the closing of the Napoleonic wars; there was no serious public debate on this issue in the Netherlands.[4] So arguably a study of Dutch decision making could be confined to a study of the mid-nineteenth-century decades, as indeed most scholars have opted to do. Emancipation may then be explained in the context of international pressure and the economic insignificance of the Dutch Caribbean, and particular the major colony, Suriname, to its metropolis.[5] The timing may be related to the eventual emergence of a modest abolitionist lobby and, indeed businesslike, to the rising income from the Dutch East Indies and the simultaneous substantial decrease in the number of slaves in the Dutch West Indies, a fortunate concurrence which helped the Dutch government to settle the indemnification of the West Indian slave-owners.

This perspective is justified. Even so, one wonders about the development, if any, of Dutch colonial ideologies regarding slavery. Both Davis, in his monumental trilogy, and Gordon Lewis, in *Main Currents of Caribbean Thought*, virtually ignore Dutch and Dutch West Indian ideologies (Davis 1966, 1975; Lewis 1983). This contribution attempts to partly fill this gap through an analysis of the contemporary literature on the major Dutch Caribbean colonies, Suriname and Curaçao.[6] In discussing current justifications for slavery and particularly representations of the Dutch West Indian slave, I focus on the influence of the Enlightenment, Christianity, and the nature of 'progressive' thinking.

The present overview cannot disclose a rich corpus of writings; in fact,

---

[4] From 1804 to 1816, as a consequence of the Napoleonic wars in Europe, the British occupied the Dutch colonies. The British abolition of the slave trade (1807) applied to the occupied territories as well. This abolition was sanctioned in 1814 and again in 1818.

[5] Van Stipriaan 1993 provides the most comprehensive economic history to date of Suriname slavery; see also Van Stipriaan 1989. From a metropolitan perspective, Suriname was an attractive proposition up to the late 1770s; in the subsequent period up to and beyond Emancipation, the colony fell short of most expectations. In both periods, and increasingly so, the Dutch East Indies commanded far more metropolitan attention and capital. In 1830, the Netherlands imported roughly the same amounts of sugar from Java (the major island of the Dutch East Indies) and Suriname; in 1850, imports from Java were five times higher, in 1860 fourteen times (Oostindie 1989:458).

[6] Prior to the Napoleonic wars, the Dutch West Indies consisted of Suriname, the three smaller, neighboring colonies of Berbice, Demerara, and Essequibo, the three Leeward Antilles (Aruba, Bonaire, Curaçao), and the three Windward Antilles (St. Eustatius, St. Martin, Saba). After the Napoleonic wars, the British acquired Berbice, Demerara, and Essequibo, which was subsequently renamed British Guiana.

after reading Davis's and Lewis's works one is hard pressed to find anything original in the relevant, predominantly Dutch-language writings. This reading therefore largely confirms established notions about the flatness of Dutch and Dutch Caribbean dialog. Even so, the prolonged absence of any serious abolitionist debates did not imply that the various discourses were static. As time progressed, and as some spokesmen thought of themselves as more humanitarian and forward-looking while others tried mainly to postpone Emancipation, they all developed definitions of slaves and of slavery, and attempted to open new fields of appropriation of the West Indian slave.

Slavery as a Non-Problem in the Dutch World

When the Dutch established commercial relations with Africa in the late sixteenth century, they were coming from a society where blacks were virtually unknown. Like the British who were equally unfamiliar with blacks, it took them only a few decades to establish a set of mostly negative representations of the African. Initially they attributed less importance to 'blackness' and inherent inferiority as such, focusing on the presumed savagery of the African instead, with paganism and licentiousness as defining features.[7] The subsequent involvement in the Atlantic slave trade and New World plantation economies soon induced Dutch spokesmen to use the whole panoply of justifications, including heredity and innate abasement. Analysis of Dutch writings on these topics does not disclose arguments absent in discourse elsewhere in the Western world. In varying admixtures, blackness, paganism, brutality, and sexual lasciviousness came to define the representation of the African, thus helping to justify the slave trade and slavery.

There was no denial of the humanity of the African; blackness, however, became associated with the curse of Noah on Cham and his descendants.[8] The infinite inferiority of the blacks was therefore somehow of God's

---

[7] Van den Boogaart (1982:53-4) provides a thoughtful analysis of these initial representations. He concludes that blackness to the Dutch was no core attribute or as such a symbol of depravity, but rather a more neutral distinguishing feature. For the British, according to Jordan (1968), blackness was one of the five core attributes in the perception of the African, the others being heathenism, savagery, beastliness, and voluptuousness. Indeed, an early eighteenth-century account of Suriname, however negative its imagery of the slaves, also found the blacks 'rather pretty,' and included an engraving of two good-looking slaves, one of each sex (Herlein 1718:94).

[8] The association of black with pagan symbols and white with Christianity was half-heartedly overcome in the sensationalist reception of the African convert Jacobus Capitein, a student at Leiden University and author of a Latin tract confirming the 'Cham ideology' and justifying slavery even of christened Africans. Capitein was honored in a poem underpinning the 'white-washing' of his soul by the workings of the gospel (Oostindie and Maduro 1986:12). On the wider symbolism of blackness, see Davis 1966:447-9, 1984:37-42. On the curse of Cham, see Davis 1984:42-3, 86-7.

making, and made it only logical that blacks served whites as slaves, even if slavery as such was not the natural condition of mankind. Enslavement by the Europeans moreover provided the Africans with an opportunity to escape the abasement and cruelty of their uncivilized continent; after all, most slaves sold to the slavers were bounties of war who otherwise would have been killed or abused by their African conquerors. Occasionally mention was made of enslavement as an avenue for Christianization; yet in the Dutch world this argument never made it to the mainstream as it did in Catholic Europe (Cohen 1980:43). Finally an occasional author such as the medical doctor D.H. Gallandat, in his manual for slave traders, voiced the more down-to-earth justification:

> 'I will only remark here that there are many occupations which would seem unjustified if they would not be of particular advantage. An argument here may be the Slave Trade, which should be acquitted of all unlawfulness solely because of the benefit it furnishes to the merchants.' (Gallandat 1769:3-4).

Even if the profitability of the slave trade did not come anywhere near the exaggerated expectations, the slave trade continued, and all Dutch colonies in the Americas came to depend on slavery. Both institutions could count on the full support both of the Dutch state and of the religious authorities. By the late eighteenth century, some French and English anti-slavery tracts had been translated into Dutch, yet apparently these did not spark a following. An exhaustive study of Dutch literature discovered only a handful of authors speaking out against slavery up to the early 1790s (Paasman 1984:98-121).

How should we account for this lack of interest, which gives the Dutch a poor showing not only in comparison to the unique British case, but even to the French and the Danes? Some tangible factors may have kept Dutch public opinion from reconsidering. The West Indies' importance to the metropolitan economy was dwarfed by the East Indies, where slavery was insignificant. Perhaps this could have helped the Dutch to discard the institution; in practice, however, it apparently led them to neglect the Caribbean colonies most of the time. The contrast with Britain is evident. Moreover, and probably working in the same direction, there was no black presence of any importance in the Netherlands.[9] This too may have helped

---

[9] Slave trading in the Netherlands was forbidden as early as the late sixteenth century, and the numbers of slaves accompanying their masters from the colonies to the metropolis was never more than a trickle. This number probably reached a peak in the third quarter of the eighteenth century. Even then, no more than some twenty slaves per year entered the Netherlands, with a roughly equal number leaving; probably there was a significant overlap. Similar migration from the main Dutch Caribbean island, Curaçao, was insignificant. Evidence of blacks in the Netherlands is circumstantial only. The status of slaves brought to the metropolis remained a matter of dispute up to Emancipation (Oostindie and Maduro 1986:

to postpone serious debates on slavery: the very subject was beyond the Dutch frame of reference. Finally, whereas in the eighteenth century the Suriname Maroon Wars – and only two slave rebellions in Curaçao – had occasionally brought the colonies into the spotlights, the nineteenth century was tranquil in terms of marronage and slave rebellions. Consequently, little reminded the Dutch of the reality of slavery in their realm.

But what about vital metropolitan interests or ideologies at stake? As Davis demonstrates, the international anti-slavery ideology derived from various sources (Davis 1984).[10] The often anti-clerical Enlightenment philosophers were crucial in opening the debate. However, the abolitionist movement derived much of its operational strength from fresh interpretations of Protestant Christianity. From the late eighteenth century onwards, abolitionism gained further momentum through its inextricable connection with new notions of human progress, industrial capitalism, and economic liberalism.

These impetuses were weak in the Netherlands. The Dutch eighteenth century has traditionally been depicted as uneventful, and its cultural ambience as boring; the Dutch Enlightenment supposedly was flat, barely radical, and never far from the mainstream of the Dutch Christian tradition (Zwager 1980:11-3, 63-4). A recent scholarly volume on the Dutch Republic in the eighteenth century succeeds in presenting a more nuanced picture – yet in spite of its debunking objectives, the overall impression remains much the same (Jacob and Mijnhardt 1992:23, 204, 212, 220, 227). In this context, it seems characteristic that in the sixteen essays on the Dutch eighteenth century and Enlightenment, the issue of slavery is not raised even once. This oversight reflects the eccentricity of the issue in contemporary thought. At the same time, it demonstrates how little subsequent scholarship tends to take attitudes towards slavery as a significant yardstick to measure modernity in the Dutch world.[11]

The establishment of the Batavian Republic (1795-1806) seemed a break with the conservative political traditions. Yet the program of its 'radical'

7, 13-7, 155-64). In 1870, a colonial author explicitly linked the virtual absence of blacks in the metropolis to Dutch ignorance regarding the West Indies (Anonymous 1870:777).

In contrast, by the 1770s current estimates put the black population in England as high as 20,000 (Walvin 1973:46-7). This figure may have been more in the order of 10-15,000; see Drescher (1986:27-30). Even so, the contrast with the Netherlands is enormous. In the 1760s and 1770s France reacted with xenophobia to an apparently growing but still very modest black presence by simply forbidding free blacks and slaves to enter the country (Cohen 1980:111).

10   On the ambiguous position of Enlightenment thinkers, see Davis 1966:391-445.
11   Mijnhardt (1992), for example, states that 'Montesquieu or Rousseau had little to offer that was relevant to the Dutch situation, except for topoi about the natural equality of humankind or the inalienable rights of the people [...].' The question whether contemporaries related these *topoi* to the issue of slavery is not raised. See also Paasman 1984:209-16.

leadership fell short of radicalism regarding the colonies. There was no intention of genuine colonial reform. Even if the radicals had earlier applauded the American Revolution, they were not prepared to see the Dutch colonies as anything but subjected sources of metropolitan wealth. Slavery was virtually ignored. The initial 1796 and 1797 prososals for a new constitution did not even mention the slave trade or slavery itself. Prompted by a few radicals, the National Assembly subsequently did appoint a committee to advise on these matters. The committee's report, however, was anything but abolitionist, and the 1798 Constitution did not consider abolition. In spite of its strong commitment to the French Revolution, the radical 'Patriot' government did not even contemplate duplicating the short-lived French abolitionist policy.[12]

If the Enlightenment did not provide a source of antislavery ideology, neither did religious dissenters. The Protestant Nederlandsch Hervormde Kerk with its dominance in Dutch society and politics remained silent until the 1850s. The influence of Catholicism was negligible. A substantial proportion of the Dutch population – even if not of its political leadership – had remained Catholic after the hard-won struggle for independence from Catholic Spain in the mid-seventeenth century. Yet full Catholic emancipation was accomplished only in the late nineteenth century, and in this process the Catholic leadership had found no expediency in championing anti-slavery policies.[13] As neither denomination created significant dissenting offspring, religious potential for abolitionism was far weaker than it had been in Britain.[14]

[12] The Batavian Republic leaned heavily on revolutionary France. The Dutch radicals were superseded by direct French rule in the so-called Kingdom of Holland (1806-1810), followed by straightforward annexation (1810-1813). During most of the 1796-1813 period, the British held the Dutch colonies in 'protective' occupation. In 1814, the Dutch ceded the colonies of Berbice, Demerara, and Essequibo to England, which united them later as British Guiana. The French revolutionary government abolished slavery in its colonies in 1794, a decision which was revoked by Napoleon in 1802. On the colonial policies of the Dutch 'Patriots,' see Schutte 1974:146-9. A first proposal for gradual abolition, co-authored by a French colonial official and a Dutch planter in Demerara, was included in the Dutch translation of Stedman's 1796 *Narrative*, Stedman 1799-1800:148-85. The proposal went largely unheeded.

[13] In 1726, the proportion of Catholics in the Netherlands was 34 per cent; in 1775, 36 per cent. Owing to the inclusion of two southern, overwhelmingly Catholic provinces, this proportion rose to 38 per cent in 1809, fluctuating between 35 and 40 per cent up to the 1970s. In 1809, members of the dominant Nederlandsch Hervormde Kerk accounted for 55 per cent of the population; the share of other Protestant denominations was 4.5 per cent. Protestant dissenters did not present a considerable numerical threat to the Nederlandsch Hervormde Kerk before the 1880s – that is, beyond the period under discussion here. All figures taken from Knippenberg 1992:23, 61, 170. Even if the Netherlands was renowned for religious tolerance, the Nederlandsch Hervormde Kerk was the only officially recognized church, and a highly privileged institution. Well into the nineteenth century, active membership was a condition for participation in the national élites.

[14] Under pressure of British Quakers, a numerically insignificant but intellectually im-

What about industrial capitalist ideology? In its 'Golden' seventeenth century, the Netherlands had been a pioneer capitalist state. Commenting on recent debates emphasizing the role of a progressive capitalist mentality in the emergence of abolitionism, Drescher indicates that precisely Dutch society should have been a case in point, but failed to live up to the theory.[15] The implications of the Dutch case for this theoretical discussion are not my main concern here. Yet it may well be argued that the pioneering quality of early Dutch capitalism had long passed. For one thing, and in striking contrast to its major competitors, during the eighteenth century the commercial and industrial sectors of the Dutch economy actually declined somewhat in comparison to agriculture (Kossmann 1992:20). Moreover, the question remains whether the early Dutch mercantile capitalist spirit may be put on a par with the later British industrial capitalist esprit. In the Netherlands, significant new industrialization came late, and so did the emergence of a class of clearly industrial capitalist orientation. If we may interpret Liberal British support for abolition partly as an expression of optimism regarding Britain's industrial future, the lack of such support in the Netherlands may also reflect a profound pessimism on the perceived decline of the nation's economy.

Either way, much of what was becoming accepted modern ideology in England, and subsequently in France and the United States, remained far from the Dutch élite's mentality and from colonial ideology. Adam Smith, in *Wealth of Nations* (1776), may well have argued for the economic inefficiency of slavery, hence suggesting that real progress even in the colonies was to be expected from the substitution of free labor for slavery. It took another half century before an isolated Dutch observer wrote on slavery in even remotely similar terms, fifty years later indeed (Van Heeckeren van Waliën 1826).[16]

In the first decades of the nineteenth century therefore, the intellectual climate in the Netherlands was hardly conducive to raising 'modern' arguments against the established practice of slavery. Only by mid-century did the Dutch élites decide to finally abolish the peculiar institution. By then even the Dutch, struggling to modernize their state and to regain the prestige that had once characterized their nation, had succumbed to the

---

portant movement within the Church, the Réveil, petitioned for abolition in 1842; yet organized action was postponed until the 1850s. Réveil spokesmen in the 1840s found the Quakers too radical, and also shied away from cooperating with Liberal abolitionists (Siwpersad 1979:73-6, 217-20).
[15] Drescher comments in his contribution in this book on the discussion in *The American Historical Review* (1985, 1987), subsequently reprinted in Bender 1992.
[16] Jacob points to a late eighteenth-century enlightened vision of industrial progress in the metropolis, but she does not suggest a link to the issue of slavery (Jacob 1992:238-9).

'peer' pressure of more advanced European neighbors.[17] In the modernizing outlook, the project of regaining respectability and rejoining the concert of progressive nations by necessity implied the dismantling of Dutch West Indian slavery.

The Colonial Perspective: Suriname

For the authors writing on the major Dutch West Indian colony, Suriname, the absence of a significant metropolitan discourse on slavery implied that there was no urgent need to justify the institution. In a way, this makes the literature more interesting. Not that it was of such remarkable quality. With fine exaggeration, Lewis has argued that Caribbean society 'was marked throughout by a spirit of cultural philistinism probably unmatched in the history of European colonialism', and that the 'planter way of life [was] at once crassly materialist and spiritually empty' (Lewis 1983:109, 327).[18] Suriname could certainly be read as a case in point. In the late 1770s, the *Essai historique* decried the colony's intellectual levels, while another author concluded that a man of letters was an exotic plant in Suriname (Nassy 1788:5, 1779:83). In the last decades of the eighteenth century, some 'Enlightened' inspiration filtered through to Suriname, resulting in the formation of European-style debating clubs and projects to raise the deplorable educational standards of the colony. Yet slavery did not rank high – if at all – on an agenda which was primarily of a utilitarian character.[19]

With the significant exception of two major historical studies, the bulk of the relevant literature was written by men with direct and often ongoing experience with Suriname slavery (Hartsinck 1770; Wolbers 1861).[20] Their writings expressed with some clarity the ambivalence of people dependent on humans to whom they had to deny their humanity. Their perspectives,

---

[17] Likewise for France: Drescher 1991:733.
[18] See also Davis 1975:184-97. 'As early as the mid-eighteenth century [...] slave societies were acquiring the image of social and cultural wastelands blighted by an excessive pursuit of private profit' (Davis 1984:80).
[19] Nor did colonial reform; see Cohen 1991:94-123. Arguing against the bad reputation of Suriname slavery became a major theme in the literature of the late eighteenth and early nineteenth century. Characteristically, no author took the pains to contradict Voltaire's indictment of Suriname slavery in the *Candide* (1759), even if this would have been an easy target in denouncing 'Enlightened' antislavery discourse; see Oostindie 1993.
[20] J.J. Hartsinck was a servant of the Dutch West Indies Company; his two-volume *Beschryving van Guiana* is based on archival sources, literature, and information supplied by Suriname planters and officials. The abolitionist historian Wolbers wrote his voluminous *Geschiedenis van Suriname* on the basis of archival research in the Netherlands. No female authors wrote on Suriname in the eighteenth or nineteenth century; in the *belles lettres* in contrast, authors such as Petronella Moens, Elizabeth Post, and Betje Wolff did publish on issues related to slavery.

however racist, testified to a continuous need to come to terms with daily realities. With some justification, Suriname planters blamed metropolitan observers for not having the slightest idea of what life in the the colony really was all about. If only they knew what blacks were like...

What *were* they like, according to the colonial authors? Of course, the bottom line is that their opinions of the slaves were low. Even so, one observes an increasing differentiation, and an apparently sharp reorientation in the early nineteenth century. The original ideology as expressed in J.D. Herlein's *Beschryvinge van Zurinamen* (1718) held sway up to the early nineteenth century at least.[21] 'The blacks are more often malicious than of good character, [they are] resentful and obstinate, therefore they need to be castigated frequently.' In terms of religion, nothing positive can be said: they are 'Heathen Slaves from the dynasty of Cham, [living] in a confused amalgam of feelings, buried in darknesses of ignorance, and curved alleys of innumerable fallacies'. Experience had taught that it was of no use to convert these people to Christianity; Herlein quoted a failed convert who explained 'that her [Afro-Suriname] Religion is far more agreeable to the senses than the Christian [doctrines]; because those People [the Christians] are more pleased by fundamental arguments than by feelings of amusement which they despise [...]'. This slave was thus implicitly used to demonstrate the higher and for blacks unattainable level of principle and abstraction of the creed of the Nederlandsch Hervormde Kerk. Otherwise Herlein did not go into any detail to justify the slave trade or slavery, as he admitted some did; he did not fail, however, to provide citations from the Bible allowing for the use of heathen slaves. Certainly the Suriname slave was no passive subject, as unfortunate uprisings had revealed, but with consistent and 'righteous' rule ('neither too cruel, nor too lenient'), the slaves did accept their status (Herlein 1718:90-121).[22]

Over the next century and a half some interpretations remained the same, others changed. 'Righteous' or 'just' rule continued to be thought of as the single most important planters' maxim – implying that the slaves would never rebel against slavery as such, but only against perceived infringements of a shared code of behavior.[23] The axiom apparently lost

---

[21] An expression of the still recent Dutch encounter with Africans, Herlein occasionally deployed the term *Mooren* (Moors) in addition to *Negers* (Negroes), *Slaven* (slaves), and *swarte* (blacks). The ambivalent *Mooren*, including Southern Mediterranean people, disappeared completely in all later writings on Suriname. In the Netherlands, it continued in use longer. See also Blakely 1993.

[22] Citations from pp. 96, 105, 94 and 86, respectively. All translations in this paper are mine; I have striven to approximate the original text as far as feasible. On a theoretical level, the axiom of just rule had already been formulated early in the sixteenth century by philosophers such as Grotius and theologians like G. Udemans. Their axiom rested on abstract juridical, respectively Christian principles rather than pragmatic grounds.

[23] See plantation regulations of 1759 and 1784; See Schiltkamp and De Smidt 1973; Pistorius

some of its respectability only by the nineteenth century, even if it remained an implicit assumption in proslavery writings. Few antislavery works addressed the theme explicitly, underlining the fact that the abolitionist ideology was informed more by European discourses than by an awareness of Suriname realities, however defined.

Well-known stereotypes were replicated when it came to describing the Suriname slaves. George Warren, in 1667, had them 'naturally treacherous and bloody,' J.J. Hartsinck, in 1770, was told that slaves were mostly 'very lazy, treacherous, cruel, given to theft, drinking and women'. The best eighteenth-century planters' manual had them cheerful, proud, haughty, and resentful.[24] Yet however denigrating or hostile, no author denied the essential humanity of the slave; the Christian dogma of the common origins of all mankind was upheld. Fairly soon, the rather casual justifications of slavery came to incorporate a time perspective. As Thomas Pistorius explained, Christian charity demanded 'that we treat as humans the slaves, who are human beings too, and share with us the same Divine Being as their Creator, even though it has *not yet* pleased him to shine the holy light of the Gospel on them as he does on us' (Pistorius 1763:98; my italics).

Yet when would the time be set for allowing the slaves to enjoy the fruits of Christianity? Unlike their counterparts in Curaçao, the Suriname colonists were notorious for disallowing any attempts to convert the slaves. Early on, Moravians had been given permission to spread the gospel among the Amerindian and Maroon populations, but arguably an interest in pacifying these potentially dangerous outsiders served as the prime motivation here. Slaves were not included in the project. Reverend J.G. Kals, in the 1730s, had cried out in vain for spreading the gospel; even if his argumentation included the economic gains to be made. Sporadic metropolitan urgings to undertake Christianization equally fell on deaf ears.[25] In Suriname, one knew that attempting to christen the slaves was to cast pearls before swine. Hartsinck underpinned the superiority of creole over African slaves by affirming that the former were 'more civilized, and are willing to confess that it was God who created all things and rules'. Nonetheless, they 'acknowledge that, being petty and sinful creatures, they cannot have access

---

1763; Hartsinck 1770, I:381, 404, 415, 1770, II:907, 918; Fermin 1770:145-7, 1778:345; Blom 1787:352-5; Stedman 1796. Hartsinck 1770, I:374 cites a leader of the 1763 slave rebellion in Berbice as saying 'that the Christians were rude to them; that they would not endure Christians or Whites in their country anymore, and that they wanted to be the rulers of Berbice; that all plantations were theirs, and that the Christians should cede these plantations to them'. Yet apparently he did not think this rebellious statement to be representative; elsewhere, he reiterated the 'just rule' axioms.

[24] Warren 1667:19; Hartsinck 1770, II:906-7. Hartsinck, like virtually all authors, implicitly took the female slaves to be more compliant. See also Blom 1787:330.

[25] Kals 1756; Van der Linde 1987; Hartsinck 1770, II:743; Wolbers 1861:265.

to that God'. The slaves therefore inevitably stuck to their own superstitions. Philippe Fermin, a physician, argued for a measure of charity in dealing with 'a folk that, even if born in slavery, nonetheless consists of humans just like us'. Some slaves did qualify for conversion, he thought; but as this in his view would have to result in manumission, spreading the gospel was not a viable strategy in Suriname. Besides, slavery provided the colonists with a rare opportunity to make fellow men happy.[26]

Others were more outspoken. Anthony Blom summed up eighteenth-century wisdom by simply stating that all efforts at Christianization were doomed to failure and should be discouraged:

> 'The best Negroes for work are those living according to the Law or Religion of their ancestors, and who have not learned anything from us but working. They are never too stupid to learn to work with the pickax and the shovel; and that way they live quietly, and are useful for a plantation.'[27]

Therefore, in a paradox not unfamiliar elsewhere in the Americas, the slaves' 'paganism' was accepted as a major justification for slavery; at the same time it was argued that conversion to Christianity, the one route to freedom, was premature. In addition, there was the more down-to-earth argument that without slavery, this colony could not exist.

Preparing for Emancipation

Throughout the eighteenth century, authors had commented on the nature of slavery in Suriname and on the character of the slave without a trace of doubt regarding the justification of the institution. Abolitionism was not even on the agenda. But in the nineteenth century, the abrupt ending of the slave trade and the growing awareness that slavery itself was under crucial attack impelled proslavery authors to be more explicit. As by the 1840s planters, travellers, politicians, and lobbyists finally engaged in polemics, the debates also gained in authenticity. Old arguments were elaborated in a proslavery discourse which ended up just struggling for postponement of the inevitable. The debate also provided an opportunity to establish what slavery had accomplished so far. The planters' lobby came to emphasize the civilizing mission of slavery, mostly avoiding the question as to why slavery, by their own standards, had so far failed to do so. The most significant new element in their policy was a remarkable reversal in attitudes towards conversion – even if partly inscribed in the strategy of playing for time.

At the turn of the century, John Gabriel Stedman, in his famous

---

[26] Hartsinck 1770, II:903; Fermin 1770, I:143, 124, 148. Traditionally, Jews, Christians, and Muslims had shared the position that religious conversion did not imply (immediate) manumission (Davis 1984:22).
[27] Blom 1787:348. See also Blom and Heshuysen 1786:391-2.

Narrative of a Five Years' Expedition Against the Revolted Negroes of Suriname, had confronted planter society with bitter accusations about its dehumanization; it was not the slaves who should be described as animals. Even if rather than urging for abolition he advocated amelioration of slavery, his views on 'Africans' were relatively favorable. However, as Richard and Sally Price in the preface to their publication of the recently uncovered original 1790 manuscript demonstrate, the editor of the *Narrative* as it appeared in 1796 made sure to substitute denigration for appreciation. The bowdlerized edition of the *Narrative* therefore likens Maroon civilization to African cultures and advances the alleged crudeness of both as an argument against premature abolition of the slave trade (Stedman 1796:lxi-lxiv).

Only a decade after the publication of the mutilated *Narrative* the slave trade was outlawed, but the same argumentation served subsequent authors well to demonstrate that the abolition of slavery itself was premature. The barbarity or animality of the slaves remained a common theme. The planters' organization Eensgezindheid characterized the slaves as 'Pagans and uncivilized people, mostly devoid of good mores or virtues: everything is inclined to barbarity'. This explained the necessity to rule by force. Similar arguments were still advanced as late as mid-century, yet by then the mainstream argumentation was that precisely slavery should be held responsible for keeping the blacks from attaining full humanity.[28]

The core attributes of the slaves as seen by most nineteenth-century authors were laziness and unreliability, on the one hand, lasciviousness and the absence of an orderly family life, on the other.[29] Abolitionists tended to blame these deficiencies on slavery, whereas proslavery ideology moved from the position that these were somehow innate characteristics to the affirmation that only further education through slavery could improve the slaves' ways. Whatever the explanations, the convergence was evident. The opinion of the slaves' actual capacities remained low on both sides. Hence most authors continued to think of immediate Emancipation as an irresponsible act.

In the search for ways to prepare the slaves for freedom, Christianization came to be seen as the central means of socialization. This was a remarkable shift, for as late as 1830 the missionary record was still confined to a century of mostly unsuccessful proselytizing among the Amerindians and Maroons. The choice of conversion was thererefore a significant innovation. At the same time, the change of policy was all but straightforward. The initial pleas

---

[28] *Verzameling* 1804:12; Kappler 1854, I:140, versus Wolbers 1861:775-6.
[29] In terms of slave revolts and marronage, this century was far more tranquil than the previous one. The emphasis on the brutality and fierceness of the slave waned accordingly. The Haitian Revolution left only a few traces in the literature on Suriname.

for spreading the gospel were strictly confined to the so-called 'slave friends'.[30] In the first 'modern' critique of Suriname slavery, juxtaposing ideas echoing Adam Smith and a plea for conversion, G.P.C. van Heeckeren van Waliën scoffed at the planters' 'incomprehensible obduracy' against the christening of the slaves. By the late 1840s, the Moravian missionary Otto Tank conceded that his brethren finally had access to a growing number of plantations. Yet his comments were biting: often the Moravians were only used 'as an instrument, to keep the Negroes in submission and under coercion, as if one foresaw that the means of the whip once will be thought of as insufficient'.[31]

This indeed is what the planters' literature suggests. In the first decades of the century, christening the slaves was at best something for the future; even if subsequently such a policy became more accepted, many continued to deny its feasibility.[32] The slaves continued to be depicted as barbaric; as 'such an exceptional kind of people that in spite of the whip which never allows their backs to heal and in spite of the heavy labor, they will concede to the most aggressive whims if only the director allows them every two or three months an occasion for dancing'; as sharing with the Indian the feeling that happiness equals doing nothing at all; as ignorant and animal-like; as ungrateful, stubborn, devoid of pride, childish, superstitious, and mendacious; as wild, too uncivilized to aspire to freedom, and actually benefitting from slavery under civilized Europeans; as mentally inferior and averse to civilization; as 'both morally and physically less sensitive [and] in everything exceptionally less accomplished than most Whites'; as lazy and childish; as understanding freedom as a condition of working little or not at all; as destined to relapse into an animal-like life if emancipated; as generally devoid of intelligence and virtue; as uncivilized, lascivious, and prone to idleness; as 'through a lack of education, lazy and indolent'; and as bound for degeneration after Emancipation, as the examples of the free coloreds, the Maroons and the emancipated slaves of the British and French West Indies demonstrated.[33] And so on, and so forth.[34]

[30] Or, before that, of foreign observers. Commenting on his visit to Suriname in the late 1770s, the French official V.P. Malouet blamed the Suriname planters for not christening their slaves and therefore not feeling inhibitions against abuse; this criticism of the planters' policies implied the conclusion that, because of the absence of Christianity, the slaves were 'reduced to animal instinct' (Malouet 1802, III:114). See also Paasman 1984:157-65.
[31] Van Heeckeren 1826:78-82, 87-8, 100-2, 127-8; Tank 1848:95. Similar criticism was voiced by the absentee plantation owner G.P.C. van Breugel (Van Breugel 1834:12). At the time of writing, a monograph on the impact of the Moravians in Suriname is in press (Lenders 1996).
[32] E.g., Eensgezindsheid 1804:19-20 and Staatscommissie 1855:294, 302.
[33] Citations from Eensgezindsheid 1804:12-14; Kunitz 1805:350; Lammens 1823:16; Van Heeckeren 1826:101; Teenstra 1835, II:186; Van Lennep Coster 1836:113-7; Lans 1842:22-3; Teenstra 1842:115, 119; Bosch 1843:147-8, 200-1; Van Emden 1848:11; Hostmann 1850, I:140-1, 1850, II:413; Kappler 1854:56; Staatscommissie 1855:97, 288-90; Winkels 1856:37; De Veer 1861:175-6. One recognizes elements of Elkins's once-celebrated Sambo-type: 'docile but

One of the problems for the abolitionists was that they actually shared many of these assessments; the above collection of characterizations draws on both proslavery and antislavery writings. Devoted to high principles of natural freedom for all, the abolitionists nevertheless were skeptical about the use the freed slaves would make of Emancipation. They therefore came to stress the benefits of Christianizing not only for the slaves' spiritual salvation but also, and perhaps even more, as a means of changing their ways and thereby helping the plantation economy survive once slavery was abolished. The advantages of christening the slaves would be twofold. First, the continuous natural decrease of the slave population confronted the plantations with a slowly eroding work force. All agreed that the alleged lascivious life of the slaves – polygamy and venereal diseases were recurring themes – caused low levels of fertility. Conversion implied imposing the norm of the monogamous nuclear family; hence, christening the slaves would result in improved demographic performance of the slaves and, after Emancipation, of the freed population. This policy was first voiced in 1828 by J. van den Bosch, a prominent adviser to the Dutch Crown sent out on a trouble-shooting mission to the colonies. It soon surfaced in many other works.[35]

Second, the imminent Emancipation faced the planters as well as the colonial state with the agonizing prospect of the freed slaves withdrawing their labor from the plantations – after all, they supposedly suffered from a stubborn leisure preference. Conversion again would be useful here, helping the slaves to accept their fate and educating them to substitute a genuine work ethic for their actual indolence, thereby facilitating the transition from work dictated by the whip to work guided by intrinsic motivation. As the 'modern' analyst Van Heeckeren stated, Christianizing would not only improve family life and hence reproduction, but equally substitute 'compliance with their fate [and] a better grasp of their duties' for their present 'stupidity and beastly life style'.[36]

---

irresponsible, loyal but lazy, humble but chronically given to lying and stealing [...] infantile [...] talk inflated with childish exaggeration [...] utter dependence and childlike attachment' (Elkins 1971:82). For a recent assessment of 'Sambo' as an ideology, see Patterson 1984:96, 207-8, 338.

[34] The earlier pragmatic justification – slaves are the only ones able to do the arduous work on tropical plantations – continued to surface, Lammens 1982:191-2; Benoit 1980:63; Lans 1842, II:16-7, 22-7, 30-1. There are interesting parallels here with the enlightened élites' perceptions of the Dutch *vulgus*. See Frijhoff 1992:292-307.

[35] Van den Bosch, cited in Oomens 1986:166; Van Heeckeren 1826:87-8, 127-8; Lans 1829:41; Lans 1842:163-5; Lans 1847:79; Staatscommissie 1855:272. See moreover Van Lier 1971:72-4, 172-6; Siwpersad 1979:85-7, 161, 185; Lamur 1985:34-43; Oostindie 1989:192-5.

[36] Van Heeckeren 1826:87-8, 101-4, 127-8. See also the opportunistic inclusion of conversion in one of the last proslavery tracts: Belmonte 1855:60-1, 120.

The initial burden of Christianization fell on the German Moravians, who since the 1730s had dedicated much effort and many brethrens' lives to missionary efforts in the colony. The results had been meagre, but they inspired confidence. As a Dutch Minister of Colonial Affairs summed it up in 1842, 'they preach the negro not only religion and morality, but also impress industry and obedience to the worldly authorities, and what is more, set the example.'[37] The Moravian brethren had indeed attempted – up to the mid-century in vain – to enhance their acceptability by emphasizing their 'neutrality' in worldly efforts: neither in theory nor in practice did they oppose slavery. As late as 1848, the Moravian leader in Suriname reassured planters that their policy was guided by the axiom that

> 'When the poor slaves patiently accept the roads whence God leads them, and when they do not complain about this and are complacent, then God will bless them for it and look upon the services that they perform obediently for you gentlemen [the planters] as if they therewith served Him.'[38]

From this perspective, the prolonged planters' resistance to conversion indeed testifies to an extremely short-term policy and an unwillingness to tolerate anything which might interfere with the established routines of plantation life.[39]

In the 1850s, the Moravians and, gradually, Catholic missionaries finally had access to all plantations. In theory, religious zeal, abolitionist ideology, and sensible demographic and economic policy all converged in the effort of converting the slaves. In practice the results were often discouraging, confirming the suspicions of the stubborn proslavery party but equally, and more painfully, the subdued apprehensions the 'slave friends' had felt all

---

[37] J.C. Baud 1842; in the same vein, J. van den Bosch 1828, and J.C. Rijk 1851; all quoted in Siwpersad 1979:200, 79, 206. Various authors confirmed that conversion would have disciplinary rather than subversive effects; Van Breugel 1834; Bosch 1843:170-3. And, in retrospect, Bartelink 1916:59.

[38] H.W. Pfenninger in Van Emden 1848:73. Similarly, Tank 1848:95. Wolbers 1861:720 commented: 'In order not to lose everything they had to give much to the slave-owners; in order to pour the poor slaves a few drops of the plentiful cup of the Gospel, they made the sacrifice of remaining silent, where keeping silent was sometimes really hard'. In exactly the same vein, the above-cited Moravian missionary Tank affirmed that the Moravians had always taught the slaves to accept their status (Tank 1848:95). On an earlier Moravian missionary's socialization towards this conformism, see Riemer 1801:90-4. For a general discussion of the relation between missionary Christianity and the slave-based social order in the Caribbean, see Lewis 1983:199-205.

[39] The contrast with the massive remarkably 'successful' Moravian mission in the eighteenth-century Danish Virgin Islands is noteworthy; Oldendorp 1987. Arguably, the major explanatory factor should be situated in the respective colonizing states. In Denmark, the monarchy and its élites were fervent protagonists of Christianizing, and simply obliged the colonists to comply. As indicated above, the eighteenth-century Dutch élites found no personal or political expediency in spreading the gospel to the colonies. Incidentally, even if the Dutch state had advocated conversion, its influence on the colonists was tenuous well into the nineteenth century.

along. M.D. Teenstra, one of the leading abolitionists, roundly admitted to serious doubts as to the results of the Moravian missionary efforts; the slaves had hearts of stone, and generally were 'very insensitive' and 'not accessible for impressions of beauty and virtue'. Two years before Emancipation, the abolitionist historian Wolbers wrote squarely about 'the rigidity of their hearts, [...] the propensity to idolatry, [and] the frivolity that still so often surface in the Negroes'.[40]

Indeed, in these last decades of slavery and those of the transition to free labor, conversion, and the imposition of Western norms of respectability, family life and work ethic proceeded with less success than was hoped for.[41] This period must have been agonizing and disillusioning to many abolitionists, who had claimed the slaves would quickly internalize 'right' standards of respectability. Applying the same yardsticks of civility, the ancient proslavery party must simply have found its pessimistic forecasts confirmed: the slaves had not yet been prepared for freedom.[42]

Curaçao: Color over Status

In 1863, 33,621 slaves or some 55 per cent out of a total population of just over 60,000 were freed in Suriname. Around 1815, at the time of the abolition of the slave trade, the number of slaves had even been some 44,000, over 75 per cent of the colony's total population. In this perspective, the numerical significance of the Antillean emancipations pales. The number of slaves freed in 1863 was only 11,654, 35 per cent of the 33,000 inhabitants of the Dutch West Indian islands. Both the limited number of inhabitants and the modest proportion of slaves corresponded to the longer run of Antillean history. In the major Dutch West Indian island, Curaçao, only 48 per cent of its 14,000 inhabitants were registered as slaves around 1815. At Emancipation in 1863, this proportion had diminished to 35 per cent out of a total population of 19,000 inhabitants.[43]

---

[40] Teenstra 1842:121, 124; Wolbers 1861:810. The militant abolitionist author W.R. van Hoëvell argued for a hierarchy of races in which Africans were situated immediately below Europeans, but above Asians and (the lowest order) Amerindians. Blacks could certainly advance, but not in Africa itself, where nature, climate and isolation combined to form 'a barrier to the progress of civilization' (Van Hoëvell 1854:237-8).
[41] In 1830, the Moravians counted less than 1800 converts among the non-white population; by 1861, this figure, according to inflated official statements, had increased to over 27,000, plus 11,000 Catholics; in both years, the total non-white population was barely over 50,000 (Van Lier 1971:173-4). Yet the missionaries themselves expressed strong doubts about the real impact of conversion (Lamur 1985; Oostindie 1989:192-5).
[42] Winkels 1856:97, 114; Kappler 1854:56; De Veer 1861; Kappler 1881:10; Siwpersad 1979: 262-70. For similar dilemmas in the British Caribbean, see Green 1976; Turner 1982; Holt 1992.
[43] Hoetink 1958:77; *Koloniaal Verslag* 1863. In 1833, slaves accounted for 40 per cent of the 15,000 *Curazoleños*.

Therefore, during the entire period from the abolition of the slave trade to the abolition of slavery itself, in Suriname both the number of slaves and their proportion of the total population – and, by implication, their significance for the local economy – exceeded the corresponding figures for the Antillean colonies by a wide margin. From this perspective, it is only logical that the Dutch debate on abolition, perfunctory as it may have been in any case, gravitated towards the case of Suriname. In contrast to the Dutch East Indies, where slavery may not have been so important but the colony as such was, the Dutch West Indian islands were characterized by both a limited significance of slavery within their territory and their own scant relevance to the metropolis.

The most telling illustration of this lack of metropolitan interest is the ending of slavery in Dutch St. Martin. When in 1848, the slaves of the French part of the island were emancipated, the slaves in the Dutch half reacted by declaring themselves free. For all practical purposes, the immediate negotiations between the (former) slaves and the powerless local planters and administration indeed confirmed the dismantlement of slavery. Yet as no final settlement – locally nor through Dutch legislation – was accorded, the issue remained unsettled right up to the general emancipation of 1863.[44]

Of the six Antillean islands, Curaçao had traditionally been the most important. From a Dutch perspective – if not necessarily as seen from the other islands – it functioned as the center of the insular Dutch West Indies. Yet again, it is striking how little the case of Curaçao figured in the debate on the abolition of slavery. Obviously, as its colonial council affirmed as late as 1847, the Curaçao slave owners did not want Emancipation.[45] Yet such statements apparently had little impact. The Staatscommissie installed in 1853 to report on slave emancipation did compose a modest volume covering both the West Indian islands and the Dutch settlement in Guinea, yet in contrast to its – more voluminous and more accommodating – parallel report on Suriname, the commission in projecting abolition in Curaçao was little inclined to bear with the objections raised by the island's slave owners (Staatscommissie 1855-56).

---

[44] Even beyond that date, St. Martin slave holders and the Dutch administration disputed the level of compensation to be paid to the former. The Hague initially maintained that no payment was required, as the compensation accorded to slave holders elsewhere in the Dutch Caribbean could not apply to St. Martin, where slavery had been abolished in 1848. The slave holders, in contrast, refused to accept that slavery had really ended in 1848. In the end, a compromise was reached, allowing for compensation but at a much lower level than the price accorded the other territories. See Paula 1993.

[45] Raad van Politie 1847, quoted in Lampe 1848:83. A decade later, their spokesman, while admitting the inevitability of full abolition, pleaded for caution and a gradual emancipation (Staatscommissie 1856:253-70).

A variety of factors explains this lack of metropolitan interest. First, there was the diminished significance of Curaçao to the metropolis, in both economics and geopolitics. During various periods in the eighteenth century, the tiny island's significance as a center for slave trading, smuggling, and financial transactions had been amazing. However, the abolition of the slave trade and the dismantlement of both the Spanish empire on *tierra firme* and the imperial mercantilisms in the region had undermined much of this function. Moreover, precisely the strong orientation of the local élites on Caribbean and Latin American networks now worked against the interests of those perhaps still hoping to influence metropolitan thinking. Even less than the Suriname plantocracy, with its long-standing, virtually exclusive orientation towards the metropolis, could the creolized – latinized – Curaçaoan élites relate to the Dutch élites. There was no question of easy access through family ties, nor through shared commercial interests. Consequently, whereas in the Netherlands the lobby for Suriname interests may have been weak, a Curaçaoan interest group was nonexistent.

One might want to add the limited number of Curaçaoan slaves as an explanatory factor. Yet this provides space for the kind of two-way reasoning also encountered in the discussion of the relevance of the insignificance of the black population in the Netherlands, or even of the limited importance of Suriname slavery to the Dutch economy. Theoretically, numerical insignificance could cause indifference as all this seemed to matter so little, yet in contrast, it could also have facilitated abolition, as the modest economic costs involved would be so easily compensated for by the moral gratification of 'doing good'.[46] It seems evident that as far as metropolitan mobilization and politics are involved, the latter pseudo-causality applies. Yet within the Dutch West Indies, a difference of sorts may be observed. Whereas in Suriname the local élites did contribute to the debate on slavery and abolition, such contributions were conspicuous by absence on the Antilles.

This failure to speak out for their own interests as slave holders is consistent with a longer tradition of both little literary activity and a predominant interest in regional affairs rather than in the relationship with the metropolis. In comparison to the 'canon' of literature on Suriname dating from the period of slavery, the few scattered publications on Curaçao are poor in quantity and quality. Moreover, virtually all were written by metropolitans, many of these only drawing on a visitor's limited experience with the island and its culture. In reviewing this small corpus, a further contrast with the literature on Suriname becomes evident. Whereas authors describing life in the latter, typical plantation society dedicated many pages

---

[46] See Teenstra 1852, II:755-6.

to the slaves and the planter-slave relation, the focus in writings on Curaçao tended towards observations regarding color rather than to status. This subtle contrast faithfully reflected the more complex economic and socio-racial structure of the island. In contrast to the typical non-Hispanic plantation colony with its overwhelming slave majority, its small and relatively homogeneous white élite, and its equally small intermediate group of free blacks and coloreds, Curaçaoan society consisted of three substantial segments: the white population, the free blacks and coloreds, and the slaves. The share of the intermediate segment increased uninterruptedly. From a modest 22 per cent in 1789, the proportion of free blacks and coloreds augmented to 32 per cent in 1817, 44 per cent in 1833, and over half the total population at Emancipation (Klooster 1994:288-9, *Koloniaal Verslag* 1863). Moreover, the white population itself was differentiated both along class and religious and cultural lines.

As H. Hoetink has forcefully argued, this particular structure of Curaçaoan society, combined with the relatively tranquil character of master-slave relations, caused the white segments to worry as much – if not more – about the free Afro-Curaçaoans as about the slaves.[47] As a seasoned expatriate in the Dutch West Indies observed:

> 'In Curaçao, the [free] coloreds are treated by the whites with far more contempt than in Suriname; yet as to the slaves, the contrary applies; the latter are better clothed and less oppressed on Curaçao than in Suriname' (Teenstra 1836, I:166).

Consequently, color even more than slavery is the recurring issue in contemporaries' accounts of élite discourse. Thus, the reverend G.B. Bosch reported on the white opinion that 'the coloreds were already too pretentious, and that the remaining distinction between the whites and [the coloreds] should be perpetuated as much as possible'. The dominant tendency in Curaçaoan politics, he argued, was the focus on maintaining the color line, defined as white versus colored and black, irrespective of status.[48] The civil servant H.J. Abbring wrote about both 'the ridiculous vanity' of the white élites regarding racial purity, the 'arrogant' mulatto aspirations to

---

[47] Hoetink 1958, 1969, 1972. Hoetink convincingly explains the comparatively mild character of slavery in Curaçao by reference to the non-plantation character of the economy, the on average limited number of slaves per slave owner, and the high level of social control on the small island. The 'mildness' of slavery in Curaçao was a recurring theme in writings on the island (Van Paddenburg 1819:75-8, Abbring 1834:84-6, Teenstra 1836, I:169). The obvious comparison was – and still is – with Suriname, with its supposedly extremely harsh slavery; on the pedigree and validity of this reputation, see Oostindie 1993. On the *hacienda*-like plantation system in Curacao, see Renkema 1981.

[48] Bosch 1829:228, 226, respectively. As to the psychological consequences of the ambivalent position of the free coloreds, he maintained that they easily felt offended, 'as if everything said to them reflects the contempt which their origins and color inspire' (Bosch 1829:103). See also Teenstra 1836, I:165-7.

membership of the white élite, and the general contempt of free blacks and coloreds regarding the slave population.[49]

The imagery of slaves was condescending and informed by paternalism, but generally not as negative as in Suriname.[50] Bosch countered stereotypes regarding the slaves' alleged stupidity, and found them in religious matters 'much less prejudiced and less superstitious than the lower classes in Europe'. Even in his summary of the 1795 slave revolt, he pictured the slaves as 'otherwise tranquil and generous' and led astray only by the dynamics of the moment.[51] Abbring likewise, apart from praising the aesthetic attractiveness of young male slaves, mentioned the slaves' humaneness; if they lacked certain virtues, this deficiency only stemmed from their bonded status (Abbring 1834:81-2, 85). M.D. Teenstra, drawing upon his own experience as an agricultural expert in Suriname, thought the Curaçaoan slaves were generally better-looking, more cheerful, educated, and industrious, and smarter than their more oppressed counterparts in the Guianas. Yet somewhat confusingly, he added a reference to the 1789 colonial report by W.A. Grovestins and W.C. Boeij, maintaining that the Curaçaoan slaves shared with the free people of color a reputation for obstinacy (Teenstra 1836, I:167). Reverend S. van Dissel in contrast maintained that 'the character of the nonwhites, in particular of the slaves, [is] generally tranquil, docile, peaceful', as well as industrious.[52] The Catholic vicar M.J. Niewindt, while pleading for more education, underlined that 'the slaves here are no coarse Africans: they know they are humans and realize very well that they should be treated as such' (Niewindt 1850, cited in Dahlhaus 1924:440).

The 1853 Staatscommissie finally heard conflicting statements. Not surprisingly, the more negative stereotyping corresponded to the plea for gradual rather than immediate emancipation, and vice versa. The following discussion between the former governor of Curaçao, J.J. Rammelman Elsevier, and the acting chairman of the commission, J.B. Heemskerk, captures that spirit:

---

[49] Abbring 1834:99. Compare Van Dissel 1857:111.
[50] Thus G.G. van Paddenburg, while taking the Christianization of the slave population as additional evidence of the mild character of Curaçao slavery, could confirm to his readership that 'The Negroes and coloreds, both free and slaves [...] have far less necessities than we, refined Europeans' (Van Paddenburg 1819:78). Perhaps the most condescending remarks were made regarding Afro-Curaçaoan promiscuity (for example, the Raad van Politie in 1818, quoted in Dahlhaus 1924:406), and the local Creole language, Papiamentu (Van Paddenburg 1819:71-3, Bosch 1829:212-9, Teenstra 1836, I:179). Then again, at least for the language if not for both issues, this criticism implicated the whites as well.
[51] Bosch 1829:220-1, 323. During the entire colonial period, two serious slave revolts were reported, one in 1750, the larger one in 1795.
[52] Van Dissel 1857:116. Van Dissel has *kleurlingen*, which is literally coloreds; from the context it is clear though that he means nonwhites in general.

'R.E.: Generally, [the Afro-Curaçaoans] are the enemies of order.
H.: So, on Curaçao too, troublemaking seems to be a constant element in the negro character.
R.E.: They are not averse to working in the fields, but [they are] very stubborn. [...] The negro thinks, I have to be free, not – where will I work, and how will I make a living.'[53]

A Curaçaoan slave owner testified in somewhat more optimistic terms, arguing that the slaves on the island were generally well-tempered and more civilized than slaves in other colonies. The latter observation was repeated in stronger terms by a priest formerly working on Curaçao, J.J. Putman, who concluded 'The slave wants to be happy too. Better than one thinks, he will know how to help himself. They are not as stupid as some portray them.' (Staatscommissie 1856:263, 275, 303).

The – comparatively – subdued and even slightly positive tone of this imagery probably reflected the relatively mild character of Curaçao slavery and the resultant absence of a feeling of continuous besiegement among the slave owners. Two additional factors may be mentioned. First, the positions taken by most authors cited echo their position as outsiders to the domestic economy. Second, the timing mattered. Most sources quoted date from the 1830s and beyond; in this period, even in Suriname the imagery of the slave as only 'as yet' uncivilized became mainstream and politically convenient.

Still, this is not the complete picture. The unconditional acknowledgement of the humanity of the slaves must have been representative even of the majority of the Curaçao élites who, in stark contrast to the Suriname planters, had tolerated the conversion of their slaves from an early stage. From the second half of the eighteenth century onwards, observers affirmed that all Afro-Curaçaoans, slaves and free alike, were Catholics. Indeed, at Emancipation in 1863, 86 per cent of all *Curazoleños* were classified as Catholic. This is a telling contrast with Suriname, where in 1863 only half the population was 'under the surveillance' of the Herrnhutters.[54]

So at least officially Afro-Curaçaoans, slave and free alike, were Christians, and in contrast to the Protestant or Jewish élites adhered to Roman Catholicism. Several observations follow. The contrast between a strong and until the 1830s successful planter opposition to conversion in Suriname versus the early opposite choice in Curaçao falsifies, most certainly for the

---

[53] Staatscommissie 1856:232, 243.
[54] *Koloniaal Verslag* 1863, no. 32, Suriname:21-2; no. 43, Curaçao:2. Of the 54 per cent of the total population in the Moravian fold, one-third were not baptized. An additional 6 per cent of the Surinamers were either baptized Catholics, or aspiring members; these were mostly former slaves too. In 1826, out of 2829 whites living on Curaçao, 15 per cent were Catholics too. With some justification, Römer-Kenepa (1992:47) argues that this group and its influence in colonial society has been neglected in historiography.

Dutch case, the decisive significance of metropolitan culture for the specifics of colonial rule. So does the prevalence, in Curaçao, of Roman Catholicism, in contrast both to the dominant religion in the metropolis and among the local whites, and to the subsequent policy of conversion through the efforts of the Protestant Herrnhutters in Suriname.

Why then the early Christianization, and why precisely Roman Catholicism? The answer to the first question is somewhat speculative. The fact that the colonists had not heeded the repeated urge of the Dutch West Indies Company to convert the imported slaves to Protestantism is not remarkable; at this early stage, there was no difference between the two major Dutch colonies. What is puzzling is the subsequent tolerance towards external, and in the context of the times even somewhat antagonistic – Spanish, Catholic – missionaries. Historical contingency certainly played a role. The peculiar location of Curaçao, just off *tierra firme*, facilitated the continuation of Spanish missionary efforts started in the pre-Dutch era, that is, from ca. 1500 until 1634. Apparently, once the initial Catholic zeal had falsified the apprehension that conversion would provoke rebelliousness among the slaves, the local élites found a continuation of this practice expedient, and perhaps even inevitable.

Two additional motives may have been of significance. First, judging from factors such as the high level of manumission and the remarkable positive demographic growth of the slave population, Curaçaoan slave owners did not face the chronic labor shortage which as late as the 1850s made Suriname planters reluctant to lose time destined for productive work to the possible indirect benefits of missionaries' visits. Finally, the gradual creolization of the Curaçaoan élites into a Hispanic Caribbean orbit may have made them more familiar with the Catholic nations' practice of 'Christian' slavery.

The contrast with Suriname indeed suggests how far apart the two worlds were. Following the more conventional wisdom reigning among the Protestant colonizing nations, Suriname planters had not seriously considered the experiment of conversion until the last decades of slavery. Arguably, their very late and opportunistic change of attitude would eventually demonstrate the shortsightedness of their ancestors, and the good judgement of their Curaçaoan peers.

To some extent, the choice of Roman Catholicism again followed from Curaçao's specific colonial history and its proximity to Spanish America. Prior to the Dutch take-over in 1634, and true to their colonial logic, the Spanish had made some efforts to Christianize the native population. In the subsequent period, priests from Caracas and Coro continued to make regular visits to the island. This Spanish domination was tolerated well into the eighteenth century; only after mid-century did the initative pass to Dutch missionaries and, subsequently, congregations. In a way therefore, the later Dutch mission only continued a pattern set by the Spanish.[55]

Yet there was more to the choice of Catholicism. With some justification, contemporaries emphasized the extreme religious tolerance of the colony. As for the whites, Protestants, Sephardic and Azhkenazim Jews all openly confessed their own religion while fully tolerating the other creeds. Moreover, even when the position of both Catholicism and the Jewish faith was still subordinated to Protestantism in the Netherlands, the Protestant Curaçaoans and the local colonial administrators had always welcomed the Roman Catholic missionaries and their activities among the slaves and free Afro-Curaçaoan population. But notwithstanding the further benefits of the proverbial religious tolerance, the hegemonic and pacifying dimension to these policies is obvious. Thus, as early as 1708, a Catholic priest wrote in his diary 'the Governor ordered me to instill in the slaves obedience and loyalty to their masters'.[56] And as for the choice of Catholicism, Reverend Bosch (1829:220, 226) remarked:

> 'Upon my arrival in Curaçao, it struck me enormously that the visitors to Catholic churches were of another color than the Protestants, as if for humans color of skin influenced religious creed; from half an hour's distance I could already notice from someone's appearance to which church he belonged.
> [...]
> However, after spending some years in Curaçao, I understood the true reason why Protestants have reserved their own churches here for people of white skin, a reason of more significance than the [presumed] appropriateness of the Roman church for ignorant people. This [rationale] is, namely, a colonial policy of contempt of people of black and brown skin. The larger one made the distance between whites and [nonwhites], the more one denigrated the latter, the stronger and longer, one thought, would colonialism remain in place [...].'

Religious tolerance and the conversion of the nonwhite population may thus have mutually reinforced one another; yet at the same time, the specific option for Roman Catholicism as the religion of the nonwhites served as a mechanism for upholding both the slave-free and the color divisions. As such, religious distinction would outlive slavery and persist until today.

Whatever the logic behind this double tradition of religious *divide et impera*, Roman Catholicism as such, and the Catholic clergy in particular,

---

[55] Lampe 1988:84, 107-10. Dahlhaus 1924, Goslinga 1956, and Lampe 1988 are the major publications on Catholicism in Curaçao; see also Allen 1992, Römer-Kenepa 1992. At times, Protestant misgivings about the prevalence of Roman Catholicism among the Afro-Curaçaoan population were voiced. See Teenstra 1836, I:174, Dahlhaus 1924:393, 444-5, Goslinga 1956:37, Klooster 1994:291-2.
[56] M.A. Schabel, cited in Lampe 1988:36.

were of particular significance in the final decades of slavery in the Dutch West Indian islands. Yet again, the impact was ambivalent. On the one hand, and for obvious reasons, the Catholic clergy had traditionally emphasized its neutrality in wordly affairs, particularly regarding the slavery issue, and its pacificying role. The first Catholic vicar, Niewindt, repeatedly argued that Catholic instruction was fundamental as a means to secure order in the colony. In 1828, he wrote to the governor, 'what is better suited to control the slaves, to keep them subordinated, to make them loyal in their service, than the influence of the Religion?' Later, he also emphasized the crucial significance of religious instruction with a view to an orderly transition to freedom.[57] In his testimony before the 1853 Staatscommissie, the Catholic priest Putman again affirmed this view, adding that earlier slave revolts had been enacted in a period 'when the slaves had not yet acquired that understanding of Religion which today has such a blessed influence among them'. The commission indeed concluded that conversion 'has contributed in no little measure to augment the susceptibility of the slaves for freedom'.[58] Likewise, after Emancipation on the first of July 1863, governor J.D. Crol explicitly thanked Niewindt's successor J.F.A. Kistemaker for the Catholic Church's assistance in the orderly enactment of full abolition (Lampe 1988:90).

On the other hand, a handful of clergymen, among whom again Niewindt, ended up adopting a stance far more critical of slavery and slave owners than the Herrnhutters in Suriname had ever ventured to express. Not surprisingly, their objections were informed by their own civilizing agenda, and were therefore particularly directed against obstacles raised by individual slave owners to religious instruction and formal marriages among slaves. Anyway, the explicitness of their argument reflected the growing strength and in the end the crucial signifiance of the Catholic Church in the social fabric of Curaçao during the last decades of slavery.

But perhaps another observation is of more relevance to the debate on Dutch slave emancipation, and the absence of a significant Curaçaoan perspective in the metropolitian debate. Much in contrast to the debate on Suriname, the available sources on Curaçao suggest a rather low-key concern about both the transition to free labor, and freedom as such.

The little concern voiced regarding possible social upheaval after Eman-

[57] Niewindt cited in Dahlhaus 1924:100, 395, and 430-1, respectively. Monsigneur M.J. Niewindt worked on Curaçao from 1824 until his death in 1860, since 1842 as the island's first vicar. In former days, he somehow personalized the Emancipation process in Curaçao (Dahlhaus 1924, Goslinga 1956; for a more balanced discussion, see Hoetink 1958:113-4, 139-43). A similar colonial benefactor did not emerge in Suriname – pride of place, if any, was reserved for King Willem III, who signed the Emancipation bill.
[58] Staatscommissie 1856:298 and 26, respectively.

cipation corresponded to the social fabric and mentality of Curaçaoan slave society. The limited number of slaves involved as compared to the already extant nonwhite free population may have helped to perpetuate the white élite's preocupation with race and color rather than juridical status. The belief that the slave population would remain in the Catholic church's fold after Emancipation added to white confidence that the transition to freedom would not jeopardize their own privileged position or their very safety. The long socializing tradition of Christianity in Curaçao indeed paid off for the white élites, a tangible reward for their traditional 'tolerance.'

The lack of anxiety regarding post-slavery labor mainly reflected the poor profile of the Curaçaoan economy, and particularly the marginality of productive slavery in the local economy. Again, the report of the 1853 Staatscommissie is instructive.[59] The commission concluded that the present situation of an excess of labor supply over its demand would be perpetuated after emancipation. As moreover the arid and densely populated island provided little room for subsistence peasant agriculture, the freed slaves would be forced to seek employment for a daily wage. In fact, the real problem was not, as in Suriname, how to keep the former slave force engaged in plantation work, but rather how to provide enough work for both the actual free population and the soon to be emancipated slaves. Both the slave owner H. van der Meulen and the priest Putman, thought that this objective was virtually beyond reach. They anticipated and even applauded an alternative strategy, already apparent among the free Afro-Curaçaoan population: emigration to Venezuela.

Post-Emancipation Agendas

If the case of Curaçao provides some interesting insights, the bottom line remains its relative insignificance to the general debate on Dutch West Indian slavery and its abolition. What is more, slavery itself never became a major issue in the Netherlands; nor did abolition, and one may want to argue that even Suriname seldom figured prominently in the Dutch public arena. Absentee owners might for a century or more have had part of their capital invested in Suriname slaves without even once raising a question regarding its moral justification, and get away with it without being frowned upon. Apparently, as late as the mid-nineteenth century the stain of slavery was easily overlooked (Oostindie 1989:362-3).

In the end, the Enlightenment and the rise of 'modernity' affected the Dutch attitude towards slavery and blacks remarkably little. The mainstream

---

[59] Staatscommissie 1856:9, 25, 30-1, 261-3, 277-8. The president of the commission indeed wondered why slaves were relatively expensive in the island, as the supply of labor far exceeded its demand (Staatscommissie 1856:278). See also Renkema 1981, especially p. 150.

authors of the proslavery movement in the eighteenth century maintained that all mankind originated from the same God. Blacks were humans too, only inferior, indolent, unreliable, and lascivious. In the nineteenth century, as abolitionism slowly gained the upper hand, both sides continued to think in much the same terms, only substituting more consistently the evolutionary 'uncivilized' for 'inferior'. The most significant pre-Emancipation change in Suriname was the embracing of conversion, a policy previously deemed useless. At first sight, it is difficult to perceive an ascendancy of enlightened or modern ideologies here. In its content, the new wave was a confirmation of traditional Christian values. But we may discern 'modernity' in the application of this package deal of religious and social values to a new subject group: the novel approach was directly inscribed in a larger policy aiming at assimilating the future free population to European norms regarding work ethics and family life.[60] Of course, the implementation of this policy was remarkable. The christening of the Suriname slaves was mostly relegated to a German missionary society first, subsequently joined by the Dutch Roman Catholic mission only. In Curaçao, again, mainstream Dutch Protestantism had sought no influence on the slaves whatsoever. Both choices again symbolize the lack of commitment in Dutch political circles, and even more so in public opinion.

In Suriname, Emancipation in 1863 was followed by a ten-year period of state supervision (Staatstoezicht) – again following the British example, but stretching the period of bondage into the 1870s. Metropolitan and colonial observers measured the results by the same yardstick and were not pleased. The effort to transform the former slave population into a rural proletariat catering on a regular basis to the needs of the plantations failed in Suriname as it had elsewhere. By the late 1880s, the plantation sector had come to rely primarily upon indentured labor from British India and the Dutch East Indies, and sugar production had plunged deep below the output during slavery and the Staatstoezicht. Moreover, the attempt to discipline the former slaves' family life and to wipe out 'paganism' seemed hopeless. The resilience of Afro-Suriname culture shattered the expectations of previous optimists, and only served to confirm the pessimism of others, both 'progressives' and 'conservatives'.

In Curaçao, the transition to a free labor economy posed a different problem. As the supply of labor exceeded its demand and as few alternatives were available locally, there was no problem of finding means to secure

---

[60] In the same period, 'enlightened' élites in the metropolis embarked on socializing policies for their own proletariat. Actually, the above-mentioned colonial trouble-shooter J. van den Bosch was in the vanguard of that movement as well. Conversely some of the more subtle socializing techniques, such as awarding medals and pecuniary prizes to 'lesser' people for voluntarily rendering outstanding services to the élites, were occasionally applied in Suriname as well (Moes 1845:129-53). See also Davis 1984:121-9, 214-26.

continued plantation labor, but rather of building alternative economic sectors. This challenge would not be effectively met until the late 1920s, when the establishment of an oil refinery redefined the entire economy. In the meantime, in spite of poverty and a lack of opportunities, society remained tranquil. Moreover, the split between a Catholic Afro-Curaçaoan majority and a Protestant or Jewish white élite remained intact. There is little reason not to accept the contemporary Catholic claim that both the smooth transition to freedom and the subsequent absence of open class conflict owed much to its strong local influence. At the same time, the Catholic church's effort to eradicate 'superstition', 'lascivity', and other presumed African traits encountered much the same obstacles as it did in Suriname.

These results could well have contributed to a subsequent rise of Dutch evolutionary, 'scientific' racism regarding blacks as it did elsewhere.[61] That this was hardly the case should probably be explained by the fact that the Netherlands did not partake in the *fin-de-siècle* scramble for Africa, and more particularly by the remoteness of Africa, Afro-America, and blacks from the public mind and eye.[62] Meanwhile, Dutch colonial rule in the West Indies continued the new policy of assimilation, attempting to socialize an increasingly plural population to Dutch standards of respectability.[63]

All in all, Dutch and Dutch West Indian discourse on slaves and blacks in general was not altogether the Same Old Song over and over again. From the beginning, a distinct tone characterized opinions in the three major sites, the Netherlands, Suriname, and Curaçao. In addition, over time, an evolutionary ideology – and with it, a civilizing and patronizing practice – came to overshadow the earlier, cruder variants of racism as a justification for slavery and colonial exploitation.

---

[61] Davis 1975:48; Davis 1984:134-6, 277-9; Cohen 1980:98-9, 181, 210-21, 260-2. Ironically, an eighteenth-century Dutch scholar, Petrus Camper, had been one of the first to link phenotype ('facial angle') with race and intellectual capacities; his theory had some acclaim elsewhere in Europe both in the second half of the eighteenth century and again in the 1840s; Curtin 1964:39-40, 366.
[62] The absence of 'scientific' racism certainly did not interfere at all with the use of (semi-) bonded labor in both the Dutch East Indies and West Indies well into the twentieth century, nor with routine racism against colonial subjects. On post-abolition 'scientific' racism in Britain and France, see Drescher 1990:440-7.
[63] Only in the 1930s and 1940s, Dutch cultural policy in Suriname encouraged the consolidation of ethnic pluralism. Yet educational policies remained firmly modelled after the metropolitan standards.

References

Abbring, H.J.
1834 *Weemoedstoonen uit de geschiedenis van mijn leven, of Mijn reis naar Curaçao, en vlugtige beschouwingen van dat eiland gedurende mijn tienjarig verblijf op hetzelve.* Groningen: Van Boekeren.

Allen, Rose Mary
1992 'Katholicisme en volkscultuur, een dialectische relatie; Een aanzet tot de studie van het "beschavingswerk" van de Curaçaose rooms-katholieke kerk in de periode 1824-1915', in: B. Boudewijnse, H. Middelbrink and C. van de Woestijne (eds), *Kerkwandel & lekenhandel; De rooms-katholieke kerk op Curaçao,* pp. 15-30. Amsterdam: Het Spinhuis.

Anonymous
1870 'Suriname en zijne vooruitzichten', *De Economist* 2:769-71.

Bartelink, E.J.
1916 *Hoe de tijden veranderen; Herinneringen van een ouden planter.* Paramaribo: Van Ommeren.

Belmonte, B.E.C.
1855 *Neêrlands West-Indië in zijne belangen en Dr. W.R. van Hoëvell in zijne 'Slaven en vrijen'; Slavernij - emancipatie - kolonisatie.* Leiden: Van den Heuvell.

Bender, Thomas (ed.)
1992 *The Antislavery Debate; Capitalism and Abolitionism as a Problem in Historical Interpretation.* Berkeley: University of California Press.

Benoit, P.J.
1980 *Reis door Suriname; Beschrijving van de Nederlandse bezittingen in Guyana [...].* Zutphen: Walburg Pers. [Original French edition 1839.]

Blakely, Allison
1993 *Blacks in the Dutch World; The Evolution of Racial Imagery in a Modern Society.* Bloomington: Indiana University Press.

Blom, Anthony
1787 *Verhandeling van den landbouw in de Colonie Suriname.* Amsterdam: Smit.

Blom, Anthony [and Floris Visscher Heshuysen]
1786 *Verhandeling over den landbouw, in de Colonie Suriname, volgens eene negentien-jaarige ondervinding zamengesteld, door Anthony Blom; En met de noodige ophelderingen en bewysredenen voorzien, door Floris Visscher Heshuysen [...].* Haarlem: Van der Aa.

Boogaart, Ernst van den
1982 'Colour Prejudice and the Yardstick of Civility; The Initial Dutch Confrontation with Black Africans, 1590-1635', in: Robert Ross (ed.), *Racism and Colonialism; Essays in Ideology and Social Structure.* The Hague: Nijhoff.

Bosch, G.B.
1829-36 *Reizen in West-Indië.* Utrecht: Van der Monde. 2 vols.

1843   Reize in West-Indië en door een gedeelte van Zuid- en Noord-Amerika; Derde deel: Reize naar Suriname, in brieven. Utrecht: Bosch.

Breugel, G.P.C. van
1834   Aansporing ter bevordering van het godsdienstig onderwijs der slaven en kleurlingen op plantaadjen, bijzonder gerigt aan eigenaren van plantaadjen in de kolonie Suriname, en aan andere weldenkende Christenen. Haarlem: Van Loghem.

Buisman, Jan Willem
1992   Tussen vroomheid en Verlichting; Een cultuurhistorisch en -sociologisch onderzoek naar enkele aspecten van de Verlichting in Nederland (1755-1810). Zwolle: Waanders.

Cohen, Robert
1991   Jews in Another Environment; Surinam in the Second Half of the Eighteenth Century. Leiden: Brill.

Cohen, William B.
1980   The French Encounter with Africans; White Response to Blacks, 1530-1880. Bloomington: Indiana University Press.

Curtin, Philip D.
1964   The Image of Africa: British Ideas and Action, 1780-1850. Madison: University of Wisconsin Press.

Dahlhaus, G.J.M.
1924   Monsigneur Martinus Joannes Niewindt, eerste apostolisch vicaris van Curaçao; Een levensschets, 27 Aug. – 12 Jan. 1860. Baasrode: Bracke-Van Geert.

Davis, David Brion
1966   The Problem of Slavery in Western Culture. Ithaca: Cornell University Press.
1975   The Problem of Slavery in the Age of Revolution, 1770-1823. Ithaca: Cornell University Press.
1984   Slavery and Human Progress. New York: Oxford University Press.

Dissel, S. van
1857   Curaçao; Herinneringen en schetsen. Leiden: Sijthoff.

Drescher, Seymour
1987   Capitalism and Antislavery; British Mobilization in Comparative Perspective. New York: Oxford University Press.
1990   'The Ending of the Slave Trade and the Evolution of European Scientific Racism', Social Science History 14:415-50.
1991   'British Way, French Way; Opinion Building and Revolution in the Second French Slave Emancipation,' American Historical Review 96:709-35.

Eensgezindheid
1804   Verzameling van uitgezochte verhandelingen, betreffende den landbouw in de kolonie Suriname; Opgesteld door het Landbouwkundig Genootschap: De Eensgezindheid, gevestigd in de devisie Matappika, binnen dezelve Kolonie. Amsterdam: Gartman/Uylenbroek.

Elkins, Stanley Maurice
1971   *Slavery; A Problem in American Institutional and Intellectual Life.* Chicago: University of Chicago Press. [Original edition 1959.]

Emden, Egbert van, H.G. Roux and J. Frouin
1848   *Onderzoek ten gevolge der circulaire van den heer Otto Tank [...].* Paramaribo: Muller Az.

Emmer, Pieter C.
1974   *Engeland, Nederland, Afrika en de slavenhandel in de negentiende eeuw.* Leiden: Brill.
1980   'Anti-Slavery and the Dutch; Abolition without Reform,' in: Christine Bolt and Seymour Drescher (eds), *Anti-Slavery, Religion, and Reform; Essays in Memory of Roger Anstey,* pp. 80-98. Folkestone: Dawson; Hamden: Archon.

Fermin, Philippe
1770   *Nieuwe algemeene beschryving van de Colonie van Suriname.* Harlingen: Van der Plaats. 2 vols.
1778   *Tableau historique et actuel de la Colonie de Surinam, et des causes de sa décadence.* Maastricht: Dufour et Roux.

Frijhoff, Willem Th.M.
1992   'The Dutch Enlightenment and the Creation of Popular Culture', in: Margaret C. Jacob and Wijnandt W. Mijnhardt (eds), *The Dutch Republic in the Eighteenth Century; Decline, Enlightenment, and Revolution,* pp. 292-307. Ithaca: Cornell University Press.

Gallandat, D.H.
1769   *Noodige onderrichtingen voor de slavenhandelaaren.* Middelburg: Gillissen.

Goslinga, Cornelis Ch.
1956   *Emancipatie en emancipator; De geschiedenis van de slavernij op de Benedenwindse eilanden en het werk der bevrijding.* Assen: Van Gorcum.

Green, William A.
1976   *British Slave Emancipation; The Sugar Colonies and the Great Experiment 1830-1865.* Oxford: Clarendon Press.

Hartsinck, Jan Jacob
1770   *Beschryving van Guiana, of de Wilde Kust, in Zuid-America [...].* Amsterdam: Tielenburg. 2 vols.

Heeckeren van Waliën, G.P.C. van
1826   *Aanteekeningen, betrekkelijk de kolonie Suriname.* Arnhem: Thieme.

H[erlein], J.D.
1718   *Beschryvinge van de volk-plantinge Zuriname [...].* Leeuwarden: Injema.

Hoetink, H.
1958   *Het patroon van de oude Curaçaose samenleving; Een sociologische studie.* Assen: Van Gorcum.
1969   'Race Relations in Curaçao and Suriname', in: L. Foner and Eugene D. Genovese (eds), *Slavery in the New World; A Reader in Comparative History,* pp. 179-87. Englewood Cliffs: Prentice-Hall.

1972   'Suriname and Curaçao', in: David W. Cohen and Jack P. Greene (eds), *Neither Slave Nor Free; The Freedman of African Descent in the Slave Societies of the New World*, pp. 59-83. Baltimore: The Johns Hopkins University Press.

Hoëvell, Wolter R. van
1854   *Slaven en vrijen onder de Nederlandsche wet*. Zaltbommel: Noman. 2 vols.

Holt, Thomas C.
1992   *The Problem of Freedom; Race, Labor, and Politics in Jamaica and Britain, 1832-1938*. Baltimore: The Johns Hopkins University Press.

Hostmann, F.W.
1850   *Over de beschaving van negers in Amerika, door kolonisatie van Europeanen [...]*. Amsterdam: Sulpke. 2 vols.

Jacob, Margaret C.
1992   'Radicalism in the Dutch Enlightenment,' in: Margaret C. Jacob and Wijnandt W. Mijnhardt (eds), *The Dutch Republic in the Eighteenth Century; Decline, Enlightenment, and Revolution*, pp. 224-40. Ithaca: Cornell University Press.

Jacob, Margaret C. and Wijnandt W. Mijnhardt (eds)
1992   *The Dutch Republic in the Eighteenth Century; Decline, Enlightenment, and Revolution*. Ithaca: Cornell University Press.

Jordan, Winthrop D.
1968   *White over Black; American Attitudes toward the Negro, 1550-1812*. Chapel Hill: University of North Carolina Press.

Kals, Joannes Guiljelmus
1756   *Neerlands hooft- en wortel-sonde, het verzuym van de bekeringe der heydenen, aangewesen en ten toon␣gespreit door drie leerredens gedaan en gemeen gemaakt door drie der voornaamste kerk-voogden in Engeland [...]; Uit 't Engelsch vertaalt, en met aanmerkingen verrykt [...]*. Leeuwarden: Koumans.

Kappler, August
1854   *Zes jaren in Suriname; Schetsen en tafereelen uit het maatschappelijke en militaire leven in deze kolonie*. Utrecht: Dannenfelser.
1881   *Holländisch-Guiana; Erlebnisse und Erfahrungen während eines 43 jährigen Aufenthalts in der Kolonie Surinam*. Stuttgart: Kohlhammer.

Klooster, Wim
1994   'Subordinate But Proud; Curaçao's Free Blacks and Mulattoes in the Eighteenth Century', *New West Indian Guide* 68:283-300.

Knippenberg, Hans
1992   *De religieuze kaart van Nederland; Omvang en geografische spreiding van de godsdienstige gezindten vanaf de Reformatie tot heden*. Assen: Van Gorcum.

Koloniaal Verslag
1863   *Koloniaal Verslag; Bijlage van het Verslag der Handelingen van de Tweede Kamer der Staten-Generaal*. 's-Gravenhage: Algemeene Landsdrukkerij.

Kossmann, E.H.
1992 'The Dutch Republic in the Eighteenth Century,' in: Margaret C. Jacob and Wijnandt W. Mijnhardt (eds), *The Dutch Republic in the Eighteenth Century; Decline, Enlightenment, and Revolution*, pp. 19-31. Ithaca: Cornell University Press.

Kuitenbrouwer, Maarten
1978 'De Nederlandse afschaffing van de slavernij in vergelijkend perspectief', *Bijdragen en Mededelingen betreffende de Geschiedenis der Nederlanden* 93:69-101.

Kunitz, J.D.
1805 *Surinam und seine Bewohner oder Nachrichten über die geographischen, physischen, statistischen, moralischen und politischen Verhältnisse dieses Landes während einer zwanzigjährigen Aufenthalts daselbst, gesammelt.* Erfurt: Beyer und Maring.

Lammens, Adriaan François
1823 *Redevoering ten betooge: dat de sterfte of het afnemen van het getal der negerslaven, in de kolonie Suriname, niet zoo zeer aan mishandelingen, maar hoofdzakelijk aan andere oorzaken moet toegeschreven worden [...].* Amsterdam: Stenvers Leeneman van der Kroe.
1982 *Bijdragen tot de kennis van de Kolonie Suriname [...] tijdvak 1816 tot 1822.* [G.A. de Bruijne (ed.).] Amsterdam: Vrije Universiteit; Leiden: KITLV/ Royal Institute of Linguistics and Anthropology. [Adapted from the original manuscript editions, 1822, 1846.]

Lampe, Armando Rudolfo
1988 *Yo te nombro libertad; Iglesia y Estado en la sociedad esclavista de Curazao (1816-1863).* Nijmegen: s.n. [PhD thesis Free University Amsterdam.]

Lamur, Humphrey E.
1985 *De kerstening van de slaven van de Surinaamse plantage Vossenburg, 1847-1878.* Amsterdam: Centre for Caribbean Studies, University of Amsterdam.

Lans, W.H.
1829 *Proeve over de oorzaken van verval en de middelen tot herstel der Surinaamsche plantaadjen.* 's-Gravenhage: Van Cleef.
1842 *Bijdrage tot de kennis der Kolonie Suriname.* 's-Gravenhage: Nederlandsche Maatschappij van Schoone Kunsten.
1847 *Emancipatie door centralisatie; Schets van een ontwerp tot behoud van Suriname.* 's-Gravenhage: Noordendorp.

Lenders, Maria
1996 *Strijders voor het lam; Leven en werk van Herrnhutterbroeders en -zusters in Suriname, 1735-1900.* Leiden: KITLV Press. [KITLV, Caribbean Series 16.]

Lennep Coster, G. van
1836 *Herinneringen mijner reizen naar onderscheidene werelddeelen.* Amsterdam: Schleijer.

Lettre sur le Gouvernement
1779 *Lettre sur le Gouvernement de Surinam; Sur l'inhumanité des blancs envers les negres [...].* London: s.n.

Lewis, Gordon K.
1983 Main Currents in Caribbean Thought; The Historical Evolution of Caribbean Society in its Ideological Aspects, 1492-1900. Baltimore: The Johns Hopkins University Press.

Lier, R.A.J. van
1971 Frontier Society; A Social Analysis of the History of Surinam. The Hague: Nijhoff. [KITLV, Translation Series 21; Original Dutch edition 1949.]

Linde, J.M. van der
1987 Jan Willem Kals; Leraar der Hervormden; Advocaat van Indiaan en Neger. Kampen: Kok.

Malouet, V.P.
1802 Collection de mémoires et correspondances officielles sur l'administration des Colonies, et notamment sur la Guiana française et hollandaise. Paris: Baudouin.

Moes, C.M.
1845 'Redevoering over de ware menschlievendheid, als den volkomensten band van alle maatschappelijke vereeniging,' Surinaamsche Almanak 1845:129-53.

Mijnhardt, Wijnandt W.
1992 'The Dutch Enlightenment; Humanism, Nationalism, and Decline', in: Margaret C. Jacob and Wijnandt W. Mijnhardt (eds), The Dutch Republic in the Eighteenth Century; Decline, Enlightenment, and Revolution, pp. 197-223. Ithaca: Cornell University Press.

Nassy, David de Is. C., et al.
1974 Historical Essay on the Colony of Surinam 1788. Cincinnati: American Jewish Archives. [Original French edition 1788.]

Oldendorp, C.G.A.
1987 History of the Mission of the Evangelical Brethren on the Caribbean Islands of St. Thomas, St. Croix, and St. John [Johann Jakob Bossard, ed.]. Ann Arbor: Karoma. [Original German edition 1777.]

Oomens, Maria
1986 'Veelwijverij en andere losbandige praktijken; Bevolkingspolitiek tegenover Surinaamse plantageslavinnen in de 19e eeuw,' Jaarboek voor vrouwengeschiedenis 7:152-71.

Oostindie, Gert
1989 Roosenburg en Mon Bijou; Twee Surinaamse plantages, 1720-1870. Dordrecht: Foris. [KITLV, Caribbean Series 11.]
1993 'Voltaire, Stedman, and Suriname Slavery', Slavery and Abolition 14-2:1-34.

Oostindie, Gert and Emy Maduro
1986 In het land van de overheerser II; Antillianen en Surinamers in Nederland, 1634/1667-1954. Dordrecht: Foris. [KITLV, Verhandelingen 100.]

Paasman, A.N.
1984 Reinhart; Nederlandse literatuur en slavernij ten tijde van de Verlichting. Leiden: Nijhoff.

[Paddenburg, G.G. van]
1819 Beschrijving van het eiland Curaçao en onderhoorige eilanden; Uit onderscheidene stukken, bijdragen en opmerkingen opgemaakt, door een bewoner van dat eiland. Haarlem: Bohn.

Patterson, Orlando
1982 Slavery and Social Death; A Comparative Study. Cambridge: Harvard University Press.

Paula, A.F.
1993 'Vrije' slaven; Een sociaal-historische studie over de dualistische slavenemancipatie op Nederlands Sint Maarten 1816-1863. Zutphen: Walburg Pers.

Pistorius, Thomas
1763 Korte en zakelyke beschryvinge van de Colonie van Zuriname [...]. Amsterdam: Crajenschot.

Postma, Johannes Menne
1990 The Dutch in the Atlantic Slave Trade 1600-1815. Cambridge: Cambridge University Press.

Renkema, W.E.
1981 Het Curaçaose plantagebedrijf in de negentiende eeuw. Zutphen: Walburg Pers.

Riemer, Johann Andreas
1801 Missions-Reise nach Suriname und Berbice; Zu einer am Surinamflusse im dritten Grad der Linie wohnende Freynegernation, nebst einige Bemerkungen über die Missionsanstalten der Brüderunität zu Paramaribo. Zittau/Leipzig: Schöpfische Buchhandlung.

Römer-Kenepa, Nolda
1992 'Onderwijs als veiligheidsklep; De rooms-katholieke kerk en het volksonderwijs op de Nederlandse Antillen 1824-1863', in: B. Boudewijnse, H. Middelbrink and C. van de Woestijne (eds), Kerkwandel & lekenhandel; De rooms-katholieke kerk op Curaçao, pp. 33-52. Amsterdam: Het Spinhuis.

Schama, Simon
1988 The Embarrassment of Riches; An Interpretation of Dutch Culture in the Golden Age. New York: Fontana Press. [Original edition 1987.]

Schiltkamp, J.A. and J.Th. de Smidt (eds)
1973 West Indisch Plakaatboek I; Suriname: Plakaten, ordonnantiën en andere wetten, uitgevaardigd in Suriname 1667-1816. Amsterdam: Emmering.

Schutte, G.J.
1974 De Nederlandse patriotten en de koloniën; Een onderzoek naar hun denkbeelden en optreden, 1770-1800. Groningen: Tjeenk Willink.

Siwpersad, J.P.
1979 De Nederlandse regering en de afschaffing van de Surinaamse slavernij (1833-1863). Groningen: Bouma; Castricum: Hagen.

Smith, Adam
1976 An Inquiry into the Nature and Causes of the Wealth of Nations. Edited by R.H. Campbell, A.S. Skinner and W.B. Todd. Oxford: Clarendon Press. 2 vols. [Original edition 1776.]

Staatscommissie
1855   *Eerste Rapport der staatscommissie, benoemd bij Koninklijk Besluit van 29 november 1853, no. 66, tot het voorstellen van maatregelen ten aanzien van de slaven in de Nederlandsche koloniën: Suriname*. 's-Gravenhage: Van Cleef.
1856   *Tweede Rapport der staatscommissie, benoemd bij Koninklijk Besluit van 29 november 1853, no. 66, tot het voorstellen van maatregelen ten aanzien van de slaven in de Nederlandsche koloniën: de Nederlandsche West-Indische eilanden en bezittingen ten kuste van Guinea*. 's-Gravenhage: Van Cleef.

Stedman, John Gabriel
1796   *Narrative, of a Five Years' Expedition Against the Revolted Negroes of Surinam, in Guiana, on the Wild Coast of South America; From the Year 1772, to 1777 [...]*. London: Johnson and Edwards. 2 vols.
1799-1800   *Reize naar Surinamen, en door de binnenste gedeelten van Guiana*. Amsterdam: Allert. 4 vols.
1988   *Narrative of a Five Year's Expedition Against the Revolted Negroes of Surinam; Transcribed for the first time from the original 1790 manuscript*. Edited, and with an introduction and notes, by Richard Price and Sally Price. Baltimore: The Johns Hopkins University Press.

Stipriaan, Alex van
1989   'The Suriname Rat Race; Labour and Technology on Sugar Plantations, 1750-1900', *Nieuwe West-Indische Gids/New West Indian Guide* 63:94-117.
1993   *Surinaams contrast; Roofbouw en overleven in een Caraïbische plantagekolonie, 1750-1863*. Leiden: KITLV Press. [KITLV, Caribbean Series 13.]

Tank, Otto
1848   'Circulaire: Aan de Heeren Eigenaars en Administrateurs van plantaadjes in de kolonie Suriname', *Berigten uit de Heiden-Wereld* 6:93-96.

Teenstra, M.D.
1835   *De landbouw in de kolonie Suriname voorafgegaan door eene geschied- en natuurkundige beschouwing dier kolonie*. Groningen: Eekhoorn. 2 vols.
1836   *De Nederlandsche West-Indische eilanden*. Amsterdam: Sulpke. 2 vols.
1842   *De negerslaven in de kolonie Suriname en de uitbreiding van het christendom onder de heidensche bevolking*. Dordrecht: Lagerweij.
1852   *Beknopte beschrijving van de Nederlandsche overzeesche bezittingen voor beschaafde lezers uit alle standen, uit de beste bronnen en eigen ervaring in Oost- en West-Indië geput*. Groningen: Oomkens. 3 vols.

Turner, Mary
1982   *Slaves and Missionaries; The Disintegration of Jamaican Slave Society, 1787-1834*. Urbana: University of Illinois Press.

Veer, G.S. de
1861   'Aanteekeningen over de Emancipatie der slaven in de Ned[erlandsche] West-Indische koloniën', *Themis* 2:169-228.

Walvin, James
1973   *Black and White; The Negro and English Society, 1555-1945*. London: Allen Lane the Penguin Press.

Warren, George
1667   *An Impartial Description of Surinam upon the Continent of Guiana in America [...]*. London: Godbird.

Winkels, W.E.N.
1856   *Slavernij en emancipatie; Eene beschouwing van den toestand der slavernij in Suriname*. Utrecht: Andriessen.

Winter, Johanna Maria van
1982   'Public Opinion in the Netherlands on the Abolition of Slavery', in: M.A.P. Meilink-Roelofsz (ed.), *Dutch Authors on West Indian History; A Historiographical Selection*, pp. 100-28. The Hague: Nijhoff. [KITLV, Translation Series 21.]

Wolbers, J.
1861   *Geschiedenis van Suriname*. Amsterdam: De Hoogh.

Zwager, H.H.
1980   *Nederland en de Verlichting*. Haarlem: Fibula-Van Dishoeck.

ROBERT ROSS

Abolitionism, the Batavian Republic, the British, and the Cape Colony

The Rights of Man

Some things might have happened earlier in Holland.[1] The story goes that in early 1806 Reinier D'Ozy, secretary to the Government at the Cape, returned there with a decree ordaining that all slaves born after a certain date be freed.[2] Unfortunately, by the time he arrived, the British had reconquered the Cape, and the decree was never issued. Emancipation would only occur some three decades later, by when British rule had been firmly established.

The problem with this story is that it is almost certainly untrue. No confirmation of it has been found in the archives of the Raad der Aziatische Bezittingen, where it would be expected, or elsewhere. D'Ozy had been sent to the Netherlands to request that additional military stores be sent to the Cape, and the despatch he took back with him, not unnaturally, was a polite and wordy refusal to divert the Batavian Republic's scarce resources to a colony which, given British supremacy at sea, could not have been defended.[3] The story has achieved a certain modest place in the historiography because historians have copied one another without verifying their references, an unfortunate but not uncommon state of affairs. On this matter Ross (1988:218), Freund (1972:250) and Schutte (1976:149) all cite J.P. van der Merwe (1926:282) who cited Sir George Cory (1910-40, III:7) who, as was his wont, cited no-one.

I have been unable to discover the source of Cory's statement. The Dutch officers accompanying D'Ozy to the Cape were able to conceal the despatches they were carrying from British eyes (Nahuys van Burgst 1993:2-3, 16). The effect of their successful subterfuge may have been to launch all sorts of

---

[1] My thanks are particularly due to Stanley Trapido for his comments on the original version of this paper and to Elizabeth Elbourne for discussions in the course of which many of my ideas on missionaries and evangelicals have developed.
[2] As Stanley Engerman has pointed out in his contribution to this book, there were already precedents for such an action in a number of Northern states of the USA.
[3] Raad der Aziatische Bezittingen to J.W. Janssens, 27 September 1805 (drafted by J.A. de Mist), Algemeen Rijksarchief (ARA), Raad der Aziatische Bezittingen 82.

rumors in Cape Town. The British probably took advantage of this circumstance to discredit the Batavians in the eyes of the Cape colonists. Imputing an abolitionist image to the Revolutionary regime would have been a useful piece of propaganda, which the British had certainly used on the occasion of their first occupation of the Cape in 1795.[4] All this is speculation, but the balance of probability is definitely that the incident never happened. However, the point is that it could have done. First, ideas to this effect had been current in Batavian discussions of slavery as early as 1797 (Schutte 1976:147-8). At that time they were entirely in the abstract, as the Netherlands was cut off from all its colonies by the British Navy. Secondly, the Cape Colony was the only one of the Dutch Atlantic possessions where the Batavian Republic was allowed a significant period of rule.[5] Following the peace of Amiens, the Dutch ruled the Cape of Good Hope for three full years, while in Suriname or the Antilles the equivalent interval before British reconquest was one of months, if not weeks. Thirdly, this had given the opportunity for the development of ideas about slavery in a less theoretical context than elsewhere and heretofore. The crucial figure in this was J.A. de Mist. An Overijssel aristocrat and moderate Patriot, he came to specialize in colonial affairs, particularly those of the Cape. In 1797 he had opposed the proposals to include emancipation in the new Batavian constitution, because there was no mechanism for effecting it. In 1802, in an effort to regain the influence he had lost in the course of the last five years, he compiled a memorandum to the Raad der Aziatische Bezittingen on the future government of the Cape which was soon to be returned to Dutch hands. In it he wrote:

> 'We do not intend to inquire into the necessity for, or the illegality and inhumanity of slave-trading in general. Religion and philosophy both pronounced sentence against it long ago; but statesmanship and self-interest, to their undoing, have appealed to the court of *necessity*, and in that court the case will not be decided for many years. Of this necessity, as far as the Cape is concerned, we are not convinced.' (De Mist 1920:251.)

The climate of the Cape, in contrast to the West Indies, was such that Europeans could work there in comfort, and 'hard working young farmers and dairymaids [should be] sent from the Netherlands'. Furthermore, if they were not treated with such harshness, the Khoisan could be persuaded to provide 'voluntary assistance'. Therefore, 'we believe that in time it will gradually become possible to give [the slaves] their freedom and to manage quite easily without them'. The slave trade should be phased out quickly.

---

[4] G.K. Elphinstone and J.H. Craig to A.J. Sluyskens and the Raad van Politie, 29 June 1795, in Theal (1897-1905, I:95-6).
[5] Even in Britain, East Indian slavery was never a major issue.

'Meanwhile, the tasks on which these people are employed should gradually be handed over to other persons, so that agriculture, stock-farming and viticulture may not suffer. In order to achieve this end, we would first of all suggest that all children in future born of slaves, should be free. At the same time, the first generation of freed slaves should be provided for. On reaching years of discretion, they should be granted plots of land for cultivation, or be assured of some definite means of livelihood, so that their freedom may not become a source of misery to them, or want and poverty drive them to thieving, and thus bring them to the gallows.' (De Mist 1920:252-3.)

These ideas De Mist maintained even as a colonial ruler. Later in 1802 he was sent to the Cape as Commissioner-General in order to establish Batavian government and to introduce reforms. While the Governor, J.W. Janssens, was nobbled by the Cape slaveowners into defending the maintenance of slavery and slave imports, De Mist remained convinced that slavery at the Cape was unnecessary and would be induced to wither away. He commented that his 'anti-slave system [does not] rest on new-fangled fragile so-called philanthropic grounds, but rather on practical maxims of state, whose falsity has at least to be shown before the contrary is defended' (Van der Merwe 1926:281; Freund 1972:244-50). Specifically he required of an unwilling Janssens that he investigate how slavery could be made to die out gradually in the Colony. By 1805 De Mist was back in the Netherlands, with a seat on the Raad der Aziatische Bezittingen. He may have given D'Ozy secret instructions of the tenet that Cory describes, but it does seem unlikely. What is clear is that the ideas he represented remained at the center of Batavian discussions about slavery, certainly with regard to the Cape of Good Hope.

Freedom from Sin

These ideas were at the highest level of Dutch politics, and even there were not central to political debate. They had little resonance beyond the political élite. As has so often been noted, there was no mass abolitionist movement in the Netherlands. Freedom in terms of the Rights of Man did not have the appeal in the Netherlands that Freedom as an essential tenet of evangelical Christianity had in Great Britain. As a result, the question that historians have to ask is not 'Why was there no mass abolitionist movement in the Netherlands which was just as much a capitalist society as Great Britain?'; rather the question should be 'Why was there no mass abolitionist movement in the Netherlands which was just as much a Protestant society as Great Britain?'

Two things follow from this reformulation. First, the exceptional nature of British abolitionism is even clearer. Logically, there is no more reason to assume that abolitionism arose from a peculiar British trajectory of Protestantism than to claim that it derived from the particular structure of British capitalism. Empirically, the former strategy is probably preferable, though it is at least arguable that the course taken by British Protestantism from the mid-eighteenth century was itself in part a consequence of the way in which the country's capitalist economy developed.

If this is indeed a correct argument, then, secondly, the roots of abolitionism have to be found in the British (and to a lesser extent North American) evangelical revival of the eighteenth century. The first point that has to be made is that the sources of that revival were just as much available in the Netherlands as in Britain. The phylogeny of the Revivals can be traced back not to the lands on the shores of the North Sea, but rather to the increased religious tension between Catholics and Protestants of the late seventeenth and early eighteenth centuries. The revocation of the Edict of Nantes and the crusading vigor of the (Catholic) Habsburg empire sent waves of ideas and refugees to the North and West (Garrett 1987; Ward 1992). The influence of the United Brethren, better known as the Moravians, on Wesley, for instance, is well known, but they were more prominent in the Netherlands, that traditional refuge from Catholic persecution, than in Britain. Much the same can be said of the Huguenot, particularly Camisard, exiles from France. The sources of the Evangelical revival were thus available in the Netherlands, and there were a few Dutchmen (and possibly women) who accepted its message in ways analogous to the British evangelicals. The most notable individual in this regard was Johannes van der Kemp, instigator of the first Dutch missionary societies, one of the most notable of the first wave of missionaries employed by British societies and, among other things, fervent opponent of slavery. Now, Johannes van der Kemp was *sui generis*. Probably the only (later) missionary to maintain a mistress in the Volmolengracht in Leiden, he was at various stages of his career cavalry officer, philosopher, medical doctor, and missionary. He was a genius, in his command of languages,[6] in the depth and breadth of his reasoning and in his ability to drive matters through to the ultimate, not a trait which made him a comfortable associate (Enklaar 1988; Elbourne 1991a). But his career does show that the ideas which led to abolitionism were available in the Netherlands (Boneschansker 1987:72-4).

To take the analogy with biological evolution somewhat further, arguments about the descent of ideas have to be allied to those of advantage in natural selection. There are at least three interlocking reasons to explain the

---

[6] For instance, he once excluded himself from missionary work in Persia because of his faulty command of Persian, a criterion which, *mutatis mutandis*, would have effectively prevented any overseas missionary work; he travelled through the wilds of Africa with a gospel in Syriac and apparently produced the only devotional work ever written in Cape Khoi, a language about as far removed from those of Northwest Europe as is possible, and one that defeated all other missionaries.

relative success of political Evangelicalism in Britain, in comparison to the Netherlands. The first has to do with the industrial revolution, to use convenient shorthand. There seems to have been an 'elective affinity', to use Weber's concept, between members of that broad social category conventionally split between the upper working and lower middle classes and Evangelical Protestantism. This was the group from which the majority of early missionaries derived and provided the rank and file of the abolitionist movement (Drescher 1986:67-88). It was obviously a group which grew sharply in numbers and political weight during the eighteenth century in Britain, but not in the Netherlands, which was relatively speaking in depression. Although they did not achieve any real political power, they were able to set the terms of debate in Evangelical circles to which Wilberforce and others had to respond.

Secondly, the second wave of Evangelical revival in Britain, in the 1780s and 1790s, saw a revitalization of Old Dissent (Elbourne 1991b). While the growth of Methodism from the 1730s on was, at the very least, politically ambivalent, the re-emergence of the Quakers and Independents, notably Baptists and Congregationalists, as a religious force towards the end of the century brought the radicalism which had slumbered since the Restoration back into the center of British political life. These groups were the carriers of the tradition which had had such a hectic life during the English Revolution, but which had never crossed the North Sea to the Netherlands. The results included a resurgence of millenarianism from the 1790s (Harrison 1979; De Jong 1970), which led fairly directly to the foundation of that most radical of organizations, both in the British Caribbean and South Africa, namely the (London) Missionary Society (Van den Berg 1956; Porter 1991).[7] The rapid conversion of the heathen was imperative, as otherwise it would be too late, and, for some missionary pioneers, their conversion would bring on the Millennium (Elbourne 1991b). Indeed the question arises whether it was the slave trade which prevented the coming of the Millennium, a question which I have never seen posed. And it was from this stage of Evangelicalism, rather from than the earlier Methodism, which abolitionism derived. True, millenarianism died away after the ending of the Napoleonic wars, which had provided it with much of its fuel. John Philip, for instance, made an exemplary transition from a millenarian position in 1813 to one which explicitly combined Christianity and the political economy of Smith and Malthus by the mid-1820s (Philip 1813, 1828).[8] Nevertheless, here too the respectable abolitionists, who were to drive the various measures

---

[7] The events surrounding the arrest and trial of John Smith in Demerara in 1823 provide Caribbean parallels.
[8] On his progress, and that of the South African mission in general, see Elbourne and Ross forthcoming.

through the British Parliament, had to respond to these sorts of movements on their ideological flank in a way which has not been incorporated into even the best studies of their movement (Turley 1991).

The third crucial difference between the development of Protestantism in the Netherlands and Great Britain was that the former had been conquered by Revolutionary France and the latter had not. What is important in this context about the ideology of the French Revolution, and of its Dutch counterpart which led to establishment of the Batavian Republic, was that it was resolutely secular. In reaction, the Dutch Protestantism in general, and its most vibrant early nineteenth-century expression, known as the Réveil, in particular, were always politically conservative. Abolitionism could not take root among those groups and tendencies within Dutch society who had most in common with the British abolitionists because it was seen as part of a revolutionary liberal ideology against which they were struggling in many aspects of Dutch life, political, theological, and social.[9]

After the restoration of the House of Orange in 1813, abolitionism was seen as part and parcel of a rejected ideology. In the reaction – in both senses of the word – to what is still disparaged as the *Franse Tijd* (French period), it was impossible to build on the ideas which a man like De Mist had expressed. Whatever the relation between abolitionism and capitalism, the connections between abolitionism and Evangelicalism are far clearer in Britain and North America. There are very good reasons why the two never came together in the Netherlands.

Cape Abolitionism and Missionary Politics

With this in mind, it is instructive to return to the question why, even after the establishment of British rule at the Cape, the abolitionist movement there remained weak. In his recent, detailed discussion of the matter, Watson (1990) demonstrates that during the 1820s a vigorous debate developed in the Cape Colony about the desirability and viability of slavery. While this was fed from metropolitan sources, it was very much an argument conducted in the Cape and in Cape terms. There were of course those who took up something approaching an abolitionist position, but they were either marginal to the society as a whole or, like John Fairbairn, editor of the *South African Commercial Advertiser*, surprisingly moderate in their anti-slavery. The only significant abolitionist society was the Cape of Good Hope Philanthropic Society, which hoped to end slavery gradually by purchasing young slave women for emancipation. In total, the Society emancipated 126 slaves, not enough to make a dent in the colony's slave population of

---

[9] In this, Dutch Protestantism had much in common with its German counterpart. See Huffman 1977:445-70.

around 36,000 (in 1834). Since many of the leading members of the society were themselves slave owners, the degree of abolitionist fervor it exhibits was not great. Thus while slavery was debated an abolitionist movement as such was more or less absent.

Now, 'weakness' is a comparative term, and Watson's explicit referent in his arguments is the United States, which is rather misleading. The United States was very rare in possessing both a large slave sector and a large area whose economy was almost entirely based on free labor, and the abolitionists came almost exclusively from the latter. Moreover, the heyday of North American abolitionism was after the emancipation of slaves in the British Empire. In comparison, say, with the abolitionist movements in Jamaica,[10] Suriname or Alabama, the Cape does come off too badly. Equally, Watson misses the degree to which there was a conscious international division of abolitionist labor. The Cape activists, notably John Philip of the London Missionary Society, left agitation for the emancipation of slaves to people in Britain and the West Indies. They concentrated their efforts on the plight of the indigenous Africans, mainly the Khoisan – and by extension the free blacks – but, after the conquest of the Western Xhosa in Hintsa's war of 1835, with them as well. Philip managed to convince Thomas Fowell Buxton the two struggles were in fact one, and after the emancipation of slaves Buxton concentrated his major efforts on the deleterious effects of colonialism on the (non-slave) colonized peoples, notably through the Select Committee (of the British Parliament) on Aborigines (Ross 1989:140-52; Elbourne 1991b:273-94, 323-30).

It was largely, though not exclusively, through the missionaries, that the political programs of evangelicalism came into the Cape Colony. As in Great Britain, the influence and fervor of political evangelicalism began to wane after the 1830s. Nevertheless, it was able to survive the disastrous consequences of a – millenarian-inspired – rebellion of many mission converts in 1851-1853 to provide the basis of later nineteenth-century Cape Liberalism. There is thus a clear ideological line of descent in South Africa from the abolitionists of the later eighteenth century down to the Christian Liberals of the twentieth. Indeed, the influence of evangelical political moralities and the Christian justification for political action passed through the missions to become an integral part of the ideological heritage of the African National Congress, and indeed of that of the élite of Botswana, one of Africa's few functioning democracies (and economies).

Nevertheless, it is self-evident that political radicalism deriving from evangelicalism was not dominant among South African whites in the early nineteenth century, or ever since. This was true no matter what language

---

[10] Watson (1990:199) admits that this was more or less non-existent.

they spoke. The main group of British immigrants, the 1820 settlers and their descendants in the Eastern Cape, had a record of racial illiberality which outdid anything the colony's Dutch could manage, as was shown by their harassment of the Xhosa and the Kat River Khoi (Kirk 1973; Crais 1992). Equally, successive colonial governors and their immediate entourages were with few exceptions high Tory soldiers. A number had West Indian experience. Except for one period in the late 1820s, they did not wish to liberalize the colony. When Lord Charles Somerset, for instance, realized that measures for the amelioration of slavery were inevitable, his reaction was to promulgate his own variety, later repudiated by the Colonial Office in London, as a preemptive strike and in the hope that he could get away with as little as possible (Rayner 1986:160; Peires 1989:472-519). After emancipation, a whole set of measures, for the control of vagrancy, squatting, and master and servant relations, continued in this vogue, although the first was in fact disallowed by the Colonial Office in London (Marincowitz 1985). And much later, slave-holding practices in the Transvaal (Boeyens 1991) were not a major source of friction between the British and the Boer Republic there until, for other reasons, the British needed to bring the Transvaal more firmly under British hegemony, and deployed all the ideological weapons at their disposal to this end (Kistner 1953; Delius and Trapido 1982).

There is thus a sense in which British political fights were replayed in South Africa. This is of course far from unusual for a colony. Nevertheless, it was also the case that even after the British conquest of the colony Dutch political disputes, or perhaps more correctly Dutch politico-theological disputes, were also played out at the Cape. In both cases, though, the choice of positions was selective. In the late eighteenth century there was a certain affinity for the Patriot movement, but this was more as a weapon with which to attack Dutch East Indies Company rule than from any great degree of ideological agreement (Schutte 1989:309-15). On the other hand, the secularism inherent in the Batavian Revolution was never attractive to a group for whom the *dominees* were still the main intellectual cadres, particularly as the lawyers, the other main section of the intellectuals, were increasingly divorced from developments in the Netherlands.[11] The ideologies of the Rights of Man, which De Mist had propagated, thus never gained a lasting foothold among Dutch South Africans.

There were those, nevertheless, who were attracted to ideas which could be said to derive from revolutionary ideas, if interpreted in very different ways. A direct line can be drawn from the Batavians through the writings of

---

[11] Pre-revolutionary Dutch law remained in force in the Cape Colony, and the Batavian codification was never enacted. In part a consequence of this, the influence of British-trained lawyers, whether English or Scotch, became paramount.

W.S. van Ryneveld,[12] to the self-consciously 'progressive' arguments of the annual *Cape Almanac*, in the middle of the nineteenth century. The introductions to this work, edited by B.J. van de Sandt and later his adoptive son B.J. van de Sandt de Villiers, form a clear location for the development of arguments about the necessity of progress in general, and for the Cape Colony in particular. By this time, the arguments of these anglicizing Afrikaners had merged with those of such British publicists as John Fairbairn to create a colony-wide progressive ethos (Du Plessis 1988:52-74).

Just as in the Netherlands, both Batavian and later progressive arguments brought forth a self-consciously reactionary counterweight from *dominees* of the Nederlandsch Hervormde Kerk. In the nineteenth century, the Cape Church was in much closer touch with developments in the Netherlands than it had ever been under Dutch East Indies Company rule, in part because it was a far livelier institution than its moribund predecessor. Even the attempts to anglicize the church ironically only increased metropolitan Dutch influence, since the several Scots who were recruited to serve at the Cape all spent a year in the Netherlands, ostensibly to learn the language, before sailing south. In general they spent the time studying at the Utrecht University, as did most of those South Africans who wished to be admitted to the ministry. There they joined the theological society (*dispuut*) Sechor Dabar, which was a prime channel for the influence of the Réveil to new generations of preachers.

The Réveil was at once a movement for the spiritual renewal of Dutch Protestantism and a movement of reaction against the secularization inherent in the Batavian revolution. Its leading figures, such as Willem Bilderdijk and Isaac da Costa (1823), were determinedly against 'the spirit of the age', and intent on glorifying the virtues of the Dutch past. It was a movement which eschewed all political radicalism, and thus did not include abolitionism within its programme until the mid-nineteenth century. By then, abolitionism was so accepted in Christian circles throughout Europe that it had ceased to be radical, and had in fact become a necessary part of a Christian movement's political programme.

In this, the new ministers influenced by the Réveil were in tune with the ethos of the Cape Church, whose leading ministers at the beginning of the

---

[12] W.S. van Ryneveld, 'Beschouwing over de veeteelt, landbouw, handel en finantie van de Kolonie de Kaap de Goede Hoop, in 1805', *Nederduitsch Zuid-Afrikaanse Tijdschrift* 8-10 [1831-1833], published posthumously. On the other hand, Van Ryneveld's 'Replies to the questions on the importation etc. of slaves into the colony; proposed by His Excellency the Earl of Macartney Etc Etc, dated 29 November 1797', were only published – very obscurely – in the *Journal of Secondary Education*, for 1931, and so can have had no immediate effect on the Cape thinking. See the extracts of both articles in Du Toit and Giliomee 1983:56-7. Van Ryneveld, who was a leading official and member of the Cape élite, did of course disseminate his ideas in general conversation.

century were themselves slave owners (Elbourne and Ross forthcoming). As a result, there was no religious impulse for social reform emanating from the Nederlandsch Hervormde Kerk, as was the case with at least some of the British Evangelical missionaries. Furthermore, the conservatives were strong enough to fight off later attempts to liberalize to Cape church (Du Plessis 1988; Du Toit 1987:48-63). They were not as yet Afrikaner nationalists. G.W.A. van der Lingen, the leading figure in this movement, was indeed a fervent *Groot-Nederlander*, before his time, and Andrew Murray jr., his successor as the dominant man within the Cape Nederlandsch Hervormde Kerk, remained more Scotch than Afrikaner, even though he was born and brought up in the Cape (Du Plessis 1988:116-25; Du Toit and Giliomee 1983:8). Nevertheless, this tradition was to be one of the blocks on which later Afrikaner nationalism was built, as Van der Lingen's heritage was transmitted to later movements through his protege Ds. S.J. du Toit (Moodie 1975:4, 57-9).

Intellectual lineages are difficult to analyze, and certainly not everything can be explained by phylogeny. Afrikaner conservatism developed as it did in dispute with its competitors, notably, in the nineteenth century, the ideas of progress, and also in reaction to the material conditions and social relations of the Cape Colony and South Africa as a whole. Nevertheless, the rejection of the sort of ideas propagated by De Mist, both in the Netherlands and in South Africa, had considerable long-term consequences. It would not have made much difference if D'Ozy had arrived a few months earlier, even if he had really been carrying the letter that rumors said he was. However, if the Batavians had had the chance to develop their colonial policies at the Cape, and if the transmission of ideas from the Netherlands to South Africa during the nineteenth century had not been so totally in the hands of their opponents, not their heirs, then the history of political philosophies, and thence of political practice, in South Africa would undoubtedly have followed a course other than that which it did. Just how different, it is impossible to say. Counterfactuals of the qualitative are outside the range of the historians' vision.

References

Berg, J. van den
1956   *Constrained by Jesus' Love; An Inquiry into the Motives of the Missionary Awakening in Great Britain in the Period Between 1698 and 1815.* Kampen: Kok.

Boeyens, Jan
1991   ' "Zwart Ivoor"; Inboekelinge in Zoutpansberg, 1848-1869', *South African Historical Journal* 24:31-66.

Boneschansker, Jan
1987   Het Nederlandsch Zendeling Genootschap in zijn eerste periode; Een studie over de opwekking in de Bataafse en Franse Tijd. Leeuwarden: Dijkstra.

Cory, Sir George
1910-1940   The Rise of South Africa; A History of the Origin of South African Colonisation and of its Development Towards the East from Earliest Times to 1857. London: Longman, Green. 6 vols.

Costa, Isaac Da
1823   Bezwaren tegen de geest der eeuw. Leiden: Herdingh.

Crais, Clifton C.
1992   White Supremacy and Black Resistance in Pre-industrial South Africa; The Making of the Colonial Order in the Eastern Cape, 1770-1865. Cambridge: Cambridge University Press.

Delius, Peter and Stanley Trapido
1982   'Inboekselings and Oorlams; The Creation and Transformation of a Servile Class', Journal of Southern African Studies 8:212-42.

Drescher, Seymour
1986   Capitalism and Antislavery; British Mobilization in Comparative Perspective. London: Macmillan.

Du Plessis, Jean
1988   'Colonial Progress and Countryside Conservatism; An Essay on the Legacy of Van der Lingen of Paarl, 1831-1875'. [MA thesis University of Stellenbosch.]

Du Toit, André
1987   'The Cape Afrikaners' Failed Liberal Moment, 1850-1870', in: Jeffrey Butler, Richard Elphick and David Welsh (eds), Democratic Liberalism in South Africa; Its History and Prospect, pp. 35-61. Middletown: Wesleyan University Press; Cape Town: Philip.

Du Toit, André and Hermann Giliomee
1983   Afrikaner Political Thought; Analysis and Documents; Volume I, 1780-1850. Berkeley: University of California Press.

Elbourne, Elizabeth
1991a   'Concerning Missionaries; The Case of Dr. Van der Kemp', Journal of Southern African Studies 17:153-64.
1991b   'To Colonise the Mind'; Evangelical Missionaries in Britain and the Eastern Cape, 1790-1837'. [PhD thesis Oxford University.]

Elbourne, Elizabeth and Robert Ross
forthcoming   'The Missions to the Cape Colony in the First Half of the Nineteenth Century', in: Richard Elphick (ed.), The History of Christianity in South Africa. Cape Town: Maskew Miller Longman.

Enklaar, Ido
1988   Life and Work of J.Th.Van der Kemp, 1747-1811. Cape Town: Balkema.

Freund, W.M.
1972   Society and Government in Dutch South Africa; The Cape and the Batavians, 1803-1806. [PhD thesis Yale University.]

Garrett, Clarke
1987	*Spirit Possession and Popular Religion from the Camisards to the Shakers.* Baltimore: The Johns Hopkins University Press.

Harrison, J.F.C.
1979	*The Second Coming; Popular Millenarianism 1780-1850.* London: Routledge and Kegan Paul.

Hilton, Boyd
1988	*The Age of Atonement; The Influence of Evangelicalism on Social and Economic Thought.* Oxford: Clarendon Press.

Hoffmann, Robert
1977	'Die Neupietistische Missionsbewegung vor dem Hintergrund des sozialen Wandels um 1800', *Archiv für Kulturgeschichte* 59:445-70.

Jong, James A. de
1970	*As the Waters Cover the Sea; Millennial Expectations in the Rise of Anglo-American Missions, 1640-1810.* Kampen: Kok.

Kirk, T.E.
1973	'Progress and Decline in the Kat River Settlement, 1829-1854', *Journal of African History* 14:411-29.

Kistner, W.
1952	'The Anti-slavery Agitation Against the Transvaal Republic, 1852-1868', *Archives Yearbook for South African History* 15:193-278.

Marincowitz, John
1985	*Rural Production and Labour in the Western Cape, 1838-1888, with Special Reference to the Wheat Growing Districts.* [PhD thesis University of London.]

Merwe, J.P. van der
1926	*Die Kaap onder die Bataafse Republiek, 1803-1806.* Amsterdam: Swets en Zeitlinger.

Mist, J.A. de
1920	*The Memorandum of Commissary J.A. de Mist.* Cape Town: Van Riebeeck Society.

Moodie, T. Dunbar
1975	*The Rise of Afrikanerdom; Power, Apartheid and the Afrikaner Civil Religion.* Berkeley: University of California Press.

Nahuys van Burgst, H.G.
1993	*Adventures at the Cape of Good Hope in 1806.* Cape Town: South African Library.

Peires, J.B.
1989	'The British and the Cape, 1814-1834', in: Richard Elphick and Hermann Giliomee (eds), *The Shaping of South African Society, 1652-1840.* Second edition. Cape Town: Maskew Miller Longman.

Philip, John
1813	*Necessity of Divine Influence; A Sermon Preached Before the Missionary Society [...] May 12 1813, by the Rev. John Philip, Aberdeen.* London: Missionary Society.
1828	*Researches in South Africa.* London: Ducan.

Porter, Andrew
1992 'Religion and Empire; British Expansion in the Long Nineteenth Century, 1780-1914', *Journal of Imperial and Commonwealth History* 20:370-90.

Rayner, Mary I.
1986 *Wine and Slaves; The Failure of an Export Economy and the Ending of Slavery in the Cape Colony, South Africa, 1806-1834.* [PhD thesis Duke University.]

Ross, Robert
1988 'The Last Years of the Slave Trade to the Cape Colony', *Slavery and Abolition* 9-3:209-19.
1989 'James Cropper, John Philip and the *Researches in South Africa*', in: Hugh Macmillan and Shula Marks (eds), *Africa and Empire; W.M. Macmillan, Historian and Social Critic*, pp. 140-52. London: Temple Smith.

Schutte, G.J.
1974 *De Nederlandse patriotten en de koloniën; Een onderzoek naar hun denkbeelden en optreden, 1770-1800.* Groningen: Tjeenk Willink.
1989 'Company and Colonists at the Cape, 1652-1795', in: Richard Elphick and Hermann Giliomee (eds), *The Shaping of South African Society, 1652-1840*, pp. 283-323. Middletown: Wesleyan University Press.

Theal, G. McC. (ed.)
1897-1905 *Records of the Cape Colony.* London: Swan Sonnenschein. 36 vols.

Turley, David
1991 *The Culture of English Antislavery, 1780-1860.* London: Macmillan.

Ward, W.R.
1992 *The Protestant Evangelical Awakening.* Cambridge: Cambridge University Press.

Watson, R.L.
1990 *The Slave Question; Liberty and Property in South Africa.* Hanover: Wesleyan University Press.

GERRIT J. KNAAP

Slavery and the Dutch in Southeast Asia

Compared to the Caribbean, the historiography of slavery in Southeast Asia is still in its infancy. This applies to both the Dutch and non-Dutch colonies in the area. Other topics have attracted more attention than slavery. For instance, the historiography of nineteenth-century Java is dominated by debates on the operation of the Cultivation System, a complex of regulations designed to exploit the local peasantry in order to generate exports of tropical crops for the European market. On the other hand, historians of seventeenth- and eighteenth-century Southeast Asia display great interest in trade and interstate relations. One topic that has received more attention recently from the latter group of historians is urban history. Although we may expect that the historiography on slavery in Southeast Asia will make some progress in the future, as a topic it will never play such an important role as it does in the Caribbean. The reason for this is simply that the institution as such was less widespread. In most of the areas in the region, slavery was only a minor element in the social fabric of the societies concerned.

F. de Haan may be called the pioneer of the study of slavery in Dutch Southeast Asia. He devoted many sections of his book on the history of Batavia (present-day Jakarta) to this topic (De Haan 1922-23). The most recent, one may even say the only, standard work on slavery in Southeast Asia in general is the collection of papers edited by Anthony Reid under the title *Slavery, Bondage and Dependency in Southeast Asia*, which appeared in 1983. Since then, a few other studies on the situation in the Dutch colonies have been published, quite often as a part of the newly revived interest in urban history. Most of these studies again concern the colonial capital Batavia, such as Jean Gelman Taylor (1983), Leonard Blussé (1986), and Susan Abeyasekere (1989). In addition, the city of Makassar (modern Ujung Pandang) has received the attention of Heather Sutherland (1986), while I have written on the city of Ambon (1991), as well as on slavery in seventeenth-century indigenous society in Ambon (Knaap 1987).

On the basis of the present state of the relevant literature, this article will give a brief discussion of the nature of slavery, both in indigenous as well as in colonial society, and the road to abolition during the nineteenth century. I shall also make a few comments on some of the issues raised in Seymour Drescher's article 'The Long Goodbye', which is reprinted in this volume.

The discussion will be limited to the developments inside Dutch-dominated Southeast Asia, present-day Indonesia, although one should bear in mind that, before the nineteenth century, the Dutch colonial empire in Asia extended as far as the Middle East and Japan. This colonial empire in (Southeast) Asia, in particular in the seventeenth and eighteenth centuries, was basically a maritime empire in which a large fleet connected various strongholds and settlements ashore. The settlements were often small cities, which, from an ethnic viewpoint, hosted a very mixed community of people. From the middle of the eighteenth century onwards, the Dutch gradually became more interested in territorial expansion. However, even by 1870, the area under direct colonial rule covered only some 25 per cent of the land surface of what is now Indonesia. Finally, it should be stressed that the views and discussions of slavery and abolition which took place in the mother country will not be treated here, as this topic is dealt with by other contributors to this volume.

The Nature of Slavery

In Southeast Asia slavery was an accepted institution in indigenous society well before the arrival of the Europeans. It was part of a long-standing tradition of vertical labor relations, which were to a large extent embedded in patron-client hierarchies. These relations of dependency could vary from outright slavery to a type in which a peasantry of smallholders was obliged to perform some sort of statute labor for the local élite. The élite was strongly motivated to bind as much labor or 'followers' to itself as possible, for the more people one controlled, the more powerful and rich one might become. This motivation was partly inspired by the shortage of labor in the region. Unlike the situation in Southeast Asia today, before the second part of the nineteenth century land was abundant but labor was scarce. 'Followers' were obtained in various ways: by violence, alliances, protection, favors, presents, and so on. When the Europeans arrived in Asia, they were struck by the fact that, in the indigenous emporia or port cities in particular, the class of people generally labelled as slaves were relatively well treated, despite the fact that indigenous law codes contained many antithetic and harsh passages on the subject (Reid 1983:6-8, 13-5, 1993:65-7).

An insight into the control of labor, including slavery, in indigenous society in South Sulawesi is given by Sutherland (1983:269-70). She provides us with a list of the dependants of a local aristocrat around 1700. He controlled 786 people, of whom 337 were slaves and 449 'free' persons. However, most of the latter were debt-bondsmen, who were obliged to work for their master until they were able to pay off their debt. Most of these people lived near the aristocrat's residence, while another group was engaged in a fishing enterprise in a nearby village. Whether one was a slave, a debt-bondsman, or a 'free follower' proved not to have any relevance to the sort of work one was expected to do. In Bali, slavery was also widespread in indigenous society. Most of the slaves here lived in or were attached to the palaces of the rulers of Bali's small principalities or to the aristocracy directly below the rulers in rank. The former seem to have possessed more than a hundred slaves each, while the latter owned some twenty to fifty slaves. The slaves were used as personal and domestic servants, concubines, and laborers on the land (Van der Kraan 1983:322).

Whereas in both South Sulawesi and Bali the majority of the slaves were fellow countrymen, in Java, on the other hand, slaves were usually non-Javanese, imported from abroad. However, around 1700 there appear to have been only a few slaves left in the indigenous societies in Java. Instead, poor Javanese were given the status of debt-bondsmen, whose position differed very little from that of free commoners who were obliged to perform statute labor in varying forms and degrees for the aristocracy. Hoadley has tried to make an estimate of the number of bondsmen in the principality of Cirebon in West Java. According to his estimate, the class concerned should have consisted of about 5 per cent of the population (Hoadley 1983:93, 97-9; Nagtegaal 1988:67-9). In seventeenth-century Ambon the slaves were also usually imported from abroad. These people worked the land or served the master or mistress in the house. During the last quarter of that century, the number of slaves in indigenous society was about 7,000, approximately 12 per cent of the population. There were villages, however, mainly the ones where the local élite was concentrated, where 30 per cent or more of the population were slaves. During these years, the class of slaves witnessed an annual growth of 1.2 per cent, which was slightly higher than the general population growth. Owing to the insufficient ratio between adult women and children, part of this growth must have been realized by continued imports (Knaap 1987:127-33).

In the colonial strongholds and settlements, the Dutch soon accustomed themselves to the phenomenon of slavery. It was the only way to solve the problem of the shortage of labor. There were not enough immigrants arriving from the mother country. Moreover, the surrounding Asian societies generally did not have the numbers to provide sufficient wage labor for the new settlements. In some cases, local rulers were reluctant to have the labor done by their subjects. Nevertheless, the ships of the colonial authorities in the roadstead had to be loaded and unloaded, the fortresses and houses ashore had to be built, and the canals had to be dug, often in collaboration with immigrant Chinese brokers and skilled Chinese workers (Blussé 1986: 60-3, 65). Soon there was also a great demand for slaves to become domestic servants, for carrying the umbrellas and the betel box when the master or mistress went out, for doing the shopping at the market and cutting firewood outside the city, for cooking and cleaning the house, and so on. Furthermore, unskilled labor was needed to man the brick and tileworks, to work in the arack distilleries, to do some fishing in the roadstead, or to perform artisanal work in the shop of the master. Moreover, many a female slave was used as a concubine. Europeans, in particular the higher echelons of the bureaucracy, gradually became the principal slave-owners, outclassing the Chinese and other ethnicities in absolute numbers of slaves employed, both collectively and individually (Abeyasekere 1983:296-302; Knaap 1991: 121-5). Among Europeans and Mestizos it even became the rule that the more slaves one owned, the more prestige one had. The treatment of the slaves varied from master to master and from mistress to mistress, as well as according to the kind of work they had to do. Matters of gender, social and ethnic background were also of importance. There were examples of fairly harmonious relations, but also of various degrees of maltreatment. In the seventeenth century fugitive slaves were found around most colonial enclaves. On the other hand, many slaves were manumitted. The latter usually entered the community of indigenous Christians surrounding the core of the European and Mestizo settlers (Hanna 1978:75; Knaap 1987:133-6, 1991:120, 124).

The one exception to the rule that slavery in the Dutch possessions was a phenomenon limited to the colonial cities and their direct surroundings was Banda in the Moluccas. Banda is a group of tiny islands south of East Seram, which was then the only place in the world where nutmeg and mace were produced. After the Dutch had conquered and depopulated the islands in 1621, it was decided to parcel out the land to Dutch and Mestizo settlers, who would exploit their piece of land using slave labor. The original idea was that each concession should measure 0.8 to 0.9 hectares and was to be worked by 25 slaves (Hanna 1978:60).

Some statistical characteristics of slavery in Dutch Southeast Asia are shown in Table 1. The period under consideration is the latter part of the seventeenth century, a time in which the colonial settlements had grown into well-established societies. Unfortunately, the number of areas for which we have information of such a statistical nature is still limited. The interpretation of the statistics remains a difficult matter. The first conclusion that might be drawn is that, considering the sex ratio among adults and the ratio between adult females and children, the conditions for slaves in indigenous society were probably better than those in the colonial enclaves. The differences between the colonial settlements are difficult to explain. For instance, it is hard to understand why the performance of overcrowded urban Batavia was as good as that of rural Banda, or why the city of Ambon's pattern deviated from that of both Banda and Batavia. On the other hand, the reason why the scores for the government-owned slaves were less favorable than those of the other categories is obvious. These people were mainly used for hard physical labor, assisting the government-employed European artisans in the shops and on the wharves.

Table 1. Slaves in Dutch Southeast Asia, c 1680

	Number of Slaves	Percent of Total Population	Adult Females per Adult Male	Children per Adult Female
Ambon, indigenous society	7,235	12.6	0.99	0.65
Banda	3,716	55.6	0.97	0.32
Ambon City	2,870	52.3	0.65	0.45
Batavia City	14,061	49.1	0.93	0.36
Batavia, government slaves	1273	–	0.48	0.42

Sources: Ambon, indigenous (Ambonese) society c 1692: Knaap 1987:127-32; Banda, 1687: Coolhaas 1975:204; Ambon City, 1694: Knaap 1991:123-5; Batavia City, 1682: Fruin-Mees 1931:1477; Batavia, government slaves, 1680: Stapel 1943:202.

The slave-holding colonial enclaves and, to a lesser extent, the indigenous societies depended largely on imports for the expansion and upkeep of their slave populations. Natural reproduction was not sufficient to keep the population stable. The levels of imports are as yet unknown. For seventeenth- and eighteenth-century Batavia the estimates vary between 1,000 and 4,000 annually, while for Ambon in 1670 a number of 600 is mentioned (Reid 1983:29; Knaap 1987:132). Most of the slaves for the colonial settlements originated from South Sulawesi, Bali, and the islands east of Bali as far as Timor (Reid 1983:30; Knaap 1991:120). The ways by which the slave market was supplied were manifold: by birth to slave parents; because of the inability of bondsmen to repay a debt; condemnation for a crime; captivity as a result of war or raids (Van der Kraan 1983:322-6; Bigalke 1983:341-3).

During the entire period under discussion, from the seventeenth to the nineteenth century, slavery in colonial circles remained limited to (sub)-urban society. The countryside, where the exports of tropical crops were generated, was mainly worked by peasant labor, at least if we exclude the nutmeg and mace from Banda. It proved fairly easy to mobilize peasant labor. Moreover, it was much cheaper than using imported slave labor (Reid 1983:17). Whether or not the colonial state expanded its sovereignty into the countryside did not matter in this respect. In particular areas, the peasants already living there were manipulated by a combination of monetary reward and coercion, sometimes by making use of the local élite and/or ruler, to grow the desired commodities. This was what happened in the early seventeenth century with Ambon cloves and in the late seventeenth century with Banten pepper in West Java and South Sumatra. This model was repeated with the introduction of coffee-growing to the highlands of West Java in the eighteenth century. Even Batavia's own lowland cash crop, cane sugar, was not exploited by making use of slave labor. Most of the workforce on the fields and in the sugar mills consisted of Chinese immigrant labor as well as Javanese seasonal labor recruited from as far away as Central Java. It is likely that among the latter category there were many bondsmen (Hooyman 1779:214; Knaap 1986:44-6, 1987:254-8).

The Road to Abolition

During the seventeenth and eighteenth centuries some publications advocating a measure of compassion for slaves were issued. The first person from within colonial circles to sound the trumpet of abolitionism was Dirk van Hogendorp. In 1800, he published a play called *Kraspoekol*, drawing attention to the brutalities which were often the lot of slaves. In the preface to the play, he advocated the prohibition of the slave trade as soon as possible and, furthermore, a gradual abolition of the institution of slavery as such (Van Hogendorp 1800:v, viii). A year later, he published a plea of the same nature, which he had apparently already written in 1796, when he was still in office in Java. In this work he scheduled the abolition of slavery for 1820 and demanded an immediate end to the slave trade, which was, according to Van Hogendorp, unlike the general treatment of the slaves, as cruel in the East as in the West (Van Hogendorp 1801:453-4, 458-60). As Van Hogendorp belonged to the very small section of opposition within Dutch colonial society, which was soon to find itself drawn into the wars of the French Revolution and its Napoleonic aftermath, his ideas found no response. Between 1796 and 1811, the Dutch colonies were almost continuously in danger of being attacked by the English. The only measure taken to limit slavery was the one introduced in 1808, which put an end to government-owned slavery in Batavia (*Encyclopaedie* 1919:803).

In 1810 and 1811, one by one, the Dutch possessions in Southeast Asia were occupied by the English. The English Lieutenant Governor General, Thomas Stamford Raffles, proved himself an enlightened reformer. In 1812, in order to obstruct slavery, he introduced a modest poll-tax on slaves and, subsequently, in 1813, he forbade the import of slaves to Java. Some years later he gave the impetus to the foundation of the Java Benevolent Institution, which aimed at promoting the abolitionist cause. After the restoration of Dutch rule in 1816, the Java Benevolent Institution continued its activities as the Javaansch Menschlievend Genootschap (Java Humanitarian Association). The restored Dutch colonial government reiterated the prohibition of seaborne slave trade, and, in 1819, introduced a better registration of slaves in order to reap the benefits of the poll-tax. In 1818 the Genootschap, in which both Protestant and Roman Catholic clergymen played an important role, called for new measures to limit slavery. The government decided to have the matter studied by a special commission. It was not until 1825 that the commission submitted its report, advising a gradual abolition of slavery. However, the authorities did not take any steps in this direction, because it was deemed to be 'against the interest of many a prominent inhabitant of the colony'. Instead, a new regulation was issued which was intended to improve the general treatment of slaves. For instance, it was decided that children who were the offspring of a liaison between a free person and a slave would be free. At the same time, the slave mother of such a child would be freed. There were no provisions for the freeing of slave fathers who had children with free women. Obviously, such things were officially not supposed to happen. Furthermore, the regulation laid down that slave families, married slaves or unmarried couples who had a child, should be kept together, while children could not be sold separately from their parents. Moreover, the masters' rights to impose physical chastisement were curtailed. Finally, the latter were obliged to provide proper food and clothing, as well as a monthly monetary remuneration to each slave who had reached the age of twelve.[1]

For the time being no further actions were undertaken, either by the abolitionists or by the government. In 1847 it was Rev. Wolter R. van Hoëvell who took up the abolitionist cause again by trying to convince the colonial government in Batavia to take measures to limit public auctions of slaves. After the government showed no signs of reacting, he published on his return to the Netherlands in 1848 a booklet in which he called for the immediate emancipation of the slaves. In return, the owners should receive financial compensation from the government. This could be raised by increasing the Chinese poll-tax. Van Hoëvell expected that the emancipated slaves would enter the fairly numerous class of house servants in the colonial settlements. Consequently, he saw no serious problem for the ex-slaves in finding a living (Van Hoëvell 1848:v-x, 51). The booklet provoked some reactions within colonial society, both positive and negative. The most negative response was a booklet published by a certain 'Ingezeten van Java' (Inhabitant of Java), who feared that widespread poverty would be the lot of the ex-slaves (Ingezeten van Java 1849:32-3).

After his return to the Netherlands in 1848, Van Hoëvell became one of the most prominent spokesmen for abolition in both the Netherlands East and West Indies. In the same year, the Dutch parliament assumed control of

[1] Van der Kemp 1918:209, 213-25. See also *Staatsblad van Nederlandsch-Indië* 44 (24 December 1825):6-7, 12.

colonial affairs. During the mid-1850s emancipation of slaves was one of the principal issues raised during the parliamentary debates on colonial affairs (Kuitenbrouwer 1978:78, 82-3). The Regeeringsreglement of 1854, the basic instructions for the government of the Netherlands East Indies, stated the intention that slavery should be abolished ultimately on 1 January 1860. This intention was not as much proposed by the Minister of Colonies, C.F. Pahud, but rather forced upon him by parliament, which urged that it be included in the instructions. The Regeeringsreglement also ordered an immediate prohibition of the public auction of slaves. By a specific regulation dated 7 May 1859, the government in Batavia, now headed by C.F. Pahud in his new capacity of Governor General, decreed the emancipation of all slaves in all directly ruled areas of the Netherlands East Indies. The compensation to be paid varied between 40 and 350 Dutch guilders per slave. The highest compensation was expected for those slaves who were between twenty and thirty years old (Margadant 1897:340, 353).[2]

Just as in the seventeenth and eighteenth centuries, during the nineteenth century slavery had never been considered a viable alternative to peasant labor for producing export crops for the world market. The Cultivation System, established on Java in 1830, which became a tremendous money-earner for the treasury of the mother country, exploited exclusively the land and labor of peasants. Meanwhile, slavery had steadily declined. Batavia, which towards the end of the seventeenth century had some 14,000 slaves in a total population of almost 30,000 (almost 50 per cent), had less than 7,000 slaves out of a population of about 45,000, (16 per cent) in 1824 (Abeyasekere 1983:289). In Java, as communications between the colonial settlements on the coast and the indigenous society in the interior improved, and as population figures showed a continuous increase, the free labor market became an increasingly better alternative to slave labor in the tertiary sector of the economy from about 1780 onwards (Boomgaard 1989: 132, 1990:45). Slavery was on the decline in other areas too. In the 1840s the number of slaves in the whole Dutch-controlled area of the Archipelago had already fallen to below the 10,000 level (*Encyclopaedie* 1919:805).

By 1860, the colonial government in Batavia expected the maximum number of slaves to be emancipated to be about 7,000 (*Verslag* 1859:24). The number turned out to be no more than 4,735, of which 1,777 in Java and 2,958 in the Outer Islands. The government paid compensation to the owners up to a total of some 784,000 Dutch guilders for 4,152 slaves, an average of 188 guilders per slave.[3]

---

[2] See also *Staatsblad van Nederlandsch-Indië* 46 (7 May 1859):1.
[3] Algemeen Rijksarchief, Ministerie van Koloniën 1850-1900, 1006, Verbaal November 22, 1860, no. 27, Letter C.F. Pahud, 17 September 1860.

Table 2. Number of Slaves Emancipated in Areas under Direct Dutch Rule by January 1, 1860

	Number of Slaves
West Java	814
Central Java	359
East Java	604
Sumatra	781
Kalimantan	9
Sulawesi	615
Nusa Tenggara	298
Moluccas	1255

Source: Number of slaves: Algemeen Rijksarchief, Ministerie van Koloniën 1850-1900, 1006, Verbaal 22 November 1860, no 27, Report W.H. du Cloux 17 July 1860.

Except for a few small pockets of direct rule in the Moluccas, slavery had become a marginal phenomenon in society. For instance, the most important slave-holding areas in Java – Batavia, Semarang, and Surabaya – had only 611, 151, and 396 slaves respectively. The proportion of slaves there had fallen to less than 0.2 per cent of the total population. By 1860, sex ratios among the slaves had improved significantly compared to those a few centuries previously. In Java, there were approximately 1.25 females to each male, while in the Outer Islands the ratio was more or less balanced. The larger concentrations of slaves to be emancipated in the Outer Islands were found in Palembang in Sumatra (602) and in Ambon (566) and Banda (514) in the Moluccas. In Palembang, the indigenous élite still had quite a number of slaves. In Banda, the concession-holders of the nutmeg and mace gardens possessed most of the slaves.[4] In Banda, the local authorities did their utmost to convince the former slaves that it was best for them to continue working on the concessions of their former masters. However, the majority of the slaves preferred to seek other occupations (*Verslag* 1859:25). Out of a group of 422 who did not return, most of the males became fishermen, while the majority of the females wanted to become seamstresses.[5]

In the indirectly ruled areas, the autonomous or self-governing indigenous states, or in the areas which had not been incorporated at all into the Dutch colonial sphere of influence, indigenous slavery continued. In 1874 the Dutch authorities declared themselves prepared to promote further emancipation in these areas as well, but only in so far as friendly relations and local tranquility allowed. Consequently, it was not until the first decade

---

[4] Algemeen Rijksarchief, Ministerie van Koloniën 1850-1900, 1006, Verbaal November 22, 1860, no. 27, Report W.H. du Cloux, 17 July 1860.
[5] Algemeen Rijksarchief, Ministerie van Koloniën 1850-1900, 1006, Verbaal November 22, 1860, no. 27, Letter H.D.A. van der Goes, 9 January 1860.

of this century that slavery was totally abolished in these regions (*Encyclopaedie* 1919:805-7). However, at the same time the colonial government still needed people who could be used to perform fairly arduous work under unhealthy conditions, for instance as laborers in mines or as coolies on dangerous military expeditions in the Outer Islands. Since 1828, this kind of dangerous and unhealthy work had been mainly performed by convict laborers, of whom there were 7,322 at the end of 1859. The upshot of this was that, by the time of Emancipation in the directly ruled areas, the slaves were already greatly outnumbered by convict laborers. During the last quarter of nineteenth century, the number of the latter group grew steadily (Reid 1993:75-6; *Verslag* 1861:Bijlage I). The growing demand for convict labor may partly be explained as a response to the abolition of slavery. It was also a result of the acceleration of the process of expansion of Dutch control and exploitation outside Java. The Outer Islands still had a low population density, which meant that the supply on the labor market was fairly limited, particularly where hard physical labor was concerned – hence the demand for convict labor.

Final Remarks

From the previous pages it should be clear that slavery in Dutch Southeast Asia was mainly an urban phenomenon. It did not resemble the plantations of the Americas in any way. Slavery as such was not a colonial invention; it already existed in pre-colonial times, where it was just one particular, unfree form in a complex spectrum of labor relations. It should be emphasized that throughout the entire period under discussion, the colonial authorities were not dependent on slave labor for the production of export crops for the world market; they exploited peasant labor, which was organized with varying degrees of compulsion. Therefore, from the viewpoint of the metropolis, the issue of slavery in Dutch Southeast Asia was not of primary importance. On the other hand, for the internal functioning of the economy in the colonial enclaves, slavery was fairly essential, at least until the beginning of the nineteenth century. Apparently, these enclaves needed an outsider such as Raffles to produce the 1813 prohibition of the slave trade. Because of this prohibition and the subsequent introduction of other regulations, the institution of slavery gradually made way for free labor. One might conclude that it had withered in the Dutch-ruled areas by the eve of Emancipation in 1860. In so far as the colonial government needed labor to do strenuous physical work, it turned to convict labor.

Before the 1840s, abolitionism tended to be overshadowed by elements in favor of slavery inside the colonial enclaves. This situation was partly due to the fact that there was no free press in the colonies. In fact, before the second half of the nineteenth century, there was no significant press at all. In this respect it is significant that Van Hogendorp and Van Hoëvell's abolitionist writings were published only after their return to the Netherlands. Another important factor was that, during the centuries under discussion, by far the largest segment of the European population was very much dependent on the colonial state for employment. A class of independent merchants, not to mention industrialists, was virtually non-existent as the colonial state itself held monopolies of the collection and export of the most lucrative crops. The colonial government in Batavia, for its part, was able to manage the affairs of the enclaves fairly autonomously, as the masters in the metropolis were content as long as the flow of tropical products to Europe was guaranteed. Furthermore, the decision-makers on colonial affairs in the mother country were not subject to parliamentary control until the reform of the constitution in 1848.

In such a situation, it is not surprising that the libertarian ideology for which the mother country was famous, and which might, as Drescher argues, have been a prerequisite for the emergence of some sort of abolitionist movement, did not have many followers in the Dutch possessions in Southeast Asia. Drescher has rightly drawn attention to the fact that the inhabitants of the colonies felt themselves to be different from metropolitan society and that the Dutch colonies were not replicas of society in Europe. In this respect, the situation was very different from that in North America. The number of settlers from Europe in the Dutch enclaves was insufficient to obtain any reasonable degree of independence. Hence, the necessity to seek co-operation with several groups of Asians in order to build up and populate the colonial settlements and maintain their interests in the areas involved. Moreover, the majority of the settlers were males, who established all sorts of legitimate and illegitimate relations with Asian women. Consequently, a 'Mestizo society' emerged, both ethnically and culturally (Gelman Taylor 1983:xix-xx). Among the features adopted from Asian societies, the institution of slavery was one of the most important.

After 1848 slavery was only a minor issue in parliamentary discussions on the East Indies. The great debate was on the continuation or the discontinuation of the Cultivation System, which had become a rather efficient device for generating export surpluses by making use of the compulsory labor of the Javanese peasantry. The opponents to the system were motivated by two arguments. First, they wanted to replace state exploitation by free enterprise; second, they wanted to improve the lot of the peasantry through the abolition of the compulsory labor required for the production of tropical cash crops. Because of the second argument, the protagonists of both the antislavery movement concerned with the Dutch Caribbean and the opposition to the Cultivation System in Java might be seen as exponents of the same phenomenon: a free labor ideology. In both cases the advocates of free labor and free enterprise, the Liberals, finally won the day. Not unlike the case of antislavery in the Americas as argued by Drescher, it is obvious that in Java an ideology stressing an extension to non-European and/or non-Christian ethnicities of the moral concept of the right of individuals to decide their own fate became victorious over an efficient and profitable system of exploitation.

References

Abeyasekere, Susan
1983   'Slaves in Batavia; Insights from a Slave Register', in: Anthony Reid (ed.), *Slavery, Bondage and Dependency in Southeast Asia*, pp. 286-314. St. Lucia: University of Queensland Press.
1989   *Jakarta; A History*. Singapore: Oxford University Press. [Original edition 1987.]
Bigalke, T.
1983   'Dynamics of the Torajan Slave Trade in South Sulawesi', in: Anthony Reid (ed.), *Slavery, Bondage and Dependency in Southeast Asia*, pp. 341-63. St. Lucia: University of Queensland Press.
Blussé, L.
1986   *Strange Company; Chinese Settlers, Mestizo Women and the Dutch in Batavia*. Dordrecht: Foris. [KITLV, Verhandelingen 122.]
Boomgaard, Peter
1989   *Children of the Colonial State; Population Growth and Economic Development in Java, 1795-1880*. Amsterdam: Free University Press. [CASA Monographs 1.]
1990   'Why Work for Wages? Free Labour in Java, 1600-1900', *Economic and Social History in the Netherlands* 2:37-56.
Coolhaas, W.Ph. (ed.)
1975   *Generale Missiven van Gouverneurs-Generaal en Raden aan Heren XVII der Verenigde Oost-Indische Compagnie*, vol. 5. 's-Gravenhage: Nijhoff. [Rijks Geschiedkundige Publicatiën, Grote Serie 150.]
Encyclopaedie
1919   *Encyclopaedie van Nederlandsch-Indië*, vol. 3. 's-Gravenhage: Nijhoff; Leiden: Brill.
Fruin-Mees, W. (ed.)
1931   *Daghregister gehouden int Casteel Batavia [...] Anno 1682*. Batavia: Kolff.
Gelman Taylor, J.
1983   *The Social World of Batavia; European and Eurasian in Dutch Asia*. Madison: University of Wisconsin Press.
Haan, F. de
1922-23   *Oud Batavia; Gedenkboek*. Batavia: Kolff. 3 vols.

Hanna, W.A.
1978   *Indonesian Banda; Colonialism and Its Aftermath in the Nutmeg Islands.* Philadelphia: Institute for the Study of Human Issues.
Hoadley, M.
1983   'Slavery, Bondage and Dependency in Pre-Colonial Java; The Cirebon-Priangan Region, 1700', in: Anthony Reid (ed.), *Slavery, Bondage and Dependency in Southeast Asia*, pp. 90-117. St. Lucia: University of Queensland Press.
Hoëvell, Wolter R. van
1848   *De Emancipatie der Slaven in Neerlands-Indië.* Groningen: Van Bolhuis Hoitsema.
Hogendorp, D. van
1800   *Kraspoekol of de Slaavernij (Een Tafereel der Zeden van Neerlands Indiën).* Delft: Roelofswaert.
1801   *Stukken rakende den Tegenwoordigen Toestand der Bataafsche Bezittingen in Oost-Indië en den Handel op dezelve.* 's-Gravenhage: Leeuwestyn; Delft: Roelofswaert.
Hooyman, J.
1779-81   'Verhandeling over den Tegenwoordigen Staat van den Landbouw in de Ommelanden van Batavia', *Verhandelingen Bataviaasch Genootschap* 1:173-262; 2:162-212; 3:297-335.
Ingezeten van Java
1849   *Beschouwingen over de Emancipatie der Slaven in Nederl. (Oost) Indië, zoodanig als die is voorgesteld in de verhandeling van Dr. W.R. van Hoëvell, door een ingezeten van Java.* Nieuwediep: Bakker.
Kemp, P.H. van der
1918   *Oost-Indië's Inwendig Bestuur van 1817 op 1818.* 's-Gravenhage: Nijhoff.
Knaap, Gerrit J.
1986   'Coffee for Cash; The Dutch East India Company and the Expansion of Coffee Cultivation in Java, Ambon and Ceylon 1700-1730', in: J. van Goor (ed.), *Trading Companies in Asia 1600-1830*, pp. 33-50. Utrecht: Hes.
1987   *Kruidnagelen en Christenen; De Verenigde Oost-Indische Compagnie en de bevolking van Ambon 1656-1696.* Dordrecht: Foris. [KITLV, Verhandelingen 125.]
1991   'A City of Migrants; Kota Ambon at the End of the Seventeenth Century', *Indonesia* 51:105-28.
Kuitenbrouwer, Maarten
1978   'De Nederlandse afschaffing van de slavernij in vergelijkend perspectief', *Bijdragen en Mededelingen betreffende de Geschiedenis der Nederlanden* 93:69-101.
Margadant, C.W.
1897   *Het Regeeringsreglement van Nederlandsch-Indië*, vol. 3. Batavia: Kolff; 's-Gravenhage: Nijhoff.
Nagtegaal, L.W.
1988   *Rijden op een Hollandse tijger; De Noordkust van Java en de VOC 1680-1743.* [PhD thesis Utrecht University.]

Nieuhof, J.
1682 *Gedenkwaerdige zee en lantreize door de voornaemste landschappen van West en Oost-Indien*. Amsterdam: Van Meurs.

Reid, Anthony
1983 'Introduction; Slavery and Bondage in Southeast Asian History', in: Anthony Reid (ed.), *Slavery, Bondage and Dependency in Southeast Asia*, pp. 1-43. St. Lucia: University of Queensland Press.
1993 'The Decline of Slavery in Nineteenth Century Indonesia', in: Martin A. Klein (ed.), *Breaking the Chains; Slavery, Bondage, and Emancipation in Modern Africa and Asia*, pp. 64-82. Madison: University of Wisconsin Press.

Reinwardt, C.G.C.
1858 *Reis naar het oostelijk gedeelte van den Indischen Archipel, in het jaar 1821*. Amsterdam: Muller.

Schutte, G.J.
1974 *De Nederlandse patriotten en de koloniën; Een onderzoek naar hun denkbeelden en optreden, 1770-1800*. Groningen: Tjeenk Willink.

Stapel, F.W. (ed.)
1943 *Pieter van Dam; Beschrijvinge van de Oost-Indische Compagnie, vol. 3*. 's-Gravenhage: Nijhoff.

Sutherland, H.
1983 'Slavery and the Slave Trade in South Sulawesi 1660s-1800s', in: Anthony Reid (ed.), *Slavery, Bondage and Dependency in Southeast Asia*, pp. 263-85. St. Lucia: University of Queensland Press.
1986 'Ethnicity, Wealth and Power in Colonial Makassar; A Historiographical Reconsideration', in: P.J.M. Nas (ed.), *The Indonesian City; Studies in Urban Development and Planning*, pp. 37-55. Dordrecht: Foris. [KITLV, Verhandelingen 117.]

Van der Kraan, A.
1983 'Bali; Slavery and Slave Trade', in: Anthony Reid (ed.), *Slavery, Bondage and Dependency in Southeast Asia*, pp. 315-40. St. Lucia: University of Queensland Press.

Verslag
1859 *Verslag van het beheer en den staat der Oost-Indische bezittingen over 1859*. 's-Gravenhage: s.n.

PIETER C. EMMER

The Ideology of Free Labor and Dutch Colonial Policy, 1830-1870

'The Dutch are little disposed to take a busy and sustained part in politics. [...] Some vital questions must be at stake, affecting the conscience, the heart or the purse of the nation to rouse them to exertion. The Pope, or the House of Orange, the finances or the colonies must be in question.'[1] This observation by Lord Napier, the British ambassador in The Hague in the 1850s, seems to imply that the West Indies should have been able to attract a public audience in the Netherlands beyond that of the political élite. However, such a conclusion would be a mistake. There was no public debate concerning colonial affairs in the Netherlands in which large sections of the population were involved. Before 1848 parliament had no say in the administration of the colonies and after 1848 colonial matters remained firmly in the hands of the political élite of the Netherlands (Oostindie 1992:147).

This situation made for some striking differences with the colonial debates and policies in the UK. First, the Dutch hardly took an interest in the abolition of the slave trade and in the emancipation of slaves in the Americas. In addition, Dutch ideas and policies regarding labor in Africa and Asia also differed from those in Great Britain during the same period, albeit to a varying degree. The main reason behind these differences was the unique, nation-wide, antislavery ideology in the UK, which was absent in the Netherlands. The inspiration of this ideology in Britain was partly religious, and partly secular. The religious antislavery campaigners stressed the fact that it was unethical to enslave a fellow human being in order to make him or her work, while the secular elements pointed out that forced labor could only be more expensive than free labor. Over time, this ideology filtered through in the British policies regarding the colonial labor supply, not only in the West Indies, but also in Africa and Asia (Temperley 1972).

Until the 1860s these convictions regarding unfree labor had not yet gained enough influence in the Netherlands to convince the Dutch political élite that slavery in the West Indies should immediately disappear as soon

---

[1] Quoted in Emmer 1980:94. My sincere thanks go to Gert Oostindie, Robert Elson, Ralph Shlomowitz and Cees Fasseur, who commented on an earlier version of this contribution.

as slave emancipation had been accepted in principle. In addition, the Dutch policies in Africa and Asia were not aimed at promoting the use of free labor. As a result, the Dutch colonial policies regarding labor were based on cost effectiveness and not on ideology. In addition, the Dutch did not spend any money on ending the international slave trade, nor did the Dutch foreign policy ever jeopardize Dutch interests in order to stamp out slavery in non-Dutch territories (Emmer 1974). The dramatic economic decline following the British and French emancipations in their Caribbean colonies (in 1833 and 1848 respectively) did not stimulate the Dutch to imitate these examples. From an economic point of view, the most advantageous labor policy in the Dutch West Indies was to continue some form of compulsion in keeping labor on the plantations by postponing emancipation and by instituting a long, transitional period of apprenticeship.

Only towards the end of the 1850s did the change towards a free labor ideology occur in the Netherlands. However, for a period of thirty years after the abolition of slavery in the British Caribbean, the Dutch enabled the planters in their West Indian possessions to continue using slave labor. Between 1830 and the 1860s the Dutch used their possessions on the African Gold Coast in order to recruit soldiers for their colonial army. The Dutch were aware of the fact that these African recruits did not have a real choice between being a slave in Africa and serving as a 'free' soldier overseas as many of the recruits were slaves of the Ashanti, who had been paid to deliver them to the Dutch. No doubt, the most prominent – and lucrative – defiance of the free labor ideology took place on Java, where the Dutch colonizers introduced a system of forced cropping.

In view of the time-lag in the breakthrough of a free labor ideology in the Netherlands, this essay will compare the social and economic advantages and disadvantages of the Dutch and British colonial labor policies between 1830 and 1870.

British and Dutch Policies in the West Indies

In the West Indies the influence of abolitionism on Dutch colonial policies regarding plantation labor remained limited not only in comparison with the policies of Great Britain but also with those of France and Denmark. First of all, slave emancipation was postponed until 1863 and the end of the period of apprenticeship in Suriname until 1873. The Dutch abolitionists never attempted to shorten the latter period as had been the case in Britain. Second, the Dutch were able to switch from the supply of apprentice labor to that of imported indentured labor without any interruption. In the British Caribbean the end of the period of apprenticeship and the beginning of the large-scale introduction of indentured labor were separated by more than a decade (Siwpersad 1979; Emmer 1984:92-5, 1993:87-113).

The slave populations of the Dutch islands in the Caribbean were not subjected to a period of apprenticeship. The islands were small and so were the number and average size of their plantations. From an economic point of view a system of apprenticeship was not required. As a matter of fact, there is evidence suggesting that on the Dutch Antilles the supply of labor was so abundant that after emancipation the employers could rid themselves of their aged and sick ex-slaves without creating a labor shortage.[2] Actually, on the Dutch Antilles emancipation might have lowered the cost of labor. In this respect the Dutch islands resembled Antigua, where the planters also relinquished their right to institute a period of apprenticeship.

After 1830 the British and the Dutch Caribbean increasingly specialized in the production of sugar, almost abandoning the cultivation of coffee and cotton. As a result of the differences between Dutch and British colonial labor policies, Suriname could double its yearly sugar output between 1830 and 1863 while the British Caribbean was forced to reduce its output by more than a quarter during that period.[3] However, every policy has its price and a comparison between British and Dutch policies regarding unfree labor should not be based on production figures alone. It stands to reason that British labor policies in the West Indies should benefit the great mass of ex-slaves while Dutch policies should benefit only the relatively small number of planters, investors, and merchants. But it is also possible to argue that the postponement of economic decline in combination with the abolitionist pressures from the metropolis both enabled and forced the planters to increase their expenditure on labor. Between 1830 and 1863 the continuation of slavery aided the planters in Suriname in paying for considerable improvements in health care, housing, food, and clothing. In fact, these improvements for the slaves were made compulsory by law and consequently all plantations in Suriname were forced to implement the amelioration policies whether they could afford them or not. In the British Caribbean there are no indications that the end of slavery brought an overall rise in personal incomes. It is more likely that the income of a considerable number of ex-slaves declined after emancipation.[4]

In many contemporaneous debates it was pointed out that colonial policies favoring the discontinuation of unfree labor in the Caribbean would be relatively expensive for all concerned. The post-emancipation decline in the production of tropical cash crops in the British and French Caribbean

---

[2] See Oostindie's contribution 'Same Old Song', in this volume.
[3] Between 1833 and 1866 the yearly sugar output of the British Caribbean declined by 25 per cent in comparison with the yearly average output during the period 1814-1833 (Green 1976:246; Van Stipriaan 1993:431-2).
[4] On the policy of amelioration: Van den Boogaart and Emmer 1977:205-25; Van Stipriaan 1993:350-60; Green 1976:304-9.

seemed to prove that the opponents of emancipation were right in this respect. This explains why the abolitionist ideology had to be very strong indeed in order to gain the upper hand. Abolitionism in the Netherlands was unable to carry so much weight as to counterbalance the strong indications that slave emancipation in the Dutch West Indies would have the same negative impact on the economy as it had in the neighboring colonies. The post-emancipation experience in the British West Indies had also shown that the introduction of indentured labor could offset the withdrawal of ex-slaves from the plantations and that a delay between the ending of the period of apprenticeship and the arrival of indentured labor would be detrimental to the West Indian economies.

British and Dutch Policies Concerning African Labor

During the period 1830-1860, British and Dutch policies concerning unfree labor in West Africa were much more similar than they were in the West Indies. As far as the availability of labor in Africa was concerned, both countries were faced with the problem that Africa did not really offer any free labor at all. Nevertheless, by using their continued presence in coastal West Africa both nations tried to obtain migrant labor. The British recruited indentured laborers for the West Indies among the liberated slaves in Sierra Leone, who had been found aboard illegal slavers. The Dutch recruited Africans who would serve as soldiers in the colonial army of the Dutch East Indies.[5]

In view of the continuation of slavery in the Dutch West Indies and of the absence of a widely spread abolitionist ideology in the Netherlands, it is not surprising that the Dutch tried to recruit labor in West Africa during the period under review and that they were not very sensitive to the charge that to an African slavery and contracts of indenture did not seem to be very different. In fact, the Dutch recruitment agency on the Gold Coast fort of Elmina and the sub-agency in Kumasi, the Ashanti capital in the interior, were both buying slaves and 'liberating' them. These 'freedmen' had no other alternative but to enlist as soldiers in the Dutch colonial army. The British authorities on the Gold Coast and in London pointed out that the Dutch recruitment caused an increase in the internal slave trade and in the enslavement of Africans. As an aside it should be mentioned that the Dutch were not alone in their attempts to obtain 'free' African labor. The British also recruited in Africa and obtained about 40,000 Africans, who were transported to the West Indies on contracts of indenture in order to serve as plantation laborers. However, the British recruitment was mainly con-

[5] On the recruitment of soldiers via the Dutch possessions in West Africa, see Emmer 1974: 63-82. On the recruitment of Africans from Sierra Leone and St. Helena, see Schuler 1986:136.

ducted among the 160,000 liberated slaves, who had been found aboard illegal slavers. Most of these slaves had been brought to Sierra Leone and could not return to their home regions in Africa as they ran the risk of being enslaved again. Thus it could be argued that the recruitment procedures of the British were not very different from those of the Dutch and that in both cases the ex-slaves were not really liberated before they signed a contract of indenture. The British, however, could claim that their recruitment did not increase the number of slaves nor that it stimulated the slave trade in Africa.

Finally, in 1862 the Dutch abandoned their attempts to obtain African recruits for their colonial army and Britain transported the last of the 'recaptives' from St. Helena to Jamaica in 1867. In total the Dutch had recruited about 3,000 Africans and the British around 40,000. Both nations could have obtained considerably more Africans if they had drawn the line between slavery and freedom differently such as had been done by the French and the Portuguese who recruited more than 150,000 'free' Africans on contracts of indenture for work on plantations overseas as well as in Africa itself. The French recruitment in Africa was almost a straight continuation of the slave trade and the same applied to the recruitment by the Portuguese. Both nations allowed the purchase of African slaves, who were subsequently called 'indentured laborers' in spite of the fact that the contents of their labor contracts were not made public. However, had there been no restraint in obtaining slaves at all, the supply of African labor would have been much larger as was demonstrated by the Cubans and the Brazilians who managed to carry more than two million African slaves to their countries between 1830 and 1870 (Clarence-Smith 1992:198).

These numbers confirm the conclusion reached previously that the attitudes of the Dutch and the British towards the continued migration of African labor were similar. On this score Britain did not stand out as the 'saintly' nation. Why the British colonial policies in West Africa deviated from the free labor ideology remains to be studied. The Dutch, on the other hand, did not behave differently in West Africa as compared to their colonial labor policies in the West and East Indies (Temperley 1972:44-6).

British and Dutch Labor Policies in Asia: The Destruction of the Myth of Cheap Labor

During the period under review the labor policies of the Dutch and the British differed widely in Asia. In India as well as in the Dutch East Indies domestic slavery declined during the first half of the nineteenth century. In India slave holding was made a criminal offence and in the Dutch East Indies all slaves were emancipated in 1860. In neither colony, however, had slaves been used in the production of cash crops.⁶ In India and Indonesia the position of slaves could be compared to that of serfs in Eastern Europe at the time. There was no way in which the plantations could draw on this type of labor.

After the abolition of slavery it took some time before another system of bonded labor was introduced in India in spite of the fact that the British authorities developed a system of indentured labor migration to their plantation colonies, starting with Mauritius in the 1830s. In the same decade the Dutch colonial authorities devised a system of forced cropping which made Java into a very successful producer of cash crops. Between 1850 and 1870, however, India's cash crop production floundered – with the exception of tea cultivation – because of the impact of the free labor ideology. Obviously, British labor policies differed in that they allowed the creation of a system of bonded labor for their plantation colonies in the Caribbean and in the Indian Ocean and that they did not allow for the creation of a supply of such labor in India until the second half of the nineteenth century. The Dutch made no such distinction.

Around 1830 Java started to succeed in producing cash crops by using peasant labor. The choice for peasant labor was made after a lengthy debate about the nature of the colonial economy. Should Java be developed by private initiative from the metropolis in combination with locally available free labor as in India? Or should the government develop a cash crop production by using unfree labor (Temperley 1972:93-110; Tinker 1974:39-60)? And if unfree labor was to be used, what role should the colonial government play in managing it, since it seemed out of the question to create another plantation-cum-slavery system on Java without strong British protests (Stevens 1982:113-5)?

Because no bonded labor was available, sugar exports from India did increase only between 1830 and 1846 when some West Indian planters organized sugar plantations in India and when Indian sugar had access to the protected British market. However, as soon as the sugar duties had been abolished after 1846, sugar exports from India declined rapidly. A similar development took place in the production of cotton. India was only able to export cotton when the US cotton exports collapsed during the Civil War (Temperley 1972:102, 108). After the Civil War had ended, India's cotton sector declined again. This development indicates that the Indian sugar and cotton plantations worked by free labor could not produce at competing prices. Obviously, the more productive sugar plantations in the British Caribbean were able to compete with Indian sugar; moreover, after 1865 the cotton plantations in the US South too drove India out of business. All this

⁶ With the minor exception of nutmeg and mace production in Banda, in the Dutch Moluccas.

occurred in spite of the fact that both the Caribbean and the US South were faced by a considerable increase in the cost of labor. The rapid decline in India's sugar production after 1846 and that of cotton after 1865 destroyed the myth that cash crop production was cheap in Asia just because that continent was so densely populated and labor costs were low (Galloway 1989:201-2).

Why cheap labor did not make for cheap sugar in India remains to be studied. The most likely explanation is that the sugar production in India remained largely in the hands of peasants and that production techniques thus remained primitive. Only investments from Europe would have been able to increase India's efficiency in producing sugar by providing for the importation of expensive milling and refining machinery. Apparently, few European investors were interested in putting their money in the existing sugar plantations in India in spite of the attractively low labor costs.

In the Dutch East Indies, the myth that cheap labor on Java would make for cheap cash crops was destroyed at an earlier stage than in India by the writings of Johannes van den Bosch, who published extensively on this topic between 1810 and 1830. Van den Bosch had visited the Dutch colonies in East and West and judged himself to be much better informed about matters concerning colonial labor than all other advisers who had been asked by the King to give their opinion on reforming the Dutch colonial administration.

Around 1830 the administration of Java was in need of a drastic change, if only because its budget showed increasingly large deficits. In order to solve this problem the King had to choose between two radically opposed policies. The first one could be called the 'free enterprise option'. This policy would encourage metropolitan and other Western investors to set up plantations on Java. These plantations would rely on the use of free labor. The establishment of a plantation sector on Java would increase the revenue of the colonial state since the taxable imports, exports, and profits of the Western plantation sector would increase. In short, Java would be developed in the same way as the plantation islands in the Caribbean (Steyn Parvé 1851:295-7).

Van den Bosch, however, suggested implementing a second policy, which was based on a combination of government intervention and of peasant production. It is interesting to note that Van den Bosch did not consider free labor as an inherently good thing. By calculating the costs of free and unfree labor, Van den Bosch came to the conclusion that cash crop agriculture on Java needed forced labor in order to be competitive on the world market.

First, Van den Bosch presented his calculations regarding the costs of slave labor in the Dutch West Indies. Slaves cost their owners about 110 guilders per year. In this amount Van den Bosch included not only the cost of the daily food rations and of the various household items, but also the interest of the capital invested in the slave in addition to a 3 per cent depreciation caused by the excess of mortality above natality in Suriname. Van den Bosch further pointed out that only one slave out of three could be expected to labor, which increased the costs of a working slave to 330 guilders per year.

Second, Van den Bosch presented his calculations regarding the cost of free labor on Java. The Javanese laborer would need at least 36 guilders per year in order to survive. However, the Javanese laborer would not work for that wage as he had to feed a family. Van den Bosch expected that a Javanese laborer would only work for about 80 guilders per year or for about 0.30 or 0.35 guilders per day (Steyn Parvé 1851:299-306).

These figures indicate that compared to Suriname the cost of labor on Java was less than a third. However, this relative advantage was offset by two factors. First of all, because of a large difference in productivity, the Suriname slave could produce 1,000 pounds of sugar on average per year and the Javanese laborer only 200. Second, the cost of shipping sugar from Java to the Netherlands was more than twice as high as from Suriname. As a result, sugar from Suriname was about 30 per cent cheaper than sugar from Java (Steyn Parvé 1851:303).

The cultivation of coffee and cotton constituted no alternative for sugar on Java. The future emancipation of the West Indian slaves would increase the supply of coffee as more and more freedmen would turn to that crop. Cotton could be best produced in the South of the US and that would not change after the ending of slavery. The inevitable conclusion was that the production of cash crops on Java would only be possible with bonded labor. Without compulsion the Javanese would use the major part of their working lives for non-productive purposes.

In a philosophical afterthought Van den Bosch pointed out that the obligation to work was strongest in Europe, where – paradoxically – the common laborer was supposed to be more independent than anywhere else. However, the Suriname slave received a higher reward for his or her labor than most laborers in the Netherlands. The Javanese peasants also had incomes which were higher than those of most free laborers in Europe. In order to cultivate enough rice for his survival the Javanese only needed 120 days a year. In addition, the Javanese had to supply labor to the nobility, but that still left many months for activities which were not connected with physical survival. The laborer in the Netherlands had to spend much more time providing for his basic needs than the Suriname slave or the Javanese peasant (Steyn Parvé 1851:316-20).

Modern research has left little doubt that Van den Bosch's analysis regarding the colonial labor market, both in the Dutch West and East Indies, was very realistic. Recent calculations have shown that the expenditure on slave labor in Suriname around 1830 indeed averaged around 1 guilder per day. The yearly maintenance costs of 110 guilders per year per slave came very close to the 113.68 guilders as calculated for the government-owned plantation 'Catharina Sophia' during the period 1848-1863. Van den Bosch was also right in assuming that only one-third of the Suriname slave population performed field labor and that the Suriname slave could produce at least 500 kilograms of sugar per year. However, the assumption that the slave population in Suriname would decline with a yearly excess of death over births of 30 per 1,000 was too pessimistic. Recent calculations have put the decline at 12 per 1,000.[7] Van den Bosch was also very well informed about the labor market on Java at the time. In a recent publication the costs of a daily laborer are estimated at between 0.18 and 0.21 guilder in the 1820s and at 0.60 guilder in the 1870s (Elson 1984:23, 135). However, Van den Bosch was wrong about the bleak prospects of coffee cultivation on Java. This crop turned out to be sometimes more profitable than sugar.

The calculations of Van den Bosch induced the King to reject the free labor option for Java and, instead, to develop a scheme of forced cropping which would enable the Dutch colonial government to market most of these crops with a profit. From 1830 onwards, the production of cash crops was forced upon the Javanese villages in addition to both the land rent tax imposed by the colonial government and the customary taxes as demanded by the village chiefs and the Javanese nobility. To the outside world the Cultivation System was presented as a system of paid labor, not as a new tax in kind and certainly not as a new kind of slavery (Van Niel 1992:122-44).

The financial outcome of the system of forced cropping exceeded all expectations. Every year the surplus on the colonial budget increased and around 1860 the costs of governing the Dutch East Indies, the African forts and the West Indian possessions had been dwarfed by the growth of the revenues of the Cultivation System. Each year, the positive balance was transferred to the general exchequer of the Netherlands and at its peak in 1860 amounted to no less than about a third of the yearly revenue of the metropolis (Fasseur 1975:204).

However, exactly at the moment when the results were higher than ever, new legislation was introduced in order to dismantle the Cultivation System on Java. Finally, the ideology of free labor had caught up with Dutch colonial policy. After the constitutional reforms of 1848 the Dutch parliament was able to discuss colonial matters and to take a vote on the colonial budget. During the 1850s there were several clashes between Conservative and Liberal MPs concerning the Cultivation System and by 1860 the majority

---

[7] Van den Boogaart and Emmer 1977:217-21; Oostindie 1989:128; Van Stipriaan 1993:338.

of the MPs in the Hague were obviously convinced that the immediate abolition of slavery could no longer be postponed and that the abolition of the Cultivation System and the introduction of free labor on Java would put an end to the inadequacies of the system and would increase the production of cash crops on Java even more (Fasseur 1975:140-2; De Jong 1989:45).

The Cultivation System, Old and New Interpretations

The assessment of the Cultivation System on Java has created a sharp divide in the historiography. Contemporaneous publications regarding the Cultivation System have pointed mainly to the distress it brought to the Javanese peasants because of the workload imposed by the system itself, in addition to an extra burden extracted by corrupt Dutch civil servants, village chiefs, and the Javanese nobility. In fact, when the Dutch public at the time took an interest in colonial matters it seemed to be more receptive to the criticisms of the Cultivation System on Java than to those regarding slavery in the Dutch Caribbean. In turn, this caused many later historians to believe that the Cultivation System was not only detrimental to the Javanese population but also to the development of the Javanese economy. Some have argued that the exploitation of Java under the Cultivation System caused a relative stagnation of the economy and that the system remained in place because the Netherlands were not able to develop a modern, capitalist economy at home until the end of the nineteenth century. In this view the growth of capitalism in the Netherlands finally created a liberal ideology in which deviations from the market were judged to be impediments to further development. Supposedly, the Cultivation System had blocked the sale of land and had hampered the growth of private investments in the Dutch East Indies (Reinsma 1955:117-24). The legislation abolishing the system of forced cropping opened the gates for a much more modern way of colonial exploitation (Fasseur 1991:34).

During the past two decades, however, a revisionist interpretation has come into existence which stresses the relatively high efficiency of the Cultivation System. Several elements of the new historiography resemble revisions on similar points in the recent analyses of plantation slavery in the New World. First of all, the revisionists point to the fact that even on densely populated islands such as Java the use of forced labor can be more profitable than that of free labor and that the benefits of the structural increase in economic growth more than made up for the incidental damage caused by abuse and mismanagement (Elson 1990:24-6). Before the introduction of the Cultivation System virtually no private investments were forthcoming to set up plantations since there was hardly any free labor available. The development of the cash crop production could not have taken place without the use of bonded labor (Van Niel 1992:210-4). On Java bonded labor had to be recruited on the island itself, since the importation of large numbers of slaves or indentured laborers from elsewhere would not have been tolerated by the British at the time.

Another revision in the historiography pertains to the profits of the system. In the case of New World slavery recent research has shown that not only the slave owners, but also the slaves themselves were able to obtain considerable material benefits from the sale of the plantation products. Revisionists have pointed out that the owners and managers of plantations had much to gain from a situation in which their slaves were healthy, lived long lives and thus could provide more labor. The demographic decline of many slave populations in the New World has not yet been fully explained, but it seems more and more unlikely that the treatment of slaves in the West Indies was the actual cause of this decline. An analogous analysis has been developed with regard to the Javanese population during the period of the Cultivation System (Boomgaard 1989:191-2). Unfortunately, the evidence on the demography of Java is too scant to allow for clear-cut indications about the detrimental or beneficiary effects of the Cultivation System. However, it seems possible to indicate that the material benefits of the system not only went to the colonial government and to the European sector in general, but also to the Javanese themselves. Recent research has indicated that the results of the Cultivation System differed from region to region and that the famines on Java could not always be connected with the operation of the system. Instead, there is new evidence showing that the system created economic growth by monetizing the society. Each forced cultivator received a money wage for his labor, which was lower than the market price of his products would have allowed for, but which left him with some money to spend since the payments he received as a forced cultivator were higher than what he had to pay in tax. In other words, the Cultivation System forced the Javanese to devote more of their time to earning money and it seems possible to argue that the system used those factors of production which had not been used before or had not been fully used. This would explain why the system was able to square the circle and to increase both the colonial revenue as well as the incomes of the Javanese (Elson 1990:49-67).

Last, but not least there is also a dramatic historiographic *volte face* regarding the abolition of the system. Until some years ago the majority of the historians believed a serious decline in the profitability and viability of the system to be the main cause for abolition. Several forced crops could only be marketed with a loss, notably indigo. New research has indicated, however, that there was a decline in output of some products, but not in revenues from the sale of all products taken together. The production of sugar remained viable. As with the abolition of slavery, ending the Cultivation System was a jump into the dark. The explanation must be that the abolition of the Cultivation System was based – among other things – on the growing impact of the free labor ideology among MPs in the Netherlands and not on clear-cut evidence that the dismantling of the system would lower costs and increase production.[8]

Yet – in contrast with many plantation areas in the West Indies – the abolition of the Cultivation System did not reduce the output of sugar. However, it would be wrong to assume that continued growth of sugar production on Java after 1870 demonstrated the superiority of free labor. That growth was based on the possibilities to continue using bonded labor. After the end of the Cultivation System the sugar plantations recruited labor by concluding collective contracts with the village chiefs in the vicinity which obliged them to supply a certain amount of labor during a certain amount of time. The abolition of the Cultivation System demonstrated that during the nineteenth century Java was one of the many tropical areas where free labor did not respond to demand as the economics text books would have it.[9]

Conclusion

During the period between 1830 and 1870 the colonial labor policies of Britain and the Netherlands deviated considerably from one another. In the Dutch West Indies slavery continued to exist until 1863 and the debate regarding slave emancipation in the Netherlands mainly focused on practical issues such as the compensation for slave owners, the duration of the period of apprenticeship, and the importation of indentured labor from Asia. The continuation of the system of slavery, the lengthy period of apprenticeship in Suriname, and the timing of the arrival of the first indentured laborers from Asia all postponed a drastic decline in the agricultural output of Suriname. As a consequence, the Suriname plantation owners, investors and merchants trading with the colony earned higher incomes or – alternatively – made smaller losses than they would have made in case the Dutch had abolished slavery in 1833 and had ended apprenticeship in 1838 as had happened in the British West Indies. Similarly, slavery and apprenticeship affected the incomes of slaves and ex-slaves many more years than these institutions had done in the British Caribbean. As a result the incomes of the 'workers in the cane' and their dependents in Suriname were not necessarily lower and probably more equally distributed than those of the freedmen in the British Caribbean during the same period.

[8] Fasseur 1980:125-9, 1991:34; De Jong 1989:66; Elson 1994:179-226.
[9] Tichelman 1987:167-72; Elson 1986:139-74; Boomgaard 1990:37-56.

In West Africa, by contrast, the colonial labor policies of the Dutch and the British hardly differed. Both countries recruited relatively small numbers of so-called free African labor and this seems to clash more clearly with the ideology and practice of the British colonial labor policies at the time than with those of the Dutch. However, compared to France and Portugal, both the Netherlands and Britain seemed to have been relatively reluctant to recruit 'voluntary' migrant labor in Africa on a massive scale during the nineteenth century.

In colonial Asia Dutch and British labor policies again differed. Both countries favored the decline and subsequent abolition of domestic slavery in India and the Dutch East Indies. Around 1830, however, the Dutch devised a scheme of forced cropping which made Java into one of the world's premier export colonies of coffee and sugar. The British labor policies in India, however, did not generate an increase in the production of cash crops. Around 1850 the main export product from India was indigo which was produced by peasants. During the crucial years right after the ending of slavery (in 1833) and of the abbreviated period of apprenticeship in the British West Indies (in 1838), India was not able to become a major exporter of sugar, coffee, and tea. The production of sugar and cotton in India decreased sharply after the abolition of the preferential duties. The production of tea only started to increase from the mid-1860s once a system of government-supervised migration of indentured labor had been devised (Tinker 1974:36).

In evaluating the free labor system of India and the system of bonded labor in Java there is ample evidence to show that private investors, shipping firms, the colonial state, and in particular the metropolitan exchequer stood to gain from the employment of unfree labor. In addition, however, new evidence shows that the average income of the Javanese increased during the operation of the system of forced cropping, while India's population did not seem to have experienced such an increase. The dramatic rise in the number of indentured and non-indentured migrants to destinations both inside and outside the colony seems to indicate that during the period 1830-1870 more and more Indians became marginalized peasants. In fact, this development might explain why in the late 1840s and again more firmly in the 1850s the colonial administrators in India seemed to have backtracked somewhat on the free labor ideology and finally agreed to setting up a system of migratory contract labor supervised by the government (Yang 1979:37-58).

The recent literature on comparative labor costs in the New World of the nineteenth century indicates that the price for the abolition of slavery as paid by the slave owners, investors, and metropolitan taxpayers should be balanced against the psychological and not the economic benefits of freedom for the ex-slaves. In comparing the free labor system in India and the system of forced labor on Java during the first half of the nineteenth century a similar observation can be made. Obviously, Britain was willing to pay the price to allow the use of only free (wage and contract) labor in its Caribbean colonies, and in India.

The Dutch were much more reluctant to pay that price and so were all the other colonial powers in Europe. In contrast with Britain, the Dutch consumers were not asked to pay for the protection of Dutch West Indian sugar in order to help their West Indian planters. In addition, the Dutch taxpayers benefitted considerably from the system of forced labor on Java. As a consequence of the large positive balance on the colonial budget, the metropolitan expenditure on railway construction and on defence could be about a third higher than the revenues from the Dutch taxpayers would have allowed for. There is no doubt that the Dutch entrepreneurs in East and West stood to gain from the postponement in applying the free labor ideology in the Dutch colonies. Similar observations can be made about the colonial labor policies of France, Spain, and Portugal. Furthermore, it has always been assumed that the introduction of free labor would cause a reduction in economic benefits to these colonial entrepreneurs and by the same token increase the benefits for the colonized. Revisionist historians have questioned this link in both East and West.

The British policies regarding the rapid abolition of slavery in the West Indies were unique and the recent research on this topic is still trying to come to grips with this. There seems to be enough evidence to conclude that during the nineteenth century the British labor policies were not only unique in the West Indies, but also in India. Similarly, the belated slave emancipation in the Dutch West Indies becomes less unique when compared to the Dutch labor policies in Asia. None of these points are made in the literature which shows a clear divide between East and West. It is about time that the comparative research on these topics should make the twain meet.

References

Boogaart, Ernst van den and Pieter C. Emmer
1977　　'Plantation Slavery in Surinam in the Last Decade before Emancipation; The Case of Catharina Sophia', in: Vera Rubin and Arthur Tuden (eds), *Comparative Perspectives on Slavery in New World Plantation Societies*, pp. 202-25. New York: Annals of the New York Academy of Sciences.

Boomgaard, Peter
1987　　*Children of the Colonial State; Population Growth and Economic Development in Java, 1795-1880*. Amsterdam: Free University Press. [CASA Monographs 1.]

1990 'Why Work for Wages? Free Labour in Java, 1600-1900', *Economic and Social History in the Netherlands* 2:37-56.

Clarence-Smith, W.G.
1992 'Emigration from Western Africa, 1807-1940', in: P.C. Emmer and M. Mörner (eds), *European Expansion and Migration; Essays on the Intercontinental Migration from Africa, Asia and Europe*, pp. 197-210. New York: Berg.

Elson, R.E.
1984 *Javanese Peasants and the Colonial Sugar Industry; Impact and Change in an East Java Residency, 1830-1940*. Singapore: Oxford University Press.
1986 'Sugar Factory Workers and the Emergence of "Free Labour" in Nineteenth Century Java', *Modern Asian Studies* 20:139-74.
1990 'Peasant Poverty and Prosperity under the Cultivation System in Java', in: Anne Booth, W.J. O'Malley and Anna Weidemann (eds), *Indonesian Economic History in the Dutch Colonial Era*, pp. 24-98. New Haven: Yale University Southeast Asian Studies.
1994 *Village Java under the Cultivation System, 1830-1870*. Sydney: Allen and Unwin.

Emmer, Pieter C.
1974 *Engeland, Nederland, Afrika en de slavenhandel in de negentiende eeuw*. Leiden: Brill.
1980 'Anti-Slavery and the Dutch; Abolition without Reform', in: Christine Bolt and Seymour Drescher (eds), *Anti-Slavery, Religion, and Reform; Essays in Memory of Roger Anstey*, pp. 80-98. Folkestone: Dawson; Hamden: Archon.
1984 'The Importation of British Indians into Surinam (Dutch Guiana), 1873-1916', in: Shula Marks and Peter Richardson (eds), *International Labour Migration; Historical Perspectives*, pp. 90-111. London: Temple Smith.
1993 'Between Slavery and Freedom; The Period of Apprenticeship in Suriname (Dutch Guiana), 1863-1873', *Slavery and Abolition* 14-1:87-113.

Fasseur, C.
1975 *Kultuurstelsel en koloniale baten; De Nederlandse exploitatie van Java, 1840-1860*. Leiden: Leidse Universitaire Pers.
1980 'Het Cultuurstelsel opnieuw in discussie', in: C. Fasseur (ed.), *Geld en geweten; Een bundel opstellen over anderhalve eeuw Nederlands bestuur in de Indonesische archipel*, vol. I, pp. 115-30. 's-Gravenhage: Nijhoff.
1991 'Purse or Principle? Dutch Colonial Policy in the 1860s and the Decline of the Cultivation System', *Modern Asian Studies* 25:33-52.

Galloway, J.H.
1989 *The Sugar Cane Industry; An Historical Geography from Its Origins to 1914*. Cambridge: Cambridge University Press.

Green, William A.
1976 *British Slave Emancipation; The Sugar Colonies and the Great Experiment 1830-1865*. Oxford: Clarendon Press.

Jong, Janny de
1989   *Van batig slot naar ereschuld; De discussie over de financiële verhouding tussen Nederland en Indië en de hervormingen van de Nederlandse koloniale politiek.* 's-Gravenhage: SDU.

Oostindie, Gert
1989   *Roosenburg en Mon Bijou; Twee Surinaamse plantages, 1720-1870.* Dordrecht: Foris. [KITLV, Caribbean Series 11.]
1992   'The Enlightenment, Christianity, and the Suriname Slave', *Journal of Caribbean History* 26:147-70. [Revised and enlarged version in the present book.]

Reinsma, Riemer
1955   *Het verval van het cultuurstelsel.* 's-Gravenhage: Van Keulen.

Shuler, Monica
1986   'The Recruitment of African Indentured Labourers for European Colonies in the 19th Century', in: Pieter C. Emmer (ed.), *Colonialism and Migration; Indentured Labour Before and After Slavery*, pp. 125-61. Dordrecht: Nijhoff.

Siwpersad, J.P.
1979   *De Nederlandse regering en de afschaffing van de Surinaamse slavernij (1833-1863).* Groningen: Bouma; Castricum: Hagen.

Stevens, Th.
1982   *Van der Capellen's koloniale ambitie op Java; Economisch beleid in een stagnerende conjunctuur.* Amsterdam: University of Amsterdam, Historisch Seminarium.

Steyn Parvé, D.C.
1851   *Het koloniale monopoliestelsel getoetst aan geschiedenis en staatshuishoudkunde.* Zaltbommel: Noman.

Stipriaan, Alex van
1993   *Surinaams contrast; Roofbouw en overleven in een Caraïbische plantagekolonie, 1750-1863.* Leiden: KITLV Press. [Caribbean Series 13.]

Temperley, Howard
1972   *British Antislavery, 1833-1870.* London: Longman.

Tichelman, F.
1987   'Problems of Javanese Labour; Continuity and Change in the Nineteenth Century', *Itinerario* 11:155-92.

Tinker, Hugh
1974   *A New System of Slavery; The Export of Indian Labour Overseas, 1830-1920.* London: Oxford University Press.

Van Niel, Robert
1992   *Java under the Cultivation System.* Leiden: KITLV Press. [Verhandelingen 150.]

Yang, Arnaud
1979   'Peasants on the Move; A Study of Internal Migration in India', *Journal of Interdisciplinary History* 10:37-58.

STANLEY L. ENGERMAN

Emancipations in Comparative Perspective
A Long and Wide View

In this article I present a number of familiar points, wishing mainly to ask three questions about the emancipation of slaves in the New World in the nineteenth century.[1] First, what accounts for the timing of the emergence of those antislavery ideas and patterns of behavior that were to lead to a British 'success' in ending slavery? Second, what accounts for the timing of the success of abolition movements, in particular times and places? What new ideas emerged and/or became more widespread, and how were these translated into political practices and procedures, directly or indirectly, that put these beliefs into operation? What changed political practices, including the nature of voting, and the relation between the public and the legislators and executives? Were the ideas long latent, awaiting (for whatever reason) political changes, or did new beliefs take a hold on more people? Third, what does the implementation and/or acceptance of alternative labor forms after slave emancipation tell us about the nature of the antislavery mind? Although we now have better answers for the Dutch and for the British cases, there remain several others for which answers to these questions would be of interest.

The Abolition of Slavery

In recent years there has been considerable new research and publications on the topics of slavery and its abolition. Studies of slavery have covered many times and places, and have led to major reinterpretations along a number of quite different fronts. Slave cultures are no longer seen as either nonexistent or very limited, but rather as demonstrating the humanity capable within even as extreme a set of conditions as were the power relations under enslavement. In regard to economic issues, the profitability and viability of slavery have frequently been demonstrated, and earlier views of slave economies as limited in growth potential have come to be seen as

---

[1] In preparing this paper I have benefitted from discussions with Seymour Drescher, David Eltis, and Robert Steinfeld, as well as from participants at the Conference 'Dutch Capitalism and Antislavery in Comparative Perspective' (Leiden, KITLV, 15 October 1993).

rather more theoretical and hypothetical than empirical propositions. That slavery, in most cases, would soon decline of its own weight is now regarded as rather dubious, based both on the ex post examination of the evidence and, perhaps more convincing, the infrequency with which those who owned slaves were willing and anxious to voluntarily let the system end. These findings have, of course, reawakened interest in explaining why slavery ever did end and why it ended at the particular times and places that it did.

While the recent studies of slavery have described the institution in many different times and places, since slavery had been one of the most ubiquitous of all the human-created social institutions, studies of emancipation seem to be rather more limited in time and space. Significantly more scholarly energy has seemed devoted to the ending of slavery in the New World in the nineteenth century, and, within that area, considerably more attention to the British ending of the slave trade in 1808 and slavery in 1834, and to the United States ending of slavery in 1865, than to the other cases of emancipation in the Americas. And this focus on the causes of the ending of nineteenth-century slavery overseas by the British, French, Danish, Swedish, Dutch, and Spanish, as well as the similarly-timed freeing of slaves by the independent nations of the United States and Brazil, has meant relatively less attention to the earlier endings of slavery in Europe itself, as well as to its subsequent endings in various parts of South America, in Africa, and in Asia. And with this emphasis on slavery, easily legally defined and in the nineteenth century often applied only outside metropolitan Europe, the nature of possible relations between the ending of slavery and the roughly simultaneous ending of serfdom throughout Europe has been relatively uninvestigated.

I wish to suggest that the primary focus on the nature of British slave abolition, an abolition which freed only one-seventh of New World slaves in the 1830s (clearly less than ten percent of all slaves and no doubt less than three percent of all legally coerced labor at the time), has meant a certain narrowness of intellectual perspective.[2] The search for a British uniqueness does, of course, open up the question of why others, particularly the Dutch who had led the British in modern economic growth, did not have significant leads and/or lagged behind the British. Yet by emphasizing the one case of Britain in the early nineteenth century, the changes of the preceding centuries and in non-European areas have been given less attention. I think that there are issues of a narrowing of time, place, and form of institution

---

[2] The estimated number of British and total New World slaves is presented in Fogel and Engerman 1974a:28. The estimate for all coerced labor includes those for serfs in Europe, approximated from the discussions in Blum 1978, and slaves in Africa, inferred from Manning 1990.

that are worth exploring before we can feel comfortable with present interpretations of the process of emancipation.

The Ending of Slavery and Serfdom in Europe

The specific timing of the ending of New World slavery comes with a number of predecessors and did not lead to immediate endings elsewhere. While the datings are often murky (itself an interesting point given the clarity of legal definitions of slavery), slavery itself had often ended in many parts of Northern and Western Europe by the early Middle Ages, certainly slavery as applied to residents of the particular area.[3] Slavery apparently had ended in England by the start of the twelfth century, roughly the same time as in France and parts of Germany. The Scandinavian regions ended slavery by the thirteenth and fourteenth centuries. In the Iberian areas slavery, which by then had been primarily of Muslim captives, had ended by the twelfth century, but only for Christians. In present-day Italy, where Muslims as well as non-Christians had been important as slaves, slavery lasted until about the seventeenth century (Phillips 1985:97-113). These areas, as well as Sicily, became, because of location or other reasons, the first in Europe to make use of slaves from Africa in the fifteenth century. African slavery in England and France was always considerably more limited (Saunders 1982:4-34, 47-61; Verlinden 1970). The Portuguese ended the slave trade to Portugal in 1761, and then slavery within Portugal twelve years later.[4]

In some areas (France, Germany) slavery was succeeded, in a manner earlier suggested by Marc Bloch, by serfdom (although the length of any profitable simultaneous existence is not clear).[5] In others, such as Scandinavia, slavery was followed by variants of 'free' labor, not serfdom, while in England, serfdom followed slavery, but declined dramatically by the end of the fourteenth century. Labor scarcity, created by the Black Death, led English landowners to forget their agreements not to bid directly for unfree labor, and did so by providing better material treatment and living conditions – including freedom (Hilton 1983).[6] As for the Dutch, Jan de Vries comments that 'serfdom [...] was rare and short-lived, leaving few traces past the twelfth century' (De Vries 1974:25). Although the timing of these changes in

---

[3] The following discussion is based primarily upon Phillips 1985:16-113; Karras 1988:5-39.
[4] See Alden 1984:625; Payne 1973, II:407-8. See also Schwartz 1985:478. The ending of the slave trade to Portugal was, however, apparently not for humanitarian reasons, but rather to increase the supply of slaves available in Brazil, where they were presumably more useful. The numbers diverted, however, could not have been too large. According to the thirteenth edition of the *Encyclopedia Britannica's* entry on Madeira, slavery there was ended by order of Pombal in 1775.
[5] Bloch 1975:1-32. See also Finley 1980:123-49; Bonnassie 1991:1-59.
[6] For a discussion of the survival of a limited number of bondsmen into the sixteenth century, see Savine 1903.

serfdom in Western Europe is only approximately accurate, the development of the so-called 'second serfdom' in Eastern Europe is similarly hard to date. It occurred sometime in the period ranging from the fourteenth to the nineteenth centuries, most importantly in the years from the fifteenth to the seventeenth centuries.[7]

With the exception of France, most areas of Northwest and Southwest Europe tended not to have a recognized form of serfdom in the eighteenth century.[8] In regard to the rest, as Jerome Blum (1978) points out, emancipation occurred in the ninety-three year period between 1771 and 1864.[9] While among the thirty-eight areas with decrees listed by Blum are some rather small places, it should be noted that they also include the largest emancipations of unfree labor: Russia, in 1861, of over twenty million; Austria, in 1848, of over twelve million; and Hungary, in 1853, of about seven million. Even the latter emancipation probably exceeded the total number of New World slaves freed by legal emancipation.[10] The timing of the emancipation of serfs given by Blum is of interest for comparisons with that of the abolition of slavery. These dates were:

Table 1. Emancipation of Serfs in Europe

Period	Number of decrees	
1771-1800	5	(including Denmark and France)
1801-1820	11	
1821-1830	0	
1831-1840	5	(all in 1831 and 1832)
1841-1850	13	(mostly German states)
1851-1864	4	

Source: Blum 1978:356.

While serfdom applied to individuals of the same race and, often, ethnic background, the debates on the economic and cultural basis of emancipation bore a distinct resemblance to those of the debates on slavery elsewhere. Unlike slaves, however, the serfs, having had a presumed right to land use,

---

[7] See Blum 1957; Genovese 1969:22-3; Topolski 1982.
[8] Most of this paragraph is based particularly on Blum 1978:356-400.
[9] For completeness in Europe, we might also add the ending of legalized 'serfdom' in the Scottish coal mines in 1799. See Whatley 1987 for a description of the Scottish coal-mining legislation.
[10] The estimate for Russian serfs is from Blum 1961:420. Blum quotes 'a contemporary [1850] apologist for serfdom' on the 'essential differences between the Russian serf and the American Negro slave': 'the serf had the privilege of taking the oath of allegiance to the tsar, paying a personal tax, and serving in the army' (Blum 1961:468-9). The estimates of the number of serfs for Austria and Hungary come from correspondence with John Komlos. The estimates for the number of serfs in France in 1789 range from 140,000 to one million. See Drescher 1987: 201-2.

were often forced to pay, in labor time and cash, for their post-emancipation benefits.

The Timing of the Ending of the Slave Trade and of Slavery

In discussing the ending of New World slavery there are several aspects that bear attention.[11] While to us the evils of slavery are rather clear, and we might anticipate that the recognition of that evil would set in process the steps to bring it to an early end, the actual process itself was rather delayed. The agreed-upon (and, at times, also the actual subsequent) ending of the transatlantic slave trade generally preceded the ending of New World slavery by at least one-quarter century.[12]

Table 2. The Timing of the Ending of Slave Trade and Slavery

	Ending of Slave Trade	Ending of Slavery
Denmark	1803	1848
England	1808	1834
United States	1808	1865
Netherlands	1814	1863
France	1815	1848[13]
Brazil	1830	1888
Spain (Cuba)	1835	1886[14]
Sweden	1794?	1847

Not only were there long lags between the apparent recognition of the evils of the slave trade and of the evils of slavery, the nature of policies introduced after these recognitions often differed. Thus the emancipation of slaves, with only limited exceptions, entailed some form of direct compensation in cash or securities, to former slaveholders. While seldom adequate to fully cover the previous prices of slaves or of land worked on by slaves, these payments were frequently supplemented by forms of compelled labor time due to the landowners by the freedpeople – a practice similar to that of the serf emancipations of the time. In the case of the Netherlands West

---

[11] This paragraph is based primarily upon material in Eltis 1987; Fogel and Engerman 1974a:33-4 and 1974b; Blackburn 1988; Davis 1975 and 1984. For the rather obscure case of Sweden, see Ekman 1975.

[12] Dating the ending of the slave trade is, for several areas (the French West Indies, Brazil, and Cuba) rather difficult given the lag between the date of signing international treaties pledging to end the slave trade, the date of the legislation ending the slave trade, and then the date of actual enforcement of these laws that effectively end slave imports. Thus dating the ending of the slave trade by the dates of the last sets of slave shipments would give: France, 1831; Brazil, 1852; and Cuba, 1867.

[13] Haiti, by 1804, is a special case.

[14] Puerto Rico, 1873.

Indies, a region with one of the last metropolitan-legislated emancipations, the major colony, Suriname, had a period of apprenticeship which lasted one decade (Emmer 1993).

Similarly, many of the slave emancipations in the Northern United States in the late eighteenth century and the newly independent states of South and Central America in the first part of the nineteenth century, had prolonged time horizons even after the initial recognition of the goal of freedom.[15] Few states, only Vermont (1777), Massachusetts (1780), and New Hampshire (1784), and few of the former Spanish-American colonies, only Chile (1823), Central America (1824), and Mexico (1829), provided immediate freedom for all of the enslaved and their offspring. All others drafted legislation to provide what would be called a 'free womb', freeing only those born after a specific date, subject to having the offspring work for the owner of the mother for a period of time generally ranging until the late teenages to 28 years, depending upon the state or country. Those born before that date were not considered free, although there were sometimes provisions for the slow emancipation of some still enslaved. Moreover, after some time, the initial law was followed by laws freeing everybody. Yet, in most cases, such legislation came more than a quarter-century after the law of the 'free womb'.

In the Northern United States the patterns were as follows:

Table 3. Slavery Laws in the Northern United States

	Law of Free Birth	Law or Provision Ending Slavery
Pennsylvania	1780	–
Rhode Island	1784	1842
Connecticut	1784	1848
New York	1799	1817 (to be ended 1827)
New Jersey	1804	1846

Some laws of emancipation, such as New Jersey's, provided that slavery would continue for those individuals unable to take care of themselves. This explains the listing of only eighteen northern slaves, in New Jersey, in the United States census of 1860. The lag between the law of the 'free womb' and the ending of slavery leaves several anomalies, such as the presence of seven-eighths as many slaves in 'free' New York in 1810 as there were in a newly expanding slave state such as Mississippi. Legislation was passed in most of the new states of the North to 'abolish' or 'prohibit' slavery, ranging

---

[15] The discussions and datings in the next paragraphs are drawn primarily from Zilversmit 1967; Fogel and Engerman 1974b, and Farnam 1938:211-24, 415-74, on the United States, and from Rout 1976; Lynch 1986, and Klein 1986, on Latin America.

in time from Ohio in 1803 through eight other states to the last of the antebellum period, Kansas, in 1859.

The lags in most Latin American nations were similar to those in the northern states of the United States, at least those that occurred before the American Civil War and the defeat of the Confederacy. The dates were as follows:

Table 4. Slavery Laws in Spanish America

	Law of Free Birth	Law or Provision Ending Slavery
Argentina	1813	1853
Peru	1821	1854
Ecuador	1821	1851
Colombia	1821	1851
Venezuela	1821	1854
Uruguay	1825	1853
Bolivia	1831	1861
Paraguay	1842	1869

While these dates of legal change are precise, it is difficult to find reliable estimates of the numbers of slaves freed by this legislation. More easy to determine are the much larger numbers of slaves freed in the last three cases of slave emancipation in the Americas:

Table 5. Slavery Laws in the Spanish Caribbean and Brazil

	Law of Free Birth	Law or Provision Ending Slavery
Puerto Rico	1870	1873
Cuba	1870	1886
Brazil	1871	1888

Even in these last cases, however, some lag between the two variants of legislated emancipation persisted. In several other ways the slave emancipations in Latin America had characteristics similar to emancipations in North America (and elsewhere). In some Latin American countries the slave trade was abolished several years before there were any limitations on the continuation of slavery, and military service was made a basis for the emancipation of individual slaves. Moreover, the antislavery legislation was applied to blacks, leaving non-enslaved Indians within the long-persisting Spanish-American *encomienda* system of labor control in a separate legal category.

Despite the variety of patterns in serf and slave emancipations by Europeans and the European settlers in the Americas, it is striking that they mainly occur within the period of about one century, from the last quarter of the eighteenth century to the last quarter of the nineteenth century; that they were mostly restricted to Europe and the Americas, with some application to European colonies of a limited geographic expanse elsewhere, and even then there was not the same date for ending slavery in the East Indies and the West Indies for both the Dutch and the British, although the timing was rather close. Further, they entailed no compensation paid by presumed 'sinners' (slave owners or serf lords) or to those presumably 'sinned against' (slaves or serfs). No doubt there are other similarities, as well as certain obvious contrasts. The relative number of slaves has been used to explain the timing of abolition. Thus, for example, Adam Smith's explanation of Quaker abolition, resting upon the relative unimportance of slaves to them in Pennsylvania, may help explain the endings of slavery in Vermont and New Hampshire, but it does little to account for the rather delayed abolition in the colonies of the Swedish and Dutch West Indies.[16] Relative magnitudes may, however, help to explain some of the factors in the relatively late slave abolitions in the United States, Cuba, and Brazil, as well as the late ending of serfdom in Russia. Nevertheless, the frequent ending of discussions of slave emancipation with the Brazilian case of 1888 leaves important parts of the story of the decline of slavery in the modern world outside of the Americas unexamined.

Ending Slavery in Africa and Asia

Slavery persisted in many parts of Africa, the Islamic Middle East, and elsewhere in Asia after 1888, often into the first half of the twentieth century.[17] It is estimated that the number of slaves in West Africa in the nineteenth century probably exceeded that in the Americas, and may have totaled as many as ten million at the start of the twentieth century (Manning 1988:26, 1990:22-3). While these slaves were dispersed among a large number of regions, the Sokoto Caliphate alone had, at the end of the nineteenth century, somewhere between one and 2.5 million slaves (Lovejoy and Hogendorn 1993:1). A basic impetus to ending slavery, albeit with rather gradual and peculiar legal measures, came from the British, French, and Germans who obtained political control of these areas, and emancipation procedures were often dictated by the metropolis against the wishes of those Europeans in Africa, whose arguments generally included both their own self-interest, but also reflected some concern with the

---

[16] Drescher 1987:51 presents an example of the 'importance of being unimportant' for maintaining slavery: 'The Swedish ambassador to France was simply unaware of slavery on Swedish St. Bartholomew until British abolitionists brought it to his notice'.
[17] For Africa, see, in particular, Lovejoy 1983; Miers and Kopytoff 1977; on the Middle East, see Lewis 1990:72-84; and for Asia, see Watson 1980; Reid 1983.

cultural and political goals of the African élite.[18] It was only by mid-century that slavery was basically abolished by law throughout most of Africa and Arabia, this abolition having been one of the major goals of western-dominated organizations such as the League of Nations and the United Nations. Within Asia, slavery existed in several nominally independent nations into the twentieth century, with the legislation ending it similar to that found earlier in western nations.[19] Thus, while British abolition was a significant historical event, it took more than one century before its effect spread around the world, often requiring a form of cultural imperialism, imposed at times by political force, from outside. And, of course, that century was marked not only by differing forms of coerced labor (to be discussed below) but some other extreme forms of human barbarity and destruction. Before turning to variant forms of coerced labor sometimes related to slavery, there remain several issues related to slave emancipation to discuss.

Slavery in Sending and Receiving Regions

The discussion thus far treats, as is customary, all slavery as involuntary and to be avoided by all individuals and families. Yet we do know that in many societies (although not the major slave societies of the New World) slavery was, at times, a voluntary action, resembling debt arrangements, for adults and for children.[20] This generally occurred in societies at relatively low levels of income, often with a high variance of income, both of which imposed threats of large-scale famines and starvations. It is still unclear if such societies ended slavery in different circumstances than in the other, more frequently discussed, cases of nonvoluntary slavery. Of course, voluntary enslavement was not the only 'solution' to problems of possible starvation, although this was a pattern apparently frequent in Africa and Asia. Another resolution to the problems of low income, apparently implanted in Western Europe in medieval and early modern times, involved population restriction (and no slavery) by the practices of infanticide, abandonment, and infant exposure.[21] Such practices may have reduced the numbers of slaves, but it does suggest the reasons why voluntary slavery might have developed in other areas.

---

[18] On the ending of slavery in Africa, see, in particular, the essays in Miers and Roberts 1988. The legislation ending slavery included a wide variety of provisions, some reflecting the actual end of enslavement, others merely making the state of slavery legally unenforceable. For the late (c 1890) ending of the slave trade from Africa to the Ottoman Empire, see Toledano 1982.
[19] See Reid 1993, and the other essays in that volume, and essays in Watson 1980.
[20] See, for example, Patterson 1982:129-31.
[21] For the earlier period, see Boswell 1988; Fildes 1988.

Most forms of slavery were applied only to outsiders of the given society, although the definition of what made for an outsider – by race, religion, nationality, ethnicity, and so on – differed over time.[22] The definition of an outsider, so important for defining slaves and emancipation, does pose a problem for the analysis of the end of slavery. Clearly, in the New World, after some initial attempts at enslaving Amerindians, slavery became restricted to Africans and their descendants. Europeans were not to be enslaved, except as a result of criminal activities, and, even then, generally with some limited time-duration (although sometimes with death). Yet before linking racism and proslavery arguments, the importance of the racist antislavery argument against introducing new slaves or continuing slavery, in Brazil, Cuba, and the United States, suggests that the equation may not so simply be used to describe emancipation.[23] Perhaps the clearest indication of the, at times, ambiguous nature of racism can be seen in the Australian sugar industry, where racism led to the import of Melanesian contract labor in the late nineteenth century, a policy ended by the racism of a 'White Australia' policy that made such imported labor undesirable.[24]

No doubt some differences existed between debates on emancipation within the New World areas and those that took place in the metropolis, where few blacks, slave or free, were to be found. These differences may reflect also differences in the class interests of labor and of landowners in the different locations. Further, the nature of the enslavement of an outsider often meant that there was some migration from point of origin to the point of settlement and labor use. In the modern world this often entailed moving Africans elsewhere for purposes of labor, seen most clearly in the transatlantic and trans-Saharan slave trades. Serfdom, however, generally entailed controls over a resident population by other members of that population. Ending serfdom was, in this sense, an internal action at the expense (or at the desire) of some members of that locality, whether by royal decree, by formal legislation, or other actions. In regard to slavery, however, we can point to two possible ways that it could have been terminated. The country of outshipment could decree the ending of a traffic in people, or, alternatively, the recipient country could refuse to permit enslaved humans to arrive and to be sold. The pattern in the New World slave trade generally saw its ending by a refusal either to permit new slave arrivals or else by some controls introduced by European shipping powers that could effect

---

[22] See Patterson 1982 and, for a different approach, Eltis 1993.
[23] Certainly the politically important 1857 antislavery tract by Hinton Helper arguing to end slavery in the US was to be seen more as anti-black than as anti-slavery, calling for policies to increase economic gains to nonslaveholding whites.
[24] On this, see, most recently, Graves 1993, as well as the extensive writings by Ralph Shlomowitz on this (and other) forms of labor movement within the Pacific region. See the list of his publications in Moore, Leckie and Munro 1990:295-6.

slave movements. The ending of indentured labor was accomplished by, at some times, restricting the outflow and, at others, by limiting the inflow, whether for ideological or economic reasons in either case. The end of Indian outmigration came in 1917, as a result of Indian nationalist pressure, while throughout the nineteenth century China, whatever its internal forms of population controls, periodically imposed restrictions on the outflow to other continents, based on the treatment provided to the migrants. The eighteenth and nineteenth centuries saw many controls on migration patterns, but most areas from which the slaves were shipped long distances did not introduce such restrictive measures, whatever may have been their freedom of action in this regard.

The possible effect of an earlier introduction of restrictions on slave exports from Africa can be seen by examining the effects upon Africa that came after the transatlantic slave trade had been limited and then ended. Once a slave acquisition and trading network had been established, ending the slave trade to the Americas could increase the supply within Africa, and thus lower the cost of using slaves within Africa. This reduction in the loss of manpower that occurred when the transatlantic slave trade ended apparently led to more use of slave labor in Africa, a shift from the exporting of slaves to the exporting of crops grown by slave labor. Thus an economic and demographic gain might have been possible if a mechanism to prohibit human exports had earlier been possible. To the receiving areas, the ending of the slave trade meant a reduced labor supply, with a higher price for scarcer labor – a reason why their direct economic interests should have been in the maintenance of international migrations. Of course, in regard to both the sending and receiving countries, it could be argued that differences in economic interests within the population meant differences in preferred migration policies. We would then need to relate these conflicting interests to internal differences in political power. Given the nature of political differences in the Americas, with the particular interests of laborers and non-slaveholding landowners, it is perhaps less surprising that the restrictions on the transatlantic slave trade came, when they did, from the receiving end, albeit influenced by international pressures from other western nations, and not from the sending end.

Variant Forms of Coerced Labor

It is now clear that slavery is one end of a rather broad spectrum of labor forms, with differing degrees of coercion, mobility across distance, material treatment, and possibilities for its status being terminated for specific individuals. Similarities to the coercion under slavery have been attributed to contract labor, debt peonage or bondage, and even to 'free' labor, with their prolonged existence of restrictions on the rights of laborers to leave employment contracts.[25] These labor control variants are based on differing sets of legal and non-legal controls and persisted for varying periods of time. In some cases the issue is how to best describe agreements presumably voluntarily entered into (given the constraints of laborer needs and their low incomes), which meant the foregoing of certain rights for a given set period of time. Noting these degrees of control indicates that there are many varieties of so-called coerced (or constrained) labor. Thus an important issue is not just the one of whether coercion exists, but rather the question of what specific form constraints will take at different times. Once emancipation is agreed to, differences could still persist regarding which forms of labor institutions are expected to take its place. The spectrum of labor forms also raises the question of why certain of these variants were permitted to continue even at the time of the successful culmination of the moral crusade against slavery. Indeed, in some cases the abolition of slavery led to a permitted (by the governments, if not by the abolitionists) increase in international movements of contract labor, an increase created in part by the decision to end slavery while the world demand for sugar and for other plantation crops remained high.

Thus, as is quite familiar, the ending of slavery in the British, French, and Dutch West Indies led to the expanded flow of contract labor from many parts of the world, mainly from India and, for the Dutch, also from Java (Emmer 1992; Engerman 1986). Even parts of the world in which slavery had not previously existed became recipients of contract labor from elsewhere in the second half of the nineteenth century. In the late nineteenth and twentieth centuries there emerged new forms of labor coercion (via land restrictions or otherwise) and contract labor in Africa, East Asia, and Oceania. With the Dutch ending of slavery and also the phasing out of the East Indies Cultivation System by the 1860s, they were followed by decades of contract labor migration from Java to Sumatra and the Outer Islands, as well as to Suriname.[26] There were possibly two million contract labor migrants within the South Pacific, both internally and to other areas, from the middle of the nineteenth century to the middle of the twentieth century, for labor in areas politically dominated by the British, French, German, and Dutch.[27] These forms of contract labor have been called a 'new system of slavery', a contention buttressed by descriptions of harsh plantation working and living conditions and of laboring people of a different color than were the landlords. Yet the crusades against them seemed to have not been as successful as might have been anticipated once *the* major evil, slavery, had been

---

[25] See the discussion in Steinfeld 1991.
[26] See Dick 1990; Boomgaard and Gooszen 1991:50-5; Fasseur 1992; Stoler 1985:25-30.
[27] The estimates are from Munro 1990. See also the other essays in that volume.

overcome. Maybe this was due to a sense that the slavery analogy was overstated, or possibly to the awareness of a world with too many other evils to permit the same concentration on contract labor as had been possible for slavery, or perhaps to a new moral hardening in attitudes towards race, labor, and the 'lower classes' due to modernization or to other nineteenth-century occurrences, or to the felt need to establish a more rigorous imperial rule. For whatever reason, however, the endings of such system lagged long behind the model presented by the British abolitionists.

Coerced Labor After Emancipation

Some insights into the politics and ideology of the attack on slavery may be obtained by looking at what institutional forms were to be advocated and/or accepted after the emancipation of slaves and serfs. Given the political circumstances that accompanied emancipation, as well as other actions in European and American societies, it will often be uncertain whether the new post-emancipation policies that actually occurred were those desired by abolitionists or whether they were forced to accept them because of a loss of political clout. The description of the emancipation process should include the basic economic changes in the systems of labor control and land ownership, and also the nature of political rights to be allowed the freedpersons, both of these in comparison with those rights which existed for those who were already free.[28] Based on political factors, as well as on such economic considerations as technology, crop mix, patterns of land ownership, and the land-labor ratio, a variety of patterns emerged, considering both what happened to the specific individuals who were freed as well as the basic systems of labor institutions that followed upon slavery and serfdom. 'Free' labor, which was the important pattern after the ending of serfdom and, in some places, slavery, was not without constraints, economically and politically. These transitions often involved payments in labor time by those freed to their former owners in exchange for freedom and rights to land. Because of low levels of income at the times of emancipation, 'free' labor became, at times, subject to debt obligations, described as peonage or bondage, that restricted opportunities and could limit labor returns in future years.

The ending of slavery in early Europe occurred in a number of quite different regions. In some areas it led, immediately or with a short lag, to serfdom. In other areas, there was a rise of 'free' labor, albeit within a significant economic or political hierarchy. Whether these differences in the subsequent forms that emerged reflected differences in economic potential, in

---

[28] For a recent examination of these questions, see the essays in McGlynn and Drescher 1992.

demographic goals, in political possibilities, or in other forces, they present the context for the range of transitions that ensued. Given the broad nature of these categories, however, when serfdom ended in England and elsewhere in Europe, it appears that only one other status, 'free' labor, was considered, although, as suggested, this includes a broad range of coercive possibilities that restricted the choices open to the nominally 'free' laborers.

When slavery ended in the Americas, after a legislated 'free womb' policy, or after periods of forced apprenticeship, or after an immediate ending, several patterns emerged. In some cases 'free' labor resulted, often with limited political rights and with these limitations, in racially discriminatory societies. In other places, slavery was replaced, at once or with some lag, with systems of contract labor, using labor drawn from other parts of the world, with relatively low living standards, but with no legal imposition upon the ex-slaves. This labor now came primarily from a continent, Asia, from which few slaves had been sent, even though there had been early controls introduced by the Dutch and British East Indies Companies. On the other hand, only relatively few contract laborers came from the continent, Africa, that had provided the majority of New World slaves. Labor from the resident populations in these areas was generated by limitations on land availability to ex-slaves. This was a critical measure that combined nominally 'free' labor with government-imposed limitations, which often also included laws regarding vagrancy, enticement, and debt, to effectively force ex-slave laborers to work for others, and not allow them to be independent farmers. While, perhaps, it is the legally distinct rights under slavery that are most easy to attack, politically and morally, examining the diverse patterns following slavery (and comparing those with what was allowed to those previously free) should provide some insight into the aims of the antislavery movement and its supporters and some understanding of the meaning to them of concepts such as slavery, free labor, and coercion.

Summary and Conclusions

The bunching of the European endings of serfdom on the continent and the emancipation of slaves in the European colonies in the Americas in the years between the last quarter of the eighteenth century and the last decade of the nineteenth century poses some significant questions for students of the abolition process. These were years in which economic development emerged within Europe, working its way from the northwest to the eastern parts of the continent. With economic change came also significant adjustments in demographic (both natural increase and migration), political, moral, religious, and ideological factors. Politically there was, in some areas, a change in the political process, with an expansion of voting rights and the development of new political practices, and ideologically there was the 'rise of the bourgeois', with emerging beliefs in individualism and greater freedoms at work and in public life. These changes need not point to the necessary emergence of a successful antislavery and antiserfdom movement. The development of slavery overseas by Europeans had come with the expansion of business interests, and a major component of any proslavery defense was its financial impact upon incomes and production. Markets had long existed in all parts of the world, although they were perhaps not everywhere as central to human life as they were to be in modern Western Europe. The puzzle of why this change in markets should have led to changing moral and ideological views in Europe and its overseas settlements, but not elsewhere, persists. That the nineteenth-century economic developments meant a growth in industrial production and the rise of the factory is clear, but whether this should have led to new relations between classes and to new attitudes to labor discipline is problematic. The changing political world that frequently accompanied economic growth in this period may have permitted the achievement of specific political, economic, and social goals by a broader part of the population than was previously possible, but the question of the evolution of specific ideological beliefs and of their moral and religious underpinnings remains.

At this time it remains difficult to give satisfactory answers to any of the three questions posed at the start of this paper. First, while the specific links remain difficult to establish, the coincidence in timing between the political and economic modernization of Western Europe and the ending of slavery throughout the world seems striking. Whatever the specifics of the arguments made by Williams, Davis, Drescher, and others, in regard to economic, religious, and ideological factors, the correlation in time is apparent. Second, the specific sequence between social change and abolition is not clear. The focus on the British as the 'first abolition' and Britain's relative ranking as an economic power made some answers seem obvious, but the pattern beyond that is considerably more diverse, suggesting the importance of considering other factors, both in the metropolis and in the slave colonies, in order to provide a fuller explanation. Third, ending slavery did not end what many have regarded as the coercion of labor, of the ex-slaves and the ex-serfs or even of those legally free before and after emancipation. Those advocating the end of slavery and serfdom may have also led the opposition to other forms of coerced labor, but they could not easily generate successful movements to end these less legally extreme institutions, whatever they may have done to ultimately expand the concepts of freedom in the modern world.

References

Alden, Dauril
1984   'Late Colonial Brazil, 1750-1808', in: Leslie Bethell (ed.), *The Cambridge History of Latin America; Vol. 2: Colonial Latin America*, pp. 601-60. Cambridge: Cambridge University Press.

Blackburn, Robin
1988   *The Overthrow of Colonial Slavery 1776-1848*. London: Verso.

Bloch, Marc
1975   *Slavery and Serfdom in the Middle Ages; Selected Essays by Marc Bloch*. Berkeley: University of California Press.

Blum, Jerome
1957   'The Rise of Serfdom in Eastern Europe', *American Historical Review* 62:807-36.
1961   *Lord and Peasant in Russia from the Ninth to the Nineteenth Century*. Princeton: Princeton University Press.
1978   *The End of the Old Order in Rural Europe*. Princeton: Princeton University Press.

Bonnassie, Pierre
1991   *From Slavery to Feudalism in South-Western Europe*. Cambridge: Cambridge University Press.

Boomgaard, Peter and A.J. Gooszen
1991   *Changing Economy of Indonesia; Vol. 2: Population Trends 1795-1942*. Amsterdam: Royal Tropical Institute.

Boswell, John
1988   *The Kindness of Strangers; The Abandonment of Children in Western Europe from Late Antiquity to the Renaissance*. New York: Pantheon.

Davis, David Brion
1975   *The Problem of Slavery in the Age of Revolution, 1770-1823*. Ithaca: Cornell University Press.
1984   *Slavery and Human Progress*. New York: Oxford University Press.

Dick, Howard W.
1990   'Interisland Trade, Economic Integration, and the Emergence of the National Economy', in: Anne Booth, W.J. O'Malley and Anna Weidemann (eds), *Indonesian Economic History in the Dutch Colonial Era*, pp. 296-321. New Haven: Yale University Southeast Asian Studies.

Drescher, Seymour
1987   *Capitalism and Antislavery; British Mobilization in Comparative Perspective*. New York: Oxford University Press.

Ekman, Ernst
1975   'Sweden, the Slave Trade and Slavery, 1784-1847', *Revue Française d'Histoire d'Outre-Mer* 62:221-31.

Eltis, David
1987   *Economic Growth and the Ending of the Transatlantic Slave Trade*. New York: Oxford University Press.
1993   'Labour and Coercion in the English Atlantic World from the Seventeenth to the Early Twentieth Century', *Slavery and Abolition* 14:207-26.

Emmer, Pieter C.
1992   'Immigration into the Caribbean; The Introduction of Chinese and East India Indentured Laborers Between 1839-1917', in: P.C. Emmer and M. Mörner (eds), *European Expansion and Migration; Essays on the Intercontinental Migration from Africa, Asia, and Europe*, pp. 245-76. New York: Berg.
1993   'Between Slavery and Freedom; The Period of Apprenticeship in Suriname (Dutch Guiana), 1863-1873', *Slavery and Abolition* 14-1:87-113.

Engerman, Stanley L.
1986   'Servants to Slaves to Servants; Contract Labour and European Expansion', in: P.C. Emmer (ed.), *Colonialism and Migration; Indentured Labour Before and After Slavery*, pp. 263-94. Dordrecht: Nijhoff.

Farnam, Henry W.
1938   *Chapters in the History of Social Legislation in the United States to 1860.* Washington: Carnegie Institution.

Fasseur, C.
1992   *The Politics of Colonial Exploitation; Java, the Dutch, and the Cultivation System.* Ithaca: Cornell University.

Fildes, Valerie
1988   *Wet Nursing; A History from Antiquity to the Present.* Oxford: Blackwell.

Finley, M.I.
1980   *Ancient Slavery and Modern Ideology.* New York: Viking.

Fogel, Robert William and Stanley L. Engerman
1974a   *Time on the Cross; The Economics of American Negro Slavery.* Boston: Little, Brown. 2 vols.
1974b   'Philanthropy at Bargain Prices; Notes on the Economics of Gradual Emancipation', *Journal of Legal Studies* 3:377-401.

Genovese, Eugene D.
1969   *The World the Slaveholders Made; Two Essays in Interpretation.* New York: Pantheon.

Graves, Adrian
1993   *Cane and Labour; The Political Economy of the Queensland Sugar Industry, 1862-1906.* Edinburgh: Edinburgh University Press.

Helper, Hinton Rowan
1857   *The Impending Crisis of the South; How to Meet It.* New York: Burdick Brothers.

Hilton, R.H.
1983   *The Decline of Serfdom in Medieval England.* Second edition. London: Macmillan.

Karras, Ruth Mazo
1988   *Slavery and Society in Medieval Scandinavia.* New Haven: Yale University Press.

Klein, Herbert S.
1986   *African Slavery in Latin America and the Caribbean.* New York: Oxford University Press.

Lewis, Bernard
1990   *Race and Slavery in the Middle East; An Historical Inquiry*. New York: Oxford University Press.

Lovejoy, Paul E.
1983   *Transformations in Slavery; A History of Slavery in Africa*. Cambridge: Cambridge University Press.

Lovejoy, Paul E. and Jan S. Hogendorn
1993   *Slow Death for Slavery; The Course of Abolition in Northern Nigeria, 1897-1936*. Cambridge: Cambridge University Press.

Lynch, John
1986   *The Spanish-American Revolutions, 1808-1826*. Second edition. New York: Norton.

Manning, Patrick
1988   *Francophone Sub-Saharan Africa, 1880-1985*. Cambridge: Cambridge University Press.
1990   *Slavery and African Life; Occidental, Oriental, and African Slave Trades*. Cambridge: Cambridge University Press.

McGlynn, Frank and Seymour Drescher (eds)
1992   *The Meaning of Freedom; Economics, Politics, and Culture after Slavery*. Pittsburgh: University of Pittsburgh Press.

Miers, Suzanne and Igor Kopytoff (eds)
1977   *Slavery in Africa; Historical and Anthropological Perspectives*. Madison: University of Wisconsin Press.

Miers, Suzanne and Richard Roberts (eds)
1988   *The End of Slavery in Africa*. Madison: University of Wisconsin Press.

Moore, Clive, Jacqueline Leckie and Doug Munro (eds)
1990   *Labour in the South Pacific*. Townsville: James Cook University of North Queensland.

Munro, Doug
1990   'The Origins of Labourers in the South Pacific; Commentary and Statistics', in: Clive Moore, Jacqueline Leckie and Doug Munro (eds), *Labour in the South Pacific*, pp. xxxix-li. Townsville: James Cook University of North Queensland.

Patterson, Orlando
1982   *Slavery and Social Death; A Comparative Study*. Cambridge: Harvard University Press.

Payne, Stanley L.
1973   *A History of Spain and Portugal in Two Volumes*. Madison: University of Wisconsin Press.

Phillips, William D. Jr.
1985   *Slavery from Roman Times to the Early Transatlantic Trade*. Minneapolis: University of Minnesota Press.

Reid, Anthony
1983   (ed.) *Slavery, Bondage and Dependency in Southeast Asia*. New York: St. Martin's Press.

1993	'The Decline of Slavery in Nineteenth Century Indonesia', in: Martin A. Klein (ed.), *Breaking the Chains; Slavery, Bondage, and Emancipation in Modern Africa and Asia*, pp. 64-82. Madison: University of Wisconsin Press.

Rout Jr., Leslie B.
1976   *The African Experience in Spanish America; 1502 to the Present Day.* Cambridge: Cambridge University Press.

Saunders, A.C. de C.M.
1982   *A Social History of Black Slaves and Freedmen in Portugal, 1441-1555.* Cambridge: Cambridge University Press.

Savine, Alexander
1903   'Bondmen Under the Tudors', *Transactions of the Royal Historical Society* 17:235-89.

Schwartz, Stuart B.
1985   *Sugar Plantations in the Formation of Brazilian Society; Bahia, 1550-1835.* Cambridge: Cambridge University Press.

Steinfeld, Robert J.
1991   *The Invention of Free Labor; The Employment Relation in English and American Law and Culture, 1350-1870.* Chapel Hill: University of North Carolina Press.

Stoler, Ann Laura
1985   *Capitalism and Confrontation in Sumatra's Plantation Belt, 1870-1979.* New Haven: Yale University Press.

Toledano, Ehud R.
1982   *The Ottoman Slave Trade and Its Suppression, 1840-1890.* Princeton: Princeton University Press.

Topolski, Jerzy
1982   'Sixteenth-Century Poland and European Economic Development', in: J.K. Fedorowicz, Maria Boguckia and Henryk Samsonowicz (eds), *A Republic of Nobles; Studies in Polish History to 1864*, pp. 70-90. Cambridge: Cambridge University Press.

Verlinden, Charles
1970   *The Beginnings of Modern Colonization; Eleven Essays with an Introduction.* Ithaca: Cornell University Press.

Vries, Jan de
1974   *The Dutch Rural Economy in the Golden Age, 1500-1700.* New Haven: Yale University Press.

Watson, James L. (ed.)
1980   *Asian and African Systems of Slavery.* Oxford: Blackwell.

Whatley, Christopher A.
1987   ' "The Fettering Birds of Brotherhood"; Combination and Labour Relations in the Scottish Coal-mining Industry, c. 1690-1775', *Social History* 12:139-54.

Zilversmit, Arthur
1967   *The First Emancipation; The Abolition of Slavery in the North.* Chicago: University of Chicago Press.

SEYMOUR DRESCHER

Epilogue
Reflections

In 1869 the English historian W.E.H. Lecky, with hyperbolic understatement, hailed his countrymen's 'unostentatious and inglorious' crusade against slavery as 'among the three or four perfectly virtuous acts recorded in the history of nations' (Lecky 1869, I:161).[1] A few years earlier Dutch colonial slavery had been ended with such unostentation that the story almost vanished from the history of nations. The scholars in this volume have demonstrated that the story of Dutch slave emancipation has heuristic value for the general history of antislavery. Beginning with analyses that zero in on the specifics of Dutch antislavery, we are successively led to view the question from the perspective of Dutch imperial expansion and, ultimately, from a planetary and millennial perspective.

It would be impossible to offer as complete a response to each individual contribution as it deserves. Within the confines of an epilogue it is best to begin by returning to the point of departure. For the past half century scholars have been attracted to the story of the rapid ending of slavery after it had endured as a publicly sanctioned institution for thousands of years. The most attractive clue to the causes of that process seemed to lie in what our last essayist calls the striking 'coincidence in timing between the political and economic modernization of Western Europe and the ending of slavery throughout the world' (Engerman). Towards the end of the eighteenth century the 'problem' of slavery changed from a problem of Western culture, as David Brion Davis calls it, into a problem of Western collective action and prohibition. More precisely, given the striking coincidence between the politicization of antislavery and the industrialization of Great Britain, the causal search could be narrowed to one point on the globe at one brief period in time. Underlying this assumption was the hypothesis that a primarily economic phenomenon, European capitalism, generated hostility and intolerance toward slavery. Whether capitalism operated directly and logically through market behavior, or indirectly and psychologically through the displacement of capitalist generated conflicts,

---

[1] I would like to express my gratitude to Pieter Emmer, Stanley Engerman, and Gert Oostindie for their helpful comments on an earlier version of this Epilogue.

the hypothesis could best be tested in the most advanced capitalist zones, Britain and France, during the age of the democratic and industrial revolutions.

Difficulties and anomalies began to be discovered in the analyses of the British and French processes. At some point in the still indecisive debate, as in the great flanking movements that followed the opening battles of the first World War, the battle front reached the Dutch frontier. 'The Long Goodbye' attempts to insert the Dutch case into the scenarios of the major Anglo- (or Franco-)centric accounts that rest upon the capitalist hypothesis. Despite, or rather because of, its marginality in most dramatic episodes of a world-historical process, the Dutch way to abolition may offer historians vital evidence on the general role of capitalism and its major variants in encouraging the world-wide dismantling of slavery.

Standing on the shoulders of an abundance of Dutch historical scholarship, I tried to broaden the perspective. Since much has been made of certain parallels in the economic, social, and religious development of early modern England and Holland, I posed a few questions: What was the potential long-term relationship between Dutch economic development and abolitionism? Was the hypothesized relationship between capitalist industrial relations and antislavery borne out by the Dutch case? Was there also a short-term 'French connection', a correlation between modernity's 'big bang', the French bourgeois-democratic Revolution, and the Batavian bourgeois-democratic Revolution? Was the relatively belated Dutch emancipation in 1863 triggered by a 'second' Dutch capitalist surge? My final question was, does the Dutch case, because it resembles most other emancipations in its minuscule abolitionism, and because it most resembled England in its early capitalist phase, suggest a different perspective on Anglo-American leadership in the turn against slavery?

Methodologically my most ambitious gambit was to widen the time frame to incorporate the Golden Age. All agree that, at least in the seventeenth century, there was no political abolitionist movement. The relatively casual response to my longer-term perspective in this collection may reflect polite skepticism that political abolitionism conceivably could have appeared 'before its (or anyone else's) time'. But some valuable comments in the essays by Kuitenbrouwer and Horlings allow me to respond to implications that Dutch development in the Golden Age cannot be compared to British economic growth in the late eighteenth century. They simultaneously raise two questions relevant to the problem of relating Dutch capitalism to Dutch antislavery: Did Britain experience an industrial 'take-off' absent in the Dutch case? On the other hand, should historians simply discard the previous emphasis on industrialization and conceive of economic growth in rather more Kuznetsian terms, as a rapid increase of per capita income in response to productivity increases?

To some extent, these two questions point in opposite directions. The growing revisionist view of slower growth during the British 'industrial revolution' seems to show no signs of abating, and many descriptions of seventeenth-century Dutch capitalism and proto-industrialization would apply equally well to British economic development until well into the nineteenth century (Berg 1985:77-83, 295-6, 313-4). Moreover, in Britain, France, and the United States, antislavery attracted more support among artisans than factory workers (Drescher 1986:128-34, 153, 159, 245 note 87, 264 note 92). Kuitenbrouwer's conclusion, that there was stronger initial opposition to slavery and the slave trade in the early seventeenth-century Netherlands than in seventeenth-century England, would seem to indicate that Dutch society was sufficiently developed and committed to free labor to stir individual disapproval, if not collective protest against slavery. Indeed, the Dutch, at the height of their economic primacy, seem to have been more reluctant to create a market in the overseas labor of their own countrymen than were their English counterparts (Eltis 1993).

However, it should also be noted that the period 1580-1650 coincided with an era of intense hostility toward Spain by the Dutch mercantile élite. Dutch participation in the slave trade met with opposition among those who believed that the Dutch were now imitating their enemies in an activity which counted as an indicator of the immorality of the Spanish empire. Early Dutch protests were reflections of the 'black legend' rather than assertions of the superiority of free labor. I will return to this point below.

As for Horlings's recommended shift of emphasis towards long-term per capita income expansion rather than industrialization, I would only note that, in Kuznetsian terms, the rate of British annual per capita growth between 1770 and 1815 was almost exactly equal to Dutch annual per capita growth over an even longer period (1580-1650) (Williamson 1990:1; Van Zanden 1993:5-26; Mokyr 1993:9). Since British abolitionism became a national social movement at a period when late eighteenth-century Britain was not growing appreciably faster than the Netherlands 150 years before, the comparison remains relevant to the hypothesized relationship between capitalism and antislavery.[2]

---

[2] At the original conference in 1993, Van den Boogaart and Klein questioned the overall economic modernity of the seventeenth-century Netherlands. This may be true but that still leaves some crucial comparative questions unaddressed: Was Great Britain, by the same (unspecified) criteria used by Van den Boogaart and Klein, also of questionable overall economic modernity during the last quarter of the eighteenth century? If the Golden Age Netherlands unquestionably resembled Britain a century later in terms of variables usually considered as benchmarks of modernity, why are these particular variables less crucial to the causal link between economic development and antislavery than others as yet unspecified?

In making the Anglo-Dutch comparison, I wanted to block a preemptive exclusion of the Dutch case by what one might call 'stage-struck' historians. Stage-struck history unconsciously assumes that slavery and antislavery are mutually exclusive preserves of different eras: mercantilist versus industrial; or early modern versus late modern. How can we be so certain that slavery is to be viewed 'part and parcel' as 'pre-modern' (Horlings)? The coexistence and co-expansion of slavery and free labor into the second half of the nineteenth century demands careful consideration before relegating one parcel to pre-modernity. By focusing exclusively on nineteenth-century antislavery historians also risk thinking anachronistically in terms of antislavery and economic development. For example, to analyze the economic or ideological context of the British abolitionist 'take-off' we must consider the British prospect in 1780 or 1820, not in 1840 or 1860. To analyze the context of Dutch emancipation we must consider the Dutch prospect in 1830 or 1860, not in 1880 or 1900. In 1860, an industrialized Netherlands was still an 'imagined economy'.

In this respect, Angelie Sens offers a convincing hypothesis about the relationship between Dutch economic decline and antislavery in the eighteenth century. Although many of the ingredients of antislavery elsewhere were in place between the Golden Age and the French Revolutionary era, the Rubicon of mass abolitionism and political abolition was clearly not crossed. There is ample evidence of awareness of, and even of hostility towards slavery. Indeed, expressions of disapprobation may have been more plentiful than historians of slavery have imagined (see also Buisman 1992:307-42). Yet antislavery did not, either in a secular or a religious context, take a political turn in the Netherlands. Dutch problems were to be solved instead by individual moral and educational reformation, what I assume to be akin to the contemporary concept of *Bildung* in Germany. Sens's context of 'commercial capitalism, operating within a national framework of decline and stagnation' strikes me as a compelling *prima facie* condition for the inhibition of a national consensus (or even a major collective movement) against slavery. In this sense Dutch capitalism was an inhibitor of abolitionism. I would only note that economic stress has sometimes been hypothesized in the British case as a major stimulus for the passage of slave trade abolition in 1806-1807. Since Sens considers antislavery more appropriate to an economic context of prosperity than of depression, I find her conclusion to be quite consistent with my analysis of the British case (Drescher 1986:140-2).

The French Revolutionary period offers an analytical opportunity for another short-term economic linkage with antislavery. The French abandoned slavery in 1794, just when they thought that they were about to lose their colonies. It required the combined threat of a massive slave uprising in

St. Domingue and the prospect of the imminent British conquest of the French colonies to discount the economic logic of the status quo. The Batavian Revolutionaries, except for a handful of representatives, did not follow the French line, even to the extent of making the issue a high priority item in parliamentary committees on colonial affairs. In discussions of the possibility of abolishing slavery during the period of the National Convention, it was agreed that such a move would only stimulate colonial planters to press for British conquest.

Sens also emphasizes non-economic factors in accounting for the fact that antislavery sentiments entered public discussion, but found no outlet in the political system. One can, of course, expand capitalism by definition to include culture, religion, and so on. Even so, it remains striking that non-economic aspects of Dutch capitalism are invoked to explain antislavery's appearance in public discourse in the late eighteenth century, while economic aspects of Dutch capitalism are used to explain antislavery's political insignificance well into the nineteenth century.

From the primarily metropolitan perspectives of Kuitenbrouwer, Horlings, and Sens, most of the details of post-Napoleonic parliamentary and public discussion reinforce my labelling of Dutch antislavery as 'Continental'. Their accounts further suggest to me that France may have played a considerable role in the precise timing of the Dutch process after 1814. If the British acted as an exogenous catalyst for generating change, the French may have offered an opportunity for not doing too much too fast. There is a rough correlation between French foot-dragging on the slave trade and slavery and moments of activity and quiescence in Dutch antislavery. British examples could be treated as anomalous until the French fell into line. Whatever may have been the seriousness and breadth of Dutch parliamentary discussions of slavery in the decade before slave emancipation, those discussions were not prodded by mass mobilizations. My use of 'perfunctory' may indeed be too dismissive a term to describe the passage of emancipation in 1863, but 'businesslike' still seems quite appropriate.

With Van Stipriaan, Oostindie, Knaap, and Ross, the scholarly focus shifts to other places and sets of actors in the abolition of the Dutch Atlantic slave system. In their discussions the colonies are geographically divided into the Caribbean islands, Suriname, and the South African Cape Colony. For the period before the emergence of North Atlantic political abolitionism in the 1780s, the Dutch slave colonies appear to have offered no economic incentive or rationale to the planters (or their trading partners in the metropolis) to consider emancipation. Neither the bursting of the investment bubble in Suriname in the 1770s nor the fall of the smaller islands' value as neutral entrepots after 1780, nor the Maroon wars extending through the entire pre-French Revolutionary period, nor the slave uprisings in the French Caribbean in the 1790s seem to have stimulated a serious reappraisal of the plantation system by colonial officials, merchants, or plantation owners. As in the British slave system, the mix of crops shifted between sugar, coffee, and cotton, always offering at least one potentially profitable alternative use of slave labor.

After 1833, the British example of compensated abolition and apprenticeship opened up an alternative to slavery. For another generation, however, there was no colonial planter movement, let alone consensus, in favor of a British-style emancipation. From the logic of high sugar prices, and of relative labor productivity, the timing of emancipation in 1863 was 'not the most appropriate moment to abolish slavery'. Indeed it was the 'worst possible moment imaginable' (Van Stipriaan; also Horlings). After 1840, the crisis of slave production in post-emancipation British Guiana and the simultaneous expansion of slave-grown sugar in Cuba were disincentives to Dutch planter abolitionism. Finally, as metropolitan emancipation grew more likely, it acted as a disincentive for capital investment in further modernization.

As in the metropolis, external pressure was the major source of change. The planters reluctantly followed their British predecessors through the familiar stages of slave trade abolition, slave amelioration, Christianization, emancipation, and apprenticeship. As in the British and French slave empires, the logic of the demographic, economic, and compensatory situation impelled the planters to hold out as long as possible for the maximum use of their slave labor (Van Stipriaan). As in the French and British colonies, non-violent slave resistance in Suriname increased problems of planter discipline enough to enter into governmental discussion, but not enough to change the situation or the thinking of the mostly recalcitrant planters.[3]

In short, late as it came, Dutch emancipation was untimely for the planters. My only reservation regarding Van Stipriaan's conclusions concern his conjecture that emancipation three or four decades earlier might have given Suriname sugar production a boost. Given severe British constraints on indentured labor recruitment from Africa to the Caribbean in the 1830s and 1840s, a more generalized Anglo-Dutch Guianese labor crisis would have been a far more likely result of simultaneous Anglo-Dutch emancipations than a probable boost to Suriname's modernization. Van Stipriaan's general conclusion, that there was no economically logical moment to abolish Dutch slavery, could also be applied to most major systems in the plantation Americas. As in the metropolis, the impetus to

---

[3] The linkage between slave resistance and British, Brazilian, and French emancipation is addressed in Drescher 1987:97-110, 1988:451-2, 1991:728-32.

Dutch transformation was largely through pressure from without.

Oostindie's essay on the slave owners in the Dutch Americas shifts the emphasis away from the narrowly economic nexus and reinforces a major point about the significance of culture in the emergence of slavery as a 'problem'. As the British colonies first showed, even slave holding societies such as eighteenth-century Virginia could generate anti-slave trade initiatives and entertain schemes to alter its slave system. Engerman's analysis of late-nineteenth century Australia's exclusion of blacks is equally applicable to Virginia's late-eighteenth century exclusion of slaves. Culture, in the form of racism, prevailed over labor economics. Virginia makes for an interesting contrast with Suriname in that both colonies experienced a brief period in the 1770s and 1780s when previous patterns of importing slaves were disrupted.

Oostindie also notes the sparseness of antislavery impulses from the Dutch metropolis either before or during the Batavian Republic. After 1780, there was apparently relatively greater leeway in the Dutch world than the British for pre-abolitionist religious rationales for slavery. Therefore the Dutch colonial world, like the metropolis, offers possibilities for auditing religious as well as economic attitudes towards slavery in the absence of strong abolitionist institutional pressures from the Netherlands. In a further comparison with Virginia, there was a weaker Dutch colonial impulse to use Christianization as a means of integrating the slaves themselves into subordinate membership in the community. Despite the well-analyzed limitations of US Southern Christianization, the gap between its variant of 'amelioration' and that of Suriname's, right down to the outbreak of the Civil War, remains striking. The contrast between Christianization in Suriname and the British Caribbean colonies is less dramatic. West Indian planters resisted exposing slaves to conversion until outside forces came into play demanding amelioration in the late eighteenth century. British missionaries initially conformed to the norm of 'neutrality' on slavery until forced into positions of greater hostility by abolitionist mobilizations in the British metropolis (Turner 1982).

Equally significant for assessing the relation between economic development and antislavery in the Dutch colonies, is Oostindie's account of the failure of abolitionism to develop in the Dutch Caribbean islands. There, in contrast to Suriname, Christianization came early, the clergy was more critical of masters, slavery was only marginally productive, and there was less fear of a crisis of post-emancipation labor (Oostindie, Van Stipriaan). In the Caribbean islands, race, rather than slavery, apparently constituted the chief barrier against slave holder conversion to emancipation. The islands imitated the mother country in that slavery never became a major issue. Mirroring metropolitan indifference, the Dutch island slave holders apparently lacked the stimulus to mobilize either for or against emancipation. Colonial opinion eased into an evolutionary ideology in an evolutionary manner.

Ross continues Oostindie's analysis of the cultural consequences of the weakness of antislavery in Dutch South Africa. Even more strongly than Oostindie, he argues that the causal chain of attitudes toward slavery (and post-slavery) are less related to economic than to cultural and religious development. Ross indicates the dampening effect of revolutionary trauma upon Dutch receptivity to change in religious groups. Here, Oostindie's statistics on the demographic weakness of Protestant dissent in the Netherlands, in comparison with Great Britain, is worth careful investigation. The abolitionist 'take-off' in Britain, allying Old and New Dissent with secular radicalism, occurred both before the outbreak of the French Wars and the rupture of conquest in the Netherlands. In the post-revolutionary period abolition quickly reemerged in Britain. Demands for political and religious reform remained closely linked to antislavery (Anstey 1980, Drescher 1994).

Ross's line of argument further suggests the utility of comparing religious development in the analysis of the timing of Dutch abolition. The French occupy an intermediate position between the British and the Dutch cases, but rather closer to the latter than to the former. French Protestantism, as minuscule as the Dutch in comparison with British Dissent, was nevertheless disproportionately well-represented among both élite abolitionists and rank and file petitioners. The largest French antislavery petition before emancipation (1847), modest compared to its earlier British counterparts, was initiated and disproportionately sponsored by French Protestants (Drescher 1980).

Ross's apocryphal opening also moves us to the most microhistorical level of the collection, a probably legendary slave trade abolition decree carried to the Cape Colony by a Dutch official on the eve of British re-conquest. The South African settlement, with the highest ratio of Europeans to non-Europeans in the Dutch empire was, as 'The Long Goodbye' suggests, the colony in which an imagined community without slavery could most easily be envisioned. One must, however, note that the suggestion of disenslavement came from a metropolitan officer, and the undocumented 'decree' came from a metropolitan official. De Mist's proposal was explicitly based upon strategic, not humanitarian or economic arguments.

Another contemporary Dutch policy suggestion even more strongly indicates the contingent character of Dutch metropolitan 'antislavery' around 1800. Some Dutch officials were apparently willing to consider committing the Netherlands to slave trade abolition in the Guianas even before 1806. In 1804, with Demerara conquered by the British and Suriname imperilled, some Dutch leaders sounded out the British on whether abolition might remove a major obstacle to Britain's peacetime restoration of the colonies (Anstey 1975:383). The Dutch Order in Council abolishing the slave trade in 1814 was similarly enacted in order to placate the British and to strengthen claims for the restoration of pre-Napoleonic Dutch possession to the Netherlands.

As Ross rightly concludes, a comparative perspective on missionary movements will be essential in any systematic analysis of the abolition process. However, despite the shift of attention to religious, as opposed to economic factors in the abolition process, the explanations of the variations of overseas missionary movements in relation to slavery must still take account of demography and economics within any given colony. If the timid antislavery impulse in the Cape Colony seems robust relative to Suriname's, or Alabama's, or Jamaica's, it was far weaker than those of Pennsylvania and Massachusetts, or even, for a time, of Virginia and Kentucky. Setting aside the vast question of post-emancipation race relations, economics and demography often weighed more heavily than intellectual traditions on the ability of abolitionists to generate pressure for the amelioration of slavery or abolition (Drescher 1986:117-22).

However, as yet another shift in our collection's geographical focus shows, the precise timing of abolition had little to do with the economic and demographic characteristics of slavery within the Caribbean, or with the desires of slave owners, of slaves, or of abolitionists in any particular colony. Despite differences in demographic and economic situations as great as those within the British Caribbean, emancipation was legislated in all slave colonies at almost the same time. The essays by Knaap and Emmer open up new comparative perspectives on the relation between economic development and the process of abolition. In addition to a relatively small system of East Indian chattel slavery, the Dutch fostered other systems of coerced labor before 1800. The Dutch empire was also comparable to the British in sponsoring the expansion of coerced labor systems during the period that European governments legislated the ending of chattel slavery.

During the nineteenth century the expanding plantation systems of Brazil, Cuba, and the United States demonstrated the viability of New World slavery in the Americas. The expanding Dutch East Indies Cultivation System offered analogous evidence for the viability of coerced labor in Asia. Emmer's discussion of Van den Bosch's cost-benefit analysis indicates that many Dutch officials assumed the uncompetitiveness of free labor in both the East and West Indies. From Knaap's account of the utility of slave labor in outlying areas such as Banda, some expansion based on the slave trade could still have fueled nineteenth-century plantation growth in low population zones. By the post-Napoleonic period, of course, this option had been ruled out by British constraint. The fact that the Dutch East Indies were 'thinly' settled by Europeans fostered adaptation to East Asian social norms (including chattel slavery) rather than to metropolitan ones. Even an economically insignificant chattel slave system lingered on without external pressure to end it. The degree of slavery's insignificance in the Dutch East Indies is evidenced by the fact that the metropolitan government had no precise idea of how many slaves it was preparing to emancipate in 1859, and considerably overestimated the number actually freed. Knaap inclines toward the conclusion that, as in the Americas, the decision for East Indian emancipation required a rejection of the logic of efficiency and of profitable exploitation.

Emmer expands the discussion in two crucial respects. Van den Bosch's accountancy of coerced versus free labor on the very eve of British emancipation is more evidence that the Dutch case allows us to audit the economic logic of overseas slavery in the absence of strong cultural and political pressures to override any attempts at cost-benefit policies. Emmer's Anglo-Dutch comparison heuristically incorporates the Americas, Africa, and Asia into the historiography of antislavery. The Dutch delay in emancipation, the length of the Dutch apprenticeship system (lasting two and one half times as long as its British predecessor), and Suriname's recourse to indentured servitude immediately after apprenticeship, testify to the absence of metropolitan pressures, the businesslike process of abolition, and to the economic disadvantages of emancipation. In Africa, the British priority was the suppression of the slave trade. That priority was not contradicted by the British recruitment of captured slaves for West Indian labor. With the end of the Atlantic slave trade in the 1860s, British recruitment of Africans ceased. The timing of Dutch abandonment of Africa as a source of labor (1862) suggests that a French connection might have been at work here. Once the French abandoned African recruitment the Dutch could no longer use the leverage of the 'French norm'.

Emmer's most important addition to the discussion of antislavery is his analysis of British and Dutch labor polices in Asia in relation to the 'free labor ideology'. Emmer notes that the British experimented with a free labor system in India for almost twenty years, with economic results analogous to what happened in the British West Indies in the first years of freedom before indentured labor. Moreover, at the very moment that the British decided to experiment with free labor in their plantation colonies the Dutch decided to expand coerced labor in the East while leaving slavery in place in the West. The Dutch therefore rejected free labor in the 1830s and only gradually dismantled the Cultivation System after 1870. Emmer's analysis of the Anglo-Dutch experience with Asian labor systems seems to have borne out Arthur Young's observation on the eve of the British abolitionist breakthrough in the 1780s: 'labour is generally *in reality* the cheapest where it is nominally the dearest' (Mokyr 1993:89). At the crucial juncture of experiments with alternative systems in Asia and America, American slavery was more competitive than nominally cheaper and freer Asian labor. Emmer's compelling conclusion, that coerced labor in East Indian sugar production remained viable and profitable during the debates over Dutch slavery only deepens the difficulty of relating capitalism and abolition.

This returns us to the difficult question of motivation: why did the Dutch, even as late as three decades after the British, 'leap in the dark'? Emmer's response is that they did so under the influence of the free labor ideology. This ideology supposedly enabled legislators to override empirical calculations such as those of a Van den Bosch, first in the British Parliament and later in the Dutch Parliament. The ideology had two components. The first was a moral and religious assertion that it was wrong, indeed criminal, to enslave human beings. The second was an economic assertion that forced labor was more expensive than free labor. (I would caution that many free labor advocates qualified their argument by stressing greater expense 'in the long run', or 'in the end'.)

In the British case, at least among the élite, faith in free labor was supposedly fortified by the increased productivity, wealth, and competitiveness and material improvement of free labor England in the generations before the abolitionist 'take-off' in the 1780s (Temperley 1977). Whether a similarly robust optimism about their own economy's performance buoyed the Dutch élite at any time between 1780 and 1860 remains unclear, although they must have been impressed by the example of economic growth and free labor in the British metropolis during that period. The strength and timing of the emergence of a Dutch 'free labor ideology' must be assessed by historians of the Dutch élite. But first, I would urge a word of caution about the British case as a comparative point of departure. Even at the peak of British antislavery faith in free labor superiority overseas was not a consensual belief among the political and intellectual élites. The superior competitiveness of free labor in the plantation Americas remained a hotly contested assertion up to the parliamentary debates on British emancipation and for a generation thereafter. My assessment is that there was an attitude of resignation among the skeptics, of 'no matter what' among the enthusiasts, and of 'you'll regret this' among the die-hard opponents. The British true believers included neither Tory Prime Ministers of the 1820s, 1830s, or 1840s, nor many political economists. More generally, a recent quantitative analysis of voting in the British House of Commons indicates that the frequently hypothesized link between votes on slavery and measures of political economy were 'either weak, ambiguous or of minimal explanatory value' (Franzmann 1994:581). Dutch legislators were certainly under less extra-parliamentary pressure, whether from colonial slaves or metropolitan abolitionists. A comparison of economic and non-economic arguments in the British and Dutch legislatures at the times of their respective emancipations would offer a valuable additional perspective.

Emmer also posits an ideological symmetry between the rationales to end the Dutch American slave system and the Eastern Cultivation System. His hypothesis is that the abolition of both systems was grounded upon the growing impact of the free labor ideology among Dutch MPs in the decades after the 1850s. The asymmetrical timing of the two policies suggest further themes for future research. Unlike their British predecessors, when the Dutch abolished slavery in 1863, they knew that they had three tested, if not optimal, safety nets of unfree labor against disaster: a temporary British-style 'apprenticeship' system; a British-style indentured labor system; and their own Eastern coerced labor system to underwrite the expenses of emancipation. Abolition legislation based upon a really secure sense of free labor superiority might have stimulated the discussion of simultaneous labor emancipations in both hemispheres. Indeed, the simultaneous termination of slavery and the Cultivation System in the early 1860s would have metamorphosed the Dutch into the abolitionist heroes of two worlds. With a single legislative stroke the Netherlands would have changed from laggard to vanguard in the termination of coerced labor. This was surely a Dutch dog that did not bark. In opening up so many new avenues for comparative analysis, Emmer demonstrates the enormous utility of the whole Dutch world for understanding the link between capitalism and slavery.

Engerman's essay brings us to the broadest assessment of the antislavery process, both temporal and geographic. Engerman's lense becomes so wide as to return the Dutch case to its traditional invisibility in historiography. In the whole galaxy of labor emancipations, even the British case is reduced to a single relatively marginal occurrence. After all, British emancipation came centuries late in a process stretching back into the murky declines of slavery and serfdom in medieval Northwestern Europe. In magnitude it was almost minuscule in relation to the tens of millions freed in subsequent emancipations of serfs in Eastern Europe, or of slaves in Africa and Asia. Moreover, a whole 'new system of slavery', indentured servitude, continued in the British empire for eight decades after colonial slave emancipation. One could pursue Engerman's brief still further afield. His sweeping survey does not even mention the termination of the vast market in human beings in imperial China or the rise and fall of the dreadful twentieth-century systems of coercion and annihilation of millions from the North Sea to the Pacific

Ocean. What additional historical sense should we make of the fact that just a century after the first metropolitan petitions submitted to the Dutch government gathered in Holland on behalf of its colonial slaves (1840s) there were more coerced European laborers working within a day's travel of the Netherlands (almost 8 million in Germany) than New World slaves at the peak of the system in the plantation Americas (Herbert 1993:149)? Still more appallingly, many of those European laborers considered themselves privileged simply to survive as slaves.

All these thoughts are suggested by Engerman's vaulting major premise – that an historical assessment of the termination of chattel slavery should be considered part of a far larger spectrum of coerced labor, extending from chattel slavery near one extreme to 'free' labor, with its own constraints, at another. Indeed, given the ubiquity of the coercion/constraint spectrum, the 'slave' metaphor can be (and has been) extended to include contemporary basketball superstars and directors of the world's Central Banks (Woodall 1994). The concept of degrees of constraint and freedom as well as the inevitable limits of liberation are important philosophical issues. Yet as Engerman himself notes, these constraints take on more historiographical importance 'once emancipation is agreed to'. In considering the emergence of antislavery and of its successes, these later, longer, and wider lenses may distract us from other, and, I hope to show, crucial historical questions: what accounts for the timing of antislavery ideas/mentality? What accounts for the emergence and the success of antislavery action? And, for the purposes of our particular focus on capitalism, what was the role of economic forces in stimulating and sustaining those ideas, those actions, and those successes?

Questions of timing presuppose moments of origin. Engerman conforms to one tradition in locating the first sustained transition to 'free labor' in medieval Northwestern Europe. If one reflects on this 'small bang', Dutch history underlines the significance of the phrase 'growth is at the margins'. Whatever the Netherlands' proportion of the world's population around 1000, it seems to have been relatively free of both slavery and serfdom at a very early date. Whether this 'first emancipation' or rather 'slaveless condition', is linked to the beginning of a long period of sustained economic growth in Northwestern Europe is a significant question.

There was nothing in Northwestern Europe in 1000 or 1500, however, comparable to the international antislavery movement, or to the abolition process of the century after 1780. A Dutch society that was far more commercialized in 1650 than in 1050 therefore embodies, better than any other place on the globe, the paradox of free labor at home and coerced labor abroad. Two centuries later, in 1850, no matter how globally or temporally one moves beyond the Dutch case, the paradox expands. The wider the range of societies incorporated into the abolition process, the more tenuous becomes the connection between the abolitions of slavery/serfdom and capitalist industrialization. Adding Central and Eastern serf emancipations from Denmark to Russia to the list hardly seems to provide candidates more likely for such a correlation – unless one emphasizes exogenous and non-economic pressures on economically underdeveloped societies rather than comparative economic development.[4]

[4] Regarding the parting suggestion on the Spanish case in Oostindie's Introduction, I should respond briefly. Before the end of the eighteenth century, the Spanish empire diverged politically and legally from its Dutch counterpart. There was no latent tension between a metropolitan zone of freedom and overseas zones of coerced labor. Slavery was a legal institution in Spain well into the nineteenth century. There was no counterpart to the Northwest European juridical and popular traditions that their air was 'too free for slaves to breathe'. Demographically, however, the Dutch and Spanish Americas converged in being preponderantly non-European, and economically Spain was even more unpropitious terrain for metropolitan economic growth than was the Netherlands during the two centuries after the formation of the Republic.

Both empires relied heavily upon bound labor in their overseas colonies to produce exportable commodities. Spanish America was considerably more dynamic economically than Spain during the last decades of colonialism, the result partly of the Bourbon reforms and partly (in the case of Cuba) of the St. Domingue Revolution. That growth did not stimulate colonial abolitionism, however, because even middle-level social groups (artisans who employed slaves for their workshops; women and families who relied on renting out slaves for income) benefitted from slavery. Neither these groups nor the landowning or mercantile élites had any incentive to do away with the existing labor system.

Abolition was thrust on Spanish America, not by economic growth (or at least not directly by economic growth), but as an unintended consequence of the struggle for independence, entailing the need to recruit nonwhite support. Forced Indian labor, Indian head taxes, and the caste regime were overturned at the same time as slavery as part of a complex negotiation with nonwhites. Abolition was a result of immediate political and economic necessity. Independence movements had no strong commitment to abolition, and rather tried to extend the life of the institution. However, the virtual elimination of the slave trade (first enacted as part of the bargain for nonwhite support, and reinforced by British pressure) soon had the same demographic and economic effects as elsewhere outside the United States. The slave population declined, and eroded élite resistance to final abolition.

Analyzing Spanish abolition from the New World side of the Atlantic may require conceptualizing a variant of abolition that is different from both the British and Continental European cases. Regional abolitions in mainland America were the consequences of local mobilizations (slave revolution in Haiti or wars of independence) where reliance on slaves proved crucial. Spanish American abolitions occurred first and fastest where slaves constituted a small proportion of the region's total workforce. It was only the second wave of Spanish slave emancipation, in the Caribbean during the 1860s and 1870s, that metropolitan abolitionism broke with the 'Continental' mold of antislavery. The Caribbean colonies played a catalytic role in radicalizing and accelerating metropolitan sentiment.

In response to Oostindie's query, what made it possible for Spanish slavery to outlast Dutch slavery was the longer duration of the slave trade to the Spanish Caribbean and the absence of antislavery mobilizations both in Spain and its colonies prior to Dutch emancipation in 1863. In the mid-1860s the colonies, especially Puerto Rico, played a vanguard role in crystallizing Spanish metropolitan abolitionism. As in most of the Atlantic world, neither of the waves of emancipation in the Spanish orbit was stimulated by industrial capitalism. For a fresh attempt to link Spanish abolitionism to the rise of laissez-faire, if not to industrial capitalism, see Schmidt-Nowara 1995. (I thank Reid Andrews for helpful suggestions on this question.)

Thus any global tour of coerced labor systems in the century after 1800 brings us full circle, back to the significance of the British empire to those systems. British abolitionism was a repository of recipes for later collective action from Canada to Brazil. The British state deployed the most formidable diplomatic and military instruments in the ending of the transatlantic slave trade. British capital fueled the expansion of slavery in the Americas, and transoceanic indentured labor from Asia. Britain provided the most formidable model of the world's economic future in discussions of serf emancipation in Europe. Britain's colonies also furnished models of the economic future in discussions of slave emancipation in the Americas. Discussions of coerced labor in the nineteenth-century Dutch world were only variants of a discourse that had touched every corner of the globe by the beginning of the twentieth century. If one looks beyond the roughly coincidental exits from slavery/serfdom to variations in motives, a second paradox reinforces the first. Engerman, like almost every other historian, recognizes that economically speaking, whatever the metropolitan constraints on enslaving Europeans or Native Americans, the development of the New World tropics was as openly permissive to economic cost-benefit calculations as any other in human history.

Whether all labor systems, like Tolstoy's happy marriages, are alike in being constrained, each form of constraint, like each unhappy marriage, is different in its own way. A major premise of Engerman's argument is the strikingly similar timings of 'endings' of New World slavery and serfdom (and, if you add a few more decades to the time-frame, in Africa, Asia, and Oceania as well). I would caution that the coincidence in timing is deceptive in certain respects. The endings of slavery and serfdom were not produced by an analogous 'antislavery and antiserfdom movement'. True, the message that freer societies, especially in Anglo-America, produced more power, stability and prosperity, increased pressure on other societies to adapt some of the recipes for power and/or prosperity emanating from Northwestern Europe. But the notion that élites or statesmen in the Eastern European empires looked to Anglo-American civil society and its economic individualism as models for their own futures misses a fundamental thrust of their aims and efforts. Russian 'Westernizing' economists and officials, for example, assumed that the backwardness of their peasants left the élite with no choice but to impose an indefinite system of close police supervision on the masses for the sake of stability (Kingston-Mann 1991:104-5). Only from a sufficient height and distance do antislaveries and antiserfdoms all look alike.

The same is true if one views slavery and its alternatives from below. From one kind of hindsight, the indentured servitude that replaced slavery in certain areas was 'a new system of slavery'. From the prospective servant's view, however, economic historians write, with equal insight: 'If they [indentured servants] were not attracted primarily by the prospects of improvements in material welfare, etc., it is not easy to comprehend why so many of them would have voluntarily made multi-year commitments to serve as indentured servants, braved discomfort and located in the adverse disease environments characteristic of the places best suited for growing sugar [...]'. So write Engerman and Sokoloff about European indentured servants in the eighteenth century (Engerman and Sokoloff 1994:9). But why should the outlook of a poor Indian in 1860 have been different from that of a poor Englishman in 1760? If indentured servitude was an affront to British abolitionists in the 1840s and to many later liberals, historians, and nationalists, to many indentured men and women it was not a 'new slavery', but a 'great escape' (Emmer 1985).

Of course, constraints always stretched before laborers to the horizon, like an ever-receding threshold of liberation. We recognize that the 'dismal spectrum' of labor history may be one field of human relations in which all forms may seem similar in being asymptotic to freedom. However, one should not overlook the certainly distinctive elements of New World slavery (Drescher 1993). For historians of antislavery the analytical difficulty created by an exclusive focus on forms or conditions of labor is that slavery, serfdom, and other variants are not only systems of labor allocation (Drescher 1986:162-3; Franzmann 1994:589; Confino 1990:1137). Had British abolitionists confined themselves to describing only conditions of labor in the colonies, it is doubtful whether slavery would have been as powerful a metaphor for political mobilization as it came to be – and ceased to be when it was replaced by other 'systems of slavery'.

The historical fact remains that antislavery had to overcome a powerful set of rationalizations that had come into play to maintain an institution for centuries: peculiar absences of free labor, peculiar climates, peculiar disease environments, peculiar crops, peculiar demographies, peculiar sources of labor. One need not rehearse the moral, political, and strategic arguments that were brought into play against New World slavery. One point remains clear for the analysis of abolition's relation to economic development. In the absence of a successful slave revolution or war, the economic arguments against slavery, *like religious and moral arguments*, were declarations of faith. For some it was an article of faith that free laborers were, in the end, superior to slave laborers. How long it took to get to 'the end' was left unclear.

Precisely because of the long-term disjuncture between an ideology of freedom at home and economic optimality abroad, the Dutch story, better than any other, reminds economically oriented historians, not just of the constraints on forms of labor, but of the constraints on forms of capital. In the end it reminds all historians, economic or otherwise, of the 'humanly devised constraints that shape all human interaction, whether they be laws, norms, ideology, government agencies, constitutions, codes of behavior, religion or conventions' (Goldin 1994). Antislavery was one of those constraints. Historians of the Dutch world have contributed a provocative new dimension to the study of that constraint – just fifty years later.

References

Anstey, Roger
1975 *The Atlantic Slave Trade and British Abolition 1760-1810*. Atlantic Highlands: Humanities Press.
1980 'The Pattern of British Abolitionism in the Eighteenth and Nineteenth Centuries', in: Christine Bolt and Seymour Drescher (eds), *Anti-Slavery, Religion, and Reform: Essays in Memory of Roger Anstey*, pp. 19-42. Folkestone: Dawson; Hamden: Archon.

Berg, Maxine
1985 *The Age of Manufacturers; Industry, Innovation, and Work in Britain 1700-1820*. Oxford: Blackwell.

Buisman, Jan Willem
1992 *Tussen vroomheid en Verlichting; Een cultuurhistorisch en -sociologisch onderzoek naar enkele aspecten van de Verlichting in Nederland (1755-1810)*. Zwolle: Waanders.

Confino, Michael
1990 'Servage russe, esclavage américain (note critique)', *Annales; Economies Sociétés Civilisations* 45:1119-39.

Drescher, Seymour
1980 'Two Variants of Anti-Slavery; Religious Organization and Social Mobilization in Britain and France, 1780-1870', in: Christine Bolt and Seymour Drescher (eds), *Anti-Slavery, Religion, and Reform; Essays in Memory of Roger Anstey*, pp. 43-64. Folkestone: Dawson; Hamden: Archon.
1987 *Capitalism and Antislavery; British Mobilization in Comparative Perspective*. New York: Oxford University Press.
1988 'Brazilian Abolition in Comparative Perspective', *Hispanic American Historical Review* 68:429-60.
1991 'British Way, French Way; Opinion Building and Revolution in the Second French Slave Emancipation', *American Historical Review* 96:709-34.
1993 'Review essay of *The Antislavery Debate: Capitalism and Abolitionism as a Problem in Historical Interpretation* [Thomas Bender (ed.)]', *History and Theory* 32:311-29.
1994 'Whose Abolition? Popular Pressure and the Ending of the British Slave Trade', *Past and Present* 143:136-66.

Eltis, David
1993 'Europeans and the Rise and Fall of African Slavery in the Americas; An Interpretation', *American Historical Review* 98:1399-423.

Emmer, Pieter C.
1985 'The Great Escape; The Migration of Female Indentured Servants from British India to Surinam, 1873-1916', in: David Richardson (ed.), *Abolition and Its Aftermath; The Historical Context, 1790-1916*, pp. 245-66. London: Cass.

Engerman, Stanley L. and Kenneth L. Sokoloff
1994 *Factor Endowments, Institutions, and Differential Paths of Growth Among New World Economies; A View From Economic Historians of the United States.* Cambridge: National Bureau of Economic Research. [Historical Paper 66.]

Franzmann, Tom L.
1994 'Antislavery and Political Economy in the Early Victorian House of Commons; A Research Note on "Capitalist Hegemony" ', *Journal of Social History* 27:579-93.

Goldin, Claudia
1994 *Cliometrics and the Nobel.* Cambridge: National Bureau of Economic Research. [Historical Paper 65.]

Herbert, Ulrich
1993 'Labour and Extermination: Economic Interest and the Primacy of *Weltanschauung* in National Socialism', *Past and Present* 138:144-95.

Kingston-Mann, Esther
1991 'In the Light and Shadow of the West; The Impact of Western Economics in Pre-Emancipation Russia', *Comparative Studies in Society and History* 33:86-105.

Lecky, William Edward Hartpole
1869 *A History of European Morals from Augustus to Charlemagne.* London: Longmans/Green. 2 vols.

Mist, J.A. de
1920 *The Memorandum of Commissary J.A. de Mist.* Cape Town: Van Riebeeck Society.

Mokyr, Joel (ed.)
1993 *The British Industrial Revolution; An Economic Perspective.* Boulder: Westview Press.

Schmidt-Nowara, Christopher Ebert
1995 *The Problem of Slavery in the Age of Capital: Abolitionism, Liberalism, and Counter-Hegemony in Spain, Cuba, and Puerto Rico, 1833-1886.* [PhD thesis, University of Michigan.]

Temperley, Howard
1977 'Capitalism, Slavery, and Ideology', *Past and Present* 75:94-118.

Turner, Mary
1982 *Slaves and Missionaries; The Disintegration of Jamaican Slave Society, 1787-1834.* Urbana: University of Illinois Press.

Williamson, Jeffry
1990   *New Views on the Impact of the French Wars on Accumulation in Britain.* Cambridge: Harvard Institute of Economic Research. [Discussion Paper 1480.]

Woodall, Pam
1994   'Central Bankers: Masters or Slaves?', *The Economist* 333 (3-9 December):106-7.

Zanden, Jan Luiten van
1993   'Economic Growth in the Golden Age; The Development of the Economy of Holland, 1500-1650', in: Karel A. Davids and Leo Noordegraaf (eds), *The Dutch Economy in the Golden Age*, pp. 5-26. Amsterdam: Nederlands Economisch-Historisch Archief.

Index

Abbring, H.J. 161-2
Aborigines 185
Africa 3, 10, 14, 19, 26, 34, 45, 99, 145-6, 151, 158, 169, 182, 185, 207-8, 210-1, 215, 219, 224-5, 230-4, 236, 248, 252, 254, 257
African National Congress 185
Alabama 185, 251
Alkmaar 127
Ambon 193, 195-8, 201
Americas *see individual territories and countries*
Amerindians 75, 95, 99, 152, 154, 158, 232, 257
Amstel Sociëteit 72
Amsterdam 32-3, 38, 41-2, 46, 69, 72-4, 80, 115, 121, 131, 134, 137-8
Anstey, Roger 67, 82
Anti-Revolutionaries 73-4, 76-9, 82-3
Antigua 118, 125, 209
April movement 73-4, 78, 81
Arabia 231
Argentina 229
Arminianism 48
Aruba 144
Ashanti 208, 210
Ashworth, John 6-7, 20, 89
Asia 3, 10, 14, 19, 26, 34, 80, 99, 158, 193-204, 207-8, 211, 213, 218-20, 224, 230-1, 234, 236, 251-4, 257
Asmodée 75, 81
Australia 232
Austria 226

Bali 195, 197
Banda 196-7, 201, 212, 251
Banten 198
Baptists 183

Barbados 118, 125
Barrau, A. 95
Batavia 13, 29, 81, 193, 196-8, 200-1, 203
Baud, J.C. 71-6, 78, 80, 82, 129
Belgium 31, 36-7, 39, 44, 68, 70, 79
Belmonte, B.E.C. 75, 129
Bender, Thomas 20
Berbice 17, 41, 144, 148, 152
Beverwijck, Johan van 34
Bilderdijk, Willem 187
Blackburn, Robin 8, 37-41, 43, 49, 67, 80-2
Blakely, Allison 4, 47
Blom, Anthony 152-3
Blum, Jerome 226
Boeij, W.C. 162
Bolivia 229
Bonaire 117, 144
Boogaart, Ernst van den 16, 245
Bosch, G.B. 161-2, 165
Bosch, Johannes van den 123, 156, 168, 213-5, 251-3
Bosch Reitz, G.C. 127, 131, 137-8
Bosch Reitz, G.J.A. 138
Botswana 185
Bourbon 256
Boxel 127
Brake, Wayne Ph. te 91
Brazil 3, 26, 44-6, 49, 122, 130, 136-7, 211, 224-5, 227, 229-30, 232, 248, 251, 257
Brederoo, G.A. 68
Breugel, G.P.C. van 155
Britain 3-4, 6, 8-11, 13-5, 18-20, 25-51, 53, 67-75, 77-80, 82-3, 89-91, 93-4, 96, 98, 101, 105-6, 124, 127-30, 135-6, 138, 143-4, 146-9, 169, 179-88,

198, 207-8, 210, 211-2, 217-20, 223-5, 227, 230-1, 234-7, 243-8, 250-8
British East Indies 10, 14, 41, 77, 180, 230
British East Indies Company 236
British West Indies 10, 14-5, 79, 125, 136-7, 155, 158, 185-6, 207-20, 230, 234, 248-9, 251-2, *see also individual territories*
Brugmans, A. 131, 137-8
Brussels 37
Buddhists 99
Bueno de Mesquita, J.J. 129
Buxton, Thomas Fowell 185
Bijlaart, H. 127

Calvinism 68, 74, 76, 79, 82, 94
Camisards 182
Camper, Petrus 93, 169
Canada 257
Cape Almanac 187
Cape Colony 10, 13-4, 17, 43, 46-8, 69, 99, 179-88, 247, 250-1
Cape of Good Hope Philanthropic Society 184
Capitein, J.E.J. 94, 145
Caracas 164
Caribbean 3, 14, 212-3, 247-8, 251, 256, *see also individual territories*
Carolinas 48
Carter, George E. 48
Catalonia 44-5
Catharina Sophia 215
Catholicism 73, 79, 91, 99-100, 146, 148, 157-8, 163-9, 182, 199, 207
Cats, Jacob 34
Cham 94, 145, 151
Chesapeake 49
Chevalier, R. le 127, 138
Chile 228
China 96, 127, 195-6, 199, 233, 254
Christianity *see individual denominations*
Cirebon 195
Clifford, G.G. 129
Cloux, W.H. du 201
Cobbett, William 81
Cobden Club 80
Colombia 229

Conan Doyle, Arthur 25, 83
Confucians 99
Congo 37, 44
Congregationalists 183
Connecticut 228
Conservatives 73-8, 80-3, 215
Continental Colonies *see* USA
Cornets de Groot van Kraayenburg, J.P. 76-7
Coro 164
Cory, Sir George 179, 181
Costa, Isaac da 187
Craig, J.H. 180
Crol, J.D. 166
Cuba 44-5, 109, 118, 126, 211, 227, 229-30, 232, 248, 251, 256
Cultivation System 14-6, 43, 71, 76, 78-80, 110, 193, 200, 203, 215-8, 234, 251-2, 254
Curaçao 3, 12, 17, 43, 99, 117-8, 143-4, 146-7, 152, 158-69

Danish Virgin Islands 157
Davis, David Brion 6-7, 20, 27, 34, 67, 80, 82, 89, 143-4, 150, 237, 243
Delaware 49
Demerara 144, 148, 183, 250
Denmark 8, 15, 25, 33, 35, 37-8, 40-1, 48, 73, 136, 146, 157, 208, 224, 226-7, 256
Dissel, S. van 162
D'Orzy, Reinier 179, 181, 188
Drescher, Seymour 4-11, 13-7, 19-20, 67-9, 77-8, 83, 90, 101, 105, 136-7, 143, 149, 193, 203-4, 237
Drie Gebroeders 127
Dutch Africa 10, 93, *see also individual territories*
Dutch Antilles 16-7, 71, 75, 77, 117-9, 136-7, 158-9, 166, 180, 209, 247, 249, *see also individual islands*
Dutch East Indies 3, 10, 13-4, 17-8, 29, 32-3, 41, 43-4, 71, 78, 99, 109-14, 144, 146, 159, 168-9, 193-204, 210-9, 230, 251-3, *see also individual territories*
Dutch East Indies Company 34, 40, 46-7, 93, 97-8, 186-7, 236

Dutch West Indies 5, 9-10, 12, 14, 16, 19, 33, 35, 40-1, 43, 46, 72, 74, 78, 81, 94-5, 99, 112, 135, 143-6, 150, 158, 160-1, 169, 180, 198-9, 204, 207-20, 227-8, 230, 234, 249, 253-4, see also individual territories
Dutch West Indies Company 16, 31-2, 34, 40, 46, 93, 97, 164

East Seram 196
Ecuador 229
Eensgezindheid 154
Elias, B.J. 129
Elkins, Stanley E. 155
Elmina 210
Elphinstone, G.K. 180
Eltis, Davis 47
Emden, E. van 127, 129, 131
Emmer, Pieter C. 5, 10, 14-5, 67, 251-4
Engerman, Stanley E. 10, 19-20, 27, 243, 249, 254-5, 257-8
England see Britain
Enlightenment 11, 37, 89-101, 144, 147, 167
Essai historique 150
Essequibo 144, 148
Europe see *individual territories*
Evangelicalism 183-4, 188

Fairbairn, J. 184, 187
Fermin, Phillippe 153
Fox, C.J. 82
France 8-9, 11, 13, 15, 25, 27-8, 31-3, 35-44, 49-51, 68-9, 72-4, 78-82, 89, 91-3, 96, 98, 130-1, 135-7, 146-50, 169, 182, 184, 208, 211, 219-20, 224-7, 230, 234, 244-8, 250, 252
Fransen van der Putte, I.D. 78
French West Indies 12, 38, 43, 72, 128, 137, 155, 209, 227, 234, 248, see also *individual territories*
Frouin, J. 129
Frijhof, Willem Th.M. 91

Gallandat, D.H. 1, 146
Gefken, J.W. 74-5, 139
Georgia 48-9
Germantown 47

Germany 46, 69, 137, 184, 225-6, 230, 234, 246
Goes, H.D.A. van der 201
Grenada 118, 125
Groen van Prinsterer, G. 71, 73-4, 76-7, 82
Groot, Hugo de (Grotius) 34, 151
Grovestins, W.A. 162
Guadaloupe 71
Guiana, British 46, 50, 71, 75, 77, 124-6, 135, 144, 148, 248, 250, see also Berbice, Demerara, Essequibo
Guiana, Dutch see Suriname
Guiana, French 46, 50, 130, 135
Guinea 159
Gulcher, P.C. 127, 138

Haan, F. de 193
Haarlem 74
Habsburg 182
Hague, the 74, 128, 135, 137, 207, 216
Haiti 8, 38, 40-2, 49-50, 77, 118, 154, 227, 247, 256
Hartsinck, J.J. 150, 152
Haskell, Thomas L. 6-7, 20, 29, 31, 35, 67, 80, 82-3, 89
Heeckeren van Waliën, G.P.C. van 149, 155-6
Heemskerk, J.B. 162-3
Heine, Heinrich 4, 25, 43
Helper, Hinton 232
Herlein, J. 145, 151
Herrnhutters 16, 46, 71, 93, 99, 129, 152, 155, 157-8, 163-4, 166, 168, 182
Hindus 99
Hoetink, Harry 161
Hoëvell, Wolter R. van 74-5, 77, 80-1, 129, 158, 199, 203
Hogendorp, Dirk van 98, 198, 203
Holmes, Sherlock 25, 83
Holsteyn, P. 95
Holt, Thomas 37
Hooyland 127
Horlings, Edwin 10-1, 16, 244-8
Houten, S. van 79
Huguenots 46, 68, 126, 137, 182
Hungary 226

Iberian peninsula 18, 35, 45, 225, *see also* Portugal, Spain
Independents 183
India, British 77, 168, 212-3, 219-20, 233-4, 256, 258
Indisch Genootschap 74
Indonesia *see* Dutch East Indies
Insinger, A.F. 80, 127
Islam 96, 99, 153, 225, 230
Israel, Jonathan I. 4
Italy 225

Jacob, Margaret C. 92, 149
Jacobins 38, 42, 69
Jakarta *see* Batavia
Jamaica 118, 125, 185, 211, 251
Janssens, J.W. 43, 179, 181
Japan 194
Java 14-6, 29, 43, 77, 79-81, 98, 110, 137, 144, 193, 195, 198-204, 208, 212-20, 234
Java Benevolent Institution 198
Javaansch Menschlievend Genootschap 198
Jews 35, 46, 68, 75, 122, 126, 137, 153, 163, 165, 169
Jordan, Winthrop 145

Kalimantan 201,
Kals, J.G. 94, 152
Kansas 229
Kemp, Johannes van der 182
Kentucky 251
Keye, Ottho 16
Khoi 182, 186
Khoisan 180, 185
Kistemaker, J.F.A. 166
Klein, Peter W. 16, 245
Knaap, Gerrit J. 10, 13-4, 247, 251-2
Kolonist 130
Kuitenbrouwer, Maarten 5, 10-1, 14-5, 244-5, 247
Kumasi 210
Kuznets, Simon 106, 245

Lans, W.H. 129
Latin America 160, 228-9, *see also individual regions and territories*

Lavigerie, Cardinal 37
League of Nations 231
Lecky, W.E.H. 243
Leewards Dutch Antilles 18, *see also* Aruba, Bonaire, Curaçao
Leiden 31-3, 69, 94, 145, 182
Leopold II 44
Lewis, Gordon K. 144, 150
Liberals 71-83, 138, 149, 185, 204, 215-6
Liberia 77
Life of Olaudah Equiano 95
Lingen, G.W.A. van der 188
London 92, 98, 210
London Missionary Society 98, 183, 185
Loudon, J. 77
Louis XIV 35

Madeira 127, 225
Makassar 193
Malay 75
Malouet, V.P. 155
Malthus, Thomas Robert 183
Maroons 17, 50, 133, 138, 147, 152, 154-5, 247, *see also* Matawai, Ndjuka, Saramaka
Maryland 49
Massachusetts 48, 228, 251
Matawai 133
Mauritius 212
Mediterranean 29, 35, 51, 151
Melanesia 232
Mennonites 96
Methodism 183
Meulen, H. van der 167
Mexico 228
Michels van Kessenich, F.B.H. 81
Middle East 194, 230
Mississippi 228
Mist, J.A. de 179-81, 184, 186, 188, 250
Moens, Petronella 94, 150
Mokyr, Joel 253
Moluccas 13, 196, 201, 212
Montesquieu 147
Moravians *see* Herrnhutters
Multatuli 81
Murray, Andrew 188

Mijer, P. 75-6
Mijnhardt, Wijnand W. 92

Napier, Lord 207
Napoleon Bonaparte 28, 35, 39, 43
Ndjuka 133
Nederlandsch Hervormde Kerk 13, 71, 73, 98-9, 148, 151, 187-8
Nederlandsch Zendeling-Genootschap 11, 91, 96, 98-100
Nederlandsche Handel Maatschappij 113, 115
Netherlands, the *passim*
New Dissent 250
New England 49
New Hampshire 228, 230
New Jersey 49, 228
New Netherland 46
New York 49, 228
Niewindt, M.J. 162, 166
Noah 145
Nusa Tenggara 201

Oceania 234, 257
Ohio 229
Old Dissent 183, 250
Oostindie, Gert J. 10, 12, 14, 18, 36, 247, 249-50, 256
Orange, House of 35, 184, 207, *see also* Willem I, II, III
Orangists 39
Ostend 36
Ottoman Empire 231
Outer Islands 200-2, 234
Ouwerkerk de Vries, J. van 130
Overijssel 113

Paasman, A.N. 70, 93, 146
Pacific 232, 234
Paddenburg, G.G. van 162
Pahud, C.F. 73-5, 200-1
Palembang 201
Papiamentu 162
Paraguay 229
Paramaribo 128, 132
Paris 38, 49
Patrimonium 82-3
Patriots 11, 39, 42-3, 69-70, 91-2, 95-7, 148, 180, 186
Pennsylvania 29, 47, 49, 228, 230, 251
Persia 182
Peru 45, 229
Philip, John 183, 185
Pierson, N.G. 80
Pistorius, Th. 152
Pombal, Sebastião José de, Marqués 225
Poncelet, J.J. 127, 131
Portugal 44, 48, 211, 219-20, 225
Post, Elisabeth 94, 150
Postma, Johannes Menne 5
Potribo 134-5
Price, Richard & Sally 154
Protestantism 13, 15, 35, 48, 73, 82, 91-2, 94, 96, 98-101, 147, 164-5, 168-9, 181-4, 187, 199, 250, *see also individual denominations*
Prussia *see* Germany
Puerto Rico 45, 227, 229, 256
Putman, J.J. 163, 166-7

Quakers 9, 29, 47, 49, 71, 89, 96, 138, 148-9, 183, 230

Raad der Aziatische Bezittingen 179-81
Radicals 81
Raffles, Thomas Stamford 198, 202
Rammelman Elsevier, J.J. 162-3
Reenen, G.C.J. van 78
Reid, Andrew 193
Resolutie 127
Réveil 71, 80, 149, 184, 187
Rhode Island 228
Rio de Janeiro 45
Rocheteau, J. 1
Rochussen, J.J. 76
Röperhoff, C.L. 127
Ross, Robert 10, 13-5, 247, 250-1
Roth, Randolph 47
Rotterdam 74, 121
Rousseau, Jean-Jaques 147
Roux, H.G. 129
Russia 226, 230, 256-7
Rijk, J.C. 72, 131, 138
Ryneveld, W.S. van 187

Saba 144
Sambo 155-6
Sandick, O.Z. van 1
Sandt, B.J. van de 187
Sandt de Villiers, B.J. van de 187
Sanna 132-3
Saramaka 133
Scandinavia 225, *see also individual territories*
Schama, Simon 4, 30, 34, 144
Schimpf, C.P. 76, 135
Schoelcher, Victor 72
Schutte, Gerrit J. 93
Scotland 186-7, 226
Scott, Rebecca J. 44
Sechor Dabar 187
Semarang 201
Sens, Angelie 10-1, 14-5, 246-7
Sicily 225
Sierra Leone 49, 210-1
Siwpersad, J.P. 5, 127
Sluyskens, A.J. 180
Smith, Adam 27, 29, 149, 155, 183, 230
Smith, J. 183
Socialism 79
Société des Amis des Noirs 89
Sokoloff, Kenneth L. 258
Sokoto Caliphate 230
Somerset Case 26, 40, 50, 70
Somerset, Charles 186
South Africa 185-8, 247, 250
South African Commercial Advertiser 184
Spain 1, 8, 16, 19, 37-8, 44-5, 48, 136, 148, 220, 224, 227, 245, 256
Spanish America 3, 19, 44, 46, 160, 164, 229, 256, *see also individual territories*
Spectator 92
St. Bartholomew 230
St. Domingue *see* Haiti
St. Eustatius 117, 144
St. Helena 210-1
St. Kitts 118
St. Martin 18, 42, 72, 117-8, 144, 159
St. Vincent 118, 125
Staatscommissie 131, 137, 159, 162-3, 166-7
Stedman, John Gabriel 42, 148, 153-4

Stipriaan, Alex van 10, 12, 14, 16-7, 247-9
Sulawesi 194-5, 197, 201
Sumatra 198, 201, 234
Surabaya 201
Suriname 1, 3, 5, 10-2, 14-8, 40, 45-6, 50, 71-7, 95, 100, 105-15, 117-39, 143-69, 180, 185, 209, 214-5, 218, 228, 234, 247, 249-52
Sweden 8, 25, 33, 35, 37, 224, 227, 230
Swedish West Indies 230

Tank, Otto 129, 155, 157
Taunay, D. 127, 138
Teenstra, M.D. 130, 158, 161-2
Thorbecke, J.R. 71-3
Timor 197
Toit, S.J. du 188
Tolstoy, Leo 257
Transvaal 186
Trinidad 125
Twente 80-1

Udemans, G. 151
Uhlenbeck, G.H. 77-8
Uncle Tom's Cabin 74, 80, 129
United Nations 231
Uruguay 229
USA 3, 9-10, 19, 26, 29, 31, 34, 39-40, 44-6, 48-51, 53, 67, 69, 77, 80, 109, 124, 136, 148-9, 179, 182, 184-5, 203, 212-4, 224, 226-32, 235-6, 245, 251, 253, 256
Usselincx, Willem 16
Utrecht 187

Veldwijk, E.G. 138
Venezuela 45, 167, 229
Vereeniging ter bevordering van de afschaffing der slavernij 74
Vereul 130
Vermont 47-8, 53, 228, 230
Virginia 34, 49, 249, 251
VOC *see* Dutch East Indies Company
Voltaire 150
Vreede, P. 70, 97
Vries, Jan de 3, 33

Wales 33
Wallerstein, Immanuel 3
Warren, George 152
Watson, R.L. 184-5
Weber, Max 183
Wedgwood, Josiah 39
Wesley, John 182
WIC *see* Dutch West Indian Company
Wilberforce, William 82, 183
Wilkens, U.H. 127, 138
Willem I 35, 43, 70, 100, 127-8, 213, 215
Willem II 71-2
Willem III 73-4, 166

Williams, Eric E. 8, 13, 26, 41, 67, 80, 237
Winter, J.M. van 5
Wolbers, J. 79, 82, 143, 150, 157-8
Wolff, Betje 94, 150
Woude, A. van der 3
Wright, H. 127

Xhosa 185-6

Yorkshire 53
Young, Arthur 48, 252

Zanden, Jan Luiten van 107

The Contributors

Seymour Drescher is University Professor of History at the University of Pittsburgh. The author of a number of works on Tocqueville, he serves on the Commission Nationale pour la Publication des Oeuvres d'Alexis de Tocqueville. During two decades of comparative study on slavery and abolition, he has authored *Econocide; British Slavery in the Era of Abolition* (1977), *Capitalism and Antislavery; British Mobilization in Comparative Perspective* (1986); and (with Rebecca Scott et al.) *The Abolition of Slavery and the Aftermath of Emancipation in Brazil* (1988). He is co-editor of *Anti-Slavery, Religion and Reform* (with Christine Bolt, 1980), and *The Meaning of Freedom; Economics, Politics and Culture after Slavery* (with Frank McGlynn, 1992). He is an editor of the *Journal of Contemporary History*, and is currently editing *The Encyclopedia of Slavery* with Stanley L. Engerman.

Pieter C. Emmer is Professor of the History of the Expansion of Europe in the Department of History, Leiden University. He has published on the history of the slave trade and of slavery as well as on the migration of indentured laborers from Asia to the Caribbean. Among his publications are the edited volumes *Colonialism and Migration; Indentured Labour before and after Slavery* (1986) and *European Expansion and Migration* (with Magnus Mörner, 1992).

Stanley L. Engerman is John H. Munro Professor of Economics and Professor of History at the University of Rochester, where he has taught since 1963. He has written articles on slavery and emancipation and is co-author of *Time on the Cross; The Economics of American Negro Slavery* (with Robert W. Fogel 1974, 1989). He has edited or co-edited several books dealing with slavery and with economic history, and most recently has been co-editing *The Encyclopedia of Slavery* with Seymour Drescher.

Edwin Horlings studied Economic and Social History at the Free University, Amsterdam. He is joint coordinator of the project 'Reconstruction of the National Accounts of the Netherlands, 1800-1940' and has recently finished his PhD thesis entitled *The Economic Development of the Dutch Service Sector, 1800-1850; Trade and Transport in a Premodern Economy* (Utrecht

University). He has published various articles on the economic development of the Netherlands during the nineteenth century.

Gerrit J. Knaap is Head of the Department of Historical Documentation and curator of the special collections of the KITLV/Royal Institute of Linguistics and Anthropology in Leiden. He obtained his degrees in History from Utrecht University. His PhD thesis, *Kruidnagelen en Christenen; De Verenigde Oost-Indische Compagnie en de bevolking van Ambon 1656-1696*, was published in 1987. He has published several selected archival collections as well as articles on Indonesian history. His present research interest is in shipping and trade in eighteenth-century Indonesia.

Maarten Kuitenbrouwer studied History and Social Sciences at the University of Amsterdam. His publications include *The Netherlands and the Rise of Modern Imperialism; Colonies and Foreign Policy 1870-1902* (1991), and *De ontdekking van de Derde Wereld; Beeldvorming en beleid in Nederland, 1950-1990* (1994). He is Associate Professor in the History of International Relations at the Department of History, Utrecht University.

Gert J. Oostindie directs the Department of Caribbean Studies at the KITLV/Royal Institute of Linguistics and Anthropology in Leiden and is Professor of Caribbean Studies at Utrecht University. He is managing editor of the *New West Indian Guide*. His research interests are history, international relations, and ethnicity, with a focus on the Dutch Caribbean and Cuba. His publications include *In het land van de overheerser II: Antillianen en Surinamers in Nederland, 1634/1667-1954* (with Emy Maduro, 1986), *Roosenburg en Mon Bijou; Twee Surinaamse plantages, 1720-1870* (1989), and, as editor, *Ethnicity in the Caribbean* (1996).

Angelie Sens is Research Assistant at the Institute for History and Culture at Utrecht University. She has conducted comparative research on eighteenth-century Dutch and French attitudes towards slavery and abolitionism. She is currently preparing her PhD thesis on Dutch images of the non-Western world, 1770-1820.

Alex van Stipriaan teaches History of the Caribbean at the Erasmus University Rotterdam. His PhD thesis on plantation slavery in Suriname was subsequently published by KITLV Press in 1993 (*Surinaams contrast; Roofbouw en overleven in een Caraïbische plantagekolonie, 1750-1863*). He published several articles on Suriname ecological and economic history, on the historical development of Afro-Suriname music and dance, on plantation and slave naming, and on slave resistance.